The Means to Prosperity

T0316314

In recent times, something of a void has emerged in discussion of fiscal policy. While recent developments in monetary theory have been fast to spread to policy analysis and practice – and one may add the media – the same is not true about fiscal policy. Issues such as its timing, cyclical adjustments, long-term sustainability, and its social implications are seen as arcane and detached from most discussions in the public sphere.

The chief aim of this book is to provide a broad assessment of the role and scope of current fiscal policy. New contributions and critical reviews of state-of-the-art research will analyze fiscal policy in terms of its viability, its potency, its consequences, and its sustainability, and also shed some light on its relation to economic and political ideas.

Per Gunnar Berglund is an Assistant Professor of Economics at Queens College/CUNY, New York. **Matias Vernengo** is Assistant Professor of Economics at the University of Utah, Salt Lake City, USA.

Routledge international studies in money and banking

The Means to Prosperity

Fiscal policy reconsidered

**Edited by Per Gunnar Berglund
and Matias Vernengo**

Routledge
Taylor & Francis Group

LONDON AND NEW YORK

First published 2006
by Routledge
2 Park Square, Milton Park, Abingdon, Oxon OX14 4RN

Simultaneously published in the USA and Canada
by Routledge
711 Third Avenue, New York, NY 10017

Routledge is an imprint of the Taylor & Francis Group, an informa business

First issued in paperback 2012

© 2006 Selection and editorial matter, Per Gunnar Berglund and
Matias Vernengo; individual chapters their contributors

Reprinted 2007

Typeset in Times by Wearset Ltd, Boldon, Tyne and Wear

British Library Cataloguing in Publication Data
A catalogue record for this book is available from the British Library

Library of Congress Cataloging in Publication Data
A catalog record for this book has been requested

ISBN 978 0 4156 4998 8

In memoriam Robert Eisner

Fiscal measures have created and destroyed industries, industrial forms and industrial regions even where this was not their intent, and have in this manner contributed directly to the construction (and distortion) of the edifice of the modern economy and through it of the modern spirit. But even greater than the *causal* is the *symptomatic* significance of fiscal history. The spirit of a people, its cultural level, its social structure, the deeds its policy may prepare – all this and more is written in fiscal history, stripped of all phrases. He who knows how to listen to its message here discerns the thunder of world history more clearly than anywhere else.

Joseph A. Schumpeter, in *The Crisis of the Tax State*

Contents

Figures

Tables

Contributors

Philip Arestis, University of Cambridge and Levy Economics Institute

Per Gunnar Berglund, Queens College CUNY

Barbara R. Bergmann, American University and University of Maryland

David Colander, Middlebury College

Robert Eisner, Northwestern University

Jeffrey A. Frankel, JFK School of Government, Harvard University and National Bureau of Economic Research

Alfred Greiner, University of Bielefeld, Germany

Alan G. Isaac, American University

Uwe Koeller, University of Bielefeld, Germany

Kenneth A. Lewis, University of Delaware

Peter Hans Matthews, Middlebury College

William A. Niskanen, Cato Institute, Washington, DC

Esteban Pérez Caldentey, Economic Commission for Latin American and the Caribbean (ECLAC), Port of Spain, Trinidad and Tobago

Max B. Sawicky, Economic Policy Institute, Washington, DC

Malcolm Sawyer, Leeds University Business School, UK

Laurence S. Seidman, University of Delaware

Willi Semmler, New School for Social Research and University of Bielefeld, Germany

Matias Vernengo, University of Utah, Salt Lake City

Ebru Voyvoda, Middle East Technical University, Ankara, Turkey

Preface

James K. Galbraith

The test of a macroeconomic theory is not elegance, nor popularity, nor whether its premises conform to certain codes of the profession, to privileged axioms laid down by guardians of faith. The test of a macroeconomic theory is whether it can explain the phenomena of the observed world in a coherent and consistent way over a very long period of time. This is true in principle, and it is even truer in practice. Theoretical doctrines in economics often rise on the power of logic and the appeal of intellectual fashion. But at the end of the day they fall when they cannot account for facts.

Thus the old-fashioned Phillips Curve collapsed when inflation coexisted, through the 1970s, with high unemployment. Thus classical monetarism, which boldly asserted that "inflation is everywhere and always a monetary phenomenon," lost its audience in the 1980s when the connection between money growth and price change disappeared. Thus the doctrine of the natural rate of unemployment, or NAIRU, faded out when unemployment fell below 6, and then 5, and then 4 percent – and inflation did not rise.

Robert Eisner was an American Keynesian economist who never accepted the Phillips Curve. Eisner never embraced monetarism in any form. And he always rejected the doctrine of the NAIRU. Eisner also resisted all latter-day versions of Say's Law; he was neither phobic about the budget deficit nor enamored of the surpluses that emerged near the time of his death.

Truly an engineer of the price system, Eisner believed in functional finance. He thought fiscal policy should serve the performance of the economy; budget balance or surpluses were in no way legitimate goals in their own right. Likewise he debunked scare stories about deficits in Social Security and in the current account, insisting always on careful measurement, correct accounting for inflation, and on careful calibration to the scale of the GDP. And he kept the larger goals in sight. For Robert Eisner the test of any policy was whether it would aid the quest for full employment prosperity, for technical and social progress, and for human freedom. In these pages, Per Gunnar Berglund describes Robert Eisner as the "greatest of the American Keynesians" and it is easy to understand why.

The essays assembled here, which culminate in a long and gracious interview Berglund conducted with Robert Eisner in 1997, share Eisner's philosophical commitments and, to a large degree, his analytical perspective. Eisner would have enjoyed their range, from formal and informal theoretical discussions of Keynesian principles to practical discussions of macro-management, and to the consequences of applying flawed theory to policy, especially in developing countries where the margin for error is tragically small.

These essays are also timely. For in the wake of the relentless non-cooperation of fact, many modern economists now find themselves virtually bereft of coherent principles, with which to guide their policy views. Eisner's adherents do not have this problem. Almost alone among macro-economists of cosmic importance, his views have withstood the test of time. It is certainly time for a school of his followers to make themselves heard.

Acknowledgments

A version of Chapter 13, "The Political Economy of the Deficit," was also published by M.E. Sharpe, Inc. as "A Debate on the Deficit. Moderated by Per Gunnar Berglund and Matias Vernengo," *Challenge*, 47(6), November–December 2004, pp. 5–45.

1 Fiscal policy reconsidered

Introduction

Per Gunnar Berglund and Matias Vernengo

Few nations can claim to have been built on the basis of a tax revolt, and even fewer can claim to have been obsessed with taxes throughout their history.[1] America, however, is a nation obsessed with fiscal policy, even if this obsession is a subconscious one. The American Revolution was based on the principle "no taxation without representation." Benjamin Franklin said, "In this world nothing is certain but death and taxes." We may add that it is all but certain that Americans will put up a fight, sometimes to death, if taxes are involved, as exemplified by Shay's Rebellion, and the Whiskey Rebellion. The obsession has not subsided with time, and the twentieth century has had its fair share of fiscal revolutions.

Herbert Stein – the head of Nixon's Council of Economic Advisers – wrote in 1969 an authoritative account of the last fiscal revolution in America at that point. The book told the story of the rise of Keynesian fiscal policies from Herbert Hoover to Lyndon B. Johnson. Policies did not change overnight. In fact, it was a long process in which the view of fiscal policy changed partly because facts changed, partly because the interpretation of facts changed. Policy priorities were guided by the experiences of the Great Depression and World War II, making full employment the prime objective, and fiscal policy served as the most important policy tool with respect to this goal.

Few anticipated the profound changes in economic environment and policy outlook that would take place in the following quarter century. The Keynesian consensus portrayed by Stein was largely abandoned in the turbulent 1970s, as economies were mired in concurrent inflation and mounting unemployment. In the course of this fiscal counter-revolution, monetarist ideas gained currency and combating inflation became first priority in economic policymaking. A new consensus gradually emerged, establishing the current hegemony of monetary policy over fiscal policy and independent central banks over Treasuries and ministries of finance.

The war on inflation has been overwhelmingly successful, even if the victory was not just won by monetary policy alone. Inflation is now virtually nonexistent in industrialized countries, and generally subdued in the developing world. The victory over inflation was, however, bought at a high cost in terms of sluggish growth, high unemployment and income inequality in many parts of the world, giving rise to a host of economic and social problems that take their toll. Social protection and the welfare state have become increasingly strained by mounting demands and deficient revenue flows, in what has sometimes been referred to as the fiscal crisis of the state.

There is now widespread discussion of the risks of general stagnation, and the specter of a liquidity trap rendering monetary policies ineffectual. The world economy is slowly recovering after three years in the doldrums. Little stimulus is to be expected from the Japanese and European economies, due not least to concerns about budgetary deficits and the limits imposed by the Stability and Growth Pact. The burden of pulling the world economy out of stagnation thus falls upon the shoulders of the United States, whose sizeable twin deficits (of the federal budget and of the current account of the balance of payments) may add further complications to this already difficult task.

Developing countries are strapped in a direr situation, if that is possible. In many cases external liberalization – forcefully pursued for more than a decade now – has meant that revenues have fallen at a time when globalization calls for increasing social spending. The increased fiscal strains derive from a fall in revenues, often associated with lower tariff revenues, and with higher spending on debt servicing, due to higher interest rates.

In these circumstances, the role of fiscal policy has become subject to renewed interest. With interest rates at their lowest levels in decades, and in some cases very close to zero, the scope for further monetary stimulus does seem limited. It is yet unclear whether monetary policy action taken hitherto will suffice to stage a broad recovery in asset prices and economic activity. Pessimists have warned that fiscal policy may be the only way to bring about the desired outcome.

The aim of this introductory chapter is to analyze the evolution of the dominant views on fiscal policy, clarify questions regarding the efficacy of fiscal policy in the short run as well as its long-run sustainability, and to explore the different dilemmas imposed on the developing world. As such, this chapter will serve as a guide for the original contributions in the subsequent chapters. The rest of this introduction is divided into three subsections. The following one will discuss briefly the changing views on fiscal policy within the profession, and provide a picture of what is the current tendency in the profession regarding short-term efficacy and long-term sustainability. The final section provides an overview of the chapters to follow and an evaluation of their convergence and divergence from conventional wisdom.

The changing consensus on fiscal policy

Most economists in recent decades would agree that future generations bear a burden resulting from public spending financed internally by public debt and taking place in the current period. The burden of public expenditure financed by debt consists of the reduced private consumption supposedly required by the withdrawal of resources from the private sector. The view of government debt as a burden on society, particularly an intergenerational burden, is however relatively new. It derives from the work of James Buchanan, starting in the 1950s, and was consolidated around the 1970s, in the midst of the crisis of Keynesian economics.

In historical perspective, economists' views on whether public debt is a blessing or a burden have changed significantly. During the eighteenth and nineteenth centuries they were dominated by the principles of sound finance and balanced budgets. Yet most laymen and politicians at the time saw government debt, albeit in moderation, as a blessing rather than a curse. For example, Alexander Hamilton, the first Treasury Secretary and main strategist of the economic system in the post-independent United States, argued for the development of a national public debt as a form of providing a strong central government. Hamilton saw government debt and a national public bank as the pillars of the British economic success that he wanted to emulate in America. Economists, on the other hand, saw public debt with apprehension.

This changed in the early part of the twentieth century. The Keynesian Revolution, and even more emphatically Abba Lerner's functional finance theory, provided the rationale for the idea that public debt would be helpful in a crisis. Functional finance established that, under certain conditions, government debt is an essential feature of a healthy economy. Within the mainstream of the profession, it was also argued that debt was a useful policy instrument. In a general equilibrium system with incomplete markets, public debt may assist capital formation and lead to higher rates of growth. Politicians, on the other hand, were not quite convinced about the positive effects of debt.

Starting in the 1950s, the benign view of public debt gradually gave way to a more pessimistic position. In most industrialized countries, the ratio of public debt to Gross Domestic Product (GDP) showed a declining tendency in post-war era, the downward trend turning only with the onset of serious unemployment and inflation in the 1970s. The change in views on the debt must therefore be attributed primarily to concerns about the potential consequences of the brisk growth in public expenditures and the expanding welfare state. The process of globalization – the liberalization of movements of goods, services and capital – since the end of Bretton Woods, has led to a proliferation as well as an increased accessibility of tax havens. Moreover, the increase in tax competition and interest rates made public debt more difficult to service. Finally, the stagflation of the 1970s, and the conservative reaction that followed, fed a tax revolt that made increasing tax burdens to finance public debt unlikely. Measures to contain spending, and to reduce the burden of debt became more common. The most well-known policy measure to curb debt is undoubtedly the

Maastricht limits on the ratio of public debt to GDP, which is imposed on the member countries of the European monetary union.

In the nineteenth century, as economics established itself as a respectable discipline with a place in the most important universities, balanced budgets were seen as essential, not just to keep the debts at sustainable levels, but also to avoid excessive burdens on the poor. William Gladstone, the prime minister that dominated British politics in the second half of the nineteenth century, believed that the miseries of the poor stemmed from the unnecessary burden of indirect taxes, which are paid mostly by the poor (Maloney, 1998, p. 32). For this very reason he fought for the imposition of income taxes.

With the depression and the advent of Keynesian economics, the role of the state changed significantly. Income tax and social security contributions became the main source of revenue, and the role of indirect taxes diminished. A progressive income tax – once advocated as a radical measure – became standard in the Western world. By the late 1970s, tax revenues in the developed countries ranged from slightly less than 30 to more than 50 percent of GDP, and some authors foresaw a fiscal crisis. According to O'Connor (1973) a structural gap developed, the ability to raise taxes was limited, and the social demands were virtually unlimited. Tanzi and Schuknecht (2000) argue that the increase in the size of government, and the pervasive fiscal deficits in the last 30 years did not lead to any social or economic advantages. According to them, since the 1960s the size of the state increased without leading to higher levels of income per capita or a better distribution of income. As a result in their view, the tax burden and expenditures should be considerably scaled down.

The growth of government measured by spending or tax revenues as a share of national income exhibits a secular trend. Wagner's Law – a positive long-run relationship between public expenditure and output – is apparently alive and kicking. The reasons for the secular growth in government are varied and related to the public view of what a government should do. The processes of industrialization and urbanization intertwine with the growth of government. Factory work and city life gives rise to pressures for the provision of public goods and social protection. It is also clear that the enlargement of the franchise and the general movement toward democratic institutions allowed for an expansion of social rights, and the number of tasks imposed on governments. The welfare state – the apotheosis of Wagner's Law – then results from technological and demographic trends, as well as democratic institutions and hard-won battles for social rights.

The impressive increase in the flows of trade and capital, that came to be denominated globalization, are seen by many authors as having dealt the last blow to the welfare state. In particular, tax competition might seem to erode the tax base, while globalization requires a more comprehensive social safety net. Globalization then forces higher spending while it erodes the ability to obtain higher revenues, leading to a fiscal squeeze. Also, the previously fiscally friendly demographic conditions, with many contributors and few recipients of pension benefits, will change in the next quarter century in most developed countries, increasing the burden of payments, and making a fiscal crisis more likely. But, like the proverbial decease of Mark Twain, rumors of a fiscal crisis may be considerably exaggerated so far.

Alarmist academic and public debate notwithstanding, trends of expenditures on social protection are stubbornly pointing upward in most parts of the world. A quarter century of sustained efforts on the part of policy-makers to check spending growth seems to have taken its toll mainly on government purchases of goods and services, with public investment suffering most drastically from the cutbacks. Although the effects of these reductions are subject to some controversy, there is widespread consensus that investment in infrastructure, education and health care are more conducive to long-term economic growth than are transfer payments. In this perspective, one cannot help noting the irony that it is the relatively productive activities of government that have been sliced while the unproductive expenditures keep pouring from the public coffers like an unstoppable lava stream. These trends carry an important a message about the sometimes-loose relationship between public discourse about political priorities on the one hand, and economic realities and necessities on the other.

While anti-government sentiments have long since permeated the political rhetoric, there is in fact no clear evidence of the death – or even a significant reduction of the size – of the state, at least in macroeconomic terms. The last 30 years, however, usually associated with globalization, have seen an increase in the size of the debt. These budgetary difficulties emerged alongside rising unemployment and sluggish growth, with the former forcing higher expenditures and the latter restraining revenues.

High levels of public debt, some fear, may reduce – for political reasons mainly – the ability of governments to run deficits in times of crisis. The impressive growth of the size of the debt over the last two centuries in most developed countries went hand in hand with the process of industrialization and capital accumulation that raised the welfare levels of their populations. However, the increase in public debt led to rising fears of a collapse of the tax state. The question of whether government debt is a blessing or a burden on society is a crucial one that economists have been groping with for the last two centuries at least.

If economists' views on the effects of government debt have swung back and forth over the years, the same is true in the political arena. For example, with the foundation of the National Debt in 1693, and the Bank of England in 1694, public finance became a major topic in political economy debates in England (Hamilton, 1947). As a general rule, conservatives saw the debt as an inappropriate increase in the power of the crown and a threat to individual liberties. On the other hand, Whigs saw public debt as the basis for the development of the financial sector, and the expansion of trade. The political conflict can be seen as a dispute between creditor's interests (Whigs) versus debtor's interests (Tories).

Among the founding fathers of political economy, David Hume and Adam Smith expressed clear ideas about government debt. The usual identification of Hume as a Tory – in particular because of his historical writings – means that his views on public debt are usually associated with the conservative country party. Hence, Rotwein (1955, p. lxxxvi) in his authoritative introduction to Hume's writings on economics argues, "what he [Hume] seeks to show is that the inevitable continued rise in debt will not only have the gravest consequences for society but will ultimately terminate in total bankruptcy."

While it is clear that Hume was concerned, and was critical of the increasing size of public debt, he was not a dogmatic critic of the fiscal policies of the crown. He clearly refers to the ill resulting from public debt, but he also claims that some good results from a national debt (Hume, 1955, pp. 90–107). Adam Smith was also more concerned about the dangers of bankruptcy than the possibilities for expanded trade that government debt facilitated (Smith, 1776, Book 5). However, one must note that Smith thought that taxes hindered capital accumulation in a way that government debt did not. As noted by Winch (1998, p. 13), McCulloch criticized both Hume and Smith, for not perceiving that output growth made the burden of debt easier to carry.

David Ricardo's contributions to the question of public finances have cast a long shadow. Ricardo was even more concerned than his predecessors about the negative effects of taxes and public debt on capital accumulation, and considered the British debt, together with the Corn Laws, one of the two great evils plaguing the nation (Winch, 1998, p. 18). For Ricardo (1817, pp. 150–2) taxes either reduce capital accumulation or force tax payers to reduce consumption. Debt, as deferred taxes, had the same effect, and hence Ricardo was for paying down government debt, and maintaining a relatively low level of taxes – measures that at that time were opposed by both Whigs and Tories. This view was later revived as the Ricardian equivalence theorem (Barro, 1974).

Thomas Malthus – personal friend and main intellectual foe of Ricardo – not surprisingly held different views regarding government debt. As a moderate Whig, Malthus was against paying down public debt, on the grounds that it allowed debt holders to expand consumption and effectual demand, a result that was prevented by Say's Law in the Ricardian system (Ferguson, 2001, pp. 129–30).

The Marginalist Revolution of the 1870s brought significant changes to the core of economic analysis – the theory of value – but left the dominant view on deficits and debt among academic economists unchanged.

It was only the Keynesian Revolution that brought a significant change in academic circles. Thirty years after Keynes (1936) *tour de force*, Tobin

(1965, p. 679) could argue that the conventional view among academic economists – but not in political circles – was that government debt is not a burden on future generations.

Keynes (1936) was opposed to deficit spending, and hence debt accumulation, as a means of stimulating consumption. However, Keynes favored government borrowing to finance capital expenditures to stimulate investment. Lerner (1943) argued that government deficits, and the consequent accumulation of debt, should be instruments for the maintenance of full employment. Colander (1984, p. 1574) suggests that while logically on Lerner's side, Keynes was unwilling to endorse functional finance for political reasons. The main political constraint to functional finance would be the possibility of persistent deficits and increasing government debt during peacetime.

The main problem raised by persistent deficits is the one of debt sustainability. Domar (1944) showed that debt-to-GDP ratios tend to increase at explosive rates when the rate of interest exceeds the rate of growth. This can be easily understood in the following way. The rate of interest on government bonds is the rate at which treasury debt increases, while the rate of growth of the economy is a proxy of the capacity to pay for the debt, since revenues rise in a booming economy. Consequently, if the rate of interest is higher than the rate of growth, then the burden of debt is rising faster than the ability to pay, and the proportion of debt to GDP must rise (Blanchard, 1990; Galbraith and Darity, 1995).

Some Keynesian authors (e.g. Modigliani, 1961; Musgrave, 1959) argue that the method of financing government expenditures, that is, either current taxes or government debt, and hence, future taxes, may affect the uses of resources. This result, one must note, contradicts Ricardian Equivalence. In this view, tax finance displaces current consumption, while debt finance displaces current investment, and has a negative impact on capital accumulation. This consolidated the mainstream Keynesian vision that fiscal deficits and the accumulation of debt have a positive effect in the short run, generating higher levels of employment, but a long-term negative effect on capital accumulation.

Note, however, that the traditional Keynesian result may be affected by market imperfections. Diamond (1965) showed that the failure of competitive markets to support optimal intertemporal allocations can stem from two sources: the divergence between the planning horizon of individuals and the horizon of economic activity, evident in economies of overlapping generations; and market imperfections, such as missing markets for the allocation of risks. Gale (1990) shows that, given financial market imperfections, public debt by introducing low-risk securities may assist capital formation and economic growth.

As Keynesian notions gained widespread currency and were embraced by the mainstream of the profession, Buchanan (1958) emerged as the most vocal mourner of Gladstonian sound finance. Buchanan blamed

Keynesian economics for the elimination of the balanced-budget constraint, which led to the lifting of the limits on politicians' natural bias towards budget deficits. Buchanan's ideas – which according to Tobin (1965, p. 680) can be reduced "to the assertion that payment of taxes is per se a burden [and,] since debt finance postpones the levy of taxes, it obviously shifts [the tax] burden to future generations" – played an important role in the conservative revolution of the late 1970s. However, most discussions about the burden of debt in academic circles are still illuminated by the old Keynesian preoccupations with the effects of debt on private incentives for investment and saving.

While most economists and politicians are concerned about the burden of debt – either because it promotes unfair intergenerational transfers or because it slows down the pace of capital accumulation – post-Keynesian authors have argued about the burden of interest rates. In this view, the problem of debt accumulation results less from the increase in social spending, but from the combination of high rates of interest and low rates of growth in the last 30 years.

Pasinetti (1997, p. 168) argues that the growth of debt is not caused by Keynesian profligacy, and that the vulnerability of fiscal accounts "usually attributed to the high size reached by the debt ... is in fact due to the high level reached by interest rates." The causes of high interest rates and low rates of growth are highly complex and related to the demise of the institutions and policy regime that were in place during the so-called Golden Age of capitalism (Glyn *et al.*, 1990). However, Pasinetti (op. cit.) argues that a revenge of the rentier – the reverse of Keynes' euthanasia of the rentier – resulting from income distribution conflict is at the heart of the process.

Interest payments as a share of GDP – representing the burden associated with government debt servicing – have increased, crowding out social spending. The Bretton Woods period, in which capital controls were widespread and interest rates were set with a view to generating full employment, allowed government social spending to increase without leading to explosive increase in government debt. The institutions and the policy regime in place during that particular period might seem to vindicate the Lernerian benign view of deficits and debt.

An overview of the book

The contributions in this volume reflect the disagreements and the changing views on the short-run and long-run efficacy of fiscal policy. The papers in the First Section tend to favor Keynesian activism in the short run – a view that we believe has maintained its respectability in academic as well as policymaking circles. In Chapter 2, Philip Arestis and Malcolm Sawyer reconsider the case for the use of fiscal policy based on a functional finance approach, which advocates the use of fiscal policy to secure high levels of aggregate demand in the context of low levels of private demand. According to this functional-finance view, any budget deficit should be seen as a response to the perceived excess of private savings over investment at the desired level of economic activity. The chapter considers the three lines of argument, which have been advanced against fiscal policy on the grounds of crowding-out. These lines are based on the response of interest rates, the supply-side equilibrium and Ricardian equivalence. The chapter advances the view that the arguments, which have been deployed against fiscal policy to the effect that it does not raise the level of economic activity, do not apply when a functional-finance view of fiscal policy is adopted. Finally the authors analyze whether the issue of sustainability of budget deficits rules out budget deficits, and conclude that in general it does not.

Laurence Seidman and Kenneth Lewis present and analyze a new automatic counter-cyclical fiscal policy, namely, triggered transfers to households. They propose in Chapter 3 that Congress pre-enact a transfer formula that authorizes an automatic triggering of a new cash transfer to households in response to a high unemployment rate. In particular, the formula prescribes a transfer-to-GDP ratio proportional to the unemployment gap. Whereas currently existing automatic stabilizers are accidental byproducts of addressing other important societal objectives – such as the ratio of government spending to GDP, the degree of progressivity of the tax system, and the level of unemployment benefits – the triggered transfer policy focuses solely on trying to achieve the optimal degree of stimulus to aggregate demand in an economic downturn. It takes as given the current automatic stabilizers enacted for other reasons, and then supplements them in order to get the desired macroeconomic stimulus. One purpose of this chapter is to encourage economists in the Keynesian tradition to resume research on the design and analysis of automatic counter-cyclical fiscal policies, and to support the enactment of such policies.

In Chapter 4, David Colander and Peter Matthews argue that a major problem of fiscal policy is finding a balance between the short-run stabilization goal and the long-run systemic stability goal. As we saw in the previous section, economists' debates about that balance have swung like a pendulum from a long-run focus to a short-run focus, back to a long-run focus. According to the authors, in the early 2000s, this pendulum is at the bottom of a swing and economists' views on fiscal policy are best described as chaotic.

Colander and Matthews believe that among the majority of academic economists, short-run discretionary fiscal policy is in ill repute both theoretically and practically. The general view held by most academic macroeconomists is that short-run fiscal policy does not work, or if it works, then it works at the wrong time. The authors conclude that the once-accepted Keynesian theories of how fiscal policy worked have given way to a variety of theoretical models that provide little guidance for policymakers.

As a pragmatic synthesis and remedy, Colander and Matthews propose a change in the budgeting procedures: Instead of using the traditional annual budgeting, government should use a moving-average budget, to which any rule that restricts fiscal policy should be made to apply. The authors contend that specifying all legal long-term budget restraints in terms of this moving average would reduce the perverse effects that long-run budget restrictions bring about under the current annual budgeting system. This chapter thus offers a complement to Seidman and Lewis' discussion (in Chapter 3) of methods to reintroduce fiscal stabilization policy.

Max Sawicky makes a case, in the last chapter of the First Section, that traditional economic arguments on the merits or demerits of public spending have become irrelevant. He contends that the predominant view in policymaking circles is that such spending cannot be afforded. Cost–benefit calculations have thus been ruled out of the political discourse. Over the past three years, the US Federal budget outlook dropped precipitously, from a projected surplus of over \$5 trillion over the coming ten years to a project deficit of similar size. It was this drastic change that lent support to the widespread view that the nation cannot afford more government spending. Sawicky swims against this tide and uses numerical examples to show that robust spending growth is not only feasible but can be accommodated within a fiscally responsible framework. His analysis is based on a stable ratio of public debt to GDP, a principle embraced by most economists but poorly understood by the public. The caveat is that the exact level that would be politically acceptable is difficult to pinpoint, and Sawicky suggests as a safe level one which is in line with recent historical experience.

The Second Section examines the impact of fiscal adjustment on economic performance for a limited but illustrative sample of developing countries, namely the Dominican Republic, Brazil and Turkey. Esteban Pérez Caldentey argues in Chapter 6 that fiscal policy in the Dominican Republic is an important constraint and burden on monetary policy and has determined to some extent the choice of exchange rate regime. Since 1990, the year marking the beginning of the implementation of the stabilization plan termed the New Economic Policy (NEP), the authorities of the Dominican Republic have been committed to orthodox macroeconomic management and trade liberalization. As part of this strategy the country has embarked on successive fiscal reforms. Two key objectives of the most recent tax and tariff reforms have been to improve the effectiveness of the tax system and to compensate for the expected loss in fiscal revenue resulting from tariff reduction. The lack of success is reflected in the relationship between two analytically useful indicators developed by Wynne Godley and Francis Cripps (1983), namely: the fiscal stance indicator has surpassed the export performance indicator, implying a potentially unsustainable debt situation.

Chapter 7 focuses on the Brazilian economy as an example of endogenous fiscal crisis. Matias Vernengo claims that under certain conditions, fiscally responsible governments facing favorable domestic and international conditions may end up dealing with a fiscal crisis. An endogenous fiscal crisis results from the normal functioning of the economic system, and the author contends that endogenous fiscal crises result from external financial liberalization. In wage-led economies, financial liberalization that promotes integration with international financial markets, when coupled with large primary fiscal surpluses, may lead to stagnating rates of output growth and high nominal deficits *cum* growing debt. The author maintains that the Brazilian economy is a good illustration of an endogenous fiscal crisis of this type.

Chapter 8 by Ebru Voyvoda discusses the Turkish economy, which bears some semblance to the Brazilian case. After more than a decade of external liberalization policies and globalization experience, fiscal policy in developing economies is generally associated with terms like debt sustainability, government solvency and fiscal crisis. There is a vast literature of both theoretical and empirical studies that investigate whether a given level of debt is sustainable and whether large and persistent deficits will eventually lead a country to default. Voyvoda cautions us that most of these studies are based on an accounting approach, which overlooks the impact on key variables such as economic growth, income distribution, employment, and the provision of public goods resulting from budget consolidation and fiscal retrenchment. She calls for a systemic approach involving general-equilibrium considerations to supplement the overly simplistic methods currently used by the International Monetary Fund as well as most other analysts in the field. Voyvoda contends that the current consensus that developing economies should maintain high primary surplus-to-GNP ratios cannot be considered as the only scientific alternative for constructing successful fiscal policies. The author uses the Turkish experience under the structural-adjustment program to show that a fiscal policy, which depends solely on attaining pre-determined levels of necessary primary surpluses, may be unable to achieve a successful debt rollover together with generating a sustained growth path.

The questions of efficacy and sustainability of fiscal policy are reintroduced in the Third Section, at a higher level of abstraction. In recent years, supply-side economists have argued that tax cuts and the resulting budget deficits may induce so much additional growth in the tax base that they end up paying for themselves in the long run. In Chapter 9, Per Gunnar Berglund juxtaposes these ideas with a long-run version of the traditional Keynesian paradox of thrift. An analogous paradox of the budget is also proposed along the lines of Vickrey (1992). Berglund develops a Keynesian growth model, which generates both these phenomena when calibrated with empirically relevant parameter values.

In Chapter 10, Robert Eisner employs pooled time-series and

cross-section analysis to analyze the impact of fiscal policy in 19 OECD countries from 1970 to 1995. This study is a continuation and extension of his long series of studies of those same relations in the context of the US economy. Eisner finds that basic hypotheses of the relation of inflation-and-cyclically-adjusted deficits to subsequent changes in unemployment and real GDP are confirmed in the pooled relations. The deficit coefficients were significantly negative for unemployment, and positive for GDP, implying that an increase of the inflation-and-cyclically-adjusted deficits is associated with a subsequent reduction of unemployment or an acceleration of real GDP growth.

Eisner finds that the absolute sizes of the coefficients were markedly less than those in the US regressions, and that the US deficit variable turned up with highly significant coefficients even when included along with all of the own-country deficit variables. This means that US deficits would appear to help the rest of the world; possibly their stimulative effect on the US economy spills over. Conversely, when US deficits come down, the rest of the world would appear to suffer, perhaps illustrating the old adage that when the United States economy develops a cold, the rest of the world develops pneumonia. Eisner contends that the time-series and cross-section estimates, their frailties notwithstanding, are remarkably consistent.

Alfred Greiner, Uwe Koeller and Willi Semmler's Chapter 11 studies the sustainability of fiscal policy for selected euro-area countries. They focus on those countries that either have a high debt-to-GDP ratio (Italy) or have recently violated the Maastricht treaty by permitting more than 3 percent of the deficit-to-GDP ratio (France, Germany and Portugal). They apply and extend an approach developed by Bohn (1998), who proposes to study whether the intertemporal budget constraint of the government holds by modeling the public debt-to-GDP ratio as a mean-reverting process, a method that is free from the arbitrary discount rates that other approaches rely upon. By controlling for the impact of other variables on this mean-reverting process, the authors conclude that for the above-mentioned countries, fiscal policy is sustainable in the long run, even if the three-percent rule of the Maastricht treaty is temporarily violated. They also compare their results from the euro-area countries to results obtained for the US fiscal policy.

Chapter 12, written by Alan Isaac, presents a theoretical post-Keynesian growth model of a conflicting-claims economy where monetary policy is assumed to follow a Taylor rule. He explores in this framework the effects of fiscal policy. Fiscal stimulus is decomposed into distinct varieties, depending on whether the initial effect is primarily on consumption or investment. Effects on output growth, employment and inflation are analyzed. The type of policy proves important for the understanding of growth, unemployment, and the distribution of income.

The last Section is composed of a Roundtable and an Interview. The former took place at the end of the conference where the papers in this volume were presented, at the Eastern Economic Association Meetings in Washington, DC, in February 2004. The latter took place in July 1997 at Robert Eisner's office at Northwestern University on Chicago's north shore.

The Roundtable (Chapter 13), mediated by Vernengo, reflects our concerns with the current fiscal stance in the US and with the changing views of Democrats and Republicans on fiscal matters. Barbara Bergmann, Jeffrey Frankel, William Niskanen, Laurence Seidman discuss "The Political Economy of the Deficit" and offer their informed, contrasting, and entertaining views on Bush's tax cuts, the bankruptcy or not of Social Security and the Democrat/Republican switch on fiscal policy.

The Interview (Chapter 14), carried out by Berglund, reflects an intellectual affinity with Robert Eisner's views on macroeconomics in general and fiscal policy in particular. It provides an overview in Eisner's own words of his life and work, and addresses numerous questions with respect to the deficit, the debt, and related issues of political economy.

Gunnar Myrdal once said that objectivity in social research presupposes honesty about one's worldview. We believe that the functional-finance approach – the idea that the merits of fiscal policies should be judged on the basis of their economic effects rather than on other grounds – provides the best available tools for analyzing fiscal policy. Also, the general tone of the contributions in this volume is cautiously favorable to fiscal activism, although the emphasis is placed more on medium-term adjustments than on short-term "fine tuning." We believe that the legacy of the last fiscal revolution has been an excessively negative view of deficits and debt. In some quarters, the profession has returned to a dogmatic view according to which fiscal austerity is always desirable. We hope that this volume will contribute to open a dialogue on fiscal issues, and to bring back a more balanced view of fiscal policy.[2]

We would like to end by thanking everybody that made the conference and this volume possible, in particular to Mary Lesser and the Eastern Economic Association, who provided facilities for the conference sessions. We would also like to thank all the conference participants whose stimulating questions and comments added vibrancy to the sessions – including those that appear in this volume and Harald Hagemann, Yong-Bok Jean, Barsha Katthry, Inge Kaul, Perry Mehrling, and Mohan Rao that were instrumental in other ways. We are much indebted to Edith Eisner, Mary Eccles, Robert Coen and James Rock for providing extensive feedback and help with the editing of both Chapter 10 and the Interview in Chapter 14.

Notes

1 Schumpeter (1918) argued that the "public finances are one of the best starting points for an investigation of society." Fiscal matters, he suggested, are one of the main vehicles of social and economic change. In that sense, fiscal issues have

a centrality in economic history to which most of the economic profession is oblivious.
2 This book shares the intellectual outlook and the same preoccupations with fiscal issues as Rock (1991).

References

Barro, Robert J. (1974), "Are Government Bonds Net Wealth?" *Journal of Political Economy*, 82(6), November–December, pp. 1095–117.

Blanchard, Olivier (1990), "Suggestions for a New Set of Fiscal Indicators," *OECD Economics and Statistics Department Working Papers*, No. 79, April.

Bohn, Henning (1998), "The Behavior of U.S. Public Debt and Deficits," *Quarterly Journal of Economics*, 113(3), August, pp. 949–63.

Buchanan, James (1958), "Concerning Future Generations," in *Public Debt and Future Generations*, edited by James M. Ferguson, Chapel Hill: University of North Carolina Press, 1964.

Colander, David (1984), "Was Keynes a Keynesian or a Lernerian," *Journal of Economic Literature*, 22(4), December, pp. 1572–5.

Diamond, Peter (1965), "National Debt in a Neoclassical Growth Model," *American Economic Review*, 55(5), December, pp. 1126–50.

Ferguson, Nyall (2001), *The Cash Nexus: Money and Power in the Modern World, 1700–2000*, New York: Basic Books.

Galbraith, James K. and William Darity, Jr. (1995), "A Guide to the Deficit," *Challenge*, July–August, pp. 5–12.

Gale, Douglas (1990), "The Efficient Design of Public Debt," in *Public Debt Management: Theory and History*, edited by Rudi Dornbusch and Mario Draghi, Cambridge, Mass.: MIT Press.

Glyn, Andrew, Alain Hughes, Alain Lipietz, and Ajit Singh (1990), "The Rise and Fall of the Golden Age," in *The Golden Age of Capitalism*, edited by Stephen Marglin and Juliet Schor. Oxford: Oxford University Press.

Godley, Wynne and Francis Cripps (1983), *Macroeconomics*, Oxford: Oxford University Press.

Hamilton, Earl J. (1947), "Origin and Growth of the National Debt in Western Europe," *American Economic Review*, 37(2), May, pp. 118–30.

Hume, David (1955), *Writings on Economics*, Madison: University of Wisconsin Press, 1970.

Keynes, John Maynard (1936), *The General Theory of Employment, Interest and Money*, London: Macmillan.

Lerner, Abba P. (1943), "Functional Finance and the Federal Debt," *Social Research*, Vol. 10, February, pp. 38–51.

Maloney, John (1998), "Gladstone and Sound Victorian Finance," in *Debt and Deficits: An Historical Perspective*, edited by John Maloney, Cheltenham, UK: Edward Elgar.

Modigliani, Franco (1961), "Long Run Implications of Alternative Fiscal Policies and the Burden of National Debt," in *Public Debt and Future Generations*, edited by James M. Ferguson, Chapel Hill: University of North Carolina Press, 1964.

Musgrave, Richard (1959), "Internal Debt and the Classical System," in *Public Debt and Future Generations*, edited by James M. Ferguson, Chapel Hill: University of North Carolina Press, 1964.

O'Connor, James (1973), *The Fiscal Crisis of the State*, New York: St. Martin's Press.

Pasinetti, Luigi (1997), "The Social Burden of High Interest Rates," in *Capital Controversy, Post-Keynesian Economics and the History of Economics: Essays in Honour of Geoff Harcourt*, Volume I, edited by Philip Arestis, Gabriel Palma and Malcolm Sawyer, London: Routledge.

Ricardo, David (1817), *On the Principles of Political Economy and Taxation*, edited by Piero Sraffa with the collaboration of Maurice Dobb, London and Cambridge: Royal Economic Society and Cambridge University Press, 1995.

Rotwein, Eugene (1955), "Introduction," in *David Hume, Writings on Economics*, Madison: University of Wisconsin Press, 1970.

Rock, James M. (1991), *Debt and the Twin Deficits Debate*, Mountain View, California: Mayfield Publishing Company.

Schumpeter, Joseph A. (1918), "The Crisis of the Tax State," *International Economic Papers*, 4, pp. 5–38, 1954.

Smith, Adam (1776), *An Inquiry into the Nature and Causes of the Wealth of Nations*, edited by Roy H. Campbell and Andrew S. Skinner, Indianapolis: Liberty Fund, 1981.

Stein, Herbert (1969), *The Fiscal Revolution in America*, Chicago: Chicago University Press.

Tanzi, Vito and Ludger Schuknecht (2000), *Public Spending in the 20th Century*, Cambridge: Cambridge University Press.

Tobin, James (1965), "The Burden of the Public Debt: A Review Article," *Journal of Finance*, 20(4), pp. 679–82.

Vickrey, William S. (1992), "Meaningfully Defining Deficits and Debt," *American Economic Review*, 82(2), May, pp. 305–10.

Winch, Donald (1998), "The Political Economy of Public Finance in the 'Long' Eighteenth Century," in *Debt and Deficits: An Historical Perspective*, edited by John Maloney, Cheltenham, UK: Edward Elgar.

Part I
Fiscal policy strikes back

2 The case for fiscal policy

Philip Arestis and Malcolm Sawyer

Introduction

The case for the use of fiscal policy and for governments to operate with an unbalanced budget (whether in surplus or deficit) arises from the simple Keynesian proposition that there is no automatic mechanism which ensures that aggregate demand is sufficient to underpin a high level of economic activity (Kalecki, 1939, Keynes, 1936). The notion that the budget should always be in balance (or even on average in balance) is rejected on the grounds that a balanced budget is generally not compatible with the achievement of high levels of aggregate demand. Further, although interest rates may have some impact on the level of aggregate demand, there are constraints on the extent to which interest rates can be varied (whether for reasons akin to a liquidity trap in operation which prevent the reduction of interest rates below a particular level or for foreign exchange considerations) and there are doubts relating to the potency of interest rates to influence aggregate demand (see Arestis and Sawyer, 2004).

Many lines of argument have been developed to the effect that budget deficits and fiscal policy are ineffectual and/or have undesired (and undesirable) effects. This paper starts from a "functional finance" perspective (discussed in the next section), which views the role of fiscal policy in terms of raising the level of aggregate demand, where it would otherwise be too low.[1] It puts forward the view that the arguments, which have been deployed against fiscal policy to the effect that it does not raise the level of economic activity, do not apply when a "functional finance" view of fiscal policy is adopted.

Fiscal policy and "functional finance"

The starting point for this paper is the argument that the nature and role of fiscal policy should be approached from the perspective of what has been termed "functional finance" (Lerner, 1943). The general proposition is that the budget position should be used to secure a high level of economic activity in conditions where otherwise there would be a lower level of economic activity. Lerner (1943) put the case for Functional Finance (capitalized in the original), which "rejects completely the traditional doctrines of 'sound finance' and the principle of trying to balance the budget over a solar year or any other arbitrary period" (p. 355). "Functional finance" supports the important proposition that total spending should be adjusted to eliminate both unemployment and inflation.

In a similar vein, Kalecki (1944a) argued that sustained full employment "must be based either on a long-run budget deficit policy or on the redistribution of income" (p. 135). Kalecki based his argument on the assumption that there would be a tendency for the level of aggregate demand to fall short of what was required for full employment. Then there was a need for either a budget deficit to mop up with the difference between full employment savings and investment, or for full employment savings to be reduced through a redistribution of income (from rich to poor).

He also argued that "although it has been repeatedly stated in recent discussion that the budget deficit always finances itself – that is to say, its rise always causes such an increase in incomes and changes in their distribution that there accrue just enough savings to finance it – the matter is still frequently misunderstood" (Kalecki, 1944b). He then set out for a closed economy the equality:

$$G + I = T + S \tag{1}$$

(where G is government expenditure, T tax revenue, I investment expenditure and S savings) and hence:

$$G - T = S - I \tag{2}$$

which can be readily modified for the open economy as:

$$G + I + X = T + S + Q \tag{3}$$

where X stands for exports and Q for imports.

From this perspective, the budget deficit is to be used to mop up "excess" private savings (over investment), and the counterpart budget surplus used when investment expenditure exceeds savings (at the desired level of economic activity). It follows, though, that a budget deficit is not required when there is a high level of private aggregate demand such that investment equals savings at a high level of economic activity (and a surplus would be required when investment exceeds savings at the desired level of economic activity). This can be expressed by saying that the government budget position should be set so that:

$$G - T = S(Y_f) - I(Y_f) + Q(Y_f) - X(WY) \tag{4}$$

where Y_f is the intended level of income (which may be thought of as equivalent to full employment or to some supply side constraint), WY is world income (which is taken as given for the purposes of $G - T$ equation). A tendency for savings to run ahead of investment leads to the view that a budget deficit is required (in the absence of any tendency for balance of trade surplus). But it is a shortfall of investment over savings that creates the requirement for a budget deficit: in the absence of any such short fall (in *ex ante* terms) there is no need for a budget deficit. The analysis of budget deficits should then be undertaken in a context, which at least allows for the emergence of an excess of (*ex ante*) savings over (*ex ante*) investment. In the absence of any such excess, the "functional finance" view would not see any cause for a budget deficit.[2]

The case for fiscal policy rests on the proposition that the equality between *ex ante* savings and *ex ante* investment at full employment income cannot be assured (or indeed at any target level of income).[3] If there were some automatic tendency, as expressed in Say's Law, for that equality to be assured, then any case for fiscal policy in the form of unbalanced budgets would disappear. Further, if the relevant rate of interest can be manipulated through monetary policy in such a way as to ensure this equality, then again there would be little room for fiscal policy. The basic Keynesian (Kaleckian) argument is that there is no assurance that this equality will be satisfied, and hence a need for fiscal policy and for an unbalanced budget.

The general presumption of Keynesians and others has been that there is likely to be a deficiency of *ex ante* investment relative to *ex ante* savings, rather than the reverse. This does not rule out that there will be occasions (as in the late 1990s in the UK, and the USA, with conditions of low unemployment) when investment runs ahead of savings. In the former case, a budget deficit is required to mop up the excess savings, while in the latter case a budget surplus results. However, the presumption that budget deficits are the more frequent outcome under the use of "functional finance" does raise the problem of cumulative budget deficits and rising government debt. Lerner (1943) and others acknowledge this possibility but saw that "No matter how much interest has to be paid on the debt, taxation must not be applied unless it is necessary to keep spending down to prevent inflation. The interest can be paid by borrowing still more" (p. 356). Lerner (1943) summarized the answers to arguments against deficit spending by saying that the national debt does not have to keep on increasing, and that even if it does the interest does not have to be paid from current taxes. Further, interest payments on bonds are an internal transfer. This question of the sustainability of budget deficits is further considered below.

Fiscal policy is often viewed in terms of the determination of government expenditure and taxation as undertaken without specific regard to the state of private aggregate demand. The "crowding out" argument, after all, assumes that there is something to be crowded out. That approach to fiscal policy suggests either that fiscal policy has no effect on the level of economic activity (since there is crowding out) or that there is a positive link between government expenditure (budget deficit) and the level of economic activity. The investigation of fiscal policy through the means of simulation of macroeconometric models is concerned (usually) with the question of what happens if government expenditure is increased, other things being equal. The results of such simulations, generally, suggest that an increase in government expenditure does have a positive effect on the level of economic activity (Arestis and Sawyer, 2003). Indeed, in the context in which these simulations are undertaken, it is somewhat surprising that positive results are obtained since such macro-econometric models generally build in a variety of ways by which there would be crowding out – the most notable one being that imposition of some form of supply-side equilibrium.

The approach to fiscal policy just described is not one that underlies the approach of this paper. Indeed we would argue that this approach has been implicit in most recent discussion of fiscal policy and "crowding out," but does not correspond to the way in which fiscal policy should be viewed. The effects of fiscal policy (especially when that takes the form of a budget deficit) from a "functional finance" perspective start from the position that budget deficits are applied when there would otherwise be a deficiency of aggregate demand (below that required for the target level of economic activity), and conversely budget surpluses applied when there would otherwise be an excess of aggregate demand. This is not to say that fiscal policy has been always (or even usually) applied in this manner. But it is to argue that fiscal policy and its effects should be evaluated against this background. The evaluation of fiscal policy should not start from the presumption that there would otherwise be adequate effective demand in that all would agree that in the context of adequate private effective demand there is no requirement for budget deficits. There have been three distinct sets of arguments to the effect that fiscal policy will be ineffective, under the general heading of "crowding out," and these are now considered in turn.

Crowding out Mark 1: interest rates

The first form of crowding, discussed in the context of the IS-LM analysis, was a partial "crowding-out" due to a rise in interest rates following a fiscal expansion which shifted the IS curve outwards. This was based on the assumption that the money supply was exogenous and fixed by government (or central bank), and that the interest rate equated the demand for and supply of money. In that context, though, it was recognized that a sufficient increase in the stock of money alongside an increase in government expenditure could prevent the rise in the interest rate, and allow the full effect on the level of economic activity of the increase in government expenditure to come through.

This argument relies on the view that monetary policy (in the form of an increase in the stock of money) does not accommodate fiscal policy, and that investment and other forms of private expenditure are sensitive to the rate of interest. It is also the case that this argument assumes that the stock of money is exogenously determined (outside of the private sector). It is clear that in industrialized economies most of what is counted as money takes the form of credit money (bank deposits). In that context, the stock of money is eventually determined by the demand for money and the level of interest rates is not set by the interaction of the supply and demand for money. Further, monetary policy no longer (if it ever did) takes the form of making changes in the stock of money (or even of targeting the rate of change of the stock of money) but rather takes the form of the setting of some key interest rate (e.g. federal funds rate, "repo" rate).

In the context of endogenous credit money with the key interest rate set by the central bank, "crowding out" through the operation of monetary policy would arise from the deliberate actions of the central bank. That is to say, that if the central bank (presumably operating on an "independent" basis) responds to a fiscal expansion by raising interest rates (say on the grounds that fiscal expansion created inflationary pressures), then there would be some form of crowding out (in so far as an increase in interest rates reduces private expenditure). Its extent would depend on the size of the interest rate rise, its feed through to other interest rates, the interest rate responsiveness of expenditure, and the phase of the business cycle. The key point here is that any "crowding out" depends on the responses of the monetary authorities: it does not occur through the response of the markets. In the short run, at least, with the key interest rate set by the central bank any "crowding out" comes from the discretionary actions of the central bank. The effect of a budget deficit on the general level of interest rates then depends on the reactions of the central bank to the budget deficit (or more generally to changes which are stimulated by the budget deficit). A "conservative" central bank which viewed a budget deficit as being to some degree inflationary (whether through a direct effect on inflation or through stimulating aggregate demand which was perceived as inflationary) would respond to a budget deficit by raising interest rates. In contrast a "Keynesian" central bank whose policy decisions were coordinated with the fiscal policy decisions would respond by making no change to the key interest rate. It is then possible that a budget deficit will be accompanied by increased interest rates, but that would be a discretionary policy decision of the central bank and not the operation of some "iron law."[4]

Others would argue that the (long-term) rate of interest is settled in the market for loanable funds, and further that the budget deficit, being the government's demand for loanable funds, will increase demand for loanable funds and thereby the rate of interest. But the "functional finance" approach views the budget deficit as filling the gap between *ex ante* savings and investment (at the desired level of economic activity). In the absence of the budget deficit, savings and investment would adjust, notably through changes in the level of economic activity. The budget deficit is required since (by assumption) the rate of interest cannot adjust sufficiently to bring *ex ante* savings and investment into line at an acceptable level of economic activity. The general expectation of the "functional finance" approach is that budget deficits have no effect on interest rates (when the budget deficit is designed to "mop up" excessive savings), and ironically this is the same conclusion, which is reached by the Ricardian equivalence literature.

Crowding out Mark 2: supply-side equilibrium

The second form of "crowding out" arose from a combination of the notion of a supply-side equilibrium (such as the "natural rate of unemployment" or the non-accelerating inflation rate of unemployment, the NAIRU), and that the level of aggregate demand would adjust to be consistent with that supply-side equilibrium. In the context of an exogenous money supply, this came through the assertion of a "real balance" effect, with changes in the price level generating changes in the real value of the stock of money, thereby generating changes in the level of aggregate demand.[5] In the context of endogenous money, it would come through the adjustment of interest rate by the central bank. This could occur if the central bank adopted some form of "Taylor's rule" under which the setting of the key interest rate depends on the "equilibrium" rate of interest, deviation of inflation from target and deviation of output from trend level (Taylor, 1993). Monetary policy can guide aggregate demand to match supply provided that interest rates are effective in influencing the level of demand and provided that the central bank's calculation of the "equilibrium rate" of interest is accurate. As has been argued above, fiscal policy has an effect on the level of aggregate demand, and "crowding out" only occurs if it assumed that the supply-side equilibrium must be attained (in order to ensure a constant rate of inflation) *and* that the level of aggregate demand would anyway be equivalent to the supply-side equilibrium. In the absence of some powerful automatic market forces or a potent monetary policy, which can ensure that the level of aggregate demand moves quickly to be consistent with the supply-side equilibrium, then fiscal policy has a clear role to play.

The supply-side equilibrium can itself be influenced by the path of aggregate demand. The size and distribution of the capital stock is a determinant of the productive capacity of the economy, and a larger capital stock would be associated with the supply-side equilibrium involving a higher level of output and employment. The level of aggregate demand (including the change in economic activity and profitability) has an impact on investment expenditure, and thereby on the size of the capital stock. The supply-side equilibrium may form an inflation barrier at any point in time, but it is not to be seen as something immutable and unaffected by the level of aggregate demand.

If the representation of the economy (economic model) is such that there are self-contained subsets of equations from which equilibrium solutions can be derived, then it is possible to speak of equilibrium positions relating to each of the subset of equations. In particular if there is a subset of equations which can be viewed as relating to the supply-side of the economy, then it is possible to speak of a supply-side equilibrium: and similarly for a demand-side equilibrium. The "natural rate of unemployment" and the NAIRU appear to fall into the category of supply-side equilibrium positions. In this context, the supply-side equilibrium seems to place a constraint on the level of output or employment (more generally the level of economic activity). In the present context, the supply-side equilibrium would appear to limit any role for fiscal policy (acting on the demand side of the economy) in that economic activity cannot be raised above the supply-side equilibrium for any length of time. However, this notion of supply-side equilibrium and the dichotomy (separation) between the supply-side and demand-side of the economy (which sometimes corresponds to the separation between the real side and the monetary side of the economy as in the classical dichotomy) raises three issues.

First, what, if any, are the mechanisms on the supply-side of the economy, which take the economy to the supply-side equilibrium position? Second, are there mechanisms, which bring compatibility between the supply-side and the demand-side of the economy? Third, are there interactions between the supply-side and the demand-side of the economy which are generally overlooked? We now look at these issues in turn.

On the first issue, it could be said little attention has been given to this. However, when the supply side is viewed as akin to a competitive (labor) market (with the "natural rate of unemployment" as the supply-side equilibrium), then an adjustment mechanism appears to be changes in real wages. In the expectations-augmented Phillips' curve, changes in real wages (expressed in terms of changes in nominal wages minus expected inflation) are linked with unemployment as a (negative) proxy for excess demand for labor. Real wages continue to adjust until the "natural rate of unemployment" is attained. This approach implicitly assumes that the cause of unemployment (and indeed over employment) arises from real wages differing from the equilibrium level. No attention is given to the level of aggregate demand, and implicitly it is assumed that the level of aggregate demand underpins the level of employment as set by the level of real wages. In the more general NAIRU approach, based on imperfect competition and wage bargaining (e.g. Layard *et al.*, 1991), there is no obvious supply-side adjustment mechanism. Wages and prices change in response to the level of demand, but there is no mechanism at work, which guides the level of real wages to its equilibrium level.[6] The adjustment in this NAIRU approach comes from the demand side alone.

With regard to the second issue, one proposed mechanism has been the operation of the real balance effect. The general price level is assumed to respond to the excess of the demand position over the supply-side equilibrium (e.g. current demand determined level of unemployment relative to the "natural rate of unemployment"), and the change in the general price level leads to a change in the real value of the money stock which then impacts on the level of aggregate demand. The level of aggregate demand is (eventually) brought into line with the supply-side equilibrium. But it is well known (at least since Kalecki, 1944c) that the real balance effect relies on "external" money with net worth to the private sector and to the stock of money remaining unchanged in the face of price changes. In a world of largely bank credit money, the amount of "external" money is relatively small: for example in the UK the ratio of M0 to GDP is less than 4 percent; a price fall of 10 percent would increase real value of M0 by the equivalent of 0.4 percent. With a wealth effect on consumption of the order of 0.02 to 0.05 (OECD, 2000, p. 192), aggregate demand would change by the order of 0.01 percent (for a decline of 10 percent in the price level). But with endogenous money the stock of money is determined by the demand for money. As prices fall, the demand for M0 would fall and hence the stock of M0 would also fall. In sum, the empirical relevance of the real balance effect can be readily dismissed.

The other adjustment mechanism postulated relates to the operation of interest rate policy by the central bank. The adoption of something akin to Taylor's rule would envisage the central bank discount rate being varied in response to the rate of inflation and to the output gap. The "equilibrium" rate of interest is then seen to be that which bring aggregate demand in line with available supply (and a constant rate of inflation). This is clearly not an automatic market mechanism, but rather arises from the discretionary operation of monetary policy (in the form of interest rates), as discussed above. In this context, the adjustment mechanism arises from an act of government (albeit in the form of the actions of the central bank) and fiscal policy could (and perhaps does) also act as an adjustment mechanism.

Turning now to the third issue, the relationship between the demand side and the supply side of the economy in the sense of changes on one side having a long-lasting impact on the other side (rather than just an adjustment process) is often seen as non-existent. However, there are reasons for thinking that is not the case. The most cited example comes under the label of hysteresis effects in the labor market: periods of low demand and high levels of unemployment are viewed as having "scarring" effects on the work force and the effective supply of labor. Without dismissing such effects, in the context of the present paper a more significant effect may come through the effects of aggregate demand on investment, and of investment on productive capacity (and hence the supply side of the economy). Fiscal policy of the "functional finance" type boosts aggregate demand, and thereby has a stimulating impact on investment, which raises the future productive capacity of the economy. Further, some advocates of "functional finance" have viewed public sector investment as a form of expenditure, which can be varied according to the state of private demand,[7] and to the extent to which the budget deficit permits additional public investment there can also be a boost to future productive capacity.[8] The growth rate of the economy may thereby be favorably enhanced by fiscal policy.

Crowding out Mark 3: Ricardian equivalence

The "Ricardian equivalence" proposition is that the future prospects of taxation to pay for a bond-financed budget deficit reduces consumer expenditure (and increases savings) which may exactly offset the boost to expenditure arising from the budget deficit. The overall level of savings (public savings plus private savings) remains unchanged.

The Ricardian equivalence proposition has been derived in the context of full employment (or at least a level of income set on the supply side of the economy) and the implicit assumption that private sector aggregate demand will underpin that level of income. Thus, the Ricardian equivalence proposition is essentially irrelevant in the context of functional finance. The Ricardian equivalence proposition relates to the question of what happens if a budget deficit were introduced into a situation where *ex ante* investment and savings were equal at full employment (or equivalent). Functional finance is concerned with the policy recommendation of introducing a budget deficit into a situation where there is a difference between *ex ante* savings and *ex ante* investment (usually an excess of savings over investment) at full employment.

The "Ricardian equivalence" proposition clearly indicates that the level of aggregate demand is invariant to the budget deficit position. But it does not indicate what that level of private demand will be, though there is perhaps the presumption that some form of Say's Law will operate, and that aggregate demand will be sufficient to underpin full employment. However, there is no particular reason for this level of aggregate demand to correspond to any supply-side equilibrium. Specifically, in the event of a shift in the supply-side equilibrium, there is no assurance that there will be a corresponding shift in the level of private demand. Estimates of the supply-side equilibrium NAIRU vary over time and across country. But there would be little reason to think that private aggregate demand would be shifting to correspond to the shifting NAIRU.

Now consider the approach of Barro (1974) which could be seen to revive interest in the Ricardian equivalence proposition under the heading of "are government bonds net wealth?" (we retain the same notation in what follows). The model is set up in terms of two generations where Generation 1 inherits a bequest of A_0^o from generation 0, and acquires assets (save) of A_1^y while they are young; during their old age they consume c_1^o and leave bequest of A_1^o. Letting r denote the rate of interest, their budget constraint in this retirement period is:

$$A_0^o + A_1^y = c_1^o + (1-r)A_1^o \tag{5}$$

so that their assets (left hand side) at the beginning of their old age is equal to their consumption, the bequest left minus the interest received on their assets.

The assets bequeathed are assumed to be acquired at beginning of period and yield interest during the period.

Generation 2 receives labor income of w, and save A_2^y (on which they receive interest), and consume c_2^y, and their budget constraint is:

$$c_2^y + (1-r)A_2^y = w \tag{6}$$

In this economy, there is net savings to provide for an increase in the capital stock which yields interest at rate r, and the net savings are equal to the assets at the end of the period minus assets at the beginning of the period. Hence it is required that:

$$A_1^o + A_2^y - A_0^o - A_1^y = \Delta K \tag{7}$$

where ΔK is the change in the capital stock set by the desire to invest.

This is equivalent to:

$$c_1^o + c_2^y + \Delta K = w + r(A_1^o + A_2^y) = y \tag{8}$$

where y stands for income. This indicates that consumer expenditure plus investment is equal to factor incomes of wages and capital income, and both are equal to national income. The presumption is then that national income is equivalent to the full employment level, and then any government expenditure has to "crowd out" private expenditure. In the "Ricardian equivalence" approach, this comes through taxation (present or perspective) reducing consumer expenditure.

But there is nothing which ensures that this equality will hold when the variables are in *ex ante* form: *ex post* there would (of course) have to be equality.

Consider the case in *ex ante* terms where:

$$c_1^o + c_2^y + \Delta K < w + r(A_1^o + A_2^y) \tag{9}$$

i.e. intended expenditure falls short of income, and equivalently

$$A_0^o + A_1^y + \Delta K < A_2^y + A_1^o \tag{10}$$

This would be a deflationary situation with (intended) expenditure falling short of (intended) income. Consider the case where income adjusts to bring equality between income and intended expenditure. We assume that consumption is a function of income (labor and capital income) and that return on capital varies proportionally with labor income (through utilization effects). Write w^* as the labor income which would result at full employment, and r^* as the rate of return at full employment, and the income and rate of return which results from a lower level of income as $m \cdot w^*$ and $m \cdot r^*$; then

$$c_1^o(m) + c_2^y(m) + \Delta K = m \cdot w^* + m \cdot r^* \cdot (A_1^o + A_2^y) \tag{11}$$

to give a solution for m ($m < 1$).

By "assumption" in this context, the intention to save will have adjusted so that:

$$A_0^o + A_1^y + \Delta K = \hat{A}_2^y + \hat{A}_1^o \tag{12}$$

where a caret refers to the *ex post* value of the variable. In equation 12 the left-hand side is treated as a given, and the right-hand side has adjusted to the indicated level.

Now introduce functional finance such that the budget deficit can "mop up" excess private savings; this would mean that

$$c_1^o + c_2^y + \Delta K + B = w^* + r^*(A_1^o + A_2^y) \tag{13}$$

where B is the budget deficit and the other variables are at the level which corresponds to full employment. Income is higher, by $(1 - m^*)$, net private savings are equal to $\Delta K + B$, and hence:

$$A_0^o + A_1^y + \Delta K + B = A_2^y + A_1^o \tag{14}$$

with

$$A_2^y + A_1^o - (\hat{A}_2^y + \hat{A}_1^o) = B \tag{15}$$

In this model, generation 2 are able to save what they wish and do so in the form of assets and bonds. Their overall savings is higher than it would have been in the absence of functional finance.

What about next period's budget constraint for generation 2? In the absence of functional finance this is:

$$\hat{A}_2^y + A_1^o = c_2^o + (1-r)A_2^o \tag{16}$$

With functional finance it is:

$$A_2^y + A_1^o = c_2^o + (1-r)A_2^o \tag{17}$$

When fiscal policy is approached in "functional finance" terms, which is a budget deficit run by the government because there is a difference between savings and investment at the desired income level, then the Ricardian equivalence approach is scarcely relevant. In the absence of a budget deficit, the excess of savings over investment cannot occur (and the discrepancy is dealt with through a fall in income reducing savings until brought into line with income).

We have argued that the Ricardian equivalence theorem relies on the assumption of Say's Law. We now suggest that when fiscal policy acts as an automatic stabilizer, then the data may suggest support for the proposition that budget deficits "crowd out" private savings even though that is not the underlying mechanism. One aspect of the "functional finance" approach is a recognition that the expenditure/tax system can act as a (partial) automatic stabilizer, with government expenditure tending to rise and tax revenue tending to fall when output slows, thereby limiting the extent of the slow down in output. This does not mean that these automatic stabilizers are sufficient since economic cycles still occur and employment is often far from being equivalent to full employment. The operation of the automatic stabilizer also indicates that the budget deficit can be an endogenous response to changes on the demand side of the economy.

Consider the case where there are demand shocks to the economy emanating from savings, investment and the foreign sector, which lead to fluctuations in the level of economic activity and the budget position. When fiscal policy is essentially passive (i.e. the automatic stabilizers operate but there is no active discretionary policy), then the budget deficit varies cyclically. However, this can give rise to the appearance of Ricardian equivalence, generated from the national income link between net private savings and the budget deficit (an equality in the simple context of a closed economy).

Next, consider a simple model in which savings are a simple function of post-tax income, i.e.

$$S = a + s(1-t)Y \tag{18}$$

and investment is autonomous, i.e.

$$I = b \tag{19}$$

Fluctuations in demand come from fluctuations in a and b, and these are simulated below as random variables. Tax revenue is a simple linear function of income, i.e.

$$T = tY \tag{20}$$

and government expenditure moves counter-cyclically, i.e.

$$G = g - hY \tag{21}$$

with g also subject to random fluctuations. All variables are written so as to be positive. The current account is CA and treated as a constant (with respect to income) but subject to random fluctuations. Then

$$G - T + CA = S - I \tag{22}$$

from which:

$$g - hY - tY + CA = a + s(1 - t)Y - I \tag{23}$$

So that income is given by

$$[h + t + s(1 - t)]Y = g + I + CA - a \tag{24}$$

Fluctuations in the savings and investment behavior lead to fluctuations in the budget deficit, as well as in the level of income. The movement of income as calculated from equation 24 was generated through taking values of $s = 0.2$, $h = 0.1$ and $t = 0.4$, and applying random shocks to the values of g, I, a and CA. In Table 2.1 we indicate the range within which the values of these variables lay: for example in the first experiment, a took values in the range ten to twenty (15 ± 5) on a randomly determined basis. For each value of these variables, the values of income, savings, and budget deficit were calculated. Each run was based on 100 observations: the regression of savings-to-income ratio on the budget deficit-to-GDP ratio was then estimated, and we also calculated the response of budget deficit to change in income. For each range of values of g, I, a and CA, 100 runs (each based on 100 observations) were undertaken. The average outcomes are reported in Table 2.1 for the results of the regression

$$S/Y = m + n(BD/Y) \tag{25}$$

and the responsiveness of the budget deficit to variations in GDP.

The results from this simple model serve to illustrate two features. First, variations in budget deficit with changes in output are of the same order of magnitude as those observed (references) in the range 0.4 to 0.7.[9] Second, the estimated coefficient on the budget deficit (relative to GDP) in a

Table 2.1 Results of simulation exercise

A	I	G	CA	N	Responsiveness
15 ± 5	22.5 ± 7.5	32.5 ± 2.5	0 ± 5	−0.745 (0.0524)	0.398
				−0.755 (0.0519)	0.408
25 ± 5	22.5 ± 7.5	32.5 ± 2.5	0 ± 5	−1.020 (0.0391)	0.706
				−0.9959 (0.402)	0.666
15 ± 5	22.5 ± 7.5	30.0 ± 5	0 ± 5	−0.790 (0.0591)	0.473
				−0.778 (0.0591)	0.550

savings ratio equation is fairly close to unity (though in most cases differ significantly from unity), and hence gives the appearance of a Ricardian equivalence even though no wealth effects have been included. The relationship between savings and the budget deficit here reflects the national income accounts relationship between private savings minus investment and the budget deficit. Thus these experiments indicate that the operation of fiscal policy as an automatic stabilizer (which partly reflects a functional finance approach) could generate (through the relationship between budget deficit, current account and net private savings) results which mimic those associated with the Ricardian equivalence approach.

The sustainability of budget deficits

The "functional finance" approach takes the view that budget deficits (or surpluses) occur as and when required to ensure high levels of economic activity. However, the "functional finance" view is that a budget deficit is not an occasional occurrence (e.g. arising from the operation of automatic stabilizers during a recession), but rather that a budget deficit may need to be a quasi-permanent feature arising from a tendency of private savings to run ahead of investment. Indeed, the experience of the industrialized economies in the post-war period has involved budget deficits in most years (see, for example, Dwyer and Hafer, 1998, p. 43, in the case of the USA).[10]

The argument is put that long-term budget deficits are unsustainable: one year's budget deficit adds to the public debt and leading to future interest payments. The continuation of a primary budget deficit (that is deficit excluding interest payments) involves the build up of interest payments, and further borrowing to cover those interest payments and the continuing primary deficit. Although the budget deficit is growing (when interest payments are included) and the public debt is also growing, their relationship with GDP depends on the growth of the economy as well as the level of interest rates. Domar (1944) provided an early analysis of this and saw "the problem of the debt burden [as] essentially a problem of achieving a growing national income" (p. 822), though when his analysis used numerical values for key variables rates of interest of 2 percent and 3 percent were assumed. Kalecki (1944*b*) argued that an increasing national debt did not constitute a burden on society as a whole since it is largely an internal transfer, and further noted that in an expanding economy the debt-to-income ratio need not rise if the rate of growth is sufficiently high (as further discussed below). But in the event that there was a problem of a rising debt-to-income ratio (and hence of interest payments to income), Kalecki (1944*b*) advocated an annual capital tax. This would be levied on firms and individuals, which would cover interest payments on the national debt which would affect "neither capitalists' consumption nor the profitability of investment" (p. 363).

It is well-known that a continuing primary budget deficit equivalent to a proportion d of GDP will lead to a debt-to-GDP ratio stabilizing at $b = d/(g - r)$ (where g is the growth rate and r interest rate, either both in real terms or both in nominal terms).[11] It is evident that the stabilization of the debt-to-income ratio (with a given primary deficit) requires that $g > r$.

In a similar vein, a continuing budget deficit of d' (including interest payments) leads to a debt-to-GDP ratio stabilizing at d'/g where here g is in nominal terms. But this implies that $b + rd = gd$, i.e. $b = (g - r)d$ and hence if g is less than r the primary budget deficit is negative (i.e. primary budget is in surplus).

However, in the functional finance approach, the budget deficit which is relevant is the overall budget position rather than the primary deficit (or surplus). To the extent that a budget deficit is required to offset an excess of private savings over investment, then it is the overall budget deficit which is relevant (see below for some caveats). Bond interest payments are a transfer payment and add to the income of the recipient, and similar in many respects to other transfer payments. In terms of sustainability, then, of a fiscal deficit, the condition under "functional finance" is readily satisfied (with the requirement of growth being positive).

If a budget deficit (of a particular size relative to GDP) is run for a number of years, then it is clear that the interest payments component of the deficit will increase, and the appearance is given that interest payments are "crowding" out other forms of public expenditure and/or leading to higher levels of taxation. However, in the case in which it is the overall budget deficit which is relevant, then a constant deficit (relative to GDP) will lead to a debt-to-GDP ratio, which converges on the ratio of the deficit to the nominal growth rate.[12]

This simple analysis of the budget deficit makes no allowance for any reaction in the willingness of the private sector to hold the public debt. If the public debt becomes an increasing part of the wealth portfolio, then the (marginal) attractiveness of holding public debt diminishes. This could have the effect of diminishing the appeal of savings, which has the beneficial effect of stimulating aggregate demand. Further, a higher rate of interest may have to be paid on public debt. The analysis of Godley and

Rowthorn (1994) incorporates aspects of that notion and includes a (pre-determined) wealth-to-income ratio for the private sector and a bond-to-wealth ratio which depends on the (exogenous) interest rate and the rate of inflation: hence there is a desired bond-to-income ratio. There is a sense in which the deficit of the public sector is then constrained by that bond-to-income ratio, and hence the non-monetized debt-to-income ratio. But this constraint may be of little relevance in the sense that the government is not seeking to run a deficit for the sake of it. It is more significant whether there is a constraint on the level of public expenditure and whether there are other constraints on the economy. On the former, we can note that in the Godley and Rowthorn model, an expansion in the level of public expenditure sets off an expansion of output and hence of tax revenue (and other changes) such that there is not an explosion in the debt-to-GDP ratio (and this does not rely on the rate of growth being greater than the rate of interest). This would suggest that there may be reactions from the private sector (arising from a reluctance to hold ever increasing amounts of government debt) which make the conditions for the sustainability of a deficit position less constraining than it first appeared.

In Table 2.2 we report some comparisons for four major countries between post-tax rate of interest and the rate of growth. The rate of growth reported is the average annual growth rate achieved over the period considered (rather than being an estimate of some underlying

Table 2.2 Comparison of growth rates and interest rates

	Nominal long-term rate	Post-tax rate of interest	Rate of inflation	Post-tax real rate of interest	Pre-tax real rate of interest	Rate of growth
1951–1997						
UK	8.45	6.34	6.22	0.12	2.21	2.31
USA	7.12	5.34	3.99	1.35	3.16	2.83
France	7.46	5.60	5.57	0.03	1.80	3.36
Germany	7.22	5.42	3.01	2.41	4.15	3.87
1969–1979						
UK	11.53	8.65	11.1	−2.45	0.85	2.42
USA	7.86	5.90	6.5	−0.61	1.65	3.66
France	8.33	6.25	8.21	−1.96	0.49	3.50
Germany	8.18	6.14	4.56	1.58	3.72	2.93
1980–1997						
UK	9.65	7.24	5.68	1.56	3.67	2.62
USA	9.84	7.38	4.4	2.98	5.21	3.44
France	10.07	7.55	4.88	2.67	4.87	1.95
Germany	7.43	5.57	2.86	2.71	4.48	2.38

Source: Based on Chadha and Dimsdale (1999), and growth rate calculations based on figures from OECD (2002), OECD *Historical Statistics*, various issues.

trend). The original source for the data provides estimates of pre-tax rate of interest, and a 25 percent tax rate has been assumed in order to calculate the post-tax rate of interest.

It is apparent that there is a tendency for the (post-tax) rate of interest to fall below the rate of growth, though not universally and less in the past two decades than formerly. Further, the difference between the rate of interest and the rate of growth is often small. Our own calculations using figures from OECD (2002) for long-term interest rates (on ten-year government bonds) and nominal GDP growth, with again an assumed 25 percent tax rate, indicates that for the 20 OECD countries for which data were complete, over the period 1985 to 2001, the growth rate and post-tax interest rate were close on average, but (averaged across countries) the growth rate exceeded the post-tax rate of interest rate most years with the period 1990 to 1993 being the main exceptions.[13]

The use of the interest rate on bonds may overstate the average cost of borrowing by government in that a government funds part of its budget deficit by the issue of the monetary base (cash and notes held by the public and reserves of the commercial banks with the central bank, which the literature labels as M0). As the demand by the public to hold M0 rises with nominal income growth this is satisfied by the government. Base money bears a zero rate of interest, and to that extent part of the budget deficit is funded at zero cost. Although this is not a substantial part of the budget deficit, nevertheless it has the effect of reducing somewhat the average cost of funding the budget deficit. An M0/GDP ratio of around 5 percent (which is not untypical) and nominal growth of 5 percent per annum would lead to an increase of M0 equivalent to 0.25 percent of GDP.

It can be noted that in the literature on Taylor's rule, it has been asserted that the equilibrium real rate of interest (central bank discount rate) is approximately equal to the real rate of growth.[14] The rate of interest relevant for the present discussion is the post-tax rate of interest on (long-term) bonds. The interest rate on bonds can generally be expected to be above the discount rate, but after allowing for taxation the post-tax rate on bonds could well be below the rate of growth. This may suggest that the relevant r and g may be close.

The payment of interest on bonds (and the replacement of other forms of public expenditure in the context of a given budget deficit) changes the composition of transfer payments and of disposable income, insofar as these interest payments accrue to the rich rather than the poor. They can be expected to raise the propensity to save and hence raise the excess of savings over investment and the required budget deficit.

The sustainability of a primary budget deficit (of given size relative to GDP) requires that the rate of growth exceed the post-tax rate of interest. We have suggested that it is often the case that that condition holds empirically. Tight monetary policy (in the form of relatively high interest rates) both directly (through impact on interest rate on bonds) and indirectly (through impact on investment and growth) harms the prospect of sustainability being achieved. It points in the direction of ensuring appropriate monetary policy rather than being too concerned over the precise size of the budget deficit. We have also argued that it is the size of the overall budget deficit which is relevant in the context of functional finance rather than the size of the primary budget deficit since it is the impact of the deficit on aggregate demand and the ability of the deficit to mop up excess savings which is relevant. For the overall budget deficit the issue of sustainability does not arise (provided that the growth rate of GDP is positive).

Concluding remarks

The levels of taxation and public expenditure and the balance between them vary for many reasons. Writing this at a time when the public expenditure consequences of USA administration's proposals for tax cuts for the rich, it is not possible to forget that the fiscal stance may change for reasons far removed from the application of the ideas of "functional finance." The case we have set out in this paper is that fiscal policy *should* be operated to secure the desired level of economic activity (and that it is a potent instrument for doing so). This "functional finance" view means that any budget deficit should be seen as a response to the perceived excess of private savings over investment at the desired level of economic activity. We have argued that the "crowding out" arguments, which have been advanced, do not take into account this view of "functional finance." The assessment of fiscal policy should relate to the circumstances in which it is intended to be employed, and then we find that the "crowding out" arguments do not apply.

Notes

1 Leaving open as to what level of economic activity is regarded as optimum or desirable.
2 One caveat to that statement is the following. A growing economy generally requires an increase in the stock of money, and within that an increase in the monetary base (M0) for which there is an increasing demand as income rises. The provision of M0 comes from a budget deficit.
3 This discussion is cast in terms of a closed economy: adjustments to account for an open economy can be readily made without undermining the basic approach pursued here.
4 In the reverse direction, the reported agreement between Clinton and Greenspan whereby the latter would reduce interest rate if the former reduced budget deficit is an example of the policy nature of links between budget deficit and interest rates. This is a clear example of monetary and fiscal policies coordination.
5 This could be a long adjustment process, but it is the "automatic" one invoked in the context of the NAIRU.
6 See Sawyer (1999) for further discussion.

7 Keynes (1980) argued for public investment to be set such that Private Investment + Public Investment = Savings, and hence that the budget deficit appeared to finance public investment. Keynes (op. cit.) also advocated that "in peace-time budgets through the Chancellor making a forecast of capital expenditure under all heads, and comparing this with prospective savings, so as to show that the general prospective set-up is reasonably in accordance with the requirement of equilibrium. The capital budget will be a necessary ingredient in this exposition of the prospects of investment under all heads. If, as may be the case, something like two-thirds or three-quarters of total investment will be under public or semi-public auspices, the amount of capital expenditure contemplated by the authorities will be the essential balancing factor. This is a very major change in the presentation of our affairs and one which I greatly hope we shall adopt. It has nothing whatever to do with deficit financing" (p. 352).

8 This would depend on the nature of the investment, e.g. investment in roads or in defense equipment, and the productivity of that investment.

9 The European Commission has, for example, estimated that the sensitivity of the budget balance to output is around 0.5 percent for the EU, that is a 1 percent fall in GDP will increase the budget deficit by 0.5 percent (Buti *et al.*, 1997, p. 7).

10 Figures in OECD, *Economic Outlook*, December 2002 reveal that there was no year in the 17 years since the mid-1980s for which data are given there when the OECD area as a whole has a budget surplus (and one year, 2000, when the deficit was zero).

11 Let the outstanding public-sector debt be D, and then the budget deficit is dD/dt and is equal to $G + rD - T$ where r is the post-tax rate of interest on public debt, G is government expenditure (other than interest payments) and T is taxation (other than that based on receipt of interest from government). With Y as national income, we have:

$$d(D/Y)/dt = (1/Y)dD/dt - (D/Y)(1/Y) \cdot dY/dt = (G + rD T)/Y - (D/Y)g$$

where g is the growth of national income. The debt-to-income ratio rises (falls) if $(G - T)/Y > (<)(D/Y)(g - r)$.

12 In that context, the Stability and Growth Pact requirements (for the operation of the European single currency) of a maximum budget deficit of 3 percent of GDP with a balance to small surplus in the budget over the business cycle and debt-to-GDP ratio of 60 percent are not compatible. An average 3 percent deficit, and 60 percent debt ratio would be compatible with a 5 percent nominal growth rate.

13 In 1990, the average difference of $r - g$ was calculated at 0.46 percent, rising to 2.17 and 2.68 in 1991 and 1992 respectively, then falling back to 1.71 percent in 1993. In those years there were some particularly large gaps, for example, Finland with a decline in nominal GDP of 4.5 percent and pre-tax interest rate of 11.9 percent. The average for the whole period across all countries was -0.16 percent (i.e. on average g exceeded r, and excluding the four years of the early 1990s the average was -0.75 percent.

14 Taylor (1993), for example, postulates a 2 percent "equilibrium" real rate of interest which he says "is close to the assumed steady-state growth rate of 2.2 percent."

References

Arestis, Philip and Malcolm Sawyer (2003), "Reinstating Fiscal Policy," *Journal of Post Keynesian Economics*, 26(1), pp. 4–25.

Arestis, Philip and Malcolm Sawyer (2004), "Can Monetary Policy Affect the Real Economy?" *European Review of Economics and Finance*, 3(3), pp. 9–32.

Barro, Robert J. (1974), "Are Government Bonds Net Wealth?" *Journal of Political Economy*, 82(6), November–December, pp. 1095–117.

Barro, Robert J. (1989), "The Ricardian Approach to Budget Deficits," *Journal of Economic Perspectives*, 3(2), Spring, pp. 37–54.

Buti, Marco, Daniele Franco, and Hedwig Ongena (1997), "Budgetary Policies During Recessions: Retrospective Application of the 'Stability and Growth Pact' to the Post-War Period," Brussels: European Commission.

Chadha, Jagjit S. and Nicholas H. Dimsdale (1999), "A Long View of Real Rates," *Oxford Review of Economic Policy*, 15(2), Summer, pp. 17–45.

Domar, Evsey D. (1944), "The 'Burden of the Debt' and the National Income," *American Economic Review*, 34(4), June, pp. 798–827.

Dwyer, Gerald P., Jr. and R.W. Hafer (1998), "The Federal Government's Budget Surplus: Cause for Celebration?" *Federal Reserve Bank of Atlanta Economic Review*, 83(3), Third Quarter, pp. 42–51.

Godley, Wynne and Robert Rowthorn (1994), "The Dynamics of Public Sector Deficits and Debts," in *Unemployment in Europe*, edited by Jonathan Michie, London: Academic Press.

Kalecki, Michal (1939), *Essays in the Theory of Economic Fluctuations*, New York: Russell & Russell.

Kalecki, Michal (1944*a*), "The White Paper on Employment Policy," *Bulletin of the Oxford University Institute of Statistics*, Vol. 6.

Kalecki, Michal (1944*b*), "Three Ways to Full Employment," in Oxford University Institute of Statistics, *The Economics of Full Employment*, Oxford: Blackwell.

Kalecki, Michal (1944*c*), "Professor Pigou on 'The Classical Stationary State': A Comment," *Economic Journal*, 54(213), April, pp. 131–2.

Keynes, John Maynard (1980), *Activities 1940–1946 Shaping the Post-War World: Employment and Commodities, Collected Writings*, Vol. 27, London: Macmillan.

Keynes, John Maynard (1936), *The General Theory of Employment, Interest and Money*, London: Macmillan.

Layard, Richard, Stephen J. Nickell, and Richard Jackman (1991), *Unemployment: Macroeconomic Performance and the Labour Market*, Oxford: Oxford University Press.

Lerner, Abba P. (1943), "Functional Finance and the Federal Debt," *Social Research*, Vol. 10, pp. 38–51. Reprinted in *Readings in Macroeconomics*, edited by Max Gerhard Mueller, New York: Holt, Rinehart and Winston, pp. 353–60.

OECD (2000), *Economic Outlook* 68, Paris: Organisation for Economic Co-operation and Development.

OECD (2002), *Economic Outlook* 72, Paris: Organisation for Economic Co-operation and Development.

Sawyer, Malcolm (1999), "The NAIRU: A Critical Appraisal," *International Papers in Political Economy*, 7(2), pp. 1–39.

Taylor, John B. (1993), "Discretion Versus Policy Rules in Practice," *Carnegie-Rochester Conference Series on Public Policy*, Vol. 39, pp. 195–214.

3 A fiscal policy to counter recessions

Triggered transfers to households

Laurence S. Seidman and Kenneth A. Lewis

The practical prescription of the Keynesian revolution can be stated simply. Use counter-cyclical fiscal policy as well as monetary policy to raise aggregate demand to combat a recession: temporarily increase cash transfers or government purchases of goods and services, or temporarily cut taxes, until a strong recovery has been engineered; complement this fiscal policy with a monetary policy that cuts interest rates, but do not rely on monetary policy alone to counter a recession. The government's announced commitment to use fiscal as well as monetary stimulus in a recession would help induce the private sector to maintain its spending at the onset of a recession. If the economy is hit with a negative demand shock that throws it into a recession, will households and business managers expect the economy to recover, or will they expect the recession to deepen or drag on? If they expect the government to act aggressively and effectively using both fiscal and monetary policy, they will continue to spend, and this behavior will sustain aggregate demand, and in itself help generate a recovery. On the other hand, if they expect the government to rely solely on monetary policy, and they observe that interest rates are already low, they may grow pessimistic, cut their spending, and thereby deepen or prolong the recession.

This straightforward Keynesian prescription for treating a recession has fallen out of fashion with many academic economists. This paper is not addressed to traditional monetarists or new classical economists; their rejection of the Keynesian prescription on theoretical grounds is discussed elsewhere (Seidman, 2003, Chapters 10 and 11). Instead, it is addressed to economists who accept the basic premises of Keynesian macroeconomics but who have become pessimistic about the timely implementation and/or effectiveness of counter-cyclical fiscal policy.

This paper will present and analyze a particular new automatic counter-cyclical fiscal policy – *triggered transfers to households* – and will try to persuade economists to advocate the enactment of automatic counter-cyclical fiscal policies and to undertake research aimed at improving their design and implementation. The idea of automatically triggering a cut in tax rates or increase in government spending to counter a recession is not new. In his classic monograph on public finance, Musgrave (1959) devoted a section to what he termed "formula flexibility":

Formula Flexibility
Formula flexibility refers to an arrangement whereby changes in tax rates and/or expenditure levels are legislated in advance, to go into effect if and when specified changes in income occur. For instance, it might be legislated that income tax rates be reduced or public expenditures raised by *x* percent if income falls by *y* percent.

(Musgrave, 1959, p. 512)

Several studies in the 1960s and 1970s analyzed the impact of automatic counter-cyclical fiscal policies (Pack, 1968; Duggal, 1975; and Seidman, 1975) and concluded that such policies would be helpful in countering recessions. But during the past three decades, work on such policies largely ceased as Keynesian macroeconomists spent the 1970s grappling with supply-shock inflation, and the 1980s and 1990s combating the new classical counter-revolution. One purpose of this paper is to try to encourage Keynesian economists to return to the constructive research agenda of designing and analyzing automatic counter-cyclical fiscal policies.

In this paper we focus on cash transfers to households. Why transfers to households rather than government purchases? After all, $50 billion of government purchases would have a stronger first round effect on aggregate demand than $50 billion of transfers because consumers spend transfers only gradually. On the other hand, transfers to households have a more even sectoral and geographical first-round effect on the economy: the first round effect would be spread evenly across all sectors and regions instead of being concentrated in particular sectors such as construction. Hence, transfers are likely to keep workers in their current jobs, while government purchases would replace some current jobs with new jobs in the targeted sectors. Thus, transfers and government purchases each have advantages and disadvantages. In this paper, we limit our analysis to transfers.

Triggered transfers versus current automatic stabilizers

How do these triggered transfers to households differ from our current automatic stabilizers? Current automatic stabilizers are not designed with the aim of providing the optimal demand stimulus to a slumping economy. For example, consider a society debating whether government spending and income taxes should be 20 percent or 40 percent of GDP. The decision, as it should be, is motivated by the debate over the proper size of government, the merits of particular government programs, and so on. The consequence for macroeconomic stability is an accident. With a 20 percent income tax, if national income drops $100 billion, tax revenue automatically drops only $20 billion, so disposable income drops $80 billion. With a 40 percent income tax, tax revenue automatically drops $40 billion, so disposable income drops only $60 billion. The society with the larger government spending (40 percent of GDP instead of 20 percent) by accident has a stronger automatic stabilizer.

The triggered transfers break the link. Consider the society that chooses government spending to be 20 percent of GDP and adopts a 20 percent income tax. Now suppose it also adopts the triggered transfers: Whenever national income drops $100 billion, automatically the Treasury mails checks to households totaling $20 billion. As a consequence, despite the 20 percent income tax rate, households' disposable income will fall only $60 billion, not $80 billion. Thus, the triggered transfers policy focuses on stabilization only. It takes as given the current automatic stabilizers that were an unintended byproduct of accomplishing other goals and supplements them in order to get the desired macroeconomic stimulus.

It must be emphasized that Congress would be free at any time to override its triggered transfers with discretionary action. The automatic policy is a default position: it occurs only if Congress fails to enact a discretionary change. Thus, the question is simply: What should happen if Congress fails to take discretionary action? Currently, tax rates stay fixed and there are no transfers. Under the proposed automatic fiscal policy, transfers would be triggered automatically according to the unemployment gap. The relationship between the magnitude of the transfers and the magnitude of the unemployment gap would be pre-enacted by Congress. Thus, under this proposal, Congress does not delegate any authority over fiscal policy, and fully retains the ability to adjust fiscal policy through discretionary action. Moreover, it is Congress that approves in advance all aspects of the triggered transfers. The automatic action is a default position in the event Congress does not take discretionary action.

Triggered transfers to households

We propose that Congress pre-enact a transfer formula that authorizes an automatic triggering of a new cash transfer to households in response to a high unemployment rate – in particular, the formula prescribes a "transfer-to-GDP ratio" that is proportional to the "unemployment gap." Specifically, the triggered transfer R would be given by

$$R/Y_{-1} = s[U_{-1} - (U^N + T)], R > 0, \tag{1}$$

where R/Y_{-1} is the "transfer ratio" and $[U_{-1} - (U^N + T)]$ is the "unemployment gap"; U_{-1} is last quarter's unemployment rate, U^N is the "normal" unemployment rate (defined as the average unemployment rate of the preceding decade), T is a threshold above the normal unemployment rate, s is the strength parameter, R is the aggregate transfer, and Y_{-1} is last quarter's GDP. Based on the advice of technical staff, Congress would pre-enact the values of T and s.

The current value of the normal unemployment rate U^N is 5.2 percent (the average unemployment rate from 1993 to 2002). Suppose T is set equal to 0.5 percent. Then the transfer would be triggered whenever the unemployment rate exceeds 5.7 percent. Suppose s is set equal to 2. For example, if last quarter's unemployment rate U_{-1} was 7.2 percent, so $[U_{-1} - (U^N + T)] = 1.5\%$, then applying the formula above, $R/Y_{-1} = 2[7.2\% - (5.2\% + 0.5\%)] = 3.0\%$, so the aggregate transfer that would be triggered this quarter would equal 3 percent of last quarter's GDP – we will say that the prescribed *transfer/GDP ratio* is 3 percent. We will refer to $[U_{-1} - (U^N + T)]$ as the *unemployment gap*, which in this example is 1.5 percent. With $s = 2$, the transfer ratio would be twice the unemployment gap.

Congress would pre-enact how the aggregate transfer R would be converted into specific dollar amounts on checks to individual households. For the 2001 tax rebate, Congress specified that each two-adult household receive the same amount ($600). If Congress pre-enacts that all households receive the same dollar rebate, then each household would receive a transfer equal to R/N, where R is the aggregate transfer given by the above formula and N is the number of households.

It is administratively feasible to trigger a transfer this quarter based on the unemployment rate (U_{-1}) and GDP (Y_{-1}) for the preceding quarter. The Bureau of Labor Statistics announces its estimate of last month's unemployment rate on the first Friday of this month. The Department of Commerce issues a preliminary estimate for the preceding quarter's GDP one month after the end of the quarter. To mail the checks out in the second and third month, the Treasury can have the addresses ready to go in advance and can enter the dollar amount per check as soon as the Commerce Department's GDP estimate is available. The actual experience with the 2001 $600 tax rebate – enacted in June, and mailed out in July, August, and September – shows that implementing the transfer policy with a one-quarter lag is feasible. Similar speed of implementation was achieved in the summer of 2003 in the advanced payment of a recently enacted increase in the child tax credit.

Are triggered transfers effective in stimulating consumption spending?

According to extreme versions of the permanent income and lifecycle hypotheses, counter-cyclical transfers to households should cause only a small increase in consumer spending in the short run. In the past decade, however, several empirical studies have challenged the validity of the extreme versions of these hypotheses. Although permanent income or lifetime wealth remains important, current disposable income turns out to have an important short-run impact on consumer spending. After surveying recent empirical studies, Mankiw (2000) writes:

> A large empirical literature ... has addressed the question of how well households intertemporally smooth their consumption. Although this literature does not speak with a single voice, the consensus view is that consumption smoothing is far from perfect. In particular, consumer spending tracks current income far more than it should.
>
> (Mankiw, 2000, p. 120)

These studies find that many households do in fact promptly adjust their consumption to changes in their disposable income. For example, Campbell and Mankiw (1989) estimate that roughly half of income goes to households that consume according to current income, and half to households that consume according to permanent (normal) income. Parker (1999) examines income changes resulting from Social Security taxes and reports that the one-quarter elasticity of expenditure on nondurable goods with respect to a decline in income is roughly one-half. Souleles (1999) studies the impact of income tax refunds and concludes that consumption increases by at least 35 percent of a refund within three months. Mankiw says imperfect smoothing occurs because some consumers may not be "rational" and may simply extrapolate their current income into the future because it is the only definite information available, and some may face borrowing constraints, as indicated by the finding that some engage in buffer-stock saving to prepare for emergencies, and by the fact that many households have virtually zero wealth. Mankiw concludes:

> Reflecting on these facts, one cannot help but be drawn to a simple conclusion: many households do not have the financial wherewithal to do the intertemporal consumption-smoothing assumed by much modern macroeconomic theory ... Acknowledging the prevalence of these low-wealth households helps explain why consumption tracks current income as strongly as it does.
>
> (Mankiw, op. cit., p. 121)

A study by Shapiro and Slemrod reported in their two articles (2003*a*, 2003*b*) appears at first glance to run counter to the other studies as well as to their earlier study (Shapiro and Slemrod 1995). They analyze consumer surveys concerning the 2001 tax rebate ($600 per family, with checks mailed from the US Treasury to households in July, August, and September) and assert that the short-run impact was small. Seidman and Lewis (2003), however, show that there are serious problems with their consumer surveys; that they do *not* obtain any direct evidence on the marginal propensity to consume (MPC) out of the rebate; and that even if their survey results were valid, simulations suggest that a tax rebate twice as large repeated for four quarters would have significantly mitigated the 2001 recession. According to a presentation by Parker (2003), preliminary results from his recent study with Souleles of the 2001 rebate finds a substantial short-run impact on consumption.

Triggered transfers in a hypothetical recession: simulation results

In a recent paper, Lewis and Seidman (2004) simulate the use of transfers to households reinforced by monetary policy to generate a recovery of a low-interest-rate economy from a negative demand shock, using the July 31, 2003 version of the Fair US quarterly macroeconometric model. The Fair model is a mainstream traditional Keynesian model that is continuously updated, re-estimated, and re-tested. Detailed information on the Fair model is given by Fair (1994, 2003). Fair (1994) comments on the relationship of his model to the Lucas critique, rational expectations, and other new macroeconometric models.

Lewis and Seidman calculate that the Fair model gives the following estimates for the marginal propensity to consume out of disposable income: one-quarter MPC = 0.20, two-quarter MPC = 0.36, three-quarter MPC = 0.47, and four-quarter MPC = 0.55. They obtain these estimates as follows. In the Fair model, real per capita consumption this quarter (C_t) is a function of real per capita disposable income this quarter (YD_t) and real per capita consumption last quarter (C_{t-1}). Suppose an increment in real per capita disposable income occurs in quarter 1 only: Without the increment, YD would have been YD_1' and with the increment YD is YD_1, so the increment is $\Delta YD_1 \equiv YD_1 - YD_1'$. This increment will raise quarter-1 consumption directly through the YD_t term in the equation, and will also raise consumption in subsequent quarters through the C_{t-1} term. Let C_i be real per capita consumption in quarter i following ΔYD_1, and C_i' be real per capita consumption in quarter i had there been no ΔYD_1. Then $\Delta C_i \equiv C_i - C_i'$ is the increment in consumption in quarter i due to ΔYD_1, and $\Sigma_{i=1}^{J} \Delta C_i$ is the cumulative increment in consumption over J quarters due to ΔYD_1. The marginal propensity to consume in one quarter – the "one-quarter MPC" – is defined as $\Delta C_1/\Delta YD_1$, and the "J-quarter MPC" is defined as $(\Sigma_{i=1}^{J} \Delta C_i)/\Delta YD_1$. Note that the time period – the number of quarters – of an MPC must always be indicated. The Fair model has an estimated consumption equation for each of the following three components of real per capita consumption spending: consumer durables, consumption of services, and consumption of non-durables. To obtain the J-quarter MPC out of disposable income for the Fair model, they calculate $(\Sigma_{i=1}^{J} \Delta C_i)/\Delta YD_1$ for each equation using its estimated coefficients. Then summing over the three components gives the J-quarter MPC.[1]

Before introducing the hypothetical recession, they describe Fair's baseline (non-recession) forecast, which, in his July 31, 2003 version of the model, begins in 2003.3. Under the Fair forecast, in the fourth quarter, the unemployment rate is 5.7 percent, the three-month Treasury bill rate is 2.1 percent, the corporate bond rate is 4.9 percent, and the mortgage rate is 5.3 percent. In the eighth quarter, the unemployment rate is 5.5 percent, the bill rate is 2.7 percent, the bond rate is 4.9 percent, and the mortgage rate is 5.5 percent.

They introduce a negative demand shock beginning in 2003.3 that generates a recession. They adjust (generally downward) the individual constant terms for eight quarters (2003.3–2005.2) in each of five equations: the equations for consumer expenditure for services, nondurables, and durables, as well as the equations for residential housing investment and business capital stock (which thereby reduces non-residential fixed investment). If (hypothetically) monetary policy is adjusted to keep the bill rate on its baseline path (projected by Fair's forecast), then in the fourth quarter (2004.2) the unemployment rate is 7.9 percent and in the eighth quarter (2005.2) the unemployment rate is 7.9 percent as well.

What would have happened in this hypothetical recession had Congress pre-enacted the transfer formula described above with a strength parameter s equal to 2, a normal unemployment rate U^N of 5.2 percent and a threshold T of 0.5 percent so that transfers are triggered when last quarter's unemployment rate exceeds 5.7 percent? They assume that consumers respond to transfers the way they respond to other disposable income, implying (from the MPC estimates given above) that 20 percent of the transfers would "be spent" by the end of the first quarter, 36 percent by the end of the second quarter, 47 percent by the end of the third quarter, and 55 percent by the end of the fourth quarter (i.e. 55 percent of the transfers is spent within a year). They judge this assumption plausible for the following reason. Contrast two scenarios. First, a transfer bumps disposable income abruptly above its normal growth path. Second, there is a recession, and a transfer keeps the growth path of disposable income closer to normal. It seems plausible that consumers might spend more of the transfer in the second scenario than in the first. To illustrate the second scenario, suppose a $50,000 employee receives a 2 percent pay increase due to recession instead of a normal 4 percent pay increase; this 2 percent shortfall would reduce the employee's pay $1,000 below normal growth. A transfer of $1,000 would restore this employee to normal salary growth. Consumers might well respond to a $1,000 rebate that sustains normal growth in the same way they would have responded to $1,000 of normal growth if there had been no recession.

Simulating the Fair model, and assuming the Federal Reserve were to respond as it usually does historically to changes in the unemployment rate and inflation rate (the Fair model contains an estimated interest rate rule equation for the historical period, indicating how monetary policy usually responds to these changes), the triggered transfers reduce the unemployment rate to 7.1 percent in the fourth quarter (versus 7.9 percent in the recession), and 6.5 percent in the eighth quarter (versus 7.9 percent in the recession).

The government debt consequences of the triggered transfers are manageable: the rise in the debt ratio due to the transfers is much smaller than the rise due to the recession *itself*. The recession itself causes an automatic fall in tax revenue that generates substantial deficits and a substantial cumulative rise in government debt. The triggered transfers raise the *debt ratio* – the ratio of government debt held by the public (excluding the central bank) to GDP – to 41.2 percent in the eighth quarter (versus 33.1 percent in Fair's baseline and 39.2 percent under the recession itself). How does this rise in the debt ratio (from 39.2 percent to 41.2 percent) due to the transfers come about? The transfers raise the *deficit ratio* – the ratio of the government deficit to GDP. For example, in the fourth quarter the deficit ratio is 7.7 percent (versus 3.2 percent in Fair's baseline and 5.1 percent in the recession itself). The cumulative effect of such deficits generates the rise in the debt ratio by the eighth quarter just reported. How large are the transfers? The transfer formula (with strength parameter $s = 2$) generates a *transfer ratio* – the ratio of the transfer to GDP – in the fourth quarter of 2.9 percent and in the eighth quarter of 1.5 percent; the new transfer is roughly a third of Fair's exogenous baseline transfer in the fourth quarter, and a sixth of Fair's exogenous baseline transfer in the eighth quarter.

Will triggered transfers cause a debt burden or inflation?

Will triggered transfers increase government debt and impose a burden on future taxpayers? It is true that triggered transfers will increase the issue of government debt – the treasury must borrow by selling new bonds when it triggers transfers to counter a recession. But automatic de-triggering when the unemployment rate comes back down below the trigger threshold reduces the risk of a long-term build up of debt.

Moreover, the burden on future taxpayers can be kept less than the debt issued by the treasury. Though the treasury is prohibited from selling bonds directly to the central bank, the central bank can simultaneously buy treasury securities from the public through open-market operations. The central bank can then exempt the treasury from paying interest or principal on the securities it purchases (Seidman, 2001, pp. 22–3). Then debt *held by the public* (*excluding* the central bank) will increase less due to these open-market purchases. To make sure the public understands this fact, the government should present official data on "government debt held by the public *excluding* the central bank."

Will triggered transfers complemented by central bank open-market bond purchases be inflationary? It is true that permanent continuous transfers plus open-market purchases would eventually generate excessive aggregate demand and cause inflation. But what is proposed is a *temporary* stimulus. The aim of the temporary transfers plus open-market purchases is to make aggregate demand normal, not excessive.

There is, of course, a risk that expansionary fiscal and monetary policy will continue even after the economy has fully recovered. There are two ways to minimize this risk. First, we propose that the transfers be automatically de-triggered by recovery. Second, there should be an institutional separation of powers between the treasury and the central bank. It is crucial that the central bank be independent of the treasury, and that the treasury be prohibited from issuing money to finance its deficits. Historically, large budget deficits have indeed often led to inflation, even hyperinflation, when they have been money-financed for a sustained period. In these historical episodes, the treasury and central bank were usually consolidated into a single unit so that "the government" simply printed money to finance its deficits. But with an independent central bank and a prohibition against printing money by the treasury, budget deficits need not lead to an excessive rise in aggregate demand.

To create a political climate receptive to using fiscal stimulus in a recession, a government should practice fiscal discipline whenever the economy is running normally, balancing its budget or even running surpluses, thereby achieving a low debt-to-GDP ratio. An advocate of aggressive fiscal policy in a recession, rather than being indifferent to the deficits and debt in a normal economy, should be especially determined to maintain fiscal discipline during prosperity.

One way to maintain fiscal discipline over the long run would be to enact a statute entitled NUBAR – a "normal unemployment balanced budget rule" (a more complete description of NUBAR is given in Seidman, 2003). NUBAR would state that Congress shall enact a *planned* budget for the coming fiscal year that technicians *estimate* will be balanced *if* the unemployment rate is normal (the average of the preceding decade). If Congress adheres to NUBAR, and the technicians are accurate, then if the economy has a normal unemployment rate, the budget will be balanced; if the economy has a boom with a below-normal unemployment rate, the budget will run a surplus; and if the economy has a recession and an above-normal unemployment rate, the budget will be in deficit. Part of the deficit will be due to the automatic stabilizers – the automatic fall in tax revenue and increase in transfers for unemployment insurance benefits; and part will be due to the new automatic fiscal policy. Of course, in a severe recession that overwhelms both monetary policy and the automatic fiscal policy, Congress should take discretionary action and suspend adherence to NUBAR in order to provide even greater stimulus through even larger transfers, tax cuts, and increases in government purchases. NUBAR would achieve even more fiscal discipline if Social Security and Medicare were placed off-budget with respect to NUBAR, so that under NUBAR the planned budget excluding Social Security and Medicare would be balanced. By running surpluses in Social Security and Medicare, and by adhering to NUBAR for the rest of the budget, fiscal discipline would be maintained, and the ratio of national debt to GDP would be kept low despite deficits that occur during recession.

Did counter-cyclical fiscal policy fail in Japan in the past decade?

In his book on the Japanese recession of the 1990s, Adam Posen (1998) provides a detailed analysis of Japanese fiscal policy. Following the bursting of the Japanese asset-price bubble at the beginning of the decade, the Japanese economy stagnated. A perception has arisen that the Japanese government aggressively pursued counter-cyclical fiscal policy to combat the recession, but that fiscal policy failed. Posen contends that this perception is incorrect. In a chapter entitled, "Fiscal Policy Works When It Is Tried," he writes:

> The reality of Japanese fiscal policy in the 1990s is less mysterious and, ultimately, more disappointing. The actual amount injected into the economy by the Japanese government – through either public spending or tax reductions – was about a third of the total amount announced. This limited quantity of total fiscal stimulus was disbursed in insufficiently sized and inefficiently administered doses, with the exception of the 1995 stimulus package. That package did result in solid growth in 1996, demonstrating that fiscal policy does work when it is tried. As on earlier occasions in the 1990s, however, the positive response to fiscal stimulus was undercut by fiscal *contraction* in 1996 and 1997. On net, the Japanese fiscal stance in the 1990s was barely expansionary.
>
> (Posen, 1998, pp. 29–30)

But doesn't the substantial rise in Japan's ratio of government debt to GDP during the 1990s indicate that a large fiscal expansion was attempted over the decade? Kuttner and Posen (2001) directly address this question:

> The effectiveness of fiscal policy in Japan in the 1990s has been at least as controversial as the currently more public disputes over monetary policy. There has been open debate over the degree to which expansionary fiscal policy has even been tried, let alone whether it has been effective, along with widespread assertions about the degree of forward-looking behavior by Japanese savers. The highly visible and rapid more-than-doubling of Japanese public debt in less than a decade speaks for itself to a surprising number of observers: the fiscal deficit has grown sharply, yet the economy has continued to stagnate, so fiscal stabilization failed...
>
> But it is easy to demonstrate from just charting publicly available

data that the bulk of the increase in Japanese public debt is due to a plateau in tax revenue rather than to increased public expenditure or even discretionary tax cuts. This of course reflects the inverse cyclical relationship between output and tax revenue. If one applied a plausible tax elasticity of 1.25 to reasonable measures of the widening output gap ... the result would be a much-reduced estimate of the structural budget deficit. In fact, using the measure of potential based on a constant productivity trend growth rate of 2.5 percent a year all but eliminates the nonsocial security portion of the deficit. Moreover, as measured by the fiscal shocks derived from our estimates in this paper, fiscal policy has been generally contractionary since 1997.

(Kuttner and Posen, 2001, p. 2)

Thus, according to Posen and Kuttner, the main reason for the run-up of government debt in Japan in the 1990s was the recession itself, not expansionary fiscal policy. If a country becomes mired in recession for a decade, low tax revenue year after year results in continuous government borrowing and a huge run-up of debt. This is the same result that Lewis and Seidman (2004) found for the US economy using the Fair macro-econometric model as reported earlier: the rise in the debt ratio due to the recession itself was much larger than the rise due to the triggered transfers.

Conclusion

This paper presents and analyzes a particular new automatic counter-cyclical fiscal policy – *triggered transfers to households*. We propose that Congress pre-enact a transfer formula that authorizes an automatic triggering of a new cash transfer to households in response to a high unemployment rate – in particular, the formula prescribes a "transfer-to-GDP ratio" that is proportional to the "unemployment gap." Current automatic stabilizers are accidental by-products of addressing other important societal objectives: the ratio of government spending to GDP, the degree of progressivity of the tax system, and the level of unemployment benefits. The triggered transfers policy focuses solely on trying to achieve the optimal degree of stimulus to aggregate demand in an economic downturn. It takes as given the current automatic stabilizers enacted for other reasons, and then supplements them in order to get the desired macroeconomic stimulus. One purpose of this paper is to try to encourage economists in the Keynesian tradition to resume research on the analysis of automatic counter-cyclical fiscal policies, and to support the enactment of such policies.

Note

1 Details of the calculation are given in Seidman and Lewis (2003).

References

Campbell, John Y. and N. Gregory Mankiw (1989), "Consumption, Income, and Interest Rates: Reinterpreting the Times Series Evidence," in *NBER Macroeconomics Annual: 1989*, edited by Olivier Jean Blanchard, Cambridge, MA: MIT Press, pp. 185–216.

Duggal, Vijaya G. (1975), "Fiscal Policy and Economic Stabilization," in *The Brookings Model: Perspective and Recent Developments*, edited by Gary Fromm and Lawrence R. Klein, Amsterdam: North-Holland.

Fair, Ray C. (1994), *Testing Macroeconometric Models*. Cambridge, MA: Harvard University Press.

Fair, Ray C. (2003), "The US Model Workbook," <http://www.fairmodel.econ.yale.edu>.

Kuttner, Kenneth N. and Adam S. Posen (2001), "Passive Savers and Fiscal Policy Effectiveness in Japan," Paper prepared for CEPR–CIRJE–NBER Conference on Issues in Fiscal Adjustment, December 2001, Tokyo, Japan.

Lewis, Kenneth A. and Laurence S. Seidman (2004), "Transfers Plus Open-Market Purchases: A Remedy for Recession," University of Delaware Economics Department Working Paper No. 2004-02, January.

Mankiw, N. Gregory (2000), "The Savers-Spenders Theory of Fiscal Policy," *American Economic Review*, 90(2), May, pp. 120–5.

Musgrave, Richard A. (1959), *The Theory of Public Finance*, New York: McGraw-Hill.

Pack, Howard (1968), "Formula Flexibility: A Quantitative Appraisal," in *Studies in Economic Stabilization*, edited by Albert Ando, E. Cary Brown and Ann F. Friedlaender, Washington, DC: Brookings Institution, pp. 5–40.

Parker, Jonathan (1999), "The Response of Household Consumption to Predictable Changes in Social Security Taxes," *American Economic Review*, 89(4), September, pp. 959–73.

Parker, Jonathan (2003), "Consumer Spending and the 2001 Tax Rebates," Presentation at an American Enterprise Institute seminar, Washington, DC, November 7.

Posen, Adam S. (1998), *Restoring Japan's Economic Growth*, Washington, DC: Institute for International Economics.

Seidman, Laurence S. (1975), *The Design of Federal Employment Programs*, Lexington: D.C. Heath and Company.

Seidman, Laurence S. (2001), "Reviving Fiscal Policy," *Challenge*, 44(3), May–June, pp. 17–42.

Seidman, Laurence S. (2003), *Automatic Fiscal Policies to Combat Recessions*, Armonk, NY: M.E. Sharpe.

Seidman, Laurence S. and Kenneth A. Lewis (2002), "A New Design for Automatic Fiscal Policy," *International Finance*, 5(2), Summer, pp. 251–84.

Seidman, Laurence S. and Kenneth A. Lewis (2003), "Is a Tax Rebate an Effective Tool for Combating a Recession? – A Reply to Shapiro and Slemrod," University of Delaware Economics Department Working Paper 2003-15, November.

Shapiro, Matthew D. and Joel Slemrod (1995), "Consumer Response to the Timing of Income: Evidence from the Change in Tax Withholding," *American Economic Review*, 85(1), March, pp. 274–83.

Shapiro, Matthew D. and Joel Slemrod (2003*a*), "Consumer Response to Tax Rebates," *American Economic Review*, 93(1), March, pp. 381–96.

Shapiro, Matthew D. and Joel Slemrod (2003*b*), "Did the 2001 Tax Rebate Stimulate Spending? Evidence from Taxpayer Surveys," in *Tax Policy and the Economy 17*, edited by James M. Poterba, Cambridge, MA: The MIT Press, pp. 83–109.

Souleles, Nicholas S. (1999), "The Response of Household Consumption to Income-tax Refunds." *American Economic Review*, 89(4), September, pp. 947–58.

4 Integrating sound finance with functional finance

David Colander and Peter Hans Matthews

A major problem of fiscal policy is finding a balance between the short-run stabilization goal and the long-run systemic stability goal. Economists' debates about that balance have swung like a pendulum from a long-run focus to a short-run focus, back to a long-run focus and ... In the early 2000s, the debate is at the bottom of a swing and economists' views on fiscal policy are best described as chaotic. Among the majority of mainstream academic economists, short-run discretionary fiscal policy is in ill repute both theoretically and practically. The general view held by most mainstream academic macroeconomists is that short-run fiscal policy doesn't work, or that if it works, it works at the wrong time. The once accepted Keynesian theories of how fiscal policy worked have given way to a variety of theoretical models that provide little guidance to policy makers. These developments in theory mean that economists have given up their voice on budgeting, allowing political interests, not economic reasoning, to guide a practical fiscal policy.

While academic macroeconomists have generally given up their voice about fiscal policy, macro-policy economists have not. However, for the most part today's macro-policy economists have given up any hope that fiscal policy can be used for short-run stabilization, and they have swung over to the long-run side of the pendulum. Given their negative view of the effectiveness of short-run fiscal policy, they have concentrated their efforts on implementing long-run systemic-stability goals for fiscal policy. Their goal is to keep politicians away from the fiscal policy levers to maintain the long-run fiscal integrity of the state. What the goal of systemic stability is designed to prevent is a situation in which the government has approached its debt borrowing limit, and yet needs to run a deficit. In that case running a deficit will not even have the desired effect, since the deficit would likely undermine confidence in the economy, and have greater offsets in investment and domestic consumption spending than the stimulative government spending. So the reason to focus on the long-run systemic stability as a fiscal-policy goal is to preserve the option of using short-run fiscal policy when it is most needed.

Their advice has led to a variety of constitutional restrictions on budget deficits, such as US states' constitutional amendments against deficits, and the European Union's Stability and Growth Pact's constraint on the budget deficit relative to GDP. While macro-policy economists agree that these constraints undermine the short-run use of fiscal policy as a tool of stabilization, the current feeling seems to be that the cost is not great and one worth paying. Thus, those who feel differently, as is the case with most of the contributors to this volume, must either lower the political and economic cost of implementing fiscal stabilization policy, or convince others of its strength.

It is generally accepted that the current restrictions on fiscal policy have not found a good balance, and that often, in balancing the long-run and short-run aspects of budgets, these restrictions create a more perverse short-run fiscal policy than is necessary, with government spending policies contributing to recessions rather than helping to stop them, and exacerbating rather than slowing booms. The paper discusses a proposal that would help in achieving a better balance between the two. Specifically, it proposes a change in governments' budgeting procedures from an annual budget to a moving-average budget, in which government uses a three-year rolling average budgeting procedure (with an underlying trend rate of increase built into it) rather than an annual budget for any rule restricting fiscal policy. It argues that specifying all legal long-term budget restraints in terms of this moving average, rather than in terms of a yearly budget, would reduce the perverse effects the long-run budget restrictions currently bring about. Thus, this paper offers a complement to Seidman's (2003) recent discussion of methods to reintroduce fiscal stabilization policy into policy.

The paper first presents a short history of fiscal policy. Second, it presents an even shorter history of the politics of fiscal policy. Third, it discusses the nature of the moving-average proposal and how the adoption of such a budgeting procedure would avoid some of problems that are currently plaguing the use of fiscal policy and how the proposal, had it been in effect, would have changed the decisions facing governments.

A short history of fiscal policy

Economists' view of fiscal policy's usefulness has fluctuated widely. Before the 1930s fiscal policy was not part of the lexicon of economists; government spending policy was discussed under the name sound finance – which held that the government budget should be balanced except in wartime. This view was primarily held on political, not economic grounds, although government spending was not large relative to total spending, and thus would not have a large stabilization effect in any case. The classical liberal tradition viewed government with suspicion, so any policy that would make it easier to increase government spending during peacetime was seen as undesirable. Sound finance principles made increasing government spending difficult, and forced government to face the costs of a spending decision simultaneously with the benefits of that spending decision, something that bond finance did not do. Economists recognized that government spending could impact the state of the economy and that, at times, unbalanced budgets could make sense, but they felt that long-run fiscal integrity of the government should override such concerns in peacetime. That long-run fiscal integrity would allow the government to have a cushion to finance a war. For Classical economists, allowing government the option of deficit spending in peacetime was similar to giving a credit card to a spendthrift child.

In the 1920s in Europe, and the 1930s in the United States, economists, such as A.C. Pigou, F. Knight, and J.M. Keynes, started questioning sound-finance principles as the economies of the world fell into a major ongoing depression, from which there seemed no escape. The depressed state of the economy created a vicious circle in which the expectations of continued depression kept investment spending low and became self-fulfilling. Given such a collapse of economic expectations, they favored, at least temporarily, giving up the sound finance principles and using government spending to stimulate the economy.

These economists' support for deficit spending was based on simple common sense reasoning, not complex underlying models; it seemed reasonable to assume that if the government spent more than it took in – ran a deficit – that the economy would be jump started; income would increase; the recipients of that increased income would spend more, creating a virtuous circle that ultimately would help pull the economy out of the recession. There were questions of how much offset would result from financing the deficit, but there was a general feeling among policy-making economists that fiscal policy could be of some use in helping pull an economy out of a severe recession and possibly even in offsetting undesirable cyclical fluctuations in output.

These changing views of the deficit were soon subsumed under the Keynesian revolution. This was unfortunate for both the Keynesian revolution and for fiscal policy because it intertwined abstract theory with pragmatic policy, obscuring both. The reality is that Keynes' *General Theory* was not about fiscal policy at all, and does not mention it as a policy tool. Keynes' support of fiscal policy predated the *General Theory* and was not dependent on it. Moreover, he maintained many of the Classical views about fiscal policy long after he wrote the *General Theory*. However, the practical and theoretical debates soon merged into a debate about "Keynesian policy." The reasons why were in large part political. Business leaders in the 1930s recognized that there was a serious problem in the Depression, and that if something were not done, it was unlikely that our economic system would continue. Given the options, liberal business leaders felt that running government budget deficits could help stimulate their demand, and was the type of intervention that would have the least effect on them. They saw it as a way to save capitalism with the least amount of government intervention.

Liberal politicians pushing for new government programs such as social security and welfare programs felt that the acceptance of deficit finance could make their introduction easier. So, they jumped on the fiscal-policy interpretation of Keynesian economics because it helped with their other goals. Thus, in our view fiscal policy was accepted because it was a conservative policy that limited government involvement in the economy, especially when compared to Keynes' proposal in the *General Theory* for socializing investment. So the debate about Keynesian policy quickly shifted to a debate about fiscal policy.

The acceptance of the fiscal-policy tool and the effectiveness of fiscal policy did not come easily. Since Keynes had not discussed fiscal policy in the *General Theory*, much of that early debate was focused on Abba Lerner's rendition of Keynesian policy (1941) that reduced it down to specific rules about monetary and fiscal policy, which he called functional finance.

Lerner was a brilliant pedagogue, and had a wonderful way of providing clear mental models that made the policies he advocated seem obvious, even if at first they seemed counterintuitive. In proposing these rules of functional finance, Lerner's stated purpose was to shift thinking about government finance from principles of sound finance that might make sense for individuals – such as a balanced budget – to *functional* finance principles that make sense for the aggregate economy in which government spending and taxing decisions affect levels of economic activity. In doing so he hoped to change the focus on the *consequences* of government financing, not on the then generally accepted, but little considered, rules of sound finance and the quantity theory of money.

In making his arguments he created a famous analogy, which saw fiscal policy as a steering wheel driving the economy. Functional finance meant using the steering wheel to guide the economy and keep it going straight; sound finance left the economy to bounce around on its own crashing again and again. The clearness of Lerner's writing, and the neatness of his models, made Lerner's story of Keynesian economics the textbook story.

Unfortunately pedagogical simplicity comes at a cost and, in specifying these rules of functional finance, Lerner simply ignored the broader arguments for sound finance, and ridiculed the balanced budget mentality of sound finance. He argued that any level of deficit and debt were possible, and that taxes should be chosen to achieve the desired level of income, not to bring in money to pay for government expenditures. Any level of government expenditures could be paid for by selling bonds or printing money – the important point was to spend to the level that would achieve full employment.[1] The only reason to tax was to fight inflation, not to finance expenditures.

Lerner's initial specification of the rules of functional finance assumed that the government's inflation and employment goals were simultaneously achievable. But it was soon found that they were not, and that therefore, generally, the rules of functional finance provided contradictory guidance. Inflation required contractionary fiscal policy; unemployment required expansionary fiscal policy, and Lerner had no rule for what to do when there was simultaneous inflation and unemployment.[2] Moreover, it was also quickly discovered that politicians, not economists, controlled the levers of fiscal policy and their imperatives for staying in office made the use of politically discretionary fiscal stabilization highly questionable. The drivers of the economic car were not economists, but groups of politicians grabbing at the steering wheel, and staying on the economic road was not their primary concern. So stagflation and the realities of politics soon led to a movement away from fiscal policy in both the texts and in macro policy.

First to go was the sense that the government could use fiscal policy to fine-tune the economy, and by the 1960s fine-tuning was no longer part of the textbook story. Fiscal policy could still be used in serious cases of recession or boom, but it certainly shouldn't be seen as a steering wheel. Among practicing macroeconomists, the second aspect of Lernerian philosophy to go was the position that the amount of debt did not matter. Most economists came to believe that it did matter because of sustainability goal; deficits have to be financed, and the financing issues ultimately place a limit on how large, and for how long, deficits can be run.

The largest fear of sustainability involves default and fear of default – where the government in question does not have the capacity to service the existing debt, or where individuals believe that the government will not have the capacity or will to do so. In this case the government may be unable to sell its bonds, leading it technically into default. If a sovereign default occurred, the solution would be either a bailout by some higher level or extra-governmental organization, or a breakdown and re-establishment of the economic system.

The debt limit is stricter for governments without a monetary authority to bail out the government if they can no longer sell their bonds. But even those governments with monetary authorities face a limit either because of international commitments on monetary policy that limit the monetary authority, or because of fear of the hyperinflation that results from such bailouts at some level. The level of these limits is ambiguous; they bite only in the uncertain future. Thus individuals can differ on where these limits are. But the academic legacy of functional finance literature is that these limits, not some mystical nature of deficits, are the reason to fear deficits.

Today, these issues are well understood by macro-policy economics, and good ones (the ones who agree with us) favor a policy that might be called *sound functional finance*, a policy that considers all these issues and tries to find a balance between the short-run and long-run goals.[3] Since short-run fiscal policy for stabilization purposes does not seem especially doable, many practicing macroeconomists turned their focus on fiscal policy on achieving these long-run goals to avoid sovereign default. This focus on long-run goals is not, however, a return to the pre-Lernerian days of sound finances. In the current macro-policy view, sound long-run finance need not involve a balanced budget; the short-run and intertemporal financing advantages of deficit finance are recognized, and built into the policy advice that policy-oriented macroeconomists give as they try to find a balance between the long-run and short-run goals. The general view is that rather than a balanced budget it is better to specify any long-run limitation on deficits relative to the taxing capacity of the government. Since GDP serves as a measure of the taxing capacity of the government, the limits are generally estimated by debt-to-GDP ratios.

While this evolution in policy economist's thinking about fiscal policy was going on, significant changes were occurring in macro-theorists' thinking as well. In these theoretical reconsiderations, not only was functional finance coming under attack; so too was the entire foundation of the Keynesian model. These attacks were so successful that by the 1990s, with the development of new classical economics, rational expectations and Ricardian equivalence, any sense that fiscal policy had a formal theoretical foundation dissolved. The new synthesis in macroeconomic theory sees macro problems within intertemporal dynamic stochastic general equilibrium models. These models of infinitely rational individuals generally come to the not surprising conclusion that deficits have no first-order impact. In an ongoing system you've got to pay for something sometime, so deficit finance is simply a rearrangement of expenditures and tax payments, which individuals can take into account and offset in their own, or their offspring's spending patterns. Ricardian equivalence tells us that financing does not matter; it is all the same. In these modern theories, deficits are simply budgeting procedures that in an economy in intertemporal equilibrium do not matter. Thus in these theoretical models, deficits make little difference, since rational agents will simply reallocate their intertemporal spending decisions to offset any government change.[4]

Most policy economists pay only slight attention to theorists, and they continued to see deficit issues in terms of finding the correct mixture of long-run fiscal restraint and short-run stabilization needs. But with the loss of any theoretical backing, their views became just one in many, and pop economic philosophies, such as supply-side economics, developed that rationalized political uses of the budget deficit. There were so many different views coming from economists that their views simply stopped being important, except to the extent that politicians wanted to use one view or another to support what they wanted to do anyway. The politicians decided that fiscal policy, and in the absence of any consistent guidance from economists on the budget, the political positions of various parties moved away from reflecting economists' recommendations, and towards the position that gave them the best political advantage.

The politics of fiscal policy

Let us now turn to a brief history of the politics of fiscal policy, focusing on the US and relating it to the Republican's and Democrat's positions on deficits. Prior to the 1930s all politicians – Democrats and Republicans alike – were against deficits; the general view held by politicians was similar to that held by Classical economists. They believed that deficit financing was to be reserved for wartime, and that in peacetime debt incurred during war would be eliminated. As we alluded to in the beginning of the paper, that view changed in the 1930s because of the severity of the economic slump. Roosevelt and the New Deal programs began a program of small deficit spending even while maintaining the rhetoric of sound finance. That change occurred as pragmatic economists of various political persuasions began considering bond-financed public works spending as a way to pull the economy out of the 1930s depression. Sound finance and concern about the long-run implications became questionable when the short-run depression left the short-run existence of the economic system in doubt.[5]

The arguments for deficits caught on among academic macroeconomists in the US in 1937, when the recovery, which had been ongoing since 1933, ended and unemployment increased, even though it was still at high levels. At that point, the political views about deficits began to shift.

World War II stopped the debate about the use of deficits as a stimulatory tool, and the economic debate turned to the problems of financing the war, and how big deficits could be run. In this debate there was little thought of sound finance, since in war time, with the survival of the state in question, deficits had always been acceptable. The war period was marked by large deficits, decreases in unemployment, significant labor shortages, and large growth rates in output. In the eyes of many the power of deficits had been demonstrated by war finance.

When the war ended in the late 1940s, both economists and politicians began to deal with the question of fiscal policy during peacetime. Many believed that the economy would fall back into depression, which was seen as a characteristic of mature capitalist economies, and that large government deficits were necessary to counteract secular stagnation. It was that time that functional finance caught on and the debate about deficits merged with the debate about Keynesian economics.

Initially, in the 1950s and early 1960s, the political sides were clear; the Democrats were Keynesian; they were the party of the deficits. Republicans were Classical; they were the party of sound finance. Consistent with these positions, Democrats pushed for increases in government programs and government spending, in part justifying these programs as increasing the size of the government budget and thereby increasing effectiveness of fiscal policy as a tool of stabilization. For example Alvin Hansen wrote that the welfare state involves "government outlays large enough to permit fiscal policy to play a controlling role in the adjustment of aggregate demand to the productive potential of which the private enterprise economy is capable." (Hansen, 1957, p. 37)

The push by Democrats for increased spending was partly offset by Republicans who pushed for tax decreases, but that push was often overwhelmed by their support of sound finance. Ultimately, Republicans found that they had to compromise on their support for sound finance and accept some level of deficits, because of the political difficulty of cutting government programs once they were started. During this time, the relative size of the government increased, and almost continual deficits were run. However, these deficits were not especially large relative to GDP, and no serious economist felt that these deficits were raising questions about the long-run financial viability of the state.

The politics of government budgets was made easier during this time period by growth and creeping inflation. Growth meant that tax revenues were increasing each year, which provided a growth dividend, and that also allowed an increasing debt even while maintaining a constant debt-to-GDP ratio. The creeping inflation similarly reduced the real debt and the debt-to-GDP ratio. This creeping inflation interacted with the progressive income tax to effectively raise the tax rate on individuals without any tax increase, thereby providing an increasing share of income going to the state, even without government specifically increasing taxes. This institutional structure allowed there to be continual deficits, and much talk about deficits, but no real concern about the deficits' effect on the long-run fiscal position of the US, which remained solid during this entire period. Thus, in the 1950s we had reached a type of political/economic equilibrium with Democrats increasing government programs and spending, and Republicans divided in their support of tax reductions and eliminating deficits. Thus, from the 1950s to 1970s government spending increased, government tax rates were reduced, and deficits were run at a level that kept the US in the middle of the ranking of countries in debt-to-GDP ratios, leaving significant borrowing capacity for the US government. On the state level, balanced budget requirements in the constitutions kept state government deficits in check, although numerous ways around these requirements were found.

The political equilibrium changed in the 1980s when the Republicans moved philosophically away from their support of a balanced budget, and began to focus solely on tax reductions. The underlying theory behind that shift was often associated with the supply-side proposition that tax cuts would increase incentives for work and investment so much that it would create growth, but few serious economists believed in the strong supply-side arguments. Instead, the sophisticated Republican reasoning was subtler and more political. Essentially, it that government spending was enormously inefficient and needed to be kept down. It also held that political forces would work to spend whatever money was available. This meant that a budget surplus, or even a deficit that did not exceed a certain level of GDP that would alarm the public, was an invitation for increased government spending. These two propositions led Republicans to eliminate their support of sound finance and a balanced budget. The new Republican supply-side position became one of "always cut taxes," and "never raise taxes." This Republican position came into being with the Reagan era; Bush the Elder violated it and his loss to Clinton was attributed to that violation, making the "tax-cut" philosophy deeply entrenched in the Republican view. This left fiscally conservative Democrats, and a few maverick Republicans, as the few reluctant supporters of sound finance, and pushed deficits higher in the 1980s.

Fear about the long-run viability of Social Security and Medicare programs, and the public's general fear of deficits led to a variety of pay-go programs to limit government spending and tax cuts and create a stronger long-run fiscal balance. But the accounting and economic issues underlying these were poorly understood by the public, and they had been written with only deficits in mind. When the economic boom of the late 1990s, combined with demographics of the baby boom, started to lead to large government budget surpluses, these pay-go programs were not renewed, and in 2002 the programs expired with hardly a mention by either side or the press. This removed the last constraint on the previous political/economic equilibrium, and opened the way for larger and larger deficits with few institutional constraints, whether or not they were needed as a fiscal stimulus.

The effects of this change in the political/economic equilibrium occurred much faster than most observers believed possible. With President Bush's election, the ending of the economic boom, the tax cuts Bush pushed through, and the increases in both social and defense spending, the seemingly large surpluses that had been predicted at the beginning of the 2000s evaporated, and were replaced by large deficits. With inflation low, these deficits were real, not nominal. Deficits relative to GDP increased, bringing back concern about sound finance and the long-run consequences of deficits. The US is, of course, a long way from its long-run limit on its borrowing capacity; it has trillions of dollars of leeway left, but with the change in the political/economic equilibrium that has led to possible $600 billion annual deficits, it will likely use up that leeway faster than many expect.

Given the current political postures of both Republicans and Democrats, more and more policy macroeconomists have come to the conclusion that some type of long-run fiscal restraint is needed. It was that concern that led to the Stability and Growth Pact in the European Union, and to constitutional amendments of states limiting budget deficits. The problem of these long-run restraints is that they affect the political/economic equilibrium in a perverse way, leading to pro-cyclical rather than anti-cyclical spending. They mean that whenever there is a slowdown in the economy, governments must cut spending, taxes must be increased, or both. This pro-cyclical state and local fiscal policy works on the up side as well. As the US economy boomed through the 1990s most state governments increased their spending or cut their taxes, maintaining only a small rainy-day fund. As they did so they contributed to the boom and kept the economy going at a rate that was unsustainable. Such pro-cyclical fiscal policy is bad for the states and bad for the national economy.

The problem is that these long-run constraints force the political system to take deficit spending into account precisely when taking it into account will have the wrong short-run effect – when the economy is going into a recession. One wants a solution that forces government to take the long-run fiscal consequences into account when the economy is in a boom – running larger surpluses in those booms. A modification of the pay-go system is one way to achieve this. It could specify that government spending restrictions become stricter when the economy is above trend, and looser when the economy is below trend, but such a change is complicated to specify and will likely be difficult to implement politically.

A proposal for a moving average budget

With that background, let us now consider the reasoning behind the proposal being suggested in this paper. It is a proposal, which we call a *moving-average budgeting proposal*, that extends the term upon which the deficit is calculated to a minimum of a three-year period, and possibly to a five-year period. Thus, in calculating the deficit, a moving average revenue period would be used.[6] A moving average budget is a budget in which revenue flows are smoothed out so that spending depends on a moving average of revenues rather than yearly revenues. Thus, the spending and tax cut limit determined by the budget is only partially determined by revenues in the current year, and are instead determined by revenues in past years. A moving average budget smoothes out revenue flows so that upward and downward adjustments are spread out over three years, rather than being made in the year. Thus, if the economy is in a boom, spendable revenues will not rise as fast as they otherwise would, and if the economy is in a recession, spendable revenues will not fall as fast as they otherwise would. If any long-run spending restriction is based on this moving-average budget, its short-run pro-cyclical effects will be partially offset.

What this proposal does is to build a rainy-season fund into the budgeting procedures by presenting the budget as one in which it automatically keeps a portion of a large increase in revenues out of the current budget. Similarly, where there is a decrease in expenditures, it keeps a portion of a decrease in revenues out of the budget so that cuts do not have to be made immediately, but instead can be spread out over a period of time. If the economy rebounds in the next time period, the spending can be increased. By using moving-average budget figures in any long-run constitutional limit on deficits, one incorporates some anti-cyclical spending into those budgeting procedures. It is an automatic stabilizer, but it is an automatic stabilizer that is not only built into the spending and taxing provisions, but into the budget itself.

The first thing to note about this proposal is that it is a proposal about budgeting procedures, not about fiscal policy. Choosing a year as the period over which to consider the state of the budget is simply an arbitrary choice that is designed to smooth out revenues and expenditure flows; few would argue that daily, weekly or monthly budgets should be balanced, or even considered since there is unevenness in both revenues and expenditures. A yearly, rather than a monthly, budget simply extends the period that is smoothed from monthly budgets to yearly budgets. A moving average budget extends it to a longer period. As long as the random fluctuations in revenues and expenditures are of shorter duration than the smoothing period, a moving-average budget rule, rather than a shorter-term budget rule, will introduce stabilizing fiscal policy into the budgeting procedures. The second thing to note about the moving-average budget is that its goal is to affect the political/economic equilibrium and how that equilibrium affects the focus that the political system gives to the long-run and short-run goals of the economy.

Our support for introducing a moving-average budgeting procedure is based on two propositions. The first proposition is that while budget procedures are only accounting phenomena; and do not *directly* affect the real economy, those budgeting procedures do *indirectly* affect real forces through their effect on people's psychology and politics. Thus policy must consider that indirect effect. Our point is that the way in which information is presented can cause people to react quite differently. Thus, budgeting procedures are important and ideally should be designed to reflect the underlying realities of the budgeting choices as best they can. We call this proposition as it relates to the long-run borrowing capacity of the government, *the principle of sound finance*.

The second proposition that the proposal is built upon is the *principle of functional finance*. This principle concerns the ability of short-run budget deficits to be simulative, because of their ability to put spending power in the hands of individuals. There is an enormous amount of theoretical and empirical work that has been done on this effect, and most of the empirical evidence suggests a small, but highly variable, positive effect in the short-run and a possible slightly negative long-run effect of a deficit due to the higher interest rates it may cause. The size of this effect will be highly uncertain, because these fiscal policy levers work significantly through expectations and consumer and investment psychology, but it will generally be there. Assuming it is, other things equal, relative to one's long-run sound-finance principle, in downturns one wants fiscal policy to be relatively simulative, and in upturns one wants it to be relatively contractionary. For that reason we expect that politically, there will be strong pushes for budget deficits whenever the economy slows. The problem is the lags in implementing discretionary fiscal policy make it almost unusable, which is why Larry Seidman (2003) has revived the arguments for built-in stabilizers that increase the deficit in contractions and decrease the deficit in expansions. The methods Seidman suggests include formula flexibility, a fiscal policy board, and establishing fiscal discipline with a normal-unemployment budget-balance rule (a variation of a rule focused on the structural rather than the cyclical deficit).

Our policy proposal operates in a similar way to formula flexibility, but it changes the very definition of deficit and surplus, and thus incorporates the stabilization into the budget procedure and the definition of deficit and surplus. It should be seen as an additional tool that can lead to a better mix of the goals. The advantage of the moving-average proposal is that it doesn't involve establishing a board, or affect tax rates, which are likely to be politically contentious. Moreover, since it takes no position on what the fiscal policy should be, but is nonetheless likely to push government toward a better balance between sound and functional finance goals of fiscal policy, it should be more politically feasible than the methods Seidman discusses.

As we stated above, this proposal should not be seen as an alternative to those other policies, but as a complement. It is also a complement to the policies that have been advanced to achieve better focus on sound finance goals, such as pay-go systems and capital-budgeting procedures. Our proposal simply involves a change in budgeting procedures; it is neutral as to the balance that government chooses between the sound and functional finance goals. Any discretionary fiscal policy can be used with it. How then will it affect the actual fiscal policy that is used? We see it working though its effect on changing the political forces that govern the spending and taxing decisions. *It gives more focus to the sound finance principle in booms and expansions, and more focus to short run goals in recessions, and thus finds a better balance between the two.*

To see the degree to which a moving average budget would stabilize revenues, depending on the nature of the fluctuations and the length of the moving average, consider the example of fluctuating flows of income and constant expenditures (of 100) shown in Table 4.1.

In the first year the 33 percent fall in income was reduced to a 20 percent fall, and in the second the 50 percent rise in income was reduced to a 6.6 percent rise in income, and so on. Thus, by using a moving-average budget, the variance of a flow of revenue available for spending can be reduced. In terms of the budget deficit or surplus, notice that it changes it significantly. For example in year seven, the current budget deficit is zero, but the moving-average budget deficit is 14.3. Thus during this expansion,

Table 4.1 A comparison of annual and moving-average (MA) budgeting

Year	1	2	3	4	5	6	7	8	9	10
Revenue	100	120	80	120	100	80	80	100	120	100
MA Revenue			100	106.6	100	100	93.3	86.6	100	100
Expenditures	100	100	100	100	100	100	100	100	100	100
Deficit	0	−20	20	−20	0	20	20	0	−20	0
MA Deficit			0	6.6	0	0	6.6	14.3	0	0

rather than the deficit not existing because of the expansion, encouraging increased spending, the budget is in deficit, reflecting the shortfall in revenue in the two previous years. That meant in years six and seven, when the economy was in a recession, the deficits were much less, and therefore there would have been less pressure to make the drastic cuts.

Instituting a moving-average budget with an unknown trend makes the underlying theory even more difficult, and presents the problem of deciding if a trend is changing or whether one is experiencing cyclical fluctuations around that trend. But these are technical issues, and are issues that have been studied significantly in the detrending literature; thus we believe that reasonable procedures can be built into the proposal. But as with many such proposals, perfection is the enemy of the politically feasible, and a simple moving-average procedure around a long-run trend may be the easiest to explain and gain political support for.

Conclusion

The problem of integrating the short-run stabilization and long-run systemic stabilities of government's fiscal policy is an ongoing one. It was not a serious problem for much of the latter twentieth century for the US because of a political/economic equilibrium that developed. Over the last couple of decades, that equilibrium has broken down, and a current problem of fiscal policy is how to integrate these. One current method of integrating them – instituting restrictions on deficits – works pro-cyclically, and often worsens the fluctuations. One way to reduce the anti-cyclical nature of the problem is to change our budgeting procedures to use moving-average revenues rather than current revenues in the calculations of budget-deficit restrictions and in the budgeting decision of the government.

These budgeting procedures matter, not because they matter inherently, but because they play a role in the political pressures which ultimately determine the fiscal policy of a country. Budgeting procedures must be considered in relation to the political/economic equilibrium that they will bring about. Moving-average budget procedures combine the long-run and the short-run dimensions of the budget process into the budget and the definition of deficit, and thereby make the reported concept of deficit better reflect the combination of long-run and short-run effects of the budget. Thus, if one is going to require some balance in a budget either absolutely, or as specified as a percentage of GDP, that balance is best specified on a moving-average budget, rather than a yearly budget. While there will still be pressures to deviate from the rule, the pressures will be less likely to undermine the initial goal of the budgeting procedure.

We fully agree that the proposal is simply an accounting change; it does not change the underlying nature of the system. Moreover, we also agree that it could be duplicated with the creation of a rainy-season fund, or by appropriate decisions on spending that take functional finance considerations into account. But the problem with these alternatives is that politically, they do not work. An effective rainy-day fund has always been politically too tempting a target in a downturn, and politically too difficult to set up in a boom. To be effective, rainy-day funds have to be much larger than anything currently conceived. They would be better seen as rainy-season funds, rather than rainy-day funds.

The moving-average budget is a change in budgeting procedure; it says nothing about what the fiscal goal of governments should be or how governments should balance functional finance and sound finance goals. It is simply meant to change when those considerations are taken into account. It is designed to lead governments to consider long-run goals more heavily in expansions, and short-run goals more in contractions. It is a budgeting procedure that can be associated with a variety of long-run spending restraint programs, or with no such program. All it does is to make whatever long-run fiscal restraint one imposes less likely to be pro-cyclical and more likely to be anti-cyclical. It is not the solution to the fiscal policy problem, but it is a small change that would help better integrate the long-run and short-run dimensions of fiscal policy into the politics of budgets.

Notes

1 Most economists of the time, including Keynes, had a hard time accepting Lerner's stark presentation of the argument. See Colander (1984).
2 Actually, Lerner latter had a proposal for how to deal with stagflation, but politically that was not adopted. See Lerner and Colander (1980) and Colander (1979, 1986).
3 We can see the various ways in which these issues play out in the current debate about the Stability and Growth Pact in the EU and in the problems of the state governments in the US, where constitutional laws in all but one state make deficits unconstitutional. However, the laws are often not followed either through accounting tricks or through outright refusal to follow them, as is currently occurring with the Stability and Growth Pact.
4 It is important to note that this shift in theoretical thinking about fiscal policy is not a movement back to the Classical position of sound finance, which provided

a strong moral voice for balancing the budget. It was a post-modern voice that nothing mattered; it all comes out in the market wash.

5 This, in our view, was what Keynes was referring to in his famous "in the long run we are all dead" statement; it meant that if we don't solve our short-run problems that can undermine the system, there would be no long run.

6 While the technical aspects of the policy are not the subject of this paper, we would expect that it most likely would be implemented quarterly, so that with a three-year moving average, every quarter the latest quarter would replace a quarter three years ago in calculating the deficit.

References

Colander, David (1979), "Rationality, Expectations and Functional Finance," in *Essays in Post Keynesian Inflation*, edited by James H. Gapinski and Charles E. Rockwood, Boston: Ballinger Publishers.

Colander, David (editor) (1986), *Incentive Based Incomes Policies*, Boston: Ballinger Publishers.

Colander, David (1984), "Was Keynes a Keynesian or a Lernerian?" *Journal of Economic Literature*, 22(4), December, pp. 1572–5.

Hansen, Alvin (1957), *The American Economy*, New York: McGraw-Hill.

Keynes, John Maynard (1936), *The General Theory of Unemployment*, New York: Harcourt Brace.

Lerner, Abba and David Colander (1980), *MAP: A Market Anti Inflation Plan*, New York: Harcourt Brace Jovanovich.

Seidman, Laurence S. (2003), *Automatic Fiscal Policies to Combat Recessions*, Armonk NY: M.E. Sharpe.

5 Regime change for the US federal budget

Max B. Sawicky

These days the merits of public spending are beside the point. The reigning presumption is that such spending is not affordable. Benefit/cost calculus is excluded from the political calculation.

Between January of 2001 and 2004, the US federal budget outlook lurched from a projected ten-year surplus of $5.6 trillion to a deficit of nearly $5 trillion. This dramatic reversal encouraged the affordability canard. This paper shows that strong growth of domestic spending is feasible, and it can be fiscally responsible. A liberal budget need not be impractical.

The discussion here is based on a precept that is widely supported among economists but little known to the public: that a fixed ratio of public debt to Gross Domestic Product (GDP) can be sustained indefinitely without economic difficulty (GAO, 1996; CBO, 1997). For instance:

> Other approaches could also create sustainable budgetary conditions. For instance, a budget that was permanently balanced would freeze the level of federal debt. Thus, as the economy grew, debt would gradually fall as a share of GDP. However, sustainable policies do not require balanced budgets. As long as deficits do not grow relative to the economy, the government could in principle keep the budget in deficit forever. Under the assumptions of CBO's long-term simulations, if the government stabilized the NIPA deficit at its current share of GDP (about 1.7 percent), the debt would remain close to its current share of GDP indefinitely.
>
> (Congressional Budget Office, March 1997)

or:

> Q. What are the key issues in evaluating the overall level of debt for the future?
> A. In assessing debt levels, it is important to focus on the right indicator of the burden of the debt. As we have noted earlier, comparing the debt to GDP provides a better indicator of the debt burden than

the debt's nominal dollar value, because it captures the capacity of the economy to sustain the debt.

(US General Accounting Office, November 1996)

The basic intuition is that a fixed debt-to-GDP ratio implies a fixed ratio of interest payments to GDP. GDP is the aggregate tax base available to the Federal government, so it is analogous to the income of an individual or family. If an expense comprising a given share of income can be carried in the present as income and that expense grow apace, the expense can be borne in the future as well. If the rent you can pay is 20 percent of your income, and both rent and income triple, you can still afford your rent.

Another assumption here is that the economy can support limited tax increases. In this dimension, the US presently ranks near the bottom of advanced industrialized nations.

Not long ago, these were uncontroversial premises. Today they have become marginalized in public debate. The strength of this marginalization stems to some extent from an unfamiliarity with simple data on budget trends, a problem this paper aims to remedy.

The analysis is confined to the next ten years. Other concerns have been raised for the outlook beyond that window (CBO, 2003). Most long-term projections imply untenable deficit increases. The long-term picture is beyond the scope of this discussion, although the decision to sideline it will be defended below.

Where we stand

Figure 5.1 shows the current "baseline" deficit projections, along with an alternative projection that reflects likely policy changes over the next ten years.

The baseline is the object of much confusion in public debate on the grounds that it is not "realistic." The purpose of the baseline calculation, however, is not to reflect reality. It is to depict the implications of current policy. If the projection looks implausible, it is because current policy is unsustainable. Rules for calculating a baseline are codified in law.

Another bum rap on the baseline is that it ignores the possibility of economic downturns. In fact, baseline calculations factor in the effect of recession by "spreading it" over the period. (There is no attempt to predict when a recession will occur, only that one is likely to occur at some point in the decade.) In general, in the wake of the misplaced "new economy" euphoria of the late 1990s, economic projections for baseline calculations from the Congressional Budget Office (CBO) tend to err on the conservative side.

Ordinarily a baseline would be a useful guide for fiscal policy decisions. Unfortunately, tax legislation since 2001 has been written with the express

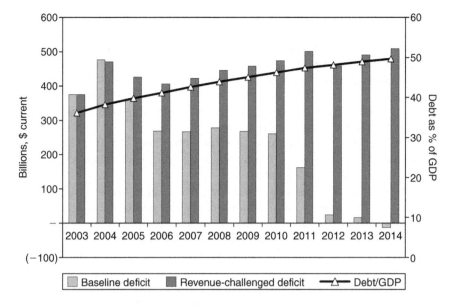

Figure 5.1 Appearance and reality in the Bush budget.

purpose of generating misleading baseline projections. The means for this obfuscation is the infamous "sunset" device, wherein tax cuts are scheduled for abrupt termination in future years, notwithstanding the expressed intention of policy-makers to forego any such termination. Legislation also provides for irrational phase-ins and phase-outs of assorted provisions.

On the spending side, the principal budget categories in this analysis are mandatory spending, net interest, defense and homeland security, and domestic discretionary. For Fiscal Year 2004, domestic spending is $420 billion. Defense/security is $475 billion. Net interest is $155 billion, and mandatory is $1,245 billion. In this context, the difficulty of balancing the budget with cuts in just the domestic category should be obvious.

A bias also affects how spending is reported in the budget. What is known as discretionary spending is projected on the basis of a simple inflation adjustment, historical experience be damned.

In both cases the motive stems from similar political considerations. The purpose of sunsets in the tax code is to generate downwardly biased deficit projections, implicitly minimizing the extent of revenue lost to tax cuts. The purpose of lowball spending projections is to provide an opportunity for critics of spending programs to characterize any increase over inflation as a fiscally irresponsible, profligate indulgence.

The baseline projection for deficits in Figure 5.1, represented by the white bars, shows the budget going to surplus within ten years. The data used here are published by the Congressional Budget Office (2004).

The adjusted baseline, represented by the black bars, is more reflective of current policy realities as far as revenue is concerned. It is based on two changes. One is to assume that tax cuts enacted in 2001 and after will be made permanent, an intention made clear by the Bush Administration and many Members of Congress.

The second pertains to an arcane provision of the individual income tax known as the Alternative Minimum Tax (AMT). The AMT was originally designed to ensure that wealthy persons who are able to claim high deductions do not escape taxation altogether.

It is basically an alternative tax system with a high standard deduction and two rates. If you owe more under AMT than under the income tax proper, you pay the AMT amount.

Currently the AMT affects fewer than five million taxpayers, but it is not indexed for inflation, as are the brackets, the standard deduction, and exemptions of the "regular" income tax. Without adjustments, every year more taxpayers absorb a tax increase by falling under the sway of the AMT. By 2014, almost 45 million taxpayers could pay the AMT (Burman *et al.*, 2004).

Nobody doubts that political pressure will force lawmakers to limit the expansion of AMT coverage. Otherwise within a decade up to 15 percent of taxpayers – those with the highest incomes – would be looking at healthy tax increases. Current law limits such relief to the current year. Allowing for AMT relief for the next ten years, plus the elimination of sunsets – meaning the extension of tax cuts – reduces projected revenues and increases projected deficits.

The line in Figure 5.1 refers to the right-hand axis. It shows the ratio of debt to GDP implied by the adjusted deficit figures (the black bars). The ratio increases over the period, a trend not sustainable over the long run, and perhaps not even for ten years. (Data underlying Figure 5.1 are shown in Appendix Table 1.)

The Bush Administration claims to exert some control over this trend, but its arguments are dubious. The Bush budget omits any cost of alleviating growing the AMT tax burden beyond FY2005. Its deficit projections are based on implicit cuts in defense spending that are contradicted by Administration defense plans (CBO, 2003; 2004). The budget was released in February. It did not include an additional $25 billion for the mission in Iraq requested by the Bush Administration in May. Only thanks to somewhat optimistic predictions of economic growth, and unimaginable reductions in non-defense spending, can the Bush Administration claim to have submitted a fiscally responsible proposal.

Table 5.1 shows non-defense discretionary spending under alternative scenarios. Homeland security is excluded from these figures. The first row shows baseline levels for the spending in question here. In this category of spending, "baseline" means no more than an inflation adjustment. For the entire period, each year's amount reflects the same purchasing power as in 2005.

Table 5.1 The spending squeeze: scenarios for domestic spending (not including homeland security) (Billions, current dollars)

	(Actual)										
	2003	2004	2005	2006	2007	2008	2009	2010	2011	2012	2013	2014
Baseline	397	420	441	452	462	471	481	492	503	514	526	539
Bush budget	397	420	431	425	423	423	424	429	437	446	456	466
Balanced budget by 2014	397	420	408	389	365	337	311	285	253	266	238	216

Source: Congressional Budget Office, author.

The premise that fixed purchasing power in 2005 reflects the cost of "current services" in 2014 is highly vulnerable to criticism. If, for instance, there are twice as many eligible children for Head Start in 2014 as in 2005, it is unlikely that today's allocation for Head Start would provide the same services for twice as many children ten years from now, even if adjusted for inflation.

Nobody expects spending to stay within the baseline. Spending usually exceeds the inflation-adjusted totals of the prior year. Since 1970, domestic discretionary spending has increased by a factor of twelve (it's twelve times as large), unadjusted for inflation. The price level has increased by a factor of less than five (OMB, 2004). Since FY2000, the comparable amounts are an overall increase of 43 percent for the spending, and 8 percent for inflation. There is no precedent for a sustained period of zero real growth in domestic spending.

The second line in Table 5.1 shows the CBO estimates of spending in the Bush FY2005 budget, projected out to ten years. It was pointed out above that the baseline levels are themselves highly unlikely. By 2014, the Bush budget implies a cut of 14 percent relative to the baseline. If defense spending held to the baseline, instead of dipping below it in the Bush budget, and added defense spending was entirely offset by reductions in non-defense spending, the implied cut in domestic outlays would be 18 percent.)

Neither of these paths generates a balanced budget in ten years. That goal is open to strong criticism, but the leaders of both major political parties uphold it.

The bottom line in Table 5.1 depicts the result if the budget is balanced squarely on the back of domestic discretionary spending. The implication is a cut of 60 percent by 2014. This is a much higher order of magnitude of unreality than the Bush budget. It implies a non-functional Federal government. It is impossible. It can't happen. The budget simply cannot be balanced by this route.

Figure 5.2 takes a different approach to the same problem, following a point made by Eugene Steuerle (2003). It shows total baseline mandatory spending, net interest, and defense spending in the bottom three regions. The bottom, mandatory component includes the cost of the new drug benefit, as estimated by CBO in January. (Subsequently, the Bush Administration released higher estimates.) The second layer is baseline defense and homeland security spending. Third are projected interest payments. The thin black area depicts the remainder of revenues available for non-defense discretionary spending, if any (negative amounts are not shown). In other words, it is the amount possible without benefit of borrowed funds – with a balanced budget.

The top white region could be considered "unfunded" baseline domestic spending. The magnitude of "unfunded" spending in later years would depend on how much interest savings would be attainable from

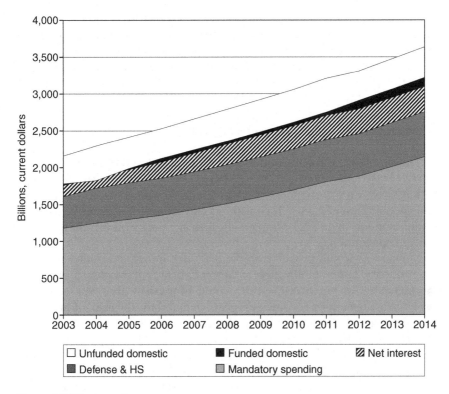

Figure 5.2 The spending squeeze.

deficit reduction; hence the white region overstates what would actually be cut on a path towards a balanced budget. As noted above, the third row in Table 5.1 factors in the benefits of interest savings for domestic spending.

Feasible spending growth

The underlying principle here has been to assume that the revenue path, including likely extensions of tax cuts and an AMT fix, is set in concrete, while non-defense discretionary spending is fair game for retrenchment. This reflects the priorities often put forward in debate and analyses. A contrary approach is now proposed. Suppose robust growth in domestic discretionary spending is postulated, and then we consider the means to finance it?

For the calculations that follow, three scenarios are adopted. One is that such spending grows a little faster than nominal Gross Domestic Product − 5 percent each year. The second is that it grows at an annual rate of 7 percent, roughly consistent with experience over the past three years, under the free-spending Republican Congress. Finally, a "maximalist" option is illustrated, beginning with annual increases of 10 percent, and then tapering off somewhat to stay close to the proposed fiscal constraint, elaborated below. (Appendix Table 2 shows the numbers for non-defense discretionary spending under three alternative assumptions, and Appendix Table 3 shows the implications for interest payments.)

The purpose here is not to advocate any of these particular paths, but to show that contrary to popular opinion, all are "affordable" over the period discussed in this paper – FY2005 through 2014. The purpose of the high-growth path is to dramatize the extent of flexibility in the budget. It is not expected that the Congress as currently constituted would adopt any such path.

The simple fiscal rule of thumb is that the debt-to-GDP ratio should be stable. This raises the question of stable at what level. Forty percent is within historical experience, it does not require wrenching changes in tax and spending policies, and for purposes of political discussion it is a nice round number. Figure 5.3 compares historical values of this ratio to the 40 percent convention.

Keynesians would properly object that such a view precludes essential discretionary fiscal stabilization policy. Of course it would, if observed mechanically. In practice, the ratio could be pushed above or below 40 percent to augment or restrain aggregate demand for the sake of maximizing employment. In this sense the 40 percent rule is meant as a long-run average, not a strict, yearly requirement.

The simple budget rule suggested here could prove inadequate to the priority of employment maximization at stable prices. More complex short-run macroeconomic frameworks are beyond the scope of this paper.

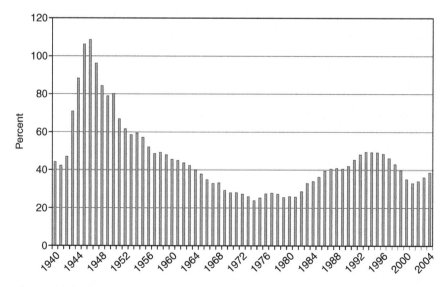

Figure 5.3 Debt as a share of GDP, 1940–2004.

The concern remains that stability in tax law, and planning for social insurance pertaining to the life cycle (such as retirement insurance) both point up the need for a fiscal planning horizon that extends well beyond the business cycle.

The second fiscal precept here is that revenues should be set at 20 percent of GDP. Remember, the purpose is to describe incremental changes and fiscal constraints that make spending growth feasible.

Figure 5.4 shows historical trends of revenues relative to GDP, again in contrast to the 20 percent level. Twenty percent is clearly outside the customary range of historical experience, but not by far. The post-1960 average is slightly more than 18 percent. For the previous business cycle it rounds to 19 percent. Increases of 2 percent of GDP are not unprecedented, as the graph shows. It must be acknowledged that a swing from the present, historically low level to 20 percent as a result of legislation would be unprecedented (Tempalski, 2003).

Table 5.2 puts together the pieces of this puzzle, showing the feasibility of liberal budgeting.

The first row is the aforementioned baseline deficit. For FY2005, revenues are projected at less than 17 percent.

The next five rows of Table 5.2 describe a revenue path that phases-up to a ratio of revenues to GDP of 20 percent by 2008. It could be more rapid, reflecting a second element of flexibility in this exercise.

The next three rows describe the costs of alleviating the growth of AMT revenue.

Next are the data (as in Appendix Tables 2 and 3) on three scenarios

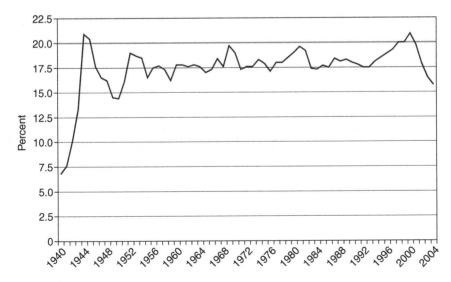

Figure 5.4 Revenue as a share of GDP, 1940–2004.

Table 5.2 Effects of policy changes on deficits

Fiscal Year	2005	2006	2007	2008	2009	2010	2011	2012	2013	2014	Total, 2005–2014
Baseline Deficit (-Surplus)	362	269	267	278	268	261	162	24	16	–13	1,894
Added Revenues	67	90	196	266	260	251	136	40	19	–15	1,312
Total Revenues	2,116	2,346	2,581	2,772	2,904	3,037	3,172	3,312	3,460	3,614	29,316
Percent of GDP	17.5	18.5	19.5	20.0	20.0	20.0	20.0	20.0	20.0	20.0	
Interest Savings	2	6	14	27	42	56	67	72	74	74	435
Deficit Reduction	69	96	210	294	302	308	204	112	93	59	1,746
AMT Fix	7	21	29	39	51	62	52	31	38	45	375
Interest Savings	–	1	2	4	7	10	13	16	19	22	94
Deficit Increase	7	22	31	43	58	72	65	47	57	67	469
Deficit Increase from Faster Spending Growth (Including interest)											
5 Percent	1	13	27	44	64	84	108	133	159	189	822
7 Percent	10	33	59	91	127	166	211	261	315	375	1,648
Maximum	24	63	110	166	231	275	324	376	433	495	2,497
Resulting Deficit											
5 Percent	301	208	114	72	88	109	131	91	139	184	1,439
7 Percent	311	227	147	118	152	192	235	219	295	370	2,265
Maximum	324	258	198	194	256	300	347	335	413	490	3,114
Resulting Debt											
5 Percent	4,694	4,902	5,016	5,088	5,176	5,286	5,417	5,508	5,648	5,832	
7 Percent	4,704	4,931	5,078	5,196	5,348	5,540	5,774	5,993	6,288	6,658	
Maximum	4,717	4,975	5,173	5,366	5,622	5,922	6,269	6,604	7,017	7,507	
Resulting Debt/GDP											
5 Percent	38.8	38.7	37.9	36.7	35.7	34.8	34.1	33.3	32.6	32.3	
7 Percent	38.9	38.9	38.4	37.5	36.8	36.5	36.4	36.2	36.3	36.8	
Maximum	39.0	39.2	39.1	38.7	38.7	39.0	39.5	39.9	40.6	41.5	

Source: Congressional Budget Office, author.

for faster spending growth. Under "Resulting deficit" is shown the deficits that result from the combined effect of these policy changes, under the three ambitious spending paths. Debt and debt-to-GDP ratio should be self-explanatory.

The key is the results in the bottom three rows of Table 5.2. It is possible to stay below the 40 percent debt-to-GDP ratio ceiling in all years but the final two under the "maximum" scenario.

Caveats

Where are the weaknesses in these numbers? First and foremost is the likely demand for ongoing increases in defense spending. The merits of such a policy are beyond the scope of this paper, though our jaundiced view of it will be obvious. Between 2000 and 2004, defense spending leaped from $294 billion to $454 billion, notwithstanding the wretched state of America's former chief adversary. Thus far, the increase has been well in excess of the costs of wars in Afghanistan and Iraq. Most homeland security is in a separate department now.

Second, the revenue path is clearly ambitious. But the object of this paper is ambitious as well.

Third, the cost of the AMT fix used here, as reported by the CBO (2004), is at the low end of the range of estimates made by others, which go as high as $800 billion for ten years (Burman, 2003).

On the other hand, it could be noted that in the 5 and 7-percent scenarios, considerable slack remains between accumulated debt and the 40 percent constraint.

The biggest question mark underlying this exercise is what happens after 2014. In Table 2 it can be seen that the debt constraint is breached in 2013 under the "maximum" program. It is obvious that if any sizable category of spending consistently grows more rapidly than revenues, there is a long-run problem of sustainability. From that standpoint, this exercise does no better than show that an elevation of spending – a considerable one – is feasible for a decade, after which growth must slow down to the same rate as that of revenues.

It is well known that the greatest problems for long-run sustainability are due to entitlement spending. The vast bulk of difficulty from this standpoint is due to Medicare and Medicaid, not to Social Security, and less to the remainder of the budget (CBO, 2003). What is the use in ignoring the post-2014 trends?

The answer is that no tenable changes in revenues or discretionary spending meet the problem posed by healthcare spending in the long-run projections. Medicaid and Medicare eventually outstrip everything else in the Federal budget, under the assumption that they grow indefinitely at double-digit rates. There is no choice but to face health care as a problem of policy design, rather than a fiscal problem. The system in this case embraces both the public and private sector and promises unsustainable cost growth across the board, accompanied by the arbitrary exclusion of the unwealthy and unhealthy from care.

The political debate seems to preoccupy itself with changes in domestic discretionary spending. But such changes cannot solve the long-run problem. Rather, they solve a political problem. It is easier for politicians to bloviate about general spending cuts outside of entitlements and defense. It is always impossible to pin them down on which programs, with what impact, and on whom. By contrast, talk of entitlement cuts can be connected immediately to popular benefit programs, and talk of defense cuts is vulnerable to "weak on defense" rhetoric.

This paper is a very long way of saying that presently, non-defense discretionary spending is a small portion of the Federal budget, and taxes are presently at extremely low ebb. Absent nostrums about balanced budgets, growth in domestic spending need not be ruled out of bounds. The long-run problem resides in an entirely different area. The point is simple, but unfortunately, in the context of Washington budget debates, it is also revolutionary. That is less a comment on the policy options described here than it is a reflection of the current low ebb of fiscal acumen in our politics.

Table 1 Appearance and reality in the Bush budget (Billions, current dollars)

Fiscal Year	2003	2004	2005	2006	2007	2008	2009	2010	2011	2012	2013	2014
Baseline deficit	375	477	362	269	267	278	268	261	162	24	16	−13
Revenue-challenged deficit	375	471	426	406	422	446	458	474	501	459	491	509
Revenue-challenged debt/GDP ratio	36.1%	38.2%	39.8%	41.1%	42.6%	43.9%	45.1%	46.2%	47.4%	48.2%	48.9%	49.7%

Sources: Congressional Budget Office, Joint Committee on Taxation, author.

Table 2 Non-defense discretionary spending: possibilities for growth (Billions, current dollars)

Fiscal Year	2004	2005	2006	2007	2008	2009	2010	2011	2012	2013	2014
GDP growth (nominal)	5.9%	5.4%	4.9%	4.4%	4.7%	4.7%	4.6%	4.4%	4.4%	4.5%	4.4%
Baseline	445	466	478	490	500	510	522	533	545	558	571
Five percent growth	445	467	491	515	541	568	596	626	657	690	725
Seven percent growth	445	476	509	545	583	624	668	715	765	818	875
Maximum growth	445	490	538	592	652	717	760	805	854	905	959

Sources: Congressional Budget Office, author.

Table 3 Effects of faster spending growth on federal outlays (Billions, current dollars)

Fiscal Year	2005	2006	2007	2008	2009	2010	2011	2012	2013	2014	Total, 2005–2114
Added program spending											
Five percent growth	1	13	25	41	58	74	93	112	132	154	704
Seven percent growth	10	31	55	83	114	146	182	220	260	304	1,406
Maximum growth	24	60	102	152	207	238	272	309	347	388	2,098
Debt service											
Five percent growth	0	0	1	3	6	10	14	20	27	35	118
Seven percent growth	0	1	4	8	13	21	30	41	54	70	242
Maximum growth	1	3	8	15	25	37	51	68	86	107	400
Totals											
Five percent growth	1	13	27	44	64	84	108	133	159	189	822
Seven percent growth	10	33	59	91	127	166	211	261	315	375	1,648
Maximum growth	24	63	110	166	231	275	324	376	433	495	2,497

Source: Congressional Budget Office, author.

References

Burman, Len, William Gale, Matthew Hall and Mohammed Adeel Saleem (2004), "AMT Relief in the 2005 Budget: A Bandaid for a Hemorrhage," Urban Institute, February.

Congressional Budget Office (1997), *Long Budgetary Pressures and Policy Options*, March.

Congressional Budget Office (1998), *Long-Term Budgetary Pressures and Policy Options*, May.

Congressional Budget Office (1998), *The Long-Term Budget Outlook*, December.

Congressional Budget Office (2004), *The Budget and Economic Outlook: Fiscal Years 2005–2014*, January.

Steuerle, C. Eugene (2003), "The Incredible Shrinking Budget for Working Families and Children," *National Budget Issues*, The Urban Institute, No. 1, December.

Tempalski, Jerry (2003), "Revenue Effects of Major Tax Bills," OTA Working Papers 81, Office of Tax Analysis, US Treasury Department, July.

Office of Management and Budget (2004), *The Budget of the United States Government, Fiscal Year 2005*.

US General Accounting Office (1996), *Federal Debt: Answers to Frequently Asked Questions*, November.

Part II
Fiscal policy in the periphery

6 Grappling with fiscal reform

The case of the Dominican Republic

Esteban Pérez Caldentey

Introduction

The macroeconomic history of the Dominican Republic is beset with episodes of balance of payments and currency crises, and debt default instances. The evolution of GDP growth marked by frequent upswings and troughs encapsulates this behavior over time (see Figure 6.1). It also comprises genuine attempts at economic stabilization. Stabilization attempts go back to the early 1980s and were definitely implemented in the 1990s under an orthodox program termed the New Economic Policy (NEP).

The NEP was designed according to the theoretical and practical canons of the Monetary Approach to the Balance of Payments (MABP). The MABP defines the balance of payments as the "net resultant inflow or outflow of international reserves." It is thus a result of a disequilibrium in the money market and hence a monetary phenomenon. The adjustment comes through the interplay of the demand for money and changes in international reserves.

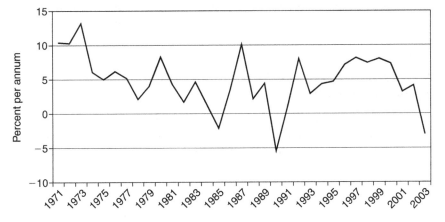

Figure 6.1 The Dominican Republic rate of growth of GDP, 1971–2003.

Assuming that inflation is stable and excluding variations in the rate of interest (on account of the assumption of a high degree of integration of capital and goods market), the rate of growth of reserves will be equal to zero, positive, or negative according as to whether output growth (i.e., income) and the income elasticity of real cash balances is equal to, greater than, or smaller than the growth of credit creation (i.e., absorption) weighted by the proportion of credit in total money supply.

Though domestic credit refers to both public and private sector credit, the former is identified as the source of the external imbalance. Thus according to the MABP, the posited causality runs from public spending to balance-of-payments disequilibrium and to the consequent loss of international reserves. Avoiding this situation involves imposing a restrictive economic policy to make absorption conform to income so that the economy in question will not lose reserves, avoiding in turn a balance-of-payments constraint.

Thus, for reasons that respond to the sheer logic of the approach, a crucial component of the NEP stabilization package was fiscal reform. The need for fiscal reform was compounded and indeed identified as a pressing issue by the fact that this stabilization package was accompanied by an outward-oriented economic policy and by the deepening of the Dominican Republic's international liaisons. The phasing-out of tariffs for a country like the Dominican Republic whose international trade tax revenue represent close to half of total current revenue underscored the urgency of fiscal reform.

This paper describes and analyzes how the Dominican Republic has approached and implemented fiscal reform from 1990 to 2002. The paper is divided into five sections. Following the introduction the second section describes the fiscal reforms of the 1990s focusing mainly on tariff reforms, which were its main component. The third and fourth sections analyze the pattern and composition of government revenue and expenditure. The final section evaluates the success of the reforms in terms of the relationship between internal and external equilibrium and in terms of the sustainability of the fiscal deficit.

An overview of tariff and fiscal reforms in the Dominican Republic, 1990–2002

Since 1990 – the year marking the beginning of the implementation of the stabilization plan termed the New Economic Policy – the country has been committed to trade liberalization. The Dominican authorities eliminated or reduced tariffs, export taxes, tariff-quotas, permits, exemptions and concessions[1] through a series of successive tax and tariff measures. During this period, the country embarked on important tariff and tax reforms meant to rationalize the tax system and, at the same time, implement measures to compensate for the expected loss of fiscal revenue resulting from tariff reduction. Tariff reforms were implemented in 1990, 1992 and 2001. Tax reforms were undertaken in 1990, 1992 and 2001.

The 1990 tariff reform was intended to rationalize and simplify the tariff structure as well as to make it more progressive. It established a new tariff structure with seven initial *ad valorem* tax rates comprised within the interval from 5 percent to 35 percent. This meant a decrease in the ceiling rate by 165 percentage points. Prior to the 1990 reform the tariff rate structure was contained within the interval from zero to 200 percent (see Table 6.1).

The tariff rates were to be applied on the CIF (cost, insurance and freight) value of the imported merchandise rather than on the FOB (free on board) value as was done prior to the reform. To avoid a sudden impact on given protection structures and ensure a soft landing, the authorities implemented a tariff surcharge set at 30 percent for 1991, 20 percent in 1992, and 10 percent in 1993. The import surcharge was finally abolished in 1994. Also a temporal tariff of 15 percent was applied to all imports with the exception of basic food products. This temporal tariff was eliminated by the second half of 1995. Finally, a 2.5 percent tax on foreign exchange transactions was implemented. This tax was later reduced to 2 percent and eventually, to 1.5 percent.

In 1991 the authorities added an additional zero-percent tariff rate to the prevailing tariff schedule. The zero-percent rate was applied to basic imports. This increased the number of tariff rates from seven to eight. In 1993, the government increased the zero-percent tariff rate to 3 percent. The 3 percent tariff rate was expanded to cover agricultural inputs that were subject to tariff rates equal or greater than 5 percent. Finally, in 1997 the authorities increased the number of tariff rates to nine as they decided

Table 6.1 Main stabilization measures adopted between 1990 and 1992

Fiscal policy	Petroleum prices were doubled. The oil tax or petroleum differential became an important source of fiscal income: 2% of GDP on average between 1991 and 1995 and 14% of all tax revenues on average between 1991 and 1995 Elimination of subsidies to electricity, sugar and wheat Temporary tax on imports initially set at 15% but to be lowered to 4% in June 1995 and that affected 40% of all imports Implementation of a foreign currency transaction of 2.5%, which was reduced to 1.5% Temporary increase in tariff rates by 1.3% and eliminated by September 1996
Monetary policy	Interest rate liberalization Internal credit reduction
Exchange rate policy	Unification of exchange rates and beginnings of a managed floating exchange rate regime

Source: On the basis of WTO (1996) and official information.

to reinstate a zero-percent tariff rate on agricultural and textile inputs (see Table 6.2).

The tariff reform somewhat simplified the tariff structure. However, according to some, the average tariff effective rate increased from 16.1 percent to 23.2 percent during 1990–1995. According to the World Trade Organization (WTO, 1996), however, the average tariff rate was 17.5 percent in 1995 (with a standard deviation of 10.2 percent and a coefficient of variation of 57 percent). In terms of sectors, the tariff rates of agriculture, mining and industry were 17.3, 6.4, and 18.1 percent, respectively. In 1997, our own calculations yield an average tariff rate of 17.3 percent.

The tariff rates most commonly found in 1995 were 5, 10, 25, and 30 percent, accounting for 10.4, 28, 13.3, and 15.6 percent of all imports. In 1997, these tariff rates accounted for 7.5, 24.1, 9.5, and 23.9 percent of all imports.

Table 6.2 Selected fiscal measures, 1995–1998

Date	Measure
January 1995	10 USD tax per passenger on all airlines with scheduled flights from and to the Dominican republic. A tax of USD 5 is established for charter airlines and air cargo lines will be subject to a tax of USD 0.03 per pound transported. The USD 0.03 tax was reduced to USD 0.02 in February.
June 1995	The 15% foreign exchange surcharge applied to 41% of imports was eliminated.
1996	Increase by 10% the tax charged to hotel, motel and apartment hotel users.
1996	Increases in subsidies to state owned firms (205 million Dominican Pesos to The Dominican Corporation of Electricity; 110 million pesos to the State Sugar Council and 35 million pesos to the Autonomous University of Santo Domingo).
1996	Oil taxes will be used for the payment of the external debt
1996	Increase of 30% in the pension earnings between 0 and 5,000 Dominican pesos and 10% those above 5,000 Dominican pesos
December 1996	The oil tax differential becomes a fixed amount per type of product. For gasoline the oil differential is fixed at 12.48 pesos per gallon and will decrease to 12.17 pesos in 1997.
1997	Application of inflation adjustment to the income tax
1997	0% tariff rate applied to the import of inputs, equipment and machinery for the agricultural and textile sectors.
1997	Creation of the Dirección General de Impuestos Internos. This institution unified the Dirección General del Impuesto sobre la Renta and the Dirección General de Rentas Internas with the aim of centralizing in one institution the task of tax collection reducing operative costs and eliminating the duplication of functions.
March 1998	Increase in the exempted tax base of the tax income.

Source: On the basis of official information.

According to the World Trade Organization (WTO), the Dominican tariff structure that emerged out of the reform was progressive (i.e., a positive effective rate of protection). The tariff rates applied to manufactured products are higher than those applied to products which are semi-elaborated (i.e., 20.7 percent for finished products, 14 percent for semi-elaborated products, and 15 percent for raw materials).

The effective rates of protection of the new tariff structure remained high. The median effective rate of protection for the Dominican industry was estimated within an interval of 133 percent to 188 percent. Other sources show that the estimated the median rate of protection to be at 123 percent for the Dominican industry in 1993.

Possible government revenue losses arising out of the tariff reform could be compensated by several other taxes applied on imports such as the value added tax (ITBIS) (8 percent) and excise taxes. The excise taxes applied to imports varied within a 5 to 80 percent range. Different excise tax rates were applied to imports and domestic products. In 1995, the rates applicable to both domestic and imported products were unified at 20 percent, and 25 percent for alcoholic beverages. Once all these trade taxes are taken into account, the effective tariff rate may be much higher than the rate derived from the tariff schedule *per se*. In fact, due to the significant effect of the reform process on the imports base, the import-duty revenue increased from 1 percent to 4 percent of GDP between 1990 and 1992. In the same vein, government revenue from trade taxes increased from 5 percent to 7 percent of GDP in the same period.

Subsequent to the trade reform, the government implemented a fiscal reform in 1992. The basic aim was fiscal balance. The reform tried to adopt simpler fiscal laws to increase the amount of revenue and the efficiency of tax collection. To this end, the fiscal reform modified personal and corporate taxes, the value-added and excise taxes on consumption.

Regarding personal and corporate tax laws, the reform increased the allotted amounts that are regarded as exempted. The reform established three tax rates that could be applied to personal income and one rate for corporate income. The new law established that public firms had to pay the same corporate taxes as private firms. Fiscal incentives were eliminated with a few exceptions (i.e., productive activities undertaken under the free trade zone regime).

The value added tax rate (ITBIS) was increased from 6 percent to 8 percent. The application of this tax was extended to cover services. All exports as well as some domestically produced and imported goods were exempted. The excise tax on consumption, which was a specific tax, became an *ad valorem* tax. Fifty individual laws that contained more than a 100 tax rates were abolished and were replaced by the new tax code. The new code included rates ranging from 10 percent to 15 percent for domestic products and seven types comprised in the interval 5 percent to 80 percent. The reform also reduced the temporary surcharge on imports established in 1987, from 15 percent to 10 percent. This surcharge was eliminated in June 1995.

In 1997 the authorities presented a tax-reform proposal, which included an increase of the exemptions and a fixed charge of 10 percent on the personal income tax; an increase in the value-added tax rate from 8 percent to 12 percent as well as an extension of its base; an excise tax on petroleum products and an increase in the tax rate applied to alcoholic beverages (Pellerano, 1997a and 1997b).

In 2000, the Dominican authorities designed a new tariff reform to further the economy's outward orientation and integration process. The reform entered into force in 2001. The reform comprised the adoption of the harmonized system for the classification of merchandise and the reduction of the dispersion and level of the tariff rates. The reform decreased the number of tariffs from the existing nine (zero, 3, 5, 10, 15, 20, 25, 30, and 35 percent) to five (20, 14, 8, 3, and zero percent).[2]

Tables 6.5 and 6.6 show, respectively, the evolution of the distribution of the tariff schedule and its basic parameters between 1990 and 2001. During 1990–1998, more than 50 percent of tariff lines were located in the upper tariff echelons ranging from 20 percent to 35 percent. In 2001, the tariff structure exhibits the opposite structure. That is, more than 50 percent of all tariff lines are assigned tariffs of 3 percent and zero percent, respectively, and thus most of the tariff lines belong to the lower echelons.

Most tariff lines are included in the tariff rate of 3 percent, which represents 41 percent of all tariff lines and are followed by 20, zero, and 8 percent, representing 27, 14, and 11 percent of the total. Thus, for all purposes it is a four-tier tariff schedule. The main consequence is the decline in the average and weighted tariff rate and the reduction of the tariff dispersion (see Table 6.3).

Table 6.3 Tariff rate distribution 1990–2001 (in percentages)

Tariff rate	Tariff schedule		
	1990–1998	*1998–2000*	*2001*
40	0	0.0	0.4
35	10.7	10.7	0.0
30	16.5	16.4	0.0
25	14.4	10.2	0.4
20	9.0	8.8	26.7
15	8.1	5.6	0.0
14	0.0	0.0	6.6
10	25.6	24.5	0.0
8	0.0	0.0	11.1
5	9.5	8.0	0.0
3	6.0	4.5	41.3
0	0.0	11.3	13.5

Source: On the basis of official data provided by the Ministry of Finance.

Overall a comparison of the 1990–1998 and 2001 tariff schedules show that the mean tariff has declined substantially from 18 percent to 9 percent. The standard deviation has also decreased from 10 percent to 8 percent. Finally the 2001 tariff schedule is more balanced in terms of its relations between the mean, the median and the mode. The median and mode coincide at 3 percent and are lower than those corresponding to the previous tariff schedules of 15 and 10 percent, respectively (see Table 6.4).

The tariff reform was accompanied by a fiscal reform whose main objective was to compensate for the consequent loss in tariff revenue. The reform contemplated the increase in the ITBIS rate from 8 percent to 12 percent. It also included the increase in excise duties applied on beer and alcoholic products and the application of marginal tax rates, ranging from zero to 80 percent, on motor vehicles. Moreover it modified the tax brackets applied on personal and corporate income. Finally, it established an additional tax on corporations, which is actually an advance payment of their income tax in the current fiscal year and equivalent to 1.5 percent of their gross monthly revenue.

More recently, as part of its participation in the Free Trade Area of the Americas (FTAA) process, which is set to culminate in 2005, the Dominican authorities have submitted a tariff-reduction proposal. As a basis for comparison and reference, Table 6.5 shows the number of tariff lines, average tariff rates, standard deviation, and tariff ranges for selected FTAA countries. In the case of the Dominican Republic, the average nominal tariff rate and the nominal tariff dispersion are below the regional FTAA average.

The tariff reduction proposal remains confidential in its details. However, to provide a rough estimate of the effects of trade liberalization on government revenue, tax revenues were estimated, using official data, under two possible tariff-reduction scenarios: a "floor" and "ceiling" schedule. The latter is a slightly modified version of the 2001 tariff schedule (See Tables 6.6 and 6.7).

Table 6.4 Basic tariff schedule parameters

	Tariff schedule 1990–1998	Tariff schedule 1998–2000	Tariff schedule 2001
Average	18.2	16.6	8.6
Weighted average	18.6	16.8	8.6
Standard deviation	10.3	11.3	8.0
Maximum	35	35	40
Minimum	0	0	0
Median	15	15	3
Mode	10	10	3

Source: On the basis of official data provided by the Ministry of Finance.

Table 6.5 Comparative tariff lines, average tariffs, standard deviation and tariff ranges: Selected FTAA countries

	Tariff lines	Average tariff	Standard deviation	Tariff range
Antigua and Barbuda	4,077	14.5	13.5	0–70
Barbados	6,469	16.5	29	0–243
Chile	5,917	8.0	–	0–35
Dominica	6,333	13.1	21.6	0–200
Grenada	6,334	11.2	10.8	0.40
Costa Rica	7,926	7	9.8	0–163
El Salvador	5,800	6.9	–	0–40
Guatemala	5,976	7	7.8	0–40
Guyana	–	10.6	–	0–40
Honduras	5,913	7.1	–	0–70
Jamaica	–	10.9	–	0.50
Mexico	11,387	16.5	14.5	0–260
Nicaragua	6,235	5.1	–	0–190
St. Lucia	6,368	10.1	12.2	0–70
St. Vincent and the Grenadines	6,237	10.9	9.81	0–40
Dominican Republic	6,719	8.6	8.0	0–40
Regional average	6,549.4	10.3	13.7	–
Standard deviation	1,604.4	3.49	6.71	–

Source: On the basis of WTO (2001–2002) and national official information.

Note
In the case of Mexico the trade weighted tariff rate is much lower (around 2 percent) due to the importance of its trade with the United States.

The main difference in both scenarios lies in the number of tariff lines included with a tariff rate of 3 percent, which would decline from 41 percent of the total in the "ceiling schedule scenario" to 6 percent in the "floor schedule scenario." As a result, the number of tariff lines with a zero percent tariff rate would increase from 14 percent to 59 percent. The reduction from 3 percent to zero percent would affect a large number of products. Also the "floor schedule" would classify 51 products as sensitive

Table 6.6 FTAA tariff basket scenarios: percentage of total tariff lines by tariff rates

Tariff rates	2001 tariff schedule	Ceiling tariff basket (modified 2001 tariff schedule)	Floor tariff basket
20	26.7	27.5	26.7
14	6.6	6.6	4.8
8	11.1	11.1	2.7
3	41.3	41.3	5.7
0	13.5	13.5	59.3

Source: On the basis of information provided by the Ministry of Finance.

Table 6.7 Revenue loss estimates using the 2000 import structure

Tariff rate	Share of imports according to the ceiling tariff basket scenario	Share of imports according to the tariff basket floor	Tax collection according to the ceiling tariff basket scenario (thousands of US$)	Tax collection according to the tariff basket floor (thousands of US$)
0	14.44	35	0.0	0.0
3	20.8	9	18,346.7	7,938.5
8	11.23	0.8	26,414.6	18,817.1
14	10.51	7.4	43,261.8	30,460.2
20	43.0	46	252,855.2	270,496.3
Total			340,878.2	327,712.1

Source: On the basis of official data provided by the Ministry of Finance.

Note
The tariff basket scenario (third column) does not show a 0.23 percent corresponding to sensitive products. The estimated loss in revenue between the adoption of both scenarios is 1.7 percent of GDP.

products. Preliminary calculations show that the difference in tax revenue collection in the adoption of the ceiling and the floor scenarios is 1.7 percent of GDP.

As the Dominican Republic progressively deepens its international ties, and reduces its tariffs on the vast majority of traded goods, the loss of revenue from tariff reductions will increase. Government can adjust on the expenditure side or the revenue side, or a combination of both. The policy choice depends on the extent to which there is room for adjustment by reducing expenditures and the scope for enhancing the revenue-collection system.

An analysis of government expenditure

Central government spending is classified (by economic function) into wages and salaries, purchases of goods and services, subsidies and other current transfers, interest payments, and capital expenditures.

Wages and salaries represent close to 6 percent of GDP and the government employs 12 percent of the labor force and 25 percent of the urban labor force (of which 40 percent public administration and defense and 60 percent other State employees, see Table 6.9). The level and composition of government employment has not undergone any significant changes in spite of the changes in government expenditure and the privatization process. This variable tends to vary pro-cyclically and, as suggested by Pellerano (2002), greater income is associated with an expansionary fiscal stance in terms of wages and salaries. This is shown in Table 6.8 where the

Table 6.8 Coefficient of correlation for cyclical variations in GDP and real government wages

	1980–1999	*1980–1991*	*1992–1999*
Correlation coefficient	0.87	0.78	0.95

Source: On the basis of ECLAC (2001).

Note
The results were obtained by separating the permanent and cyclical fluctuations component of the real government wages and real GDP.

correlation coefficient for the cyclical variation of real GDP and wages between 1980 and 1999 was 0.87 and 0.95 for 1992–1999. For this reason, it may not be the best adjustment or leverage variable available.

Moreover in the last two years as indicated in Table 6.9 there has been a marked increase in public-sector employment, reflecting a conscious decision on the part of the authorities to strengthen the government base.

Central government purchases of goods and services account for 2 percent of GDP and are indeed an endogenous variable that has responded to the greater attention paid to the social welfare of the population, and to the increase in prices of raw materials.

The most important component of current transfers is subsidies, which currently account for 1.3 percent of GDP and 8 percent of total expenditures (Pellerano, 2002). Within this item, subsidies to the electricity service and the state-owned electrical corporation have been the most important components. In the last decade, subsidies to the electrical sector account for on average 4 percent of total public expenditure, and close to a third of all non-financial public firms. Subsidies on electricity services are followed by subsidies to gas and water services. Subsidies can be reduced especially to electrical services as long as the price of electricity declines, which basically means an additional reform of the electrical sector and which may in

Table 6.9 Composition of government employment

	Public administration and defense	*Other government employees*	*Total*
1996	100,702	196,451	297,153
2001	151,662	229,837	381,499
	Rate of growth	*Rate of growth*	*Rate of growth*
1997	0.7	2.0	1.6
1998	3.4	6.2	5.3
1999	1.7	−2.4	−1.1
2000	25.3	9.4	14.8
2001	13.6	1.1	5.7

Source: On the basis of official information.

fact be a long-term reform and not a particularly useful variable to be used as a fiscal equilibrating tool. Interests and amortization components of the debt are likely to increase as the country has increased its external indebtedness.

The last component of public expenditure is capital expenditure, which has a clear political component and a marked political cycle. Figure 6.2 shows how capital expenditures as a percentage of total expenditures vary according to different governments. In the last few years the importance of capital expenditures has declined. Capital expenditures comprise, as shown in Table 6.10, real investment representing 2 percent of GDP, capital transfers (1.7 percent of GDP) and debt amortization payments (2.5 percent of GDP, of which 83 percent payments on the external debt).

The analysis of government expenditure indicates that the scope is limited for government expenditures to serve as a stabilization tool with a view to bringing about fiscal balance or offsetting the decline in government revenue resulting from tariff reduction. The fiscal adjustment must

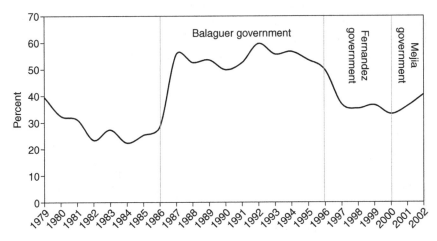

Figure 6.2 Capital expenditures as a percentage of total expenditures, 1979–2002.

Table 6.10 Composition of capital expenditure as percentage of GDP, 1980–2001

	1980–1991	1992–1996	1997–2001
Capital expenditure	5.0	8.4	6.1
Investment	2.5	4.7	2.5
Capital transfers	1.8	2.2	1.5
Amortization of debt	0.4	1.1	1.8*

Source: On the basis of official data provided by the Ministry of Finance.

Note
*2.5 in 2001.

be focused on the revenue side. While this finding is symptomatic of "real-world" constraints on fiscal policy management, it is somewhat contrary to MABP policy prescriptions.

An analysis of government revenue

Table 6.11 classifies government revenue from 1980 to 2001 according to whether it depends on domestic or external sources. External sources of revenue comprise duties, supplementary taxes, the exchange-rate surtax, the value-added tax levied on imports, as well as transportation and export taxes. All other taxes are considered as based on internal sources of revenue.

Traditionally, the Dominican Republic has been one of the most dependent countries in Latin America and the Caribbean on taxes related to international trade. If only trade taxes proper are considered, their ratio to total revenue reached 31 percent in 1999 ranking nine for FTAA countries and largely above the average for South American, Central American and Caribbean countries (see Table 6.14). The inclusion of other taxes relating to international trade increases this dependency ratio to 45 percent in 2000 prior to the fiscal reform and is currently 32 percent.

The fiscal vulnerability resulting from the dependency of government revenue on trade taxes is compounded by their volatility. Tables 6.15 and

Table 6.11 Composition of government current revenue as percentages of total current revenue, 1980–2001

	1980–1991	*1992–1995*	*1996–2000*	*2001*
Internal sources of revenue	43.1	37.3	40.8	47.3
Income taxes	21.3	18.3	20.5	26.6
Property taxes	2.1	1.1	1.6	1.6
Excise taxes	9.6	3.9	6.2	6.5
Taxes on other consumption goods	10.1	14.1	12.5	12.6
ITBIS (internal)	4.3	8.2	9.8	14.2
External sources of revenue	36.1	42.7	39.9	32.1
ITBIS (external)	2.9	8.1	9.0	9.6
Sales of tickets to the outside	1.5	1.5	0.9	0.0
Airport tax	0.5	0.8	1.1	0.9
Import duties	7.7	27.7	26.7	15.7
Complementary taxes	16.8	1.7	1.8	0.5
Foreign exchange surcharge	3.7	2.8	0.2	0.0
Export taxes	3.0	0.0	0.3	5.4

Source: On the basis of information provided by the Ministry of Finance and the Central Bank of the Dominican Republic.

Note

This classification only considers the main sources of revenue and does not include among others non-tax revenue. Taxes on other consumption goods refer mainly to the petroleum and natural gas taxes.

6.16 show the relative volatility of trade-based taxes (or of a sample of these whenever data was not available) for 1990–2000. The relative volatility was computed as the ratio to real GDP of the absolute volatility (measured by the standard deviation) of trade taxes measured in real terms. To obtain a value of tax collection in real terms two approaches were followed.

The first involved the use of the GDP deflator. The second involved the use of different deflators according to tax categories, which is a more accurate way of measuring purchasing power. According to both methods the relative volatility ratio is greater than one. That is, the absolute volatility of taxes is greater than that of GDP for the greater majority of the cases pointing to the difficulty in securing a stable stream of revenue over time without resorting to discretionary and once-and-for-all tax compensation measures (See Tables 6.13 and 6.14).

Excluding complementary taxes (which exhibit the highest degree of volatility of all according to the second method used to determine relative volatility) external sources of revenue during the 1990s accounted for 39 percent of the total on average with a 2.6 percent standard deviation. The fiscal reforms carried out in the 1990s and the different policy measures regarding tariffs that we have described reduced in part the weight of trade-based taxes in total revenue and the tax effort, which shows as a declining trend during the 1990s.

Trade-based taxes expressed as a percentage of GDP increased markedly following the 1990 reform (from 2.7 percent to 5.5 percent between 1990 and 1993) and then declined to 4.3 percent in 2000 and to 4.1 percent in 2001.

The most important taxes related to trade are import duties and the ITBIS applied on imports. Import duties, though still accounting for a quarter of total trade-based tax revenues during 1990–2000, have declined in importance in tandem with the efforts to decrease the country's fiscal vulnerability. Import duties, which represented 4 percent of GDP following the 1991 reform, reaching 4.7 percent in 1993 declined to 3.8 percent in 2000 and to 2.6 percent in 2001.

The behavior of import duties may be analyzed from three perspectives. First, regression analysis of import-duty revenue shows that revenues respond positively to movements in the tax base as measured by the ratio of local merchandise imports to GDP. Table 6.15 shows the results of running a regression of import duties as a percentage of GDP on imports as a percentage of GDP and dummy variables to capture the effects of the tax and tariff reforms of 1992 and 1995 and that of 2001 on import duty collection. Two lagged terms for the import base variable were included as both were found to be significant whereas the contemporaneous variable was excluded since it was not statistically significant. The results are consistent with the observed results of tariff and tax reform. Indeed, the coefficient for the 1992–1995 dummy variable has a positive sign and that

Table 6.12 Trade tax revenues (as a percentage of total tax revenue), ranking of FTAA countries, 1990–1999

	1990	1991	1992	1993	1994	1995	1996	1997	1998	1999	Average
Bahamas	62.0	66.4	66.0	64.6	67.9	67.1	65.5	66.5	66.1	65.8	65.8
Antigua & Barbuda	57.9	65.6	66.1	66.2	66.2	67.7	67.1	66.7	67.4	66.1	65.7
Grenada	75.8	62.8	58.9	57.1	56.4	53.5	60.4	63.9	64.4	61.1	61.4
St. Kitts & Nevis	64.8	62.7	62.1	64.2	61.6	59.2	54.4	53.9	49.7	50.6	58.3
St. Lucia	62.8	56.1	50.2	51.7	53.1	55.0	54.2	56.4	59.5	59.4	55.8
Dominica	57.9	54.7	55.1	55.6	56.4	54.1	53.2	54.3	53.8	54.6	55.0
Belize	62.3	61.5	61.1	56.9	56.3	56.3	58.8	33.8	36.8	39.3	52.3
St. Vincent & the Grenadines	52.3	51.9	51.1	53.5	50.7	52.8	49.3	50.8	49.3	50.3	51.2
Costa Rica	28.2	30.2	25.1	23.3	22.4	51.8	46.5	46.0	47.6	43.2	36.4
Dominican Republic	38.7	34.0	41.0	37.1	31.5	29.1	28.9	28.6	28.6	31.3	32.9
Honduras	38.0	36.8	31.8	29.5	29.7	25.9	26.5	24.9	17.7	14.7	27.6
Jamaica	21.0	23.1	24.7	28.3	26.1	30.7	29.0	29.8	30.0	30.1	27.3
Ecuador	31.6	28.2	24.0	22.9	23.8	23.0	19.3	24.5	31.6	25.6	25.5
Colombia	26.0	26.0	21.3	26.1	26.8	27.5	24.5	24.7	26.7	20.4	25.0
Venezuela	35.6	42.2	37.2	25.9	18.9	18.2	17.1	16.5	19.2	16.8	24.8
Nicaragua	21.5	20.3	20.3	21.5	21.7	23.2	22.6	24.1	28.0	31.2	23.4
Panama	22.0	19.1	19.7	28.1	28.5	19.1	20.3	20.2	22.8	19.8	22.0
Paraguay	25.4	22.9	18.3	18.4	18.2	22.9	19.4	19.6	19.3	14.9	19.9
Guatemala	22.5	19.2	25.4	22.7	23.6	23.6	17.5	15.0	14.5	13.6	19.8
Haiti	18.9	21.0	16.1	16.4	13.1	19.0	15.6	21.8	21.0	21.5	18.4
El Salvador	21.6	21.3	18.2	19.3	19.4	17.4	14.0	11.8	11.9	11.4	16.6
Guyana	16.3	16.3	12.5	16.0	15.4	15.0	14.6	13.9	14.3	14.4	14.9
Chile	16.6	13.8	12.7	12.2	11.4	12.4	12.1	10.8	10.1	9.5	12.2
Barbados	13.0	9.3	8.1	7.9	17.9	17.0	14.2	10.2	10.4	10.3	11.8
Bolivia	16.6	13.0	12.1	11.5	11.5	11.5	10.6	9.7	9.4	8.3	11.4
Peru	10.4	10.0	10.6	12.4	12.4	13.2	12.2	10.9	11.1	10.9	11.4
Trinidad & Tobago	8.9	9.1	10.2	10.9	11.9	9.1	8.5	9.2	9.9	9.7	9.7
Uruguay	15.3	13.4	11.2	8.0	8.2	6.8	6.4	6.7	6.8	6.1	8.9
Mexico	8.4	10.1	10.6	9.3	8.2	6.7	6.6	5.8	5.3	5.3	7.6
Argentina	12.1	5.9	5.9	6.2	6.3	4.6	4.9	5.7	5.1	4.5	6.1
Brazil		0.0	5.0	4.2	3.9	6.0	4.6	4.7	5.0	5.2	4.3

denoting the 2001 tariff and tax reform has a negative sign. Both coefficients are significant at the 5 percent significance level.

The parameter corresponding to the tax base (imports as percentage of GDP) is also statistically significant and is either equal or very close to one. However, due to an insufficient number of observations, this result fails to capture a key change in the response of import taxes for a given import base that occurred following the 1991 reform. Following the

Table 6.13 Relative volatility of trade-based taxes using the GDP deflator, 1990–2001.

	90–01	79–90	92–01	93–01	95–01	96–01
Total external sources of revenue as % of GDP	1.93	2.06	1.62	1.39	1.63	1.75
ITBIS (external)	1.09	3.86	1.09	0.66	0.89	1.16
Sales of tickets to the outside	2.65	4.00	2.51	2.16	1.14	1.29
Airport tax	1.97	0.31	1.46	1.24	1.51	1.65
Import duties	14.68	28.42	5.56	1.00	1.01	1.21
Complementary taxes	2.42	9.78	2.20	1.65	0.26	0.00

Source: On the basis of official data.

Table 6.14 Relative volatility of trade-based taxes using different implicit price deflators, according to tax category, 1990–2001.

	90–01	79–90	92–01	93–01	95–01	96–01
Total external sources of revenue as % of GDP	1.23	2.28	1.19	0.87	1.03	1.07
ITBIS (external)	2.04	2.13	1.58	1.36	1.51	1.60
Sales of tickets to the outside	1.19	3.86	1.46	1.47	1.84	2.21
Airport tax	2.89	4.00	2.52	2.12	1.11	1.15
Import duties	1.70	0.45	1.03	0.80	0.98	1.10
Complementary taxes	14.45	28.42	8.53	8.83	11.53	14.14
Foreign exchange surcharge	3.57	16.15	2.40	1.47	0.64	0.80

Source: On the basis of official data.

reform, import duties became more responsive to a given tax base indicating perhaps an increase in the efficiency of import duty collection.

The simple correlation coefficient between imports as a percentage of GDP and duty collections as a percentage of GDP is 0.37 for the period prior to the reform (1979–1991) and to 0.64 for the period following the reform (1992–2001). In addition, a scatter diagram (Figure 6.3) shows a clear change in the slope of the relationship between both variables before and after the reform.

The value-added tax (ITBIS), which is the main source of compensating for the revenue losses arising from tariff reductions, has yielded higher revenues over time (1.6 percent, 3 percent and 4 percent of GDP in 1991, 1999, and 2001). However, by known empirical standards the ITBIS is a comparatively inefficient tax, that is, its revenue collection is below its potential.

Table 6.16 shows two measures that are used in the tax literature to gauge the efficiency of a tax (Ebrill *et al.*, 2001). These are the efficiency and C-efficiency ratio. The efficiency ratio is defined as the ITBIS revenue as a percentage of GDP divided by the tax rate. The C-efficiency ratio is the ratio of ITBIS revenues to consumption divided by the tax rate. The

Table 6.15 Results of regression analysis of import duties as a percentage of GDP on the import base and tariff reforms, 1980–2001

Variable	Parameter estimate	T-statistic
Constant	0.07	1.33
Import base as percentage of GDP(-2)	1.02	2.24
Import base as percentage of GDP(-3)	0.92	2.20
Tariff and tax reform 1992–1995	0.40	2.27
Tariff and tax reform 2001	-0.56	-2.45
N = 19		
R^2 (adjusted) = 0.43		
Schwarz Criterion = -2.56		
Akaike Criterion = -2.82		
Statistical tests		
Residual tests:		
Box-Pierce	$\chi^2(1) = 1.15$	
Ljung-Box	$\chi^2(1) = 2.31$	
Breusch-Godfrey	$\chi^2(1) = 2.63$	
Functional form tests:		
Ramsey Reset Tests	$\chi^2(1) = 0.04$	
Heteroscedasticity Test:		
Breusch-Pagan	$\chi^2(4) = 2.97$	
Arch Process Test	$\chi^2(2) = 0.99$	

Source: On the basis of data provided by the Ministry of Finance and the Central Bank of the Dominican Republic.

Note
Estimations were carried out with the Modler (250) software.

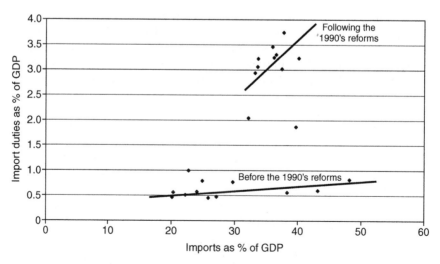

Figure 6.3 Import duty collection and import base, 1980–2001.

Table 6.16 Value added tax: Efficiency and C-efficiency ratios for the Dominican
Republic and other geographic regions

	Sub-Saharan Africa	*Asia and the Pacific*	*Americas*	*Dominican Republic Average 95–00*	*Dominican Republic 2001*
Efficiency ratio	27	35	37	34	33
C-efficiency ratio	38	58	57	42	44

advantage of the latter over the former is that it takes into account the fact
that the value added tax is levied on consumption. More important, it
avoids making policy recommendations seeking to increase the tax base by
incorporating into the tax structure other components of aggregate
demand such as investment (ibid. p. 41). A low value of these ratios is an
indication of tax evasion or tax erosion.

The results for the Dominican Republic show that the efficiency ratio in
1991, which is the year prior to the 1992 reform, was 0.25, and that in 2000
(the year prior to the implementation of the following tax reform) it was
equal to 0.33. The first figure means that in 1991, an increase of 2 percentage points in the tax rate would have resulted, other things being equal, in
an increase of 0.50 percent in the ITBIS-to-GDP ratio. The increase of 2
percentage points in the ITBIS rate from 6 percent to 8 percent yielded an
increase in the ITBIS-to-GDP ratio remarkably close to this relationship.
The ITBIS-to-GDP ratio increased from 1.52 to 2.13, that is, an increase of
0.61 percentage points.

Similarly, the efficiency ratio in 2000 was 0.34, indicating that an
increase of one percentage point in the tax rate would increase the ITBIS-
to-GDP ratio by 0.34 percent. The increase in the ITBIS rate from 8
percent to 12 percent resulted in an increase of 1.26 percent percentage
points in the ITBIS-to-GDP ratio, which is very close to that predicted by
the efficiency ratio (1.36 percent).

When compared to other countries that have adopted the value added
tax or the consumption tax, the efficiency ratios for the ITBIS in the
Dominican Republic are low. In fact, as Table 16 shows they are below the
Latin American averages. The International Monetary Fund (IMF) calculations indicate that the efficiency ratio for Latin America is 37 percent
(Ebrill, *et al.*, 2001). According to this author's computations the efficiency
ratio for the Dominican Republic is 33 percent. In terms of the
C-efficiency ratio, the coefficient yielded an average of 42 percent and a 44
percent for 2001. For Latin America the C-efficiency ratio is 57 percent.

Also more recent estimations for smaller economies validate this conclusion, that is, the Dominican Republic lags in tax efficiency relative to
other countries in the hemisphere. Table 6.17 shows selected Latin

Table 6.17 Value added tax in the Dominican Republic and selected Caribbean countries

Country	Population (millions)	Introduction of VAT	VAT rates	VAT percentage of total tax revenue	VAT percentage of GDP	C-efficiency ratio
Barbados	0.3	1997	15	32.7	9.5	110.2
Belize	0.2	1996	8			56.2
Costa Rica	3.7	1975	13		4.0	87.4
Dominican Republic	8.5	1983	12	25	4.0*	44
Jamaica	2.6	1991	15	35.8	8.8	83.5
Nicaragua	4.8	1975	15			34.6
Panama	2.7	1977	5			67.3
Trinidad and Tobago	1.7	1990	15	23.6	4.3	46.8

Source: On the basis of official data.

Note
*2001.

American and Caribbean countries, the date of introduction of the VAT and the computed C-efficiency ratio. With the exception of Nicaragua, the C-efficiency ratio in the case of the Dominican Republic is below that of other countries.

The decomposition of the efficiency ratio into its internal and external component does not improve the overall picture of inefficiency of the tax. The efficiency and C-efficiency ratios for the ITBIS as a whole are equally divided for its internal and external component.

These results would indicate that trying to recover the revenues lost in tariff reduction by increasing the ITBIS rate is by no means optimal. This policy measure, given the inefficiency of the ITBIS, may involve placing an unjustified burden on the consumer and his welfare. It also means increasing the complexity of the tax system by introducing discretionary and temporary change in the tax structure, which is a well-known feature of Dominican economic history. Moreover, it causes unwarranted changes in macroeconomic variables, leading authorities to react by undertaking measures that are believed to maintain stability in the face of a change in external conditions when, in fact, it is a reaction provoked by the inefficiency of the tax system. If the efficiency ratio were higher than the actual one (34 percent), say 40 percent, a four percentage-point increase in the tax rate (like the one that Dominican authorities implemented in 2001) would have increased the revenue potential of the ITBIS from 1.3 percent to around 1.6 percent of GDP. If the efficiency ratios were closer to those of Caribbean economies, the Dominican Republic would significantly soften its budget constraint.

These arguments become even more relevant when the relationship between the import duties as a percentage of GDP and external ITBIS is examined. Due to the fact – as presented in the first section of this paper – that the external tax structure is a cascading one, both variables should be closely related. Both variables were relatively closely associated from the inception of the ITBIS in 1983 to 1989. The coefficient of correlation was 0.47. Following the 1990 reforms both variables seem to be dissociated and the coefficient of correlation declined to 0.22.[3]

Fiscal reform in the Dominican Republic: an assessment

Fiscal reform in the Dominican Republic became a pressing need as the Dominican Republic adopted an outward-oriented policy and pursued a deeper international integration. However, the implementation of fiscal reform was limited in its scope by the absence of attention paid to institutional and political factors, and to efficiency considerations.

Ultimately, as will be shown below using a framework developed by Godley and Cripps (1983), fiscal reform was not able to fulfil its original aim (as set in the Monetary Approach to the Balance of Payments) of bringing absorption in line with income. In fact fiscal reform did nothing to alter the relationship between the internal and external conditions characterized during most of the period here analyzed by joint fiscal and external deficits.

Using national accounts it is possible to demonstrate that in a "quasi steady state" the value of the flow of national income is a weighted average of the export performance ratio and the fiscal stance (Godley and Cripps, 1983; Anyadike-Danes, 1996). The export performance ratio is the ratio of the value of exports to the average propensity to import. The fiscal stance is equal to the ratio of the value of government expenditure to the tax to GDP ratio. Formally,

$$Y = \omega_1(X/\mu) + \omega_2(G/\theta) \tag{1}$$

where:
Y = national income
ω_1 and ω_2 = weights
X = value of exports
μ = average propensity to import
G = value of government spending
θ = the government's share or tax collections to national income (tax-to-GDP ratio)

Since the flow of national income is a weighted average of the export performance ratio and the fiscal stance, when the fiscal stance is greater than the export performance ratio, national income is smaller than the former and greater than the latter (Anyadike-Danes, 1996, p. 716). That is,

$$G/\theta > X/\mu \Leftrightarrow G/\theta > Y > X/\mu \tag{2}$$

In turn this implies that a budget deficit will be by definition accompanied by a deficit in the balance of payments. In other words,

$$G/\theta > Y \Leftrightarrow G > \theta Y \text{ and } X < \mu Y \tag{3}$$

Since $\theta = T/Y$ and $\mu = M/Y$, where T are taxes and M imports,

$$G > \theta Y \Leftrightarrow G > (T/Y)Y \Leftrightarrow G > T \Leftrightarrow G - T > 0 \quad \text{(Fiscal deficit)}$$
$$X < \mu Y \Leftrightarrow X < (M/Y)Y \Leftrightarrow X < M \Leftrightarrow X - M < 0 \quad \text{(Current account deficit)} \tag{4}$$

Using this logic, as long as the fiscal stance exceeds the export performance ratio, a country will experience a twin deficit situation.

As seen in Figure 6.4, in spite of the reforms, the fiscal stance has persistently surpassed the export performance ratio, leading, in the absence of net asset accumulation, to a persistent twin-deficit situation (see Figure

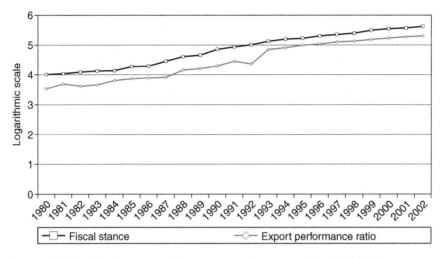

Figure 6.4 The fiscal stance and the export performance ratio, 1980–2002.

6.5).[4] This, in turn, has led to an unsustainable debt situation as seen from the following debt-sustainability analysis.

A budget deficit is said to be unsustainable when it leads to uncontrolled increases in the public debt or when interest payments are perceived as being too much of a burden as they are imposed on taxpayers through excessive tax rates or through an unequal distribution of the burden of the debt (Sawyer, 1998). The concept of fiscal sustainability can

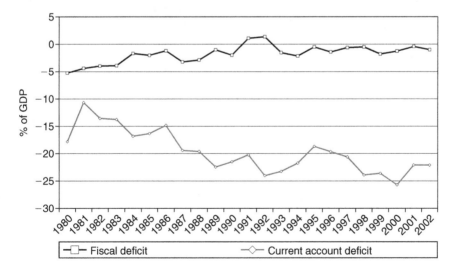

Figure 6.5 The fiscal and current account deficits in the Dominican Republic as a percentage of GDP, 1980–2002.

be examined using an equation that relates four variables: government expenditures, government revenues, rate of growth of real GDP, the real interest rate and the outstanding public debt. More specifically the equation says that the primary budget surplus as percentage of GDP equals the difference between the real interest rate and real GDP growth multiplied by the share of public debt to GDP (Pasinetti, 1998).

This concept can be expressed formally as follows,

$$S/Y = (r - g)D/Y \tag{5}$$

where:
  S = primary budget surplus
  Y = nominal output
  r = real rate of interest
  D = internal debt
  g = real growth rate of GDP

Equation (5) provides the boundary line between an unsustainable and a sustainable budget surplus or deficit. If $S/Y > (r - g)D/Y$ then the surplus or deficit is said to be sustainable. This is illustrated in Figure 6.6 for a case of a developing country where real interest rates chronically exceed the rates of growth of real output.

Notice that the formula considers only internal debt. It would thus at best provide a rough approximation to deficit sustainability in developing countries since external debt often places an important constraint on fiscal accounts. Including external debt in Equation (5) and expressing the surplus or deficit boundary line in national currency we obtain,

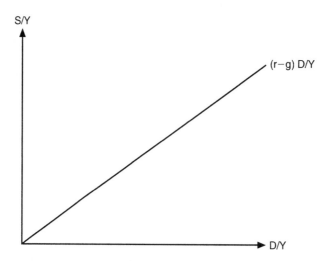

Figure 6.6 The boundary between sustainable and unsustainable deficits.

$$S/Y = (r_i - g)D_i/Y + (r_e + \delta - g)D_e/Y \tag{6}$$

where:

r_i = internal real rate of interest
D_i = internal debt
r_e = foreign real rate of interest
D_e = external debt
δ = exchange rate depreciation

This second case, which is more akin to that of the Dominican Republic, includes external debt. The possibilities for obtaining fiscal balance become more complex as there are four variables determining fiscal balance. Table 6.18 shows the computations for 1991 through 2002 of estimated fiscal sustainability and compared these results to actual fiscal performance.

As Table 6.18 indicates, the actual fiscal result has been below the sustainability level and the gap to achieve sustainability has widened since the start of the stabilization reforms.

As shown from the entire previous analysis, fiscal reform has not only been unsuccessful but also, by generating a fiscal stance over and above the export performance ratio, it has led to an unsustainable debt situation.

According to the framework used in this section, this situation could have been avoided in the past, and can be avoided in the future, if it were a main goal of fiscal policy to attune the fiscal stance to the export performance ratio. In this sense, export performance sets the limit and scope to fiscal policy. Economic policy must focus not on credit restraint as recommended by the Monetary Approach to the Balance of Payments, on softening the external constraint. In other words, fiscal policy can be made to work for development only if the external conditions allow it to work without paying too much attention to fiscal balance. Otherwise any country, such as the case of the Dominican Republic, may find itself in a process of continuous fiscal adjustment whose main consequences are output and employment losses.

Table 6.18 Stability surplus boundary with internal and external debt

Years	D_i/Y	D_e/Y	r_i	$r_e + \delta$	g	*Stability surplus boundary*	*Actual fiscal result*	*Sustainability gap*
1991	3.0	60.3	25.7	14.6	1.0	8.20	3.3	−4.9
1995	6.2	31.7	18.7	5.78	4.8	1.17	0.7	−0.47
1998	6.2	21.3	16.0	16.68	7.3	2.52	1.0	−1.52
2000	5	18.5	17.5	18.22	7.3	2.5	2.0	−0.5
2002	5	19.8	18.3	26.3	4.1	5.1	2.6	−3.3

Source: Elaborated on the basis of information provided by the Central Bank of the Dominican Republic (1991–1998) and Pellerano (1999).

Notes

1 A majority of import quotas and permits were abolished in 1990 and 1998. Export taxes were eliminated in 1992.
2 As can be seen in the next section, tariff rates of 25 percent and 40 percent are still applied on some tariff lines. Also two tariff lines still maintain a 15 percent tariff rate.
3 Furthermore the relationship between the ITBIS external tax base and the ITBIS revenue collection is weak as preliminary econometric analysis undertaken showed.
4 In Figure 6.5 the data for the fiscal deficit correspond to the central government. The correct variable is the fiscal deficit of the consolidated public sector for which a coherent time series is not available. The deficit of the consolidated public sector is higher than that of the central government.

References

Anyadike-Danes, Michael K. (1996), "Run in the Sand? The Limits to Growth in Barbados," *Cambridge Journal of Economics*, 20(6), November, pp. 715–28.
Ceara Hatton, Miguel (1990), *Tendencias Estructurales y Coyunturales de la Economía Dominicana, 1968–1983* ("Structural and Short-Term Trends of the Dominican Economy, 1968–1983"), Santo Domingo: SIECA.
CEDOPEX (1997*a*), *Report of the Dominican Republic*, Santo Domingo: Dominican Center for the Promotion of Exports (CEDOPEX).
CEDOPEX (1997*b*), *Integración de la República Dominicana al CARICOM* ("Integration of the Dominican Republic to CARICOM"), Santo Domingo: Dominican Center for the Promotion of Exports (CEDOPEX).
CEDOPEX (1998), *Estado Actual del Acuerdo de Libre Comercio entre Centroamérica y la República Dominicana* ("Current Status of the Free Trade Agreement between Central America and the Dominican Republic"), Santo Domingo: Dominican Center for the Promotion of Exports (CEDOPEX).
CEDOPEX (1998), *Protocolo al Tratado de Libre Comercio Centroamérica-República Dominicana Suscrtito el 16 de Abril de 1998* ("Protocol to the Free Trade Agreement between Central America and the Dominican Republic Subscribed on 16 April 1998"), Santo Domingo: Dominican Center for the Promotion of Exports (CEDOPEX).
Central Bank of the Dominican Republic (1996), *Operaciones Fiscales del Gobierno Central, Enero 1990 – Diciembre 1995* ("Fiscal Operations of the Central Government, January 1990 – December 1995"), Santo Domingo: Central Bank.
Central Bank of the Dominican Republic (1997*a*), *Nueva Literatura: Economía Dominicana* ("New Dominican Economic Literature"), Santo Domingo: Central Bank.
Central Bank of the Dominican Republic (1997*b*), *Estadísticas Monetarias, Bancarias, Financieras y de Precios 1990–1996* ("Monetary, Banking, Financial and Price Statistics, 1990–1996"), Santo Domingo: Central Bank.
Central Bank of the Dominican Republic (1997–1999), *Informe de la Economía Dominicana, 1996–1997–1998* ("Report of the Economy of the Dominican Republic, 1996–1997–1998"), Santo Domingo: Central Bank.
Central Bank of the Dominican Republic (1999), *Boletín Trimestral* ("Quarterly Bulletin"), 53(10–12), October–December 1998, Santo Domingo: Central Bank.

Central Bank of the Dominican Republic (1985–1998), *PIB Nominal y Real, 1970–1998; Tipos de Cambio Mensual del Mercado Oficial, Bancario y Extrabancario, 1985–1998* ("Real and Nominal GDP, 1970–1998, Official, Market and Parallel Monthly Nominal Exchange Rates"), Santo Domingo: Central Bank.

CNZFE (1999), *Informe Estadístico del Sector de Zonas Francas, 1998* ("Statistical Report of the Free Trade Zones, 1998"), Santo Domingo: National Council of Free Trade Zones (CNZFE).

Coutts, Kenneth J., Cury H. Guiliani and Fernando Pellerano (1986), "Stabilization Programmes and Structural Adjustment Policies in the Dominican Republic," *Labour and Society*, 11(3), 361–78.

Customs Office (1997), *Arancel de la República Dominicana* ("Tax Schedule of the Dominican Republic"), mimeo.

Dauhajre, Andrés and Jaime Aristy (editors) (1996), *Programa Macroeconómico de Mediano Plazo para la República Dominicana: 1996–2000,* ("Medium-Run Macroeconomic Program for the Dominican Republic: 1996–2000"), Santo Domingo: Fundación Economía y Desarrollo.

Dauhajre, Andrés and Jaime Aristy (editors) (1996), *Programa Macroeconómico de Mediano Plazo para la República Dominicana: 1996–2000: Resumen Ejecutivo* ("Medium-Run Macroeconomic Program for the Dominican Republic: 1996–2000. Executive Summary"), Santo Domingo: Fundación Economía y Desarrollo.

Ebrill, Liam P., Michael Keen, Jean-Paul Bodin and Victoria Summers (2001), *The Modern VAT*, Washington, DC: International Monetary Fund.

ECLAC (1995–1998), *The Dominican Republic: Economic Reports*, Mexico City: Economic Commission For Latin America and the Caribbean (ECLAC).

ECLAC (1980–1998), *ECLAC Data on the Dominican Republic Elaborated On the Basis of Official Information*, Mexico City: Economic Commission For Latin America and the Caribbean (ECLAC).

Edwards, Sebastian (1995), *Crisis and Reform in Latin America: From Despair to Hope*, New York: Oxford University Press.

Franco, Gustavo H.B. (1986), *Aspects of the Economics of Hyperinflations: Theoretical Issues and Historical Studies of Four European Hyperinflations of the 1920s (Inflation, Stabilization, Indexation, Adjustment, Dollarization)*, PhD Dissertation: Harvard University.

Godley, Wynne and Francis Cripps (1983), *Macroeconomics*, New York: Oxford University Press.

IDB (1998), *República Dominicana: Programa de Reforma de Empresas Públicas; Ayuda Memoria del Sector Hidrocarburos* ("Dominican Republic: Program of Reforms of Public Sector; Aide Memorandum on the Hydrocarbon Sector"), Inter-American Development Bank.

International Monetary Fund (1996), *Dominican Republic: Recent Economic Developments*, Washington, DC: International Monetary Fund.

International Monetary Fund (1997), *Government Finance Statistics Yearbook*, Washington, DC: International Monetary Fund.

León-Ledesma, Miguel A. (1999), "An Application of Thirwall's Law to the Spanish Economy," *Journal of Post Keynesian Economics*, 21(3), Spring, 431–9.

Martí Gutierrez, Adolfo (1997), *Instrumental para el Estudio de la Economía Dominicana* ("Set of Instruments for the Study of the Dominican Republic"), Santo Domingo: Buho.

Ministry of Finance (1996–1998), *Estadísticas Mensuales de Ingresos y Gastos del Gobierno Central* ("Monthly Revenue and Expenditure Statistics of the Central Government"), Santo Domingo: Ministry of Finance.

Moya Pons, Frank (1995), *The Dominican Republic: A National History*, New Rochelle: Hispaniola Books.

ONAPLAN (1996), *Informe Preliminar del Comportamiento de la Economía Dominicana en 1995* ("Preliminary Report on the Evolution of the Dominican Economy in 1995"), Santo Domingo: Oficina Nacional de Planificación (ONAPLAN).

Pasinetti, Luigi L. (1998), "The Myth (or Folly) of the 3 Percent Deficit/GDP Maastricht 'Parameter'," *Cambridge Journal of Economics*, 22(1), January, pp. 103–16.

Pellerano, Fernando (editor) (1991), *Apertura y Reformas Estructurales: El Desafío Dominicano* ("Outward Orientation and Structural Reforms: The Dominican Challenge"), Santo Domingo: CEIA.

Pellerano, Fernando (1997*a*), "Los Agujeros del Paquete Tributario" ("The Loopholes of the Tax Package"), *La Revista Económica*, January–February.

Pellerano, Fernando (1997*b*), "Liberalización y Estructura Tributaria" ("Liberalization and Tax Structure"), *La Revista Económica*, 111(67), March.

Pellerano, Fernando (1997*c*), "El Efecto Fiscal de una Devaluación" ("The Fiscal Effect of a Devaluation"), Ministry of Finance, mimeo.

Pellerano, Fernando (1999), "Finanzas Públicas y Política Fiscal: Año 1998 y Proyección 1999" ("Public Finances and Fiscal Policy for 1998 and Forecast for 1999"), Ministry of Finance, mimeo.

Pellerano, Fernando (2002), "Notes on Fiscal Policy in the Dominican Republic," Ministry of Finance, mimeo.

Presidency of the Republic, Unit of Economic Analysis, (1996), *Carácter de la Política Económica del Primer Año de Gobierno* ("Orientation of Economic Policy in the First Year of Government"), August 1996/August 1997, mimeo.

Sawyer, Malcolm C. (1998), "Financial Constraints on Keynesian Macroeconomic Policies," in *John Maynard Keynes: Keynesianism into the Twenty-First Century*, edited by Soumitra Sharma, Cheltenham, UK: Edward Elgar, pp. 240–9.

World Bank (1988), *World Development Report 1988*, New York: Oxford University Press.

World Trade Organization (1996), *Trade Policy Review: The Dominican Republic. Report by the Secretariat*, Geneva: World Trade Organization.

World Trade Organization (1996), Trade Policy Review Body: The Dominican Republic; *Report by the Secretariat – Summary Observations*, Geneva: World Trade Organization.

7 Globalization and endogenous fiscal crisis

Theory and Brazilian experience

Matias Vernengo[1]

Introduction

It is quite hard to define precisely a fiscal crisis. Fiscal crises are often associated with severe social or external problems, such as revolutions and wars. In those situations fiscal deficits soar, and public debt consequently explodes. However, defaults of domestic public debt are very rare, in contradistinction to defaults on foreign debt.[2] For that reason we will define a fiscal crisis as a situation in which public deficit is high and debt grows fast for a relatively long period.[3]

Using this definition, most economists would agree that fiscal crises result from exogenous factors. In other words, the causes of fiscal crisis are the result of exogenous social emergencies, and/or of bad decisions by policy makers – that is, macroeconomic populism (Dornbusch and Edwards, 1990; Bresser Pereira and Dall'Acqua, 1991). In that respect, there is little that can be done to avoid fiscal crisis beyond educating the public and the political community and hoping for the best.

Fiscal crises in developing countries are usually seen as resulting from exogenous causes, a mix of bad luck and populism. However, under certain conditions, fiscally responsible governments may end up dealing with a fiscal crisis. An endogenous fiscal crisis results from the normal functioning of the economic system, and policy interventions would be essential in eliminating them.[4] The analysis of endogenous fiscal crisis is the main focus of this paper. The paper argues that globalization, understood as liberalization of the balance of payments accounts,[5] leads to a fiscal squeeze of social spending (Grunberg, 1998), on the one hand, and to a fiscal crisis, on the other.

Beyond the question of whether fiscal deficits are exogenous, or endogenous, the most important question from a policy perspective is what are the effects of persistent deficits and a fast growing debt on the economic system. The conventional reply is that sustained budget deficits tend to reduce national savings, and reduce investment, leading to lower levels of income per capita in the future. In other words, public deficits crowd out investment, and lead to lower rates of growth in the long run.[6]

It will be argued in this paper that endogenous fiscal deficits affect the composition of the budget, spending in particular, and its effects on growth depend largely on the structure of spending rather than any direct effect on national savings.

The following section discusses the notion of endogenous fiscal crisis in developing countries within the context of globalization. A heuristic model adapted to endogenous fiscal crisis in developing countries is worked out. Some general conclusions are drawn. The following section uses the heuristic model to analyze the Brazilian experience during the 1990s. The final section pulls the results together for a general evaluation, and raises questions about fiscal policy objectives in developing countries.

The heuristic framework

A developing economy with a relatively well-developed domestic financial market and a reasonably big government – in terms of spending and revenues relative to GDP – in an environment of open international financial markets is the object of analysis. In this economy, the domestic interest rate (i) is determined by the monetary authority, which sets it equal to the foreign interest rate (i^*) plus a premium (μ). The premium is the amount paid over international rates to maintain the foreign exchange stable. We have

$$i = i^* + \mu \tag{1}$$

In other words, the monetary authority follows a simple uncovered interest parity rule.[7] Further, we assume that the domestic public debt is all denominated in domestic currency, to avoid questions of how the exchange rate affects debt dynamics, and presuppose that all the public debt is indexed to the domestic interest rate, allowing us to ignore questions related to interest rate term structures. In that respect, the interest payments on outstanding debt are directly connected to the functioning of international financial markets.

The fiscal stance can be divided in three sub-items, according to whether we include or not interest payments and adjustments for inflation. Table 7.1 shows the nominal deficit, the primary deficit, and the operational deficit. The nominal deficit is the most inclusive measure of deficit and includes the difference of all spending and revenues, while the primary deficit is the less inclusive, excluding all interest payments. Nominal interest payments correspond to real interest payments and the payments resulting from adjusting the debt to inflation. The differences between nominal and operational deficits in the context of inflationary processes can be significant. For simplicity we will assume that the price level is stable and hence the operational and nominal definitions of public deficit collapse. Note that if international financial markets determine the

Table 7.1 Public deficit

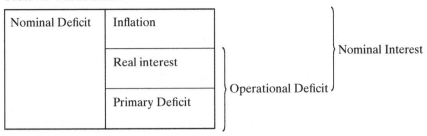

rate of interest, hence, the domestic authority does not directly control the gap between the nominal and primary deficits.

Finally, we assume that the country is dependent on foreign exchange to close the balance of payments, and as part of an agreement with the International Monetary Fund (IMF) it consents to a target primary surplus.[8] As a result, the nominal deficit becomes endogenous, since international markets determine interest payments, and the primary deficit is also determined as a result of international considerations.

Debt dynamics in this case can be described as follows. For simplicity we assume that all deficits are financed with debt and that no monetization takes place. Then, the primary deficit is described as

$$(G - T) = \dot{D} - iD \tag{2}$$

Dots represent changes in levels; hence, the primary deficit is the difference between spending and tax revenue, which equals the change in debt minus interest payments on outstanding debt. A high operational deficit may very well persist even in the case domestic government maintains permanent primary surpluses, if the interest on outstanding debt is sufficiently high. Hence, as we suggested earlier, a fiscally responsible government may end up with high deficits. To understand the endogenous fiscal crisis, though, we must also look at debt dynamics.

A typical measure of domestic debt sustainability is the debt-to-GDP ratio $(d = D/Y)$. The rate of growth of the debt-to-GDP ratio is defined as the rate of growth of debt minus the rate of growth of output (g). That is

$$\frac{\dot{d}}{d} = \frac{\dot{D}}{D} - g \tag{3}$$

Substituting (1) and (2) into (3) we get

$$\frac{\dot{d}}{d} = \frac{(G-T) + (i^* + \mu)D}{D} - g = (i^* + \mu - g) + \frac{(G-T)}{D} \tag{4}$$

For the growth of debt-to-GDP ratio we have, then

$$\dot{d} = (i^* + \mu - g)d + \frac{(G - T)}{Y} = (i^* + \mu - g)d + \tau \tag{5}$$

That is, the debt-to-GDP ratio depends on two different effects. The ratio of debt to GDP will grow if the foreign interest plus the risk premium is higher than the rate of growth of GDP, when the target primary deficit (τ) is negative, that is, when there is a primary surplus. Also, if the ratio of primary deficit to GDP (Y) is positive and high, then debt may grow, even if the rate of growth of the economy is higher than the interest rate.

As a result, a fiscal crisis, characterized by high deficits (nominal) and growing debt could occur even if the government is fiscally responsible – maintains primary surpluses, that is, so that τ is negative – if the foreign interest rate, and/or the risk premium are sufficiently big. Once the government fixes the primary fiscal target, the final result of the fiscal accounts, measured by the nominal result, is not directly controlled by the domestic authority, and, in this particular sense, is said to be endogenous, that is, determined by the economy.

One additional caveat must be analyzed in this context. It may be argued that primary surpluses are necessary in order to reduce the risk premium (μ) paid by government over international interest rates. In other words, credibility is necessary for the debt-to-GDP ratio to be stable, and to avoid a fiscal crisis. Note that we assumed that public debt is denominated in domestic currency. If government borrowing is done internally in the country's own currency, then high debt-to-GDP ratios do not lead to defaults. Hence, there is no obvious limit to counter-cyclical fiscal policy. In this view, society owes the debt to itself, paraphrasing Alvin Hansen,[9] and one should not be overly concerned with the size of the debt.[10] The results are quite different if debt is in foreign currency. In this case, the government cannot monetize the deficit, since it does not have seigniorage privileges over foreign currency, and default is more likely.[11]

Arguably, the only risk associated with public debt denominated in domestic currency is that the monetization of debt would lead to hyperinflation, a view often associated with recent Latin American experiences. One must note that that presumes that the economy is near full employment, and, as a result, that monetization leads to higher private spending and inflation.[12] One problem with this line of reasoning is that the very notion of full employment – as defined by the natural rate of unemployment and the NAIRU – is vague. Some attribute to Solow the joke according to which the natural rate is whatever the rate of unemployment had been in the last three years. In fact, empirical evidence suggests that Solow was right on the mark and, hence, that there is no fixed unemployment rate at which inflation accelerates (Staiger *et al.*, 1997).

The empirical evidence seems to indicate that the natural rate varies with time, and that an economy that is operating near full capacity would tend to have a low natural rate. In other words, there is hysteresis in the unemployment determination process (Blanchard and Summers, 1987; Gordon, 1996). In this case, we can close the heuristic model with two equations that incorporate the stylized fact that higher levels of growth lead to higher levels of potential growth (equivalent to lower unemployment reducing the natural unemployment level, as should be clear from Okun's effect). Potential GDP growth depends positively on actual growth and on productivity growth. Actual growth (g) can be written as follows:

$$g = az + b\lambda - fi \tag{6}$$

That is, growth depends positively on autonomous demand (z), which includes non-interest government spending, and on productivity growth (λ), and negatively on interest rates that reduce non-interest government spending for a given level of total spending, as well as private consumption. Finally, productivity is positively affected by growth, meaning that an economy at full speed tends to lead to faster rates of technological innovation, as in Verdoorn's effect. That is,

$$\lambda = \lambda_a + cg \tag{7}$$

The above equations indicate that the rate of growth depends on demand growth, and since demand growth leads to higher productivity, this means that the potential rate of growth of the economy grows with the expansion of demand, and that the natural rate of unemployment falls concomitantly. The closure follows the Kaldorian model of growth and cumulative causation (Kaldor, 1970). An important implication of the model is that monetization of public debt may lead to higher output and productivity, and because potential growth is accelerating, the debt-to-GDP ratio may very well be falling.[13] Even if the debt-to-GDP ratio is growing there is no real threat of default. Growing productivity reduces the risk of demand-pull inflation. In this view, the necessary complement of expansionary fiscal policy is low interest rates, to reduce the financial component of government debt servicing.[14] The thrust of the model follows, as it can be noted from the main conclusions, Abba Lerner's functional finance approach.

How deficits affect a peripheral economy

The conventional view of fiscal deficits is that in the short run they stimulate the economy in Keynesian fashion, but in the long term, given that national savings equal domestic investment and net foreign investment, then a fall in national savings must lead to a fall in capital formation or net foreign investment. In both cases the level of growth must fall. Put simply, deficits are good in the short run, but not in the long run.

Sometimes the negative long-term effect on growth is presented as the result of rising interest rates leading to lower capital accumulation. The higher rates of interest result from the decrease in national savings. In other words, public spending crowds out private spending. Leaving aside the logical problems with the crowding-out argument – tackled long ago when Keynes debated the so-called Treasury view[15] – there is very little evidence that deficits affect the rate of interest in a significant manner (Gale and Orszag, 2003, p. 475).[16] Further, the heuristic model of the previous section suggests that, when the monetary authority follows an interest parity rule, and the public debt is indexed to that rate, the causality between interest rate and fiscal deficit is reversed. That is, a higher interest rate will lead to higher interest payments on debt, and higher nominal deficits. This closure might be more relevant for developing countries.

Whatever the effects of public deficits on growth, then, those results cannot be brought about by higher rates of interest within the framework developed in the previous section. Income distribution is, however, affected by a fiscal crisis. A primary surplus together with a nominal deficit implies that the government is paying the difference to debt holders. Usually debt holders are wealthy individuals, corporations, and banks. In other words, the combination of primary surplus *cum* nominal deficit represents a transfer of resources from society as a whole to wealthy debt holders. The redistributive process is quite strong since in most cases primary surpluses imply that social spending has to be squeezed (Grunberg, 1998).

Therefore, the effects of fiscal deficits on the level of activity are mediated by income distribution rather than the rate of interest. In wage-led economies, redistribution towards debt holders with lower propensities to consume should lead to output stagnation. In other words, in wage-led economies, financial liberalization that promotes integration to international financial markets, coped with large primary fiscal surpluses, promotes stagnating rates of output growth, and a fiscal crisis. The stagnationist scenario would be reversed in a profit-led economy. However, anecdotal evidence suggests that developing countries tend to be wage-led, resulting in a more likely stagnationist scenario. In that sense, the long-run effects of the fiscal crisis are negative, but the reasons have nothing to do with public spending crowding out private spending.

The question to be asked then is why a country would promote a severe fiscal adjustment, in terms of the primary target, if the final effects turn out to be low levels of output growth. The primary deficit is a very narrow concept, and it is well known since the times of Keynes that actual deficits are not good measures of the fiscal stance. In other words, primary targets do not allow controlling aggregate demand. That is the reason why authors like Abba Lerner, as noted before, proposed a full-employment deficit as the correct measure of fiscal stance (Colander, 1984).

The reason for using the primary deficit as target for policy, with the implicit objective of maintaining a stable debt-to-GDP ratio, is related to the effects of globalization. In an open economy the rate of interest is set to keep the foreign exchange under control, as assumed in the monetary policy rule. As a result, the interest payments on debt cannot be controlled, in particular, because the debt is indexed to the base rate of interest determined by the monetary authority. Accordingly, the only variable left for the government to try to control the debt-to-GDP ratio is the primary surplus.

In this respect, one should reaffirm that primary surpluses have little, if anything, to do with generating credibility. Foreign investors, concerned with foreign debt, should look at the export performance of the country, the only secure source of foreign reserves, rather than primary fiscal balances. Unless one assumes that foreign investors are irrational, the credibility argument seems of limited relevance. Also, domestic investors should not be concerned about the ability to repay, since monetization is always an alternative. If the economy is at full employment, demand pressures would build up and inflation might result. If the economy is not at full employment, the danger of inflation comes from another source. If the government monetizes the debt, the public can use the money to buy foreign exchange and force depreciation, increasing the costs of imported goods and leading to inflation. In both cases, the monetary authority can just keep interest rates sufficiently high in order to avoid the switch from domestic debt to foreign assets.

If the primary target is the only instrument to control, even imperfectly, the debt-to-GDP ratio, then one may ask what the reason behind the monetary policy rule is. The interest rate is set to maintain the exchange rate relatively constant, as already noted. The first and foremost important reason is that in many developing countries the pass-through effect from import costs to prices is quite high and severe depreciations are followed by high inflation. Therefore a central bank targeting low levels of inflation must control the exchange rate, which, in the context of an open capital account, can only be done by manipulating the rate of interest. Also, one must note that the exchange rate is usually maintained stable at a level that allows domestic exports to be competitive, so as to allow the country to obtain enough foreign reserves as to avoid a balance of payments crisis.

In sum, within the framework here developed, fiscal policy is constrained by the balance of payments necessities of the economy. Anti-inflationary policy promotes high rates of interest, leaving only the very limited instrument of the primary balances to control debt sustainability. One should note that external financial crises are not caused by an alert private sector pouncing upon the public sector's imprudent actions such as running an unsustainable fiscal deficit (Perry and Herrera, 1994), but on the contrary, fiscal crises are the result of a prudent public sector forced into financial distress by international financial markets.[17]

More importantly, the policy mix of high interest rates and permanent primary surpluses has the effect of reducing actual and potential growth, leading to higher unemployment. As growth slacks and interest rates increase, debt-to-GDP ratios increase. A fiscal crisis then results in the midst of stagnation. Also, one must note that a fiscal squeeze caused by permanent primary surpluses affects growth in particular through its effects on public investment in infrastructure (Câmara and Vernengo, 2004–2005). Most developing countries that sign agreements with the International Monetary Fund (IMF) assent to reaching the primary fiscal targets that the IMF staff deem necessary for fiscal stability. An especially troubling effect results from the fact that investment expenditures of public firms in most developing countries are accounted for as part of total government's expenses. Effectively that means that public firms have their ability to invest – chiefly in infrastructure – severely restricted, adding to the fiscal crisis.

The Brazilian experience in the 1990s

This section will use to the heuristic model developed in the previous sections to discuss the Brazilian experience in the 1990s. In many respects – as might be clear to the reader – the heuristic model was developed with the Brazilian economy at the back of the mind.[18] The discussion of the Brazilian fiscal performance during the 1990s is not exhaustive, and is intended to illustrate the questions raised by the analytical framework.[19]

The heuristic model presupposes that monetary policy is set to maintain a relatively stable exchange rate. During the second half of the 1990s, and arguably ever since the Real stabilization plan, the exchange rate has been the main instrument to control inflation. Further, the model assumes that public debt is for the most part indexed to base interest rate. Figure 7.1 shows the percentage of domestic public debt indexed to the overnight rate set by the monetary authority since 1990. With the exception of the hyperinflationary period of the early 1990s, around 60 percent is indexed. It is evident that the assumption that 100 percent of public debt is indexed is an exaggeration, but it may be useful as a first approximation. Hence, it seems reasonable to conclude that monetary policy has a great impact on the fiscal results. As we will see though, monetary authorities do not set interest rates with fiscal results in mind.

One should note that in the case of the Brazilian economy, to avoid a complete fiscal squeeze, the federal government promoted a centralization of revenues, a severe adjustment of the accounts of the lower levels of administration and a sizeable increase of tax revenues, all as part of a Law of Fiscal Responsibility. Figure 7.2 shows the increase in tax revenues as a share of GDP during the 1990s.

The following figures show the primary, operational and nominal balances of the Brazilian government. The first one shows those results going back to the mid-1980s, while the second restricts the period to the post-

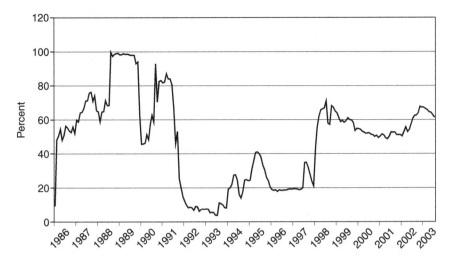

Figure 7.1 Indexed portion of debt (% GDP).

Real Plan period. From the mid-1980s to the Real Plan nominal deficits are enormous, reflecting the high levels of inflation. In this respect the operational measure gives a better picture of the actual financial commitments of the Brazilian administration during the high inflation period. In the period from 1985 to 1994, the operational deficits averaged 2.6 percent of GDP, and peaked at more than 7 percent in 1989.

In the same period, only in two years – 1987 and 1989 – did the government run primary deficits, both at around 1 percent of GDP. Primary sur-

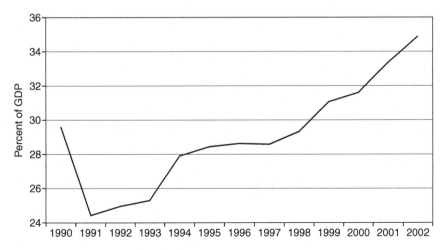

Figure 7.2 Tax revenue (% GDP).

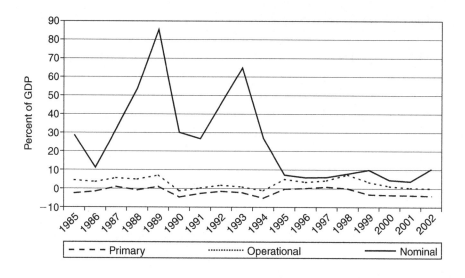

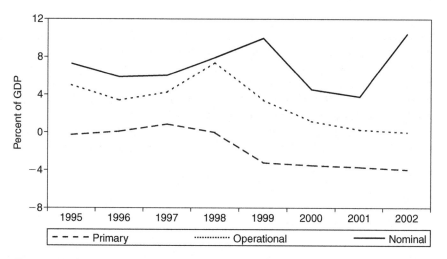

Figure 7.3 Fiscal results, 1985–2002 and 1995–2002.

pluses were the norm rather than the exception even in the high-inflation period. If one takes the primary balance as a measure of fiscal rectitude, one is forced to conclude that the Brazilian administrations have been remarkably austere. This, in fact, suggests that imprudent fiscal behavior is not behind the Brazilian fiscal crisis of the 1990s.

In the post-stabilization period, nominal deficits fell *in tandem* with inflation. Primary surpluses averaged around 2 percent of GDP, but there is a clear trend of higher surpluses following the stabilization plan. It is true that if one breaks the Fernando Henrique Cardoso's administration into its two periods – 1995 to 1998 and 1999 to 2002 – one notes that there were primary deficits in two years in the first period and none in the second term. However, we believe that this does not justify Giambiagi and Ronci's (2004) position according to which the principal cause of the fiscal deterioration in the first Cardoso administration was the deterioration in the primary balance rather than the increase in the interest payments on public debt.[20] The two primary deficits were of around 1 percent of GDP, and had little effect on debt growth when compared to the effects of rates of interest that were above 40 percent in the aftermath of the Tequila crisis.[21]

It is also worth noticing that in the post-1994 period, the gap between primary and nominal deficits fluctuates around 8 percent of GDP, getting wider toward the end. If we still take the operational deficit – adjusting for inflation and looking only at real interest payments – the gap is quite sizeable, around 4 percent of GDP. This means that the fiscal efforts associated with the primary target were basically lost in the financial transfers to debt holders.

As the debt-to-GDP ratio depends on the nominal deficit, that variable continues to rise throughout the 1990s. Figure 7.4 shows the debt-to-GDP ratio excluding the public external debt, that is, the public debt denominated in foreign currency, which corresponds to approximately a third of the total public debt. It is clear that that debt is growing despite all the commitments to the IMF, which have been kept for the most part, on maintaining primary surpluses.[22] The growth in the debt-to-GDP ratio is not problematic *per se*, at least not from a functional finance perspective. The matter of concern is that debt has been accumulated with little gain in terms of economic growth and reduction of unemployment.

In sum, the Brazilian economy has experienced a severe fiscal adjustment, raising revenues and cutting spending in non-financial categories.

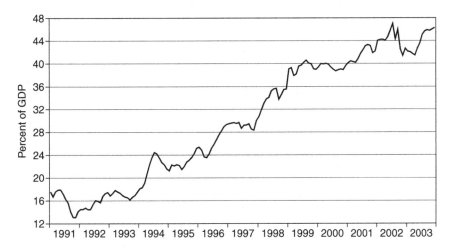

Figure 7.4 Public debt (% GDP).

Table 7.2 Functional Income Distribution (%GDP)

Year	Operational surplus	Wages
1990	32.55	45.37
1991	38.49	41.65
1992	38.03	43.54
1993	35.38	45.14
1994	38.39	40.11
1995	40.27	38.27
1996	40.97	38.54
1997	42.77	37.46
1998	41.57	38.86
1999	40.52	38.15
2000	40.63	37.87
2001	40.97	37.00

Source: IPEA Data.

However, nominal deficits continued high and the debt piled up. One should note that income distribution has gotten considerably worse (Table 7.2), as predicted by the heuristic framework. The share of wages in total income was approximately 45.4 percent in 1990 and only 37 percent in 2001 (see Table 7.2). The flip side of the reduction in the participation of wages is the increase in the net operating surplus (interest, profits, rents, etc.) from 32.5 to almost 41 percent in the same period.

Finally, as noted above, the economy has stagnated during the 1990s. It is clear that stagnation did not start with external liberalization in the 1990s, but it became worse afterwards. The real GDP growth was on average 7.45 percent from 1948 to 1980, and it slowed down to only 2.47 percent in the 1981–2000 phase. The real rate of growth in the 1980s was 3.94 percent. In the 1990s growth has been even lower, at 1.78 percent for the whole decade, 2.69 percent if we exclude the 1990 recession, 2.62 percent for the period after stabilization, and 2.41 percent for the whole Fernando Henrique Cardoso's administration. Things have not improved in the first half of Luis Inácio Lula da Silva's administration. Primary surpluses were not sufficient to reduce the growth of public debt during the 1990s, and hence debt piled up with the only obvious effect of increasing the share of income that goes to the wealthy, in an already very unequal society.

Concluding remarks

The analytical framework developed in this paper intends to illustrate some problems with fiscal policy in developing countries. The conclusions are only preliminary, since the topic is complex and highly controversial. However, the current consensus that developing countries should maintain high primary surpluses, something imposed in every IMF package, and accepted without criticism by most governments, including those on the left like Cardoso and Lula's administrations in Brazil, seems astounding.

Primary surpluses are incapable of controlling the debt-to-GDP ratio. The reason for higher debt-to-GDP ratios is that, in a globalized economy, interest rates tend to be high and nominal deficits high as a result. The consequence is that income is redistributed to the wealthy, and the government ability to spend is restricted. Both income redistribution and lower spending imply that the economy stagnates. Not only is fiscal crisis endogenous in that environment, but primary surpluses, as instigated by a narrow view of fiscal responsibility, result in a Pyrrhic victory.

Alternative policies should try to constrain the nominal deficit, while also allowing for a primary deficit. As noted by Vickrey (1997, p. 497) deficits and growing debt are still required to maintain full employment. In fact, it is not clear why economies with high levels of unemployment, and debts that are below 50 percent of GDP cannot experience, at least for some time, growing levels of debt. The current mood with respect to fiscal policy around the world, as noted by Stiglitz (2003, p. 49) is related to the apparent success of Clinton's fiscal consolidation, even though Clinton "pushed deficit reduction too far." This view has been counterproductive in the developing world. Stiglitz (2003, p. 55) correctly points out that "sometimes,... the IMF, wedded to pre-Keynesian ideas – and finding support in the Clinton administration's deficit reduction rhetoric – ...forced them [developing countries] to do the opposite of what they know to be their best interests."

The main question, then, is not whether deficits and debts are growing, but for what purpose the deficit is being run and the debt is being accumulated. The question is what the best interests of developing countries are, and how fiscal policy can serve them efficiently. For developing countries trying to close the income gap *vis-à-vis* the developed world, growth, employment generation and reduction of income inequalities should be the overriding reasons for running fiscal deficits and for debt accumulation, and the ultimate measure of responsible fiscal performance.

Notes

1 I would like to thank Per Berglund, Robert Blecker, Lauro Gonzalez, Harald Hagemann, Inge Kaul, Esteban Pérez, Malcolm Sawyer, Willi Semmler, José Antônio Pereira de Souza and other conference participants for their comments. The usual caveat applies.

2 Defaults on internally held public debt do not take place in the literal sense, since the debt can always be monetized. In fact, instead of defaulting on public debt the usual mechanism used by governments that are financially strapped is to let inflation erode the value of outstanding debt. For a discussion of hyperinflation see Câmara and Vernengo (2004).

3 The definition only stands if the economy is near full employment, in which case there is a danger of overheating the economy. Note that these definitions are arbitrary, since high deficits and fast-growing debt are not clearly defined.

Most discussions of deficit and debt, however, use some arbitrary thresholds to determine the sustainable and acceptable levels of public spending and debt accumulation. This is particularly the case in stock-flow models (e.g. Godley and Cripps, 1983). Schumpeter (1918) defines a fiscal crisis as one in which the demands for public spending are not matched by society's ability or willingness to pay. See also O'Connor (1973) for a radical view of fiscal crises, and Musgrave (1992) for an analysis of Schumpeter's views.

4 It is well known that tax revenues are pro-cyclical and some spending categories are counter-cyclical, and that the public deficit is endogenous in that respect. Here we mean something else. Once the fiscal policy target is set, the government does not have control over the final fiscal stance, which is endogenously determined by the functioning of the economy. The clarification of the definition used here hinges on breaking the concept of the deficit into its component parts.

5 The paper will emphasize the liberalization of the capital account rather than the trade account of the balance of payments. Trade liberalization impacts the fiscal accounts by reducing tax revenues, a pressing problem for the poorest developing countries (Grunberg, 1998; Toye, 2000). Capital account liberalization affects interest rates and, therefore, the financial component of government spending.

6 Auerbach (2003), Ball and Mankiw (1995) and Gale and Orszag (2003) are good surveys on the conventional view on the effects of budget deficits.

7 A more complex rule à la Taylor, where the level of employment and inflation could also be taken into consideration, but would not affect our main conclusions.

8 The targeted primary surplus only affects the ability to obtain foreign reserves to the extent that a surplus contracts domestic demand and reduces imports. It seems, then, that the IMF concentration on primary surpluses is at the expense of the domestic level of activity.

9 For Hansen's remark see Barbara Bergmann in this volume.

10 Abba Lerner's functional finance analysis provided the rationale for the idea that public debt would be good in a crisis. Lerner (1943) argued that government deficits, and the consequent accumulation of debt, should be instruments for the maintenance of full employment.

11 In fact, very often a balance of payments crisis forces government to attract foreign currencies, raising interest rates on the one hand, and depreciating the domestic currency on the other. Higher interest rates imply higher debt servicing, and depreciation increases the cost of foreign denominated debt. The fiscal crisis is then the result of a balance of payments crisis (Câmara and Vernengo, 2004).

12 Eisner (1989) argues that there is little evidence of a correlation between fiscal deficits, excess demand and inflation. In fact, the real story of the inflation of the 1970s and the 1980s deflation is associated to supply side shocks. See also Kaldor (1976).

13 This is not to say that monetization will never lead to inflation. The model suggests though that inflation will not come from the economy working at full capacity, since potential capacity increases with actual capacity. However, if monetization leads to depreciation, then cost inflation from rising input costs may follow.

14 Historically, central banks have financed government spending at low rates of interest, particularly in moments of crisis. For example, the Bank of England financed the Treasury during the Napoleonic Wars, and debt-to-GDP ratios went to approximately 300 percent, and the Federal Reserve did the same during World War II, when debt-to-GDP escalated to more than 100 percent.

15 For Keynes' views on the effects of fiscal deficits in the long run, see Colander (1984).
16 Gale and Orszag (2003) argue that the evidence is mixed at best, but that most macroeconometric models in the United States imply a very small but significant positive correlation between interest rates and public deficits. Causality is never questioned though.
17 For criticisms of the conventional view on balance of payments crisis, see Taylor (1998) and Erturk (2003).
18 Reading Damill, Frenkel, and Juvenal (2003) indicates that the heuristic model would also fit quite well to the Argentinean experience.
19 For a more thorough discussion see Câmara and Vernengo (2002) and Lopreato (2002).
20 See also Blanchard (2004) on the Brazilian debt dynamics. According to Blanchard a central-bank-engineered increase in the real interest rate may increase the probability of default on the debt, making domestic government debt less attractive, and leading to a real depreciation. Further, Blanchard suggests that outcome is the higher the higher the proportion of foreign-denominated debt. We would argue that is only relevant because a sizeable part of the public debt – 30 percent – is denominated in foreign currency. The policy conclusion is that governments should try to maintain the foreign portion of public debt to a minimum.
21 More importantly, it is clear that throughout the Cardoso administration – and in fact since the debt crisis – the Brazilian government has pursued austere fiscal policies, and that the primary balance has been on average positive, hence contributing to decrease the size of public debt. The logical conclusion is that it is the interest rate that leads to growing debt, exactly the opposite that Giambiagi and Ronci (2004) argue. Therefore their conclusion that "to preserve the hard-won fiscal discipline, the authorities recent [sic] austere fiscal attitude should be permanently embedded into the fiscal institutions," seems still more bizarre. Permanent fiscal adjustment, no matter what the cyclical position of the economy is, might be pushing austerity too far.
22 For a specific critique of the fiscal policies implemented within the Washington Consensus agenda, see Câmara and Vernengo (2004–2005).

References

Auerbach, Alan J. (2003), "Fiscal Policy, Past and Present," *NBER Working Papers*, No. 10023, October.
Ball, Laurence and N. Gregory Mankiw (1995), "What Do Budget Deficits Do?" *Budget Deficits and Debt: Issues and Options*, Kansas City: Federal Reserve Bank of Kansas City, pp. 95–119.
Blanchard, Olivier J. (2004), "Fiscal Dominance and Inflation Targeting: Lessons from Brazil," *NBER Working Paper* No 10389, National Bureau for Economic Research, March.
Blanchard, Olivier J. and Lawrence H. Summers (1987), "Hysteresis in Unemployment," *European Economic Review*, 31(1–2), February–March, pp. 288–95.
Bresser Pereira, Luiz Carlos and Fernando Dall'Acqua (1991), "Economic Populism versus Keynes: Reinterpreting Budget Deficits in Latin America," *Journal of Post Keynesian Economics*, 14(1), Fall, pp. 29–38.
Câmara Neto, Alcino F. and Matias Vernengo (2002), "Uma Releitura Heterodoxa de Bresser e Nakano," *Brazilian Journal of Political Economy*, 22(4), October–December, pp. 152–5.

Câmara Neto, Alcino F. and Matias Vernengo (2004), "Allied, German and Latin Theories of Inflation," in *Contemporary Post Keynesian Analysis*, edited by Mathew Forstater and L. Randall Wray, Cheltenham, UK: Edward Elgar.

Câmara Neto, Alcino F. and Matias Vernengo (2004–2005), "Fiscal Policy and the Washington Consensus," *Journal of Post Keynesian Economics*, 27(1), Winter.

Colander, David (1984), "Was Keynes a Keynesian or a Lernerian?" *Journal of Economic Literature*, 22(4), December, pp. 1572–5.

Damill, Mario, Roberto Frenkel and Luciana Juvenal (2003), "Las Cuentas Públicas y la Crisis de la Convertibilidad en la Argentina," *Desarrollo Económico*, 43(170), July–September, pp. 203–29.

Dornbusch, Rudi and Sebastian Edwards (1990), "Macroeconomic Populism," *Journal of Development Economics*, 32(2), April, pp. 247–77.

Eisner, Robert (1989), "Budget Deficits: Rhetoric and Reality," *Journal of Economic Perspectives*, 3(3), March–May, pp. 73–93.

Erturk, Korkut A. (2003), "On the Changing Nature of Currency Crises," University of Utah, Economics Department Working Papers, No. 2003-02.

Gale, William and Peter Orszag (2003), "Economic Effects of Sustained Budget Deficits," *National Tax Journal*, 56(3), September, pp. 462–85.

Giambiagi, Fabio and Marcio Ronci (2004), "Fiscal Policy and Debt Sustainability: Cardoso's Brazil, 1995–2002," *IMF Working Papers*, No. 156, Policy Development and Review Department, Washington, DC, August.

Godley, Wynne and Francis Cripps (1983), *Macroeconomics*, New York: Oxford University Press.

Gordon, Robert J. (1996), "The Time-Varying NAIRU and its Implications for Economic Policy," *NBER Working Papers*, No. 5735, National Bureau for Economic Research, August.

Grunberg, Isabelle (1998), "Double Jeopardy: Globalization, Liberalization and the Fiscal Squeeze," *World Development*, 26(4), April, pp. 591–605.

Kaldor, Nicholas (1970), "The Case for Regional Policies," in *The Essential Kaldor*, edited by Fernando Targetti and Anthony P. Thirlwall, London: Duckworth, 1989, pp. 311–26.

Kaldor, Nicholas (1976), "Inflation and Recession in the World Economy," in *The Essential Kaldor*, edited by Fernando Targetti and Anthony P. Thirlwall, London: Duckworth, 1989, pp. 516–32.

Lerner, Abba P. (1943), "Functional Finance and the Federal Debt," *Social Research*, Vol. 10, February, pp. 38–51.

Lopreato, Francisco Luiz C. (2002), "Um Olhar sobre a Política Fiscal Recente," *Economia e Sociedade*, 11(2), July–December, pp. 279–304.

Musgrave, Richard A. (1992), "Schumpeter's Crisis of the Tax State," *Journal of Evolutionary Economics*, 2(2), pp. 89–113.

O'Connor, James R. (1973), *The Fiscal Crisis of the State*, New York: St. Martin's Press.

Perry, Guillermo and Ana María Herrera (editors) (1994), *Public Finances, Stabilization and Structural Reform in Latin America*, Washington, DC: Inter-American Development Bank.

Schumpeter, Joseph A. (1918), "The Crisis of the Tax State," *International Economic Papers*, Vol. 4, pp. 5–38, 1954.

Staiger, Douglas, James H. Stock and Mark W. Watson (1997), "The NAIRU,

Unemployment and Monetary policy," *Journal of Economic Perspectives*, 11(1), Winter, pp. 33–50.

Stiglitz, Joseph E. (2003), *The Roaring Nineties: A New History of the World's Most Prosperous Decade*, New York: W.W. Norton.

Taylor, Lance (1998), "Lax Public Sector, Destabilizing Private Sector: Origins of Capital Market Crises," *CEPA Working Paper*, No. 11, Center for Economic Policy Analysis, October.

Toye, John. (2000), "Fiscal Crisis and Fiscal Reform in Latin America," *Cambridge Journal of Economics*, 24(1), January, pp. 21–44.

Vickrey, William S. (1997), "A Trans-Keynesian Manifesto," *Journal of Post Keynesian Economics*, 19(4), Summer, pp. 495–510.

8 Fiscal programming and alternatives in debt management

The Turkish experience

Ebru Voyvoda[1]

Introduction

After more than a decade of external liberalization policies and globalization experience, fiscal policy in developing economies is generally associated with terms like "debt sustainability," "government solvency" and "fiscal crisis." There is a vast literature, both theoretical and empirical, that investigates whether a given level of debt is sustainable and/or whether large and persistent deficits will eventually lead to default.[2] The debt position of the public sector in developing countries is considered to be the major element in constraining persistent growth. Therefore, fiscal policy in these countries is reduced to serious fiscal austerity under the structural adjustment programs, which usually involves large cuts in (non-interest) public expenditures with the aim of achieving "stability."[3]

The conventional wisdom implies that fiscal prudence is correlated to economic growth. Barro (1991), Fischer (1993), Easterly and Rebelo (1993) and in a recent survey Auerbach (2003) argue that high-deficit periods are usually associated with low growth rates and fiscal surplus is generally regarded as a signal of stability. However, a better understanding of the effects of fiscal policy on the economy as a whole depends to a great extent on the sources of public revenue and to the spending patterns of the public sector. This is particularly true in developing countries, where the public sector has traditionally been an engine of growth.[4]

The discussion on fiscal policy is of remarkable importance to the Turkish economy, which has been following the IMF-supervised structural adjustment program known as *Turkey's Program for Transition to a Strong Economy* (TPSE) since 2001 and planned to be operative at least until 2006.[5] TPSE incorporates most of the conventional measures: drastic cuts in public spending, monetary contraction, flexible exchange rate management, reduction in wages as well as reduction in wages for public employment. Nevertheless, the most emphasized goal of the program is the guarantee of long-term sustainability of fiscal policy. Particular importance is attributed to budgetary discipline to attain the pre-determined levels of required primary surpluses. The program targets a primary surplus of more than 6 percent of GDP, every year at least until 2006, with the aim of reducing the public debt stock to 63.9 percent of GDP (90.9 percent at the time of the program's enactment) by the end of that year.

This orthodox fiscal policy package leaves itself open to criticism based on the argument that it focuses solely on austerity measures to correct balance-of-payments (BOP) difficulties. The stabilization policy advice reflects a dogmatic preference for fiscal prudence. It ignores the likely negative implications for economic growth and income distribution. In the case of Turkey, some of the negative effects that have already been observed are the high levels of interest rates on government debt instruments (GDIs), rising unemployment, stagnating fixed investment and falling real wages. Defenders of the program claim that severe cuts in (non-interest) public expenditures would signal a commitment to stability, which will reduce country risk and eliminate the upward pressure on the interest rate, leading to increasing investment and growth. This mechanism, which has recently been identified with the non-conventional phrase *expansionary fiscal contraction*, is expected to give rise to a sustainable growth path, through a process of *reversed crowding-out*. In that sense, one might argue that, the current IMF-led austerity program in Turkey provides a crucial test of the expansionary attributes of such fiscal contraction, and will likely have a major impact on the Fund's credibility as a policy adviser (and as international lender of last resort).[6]

Yet it remains an open question whether the Turkish economy will be able to enact such high degree of contraction in public expenditure, and whether fiscal contraction will be able to generate a sustained growth path. A primary surplus in a highly indebted country, with (domestic) interest payments on the current stock of public debt reaching 22 percent of GDP, implies that the government is actually transferring resources away from the society to the holders of public debt. Further, the imposition of high primary surpluses implies that the fiscal authority has been deprived of any viable funds to sustain its public services on health, education, environmental protection and provision of social infrastructure.[7] Nonetheless, the program has been presented to be the only scientific methodology to attain fiscal sustainability, and massive media propaganda suggests that there are no alternatives.[8]

The purpose of this study is to investigate the theoretical basis of the current fiscal program in Turkey and discuss its relevance in generating expected reductions in real interest rates and aggregate stock of public debt. Presenting the fact that through the liberalization experience in 1990s, the public sector has lost its role in production and accumulation processes of the economy, I shall argue that the current fiscal austerity program is to be considered as a complementary step to further support the functioning of the central budget solely as an income transfer mechanism. Finally, a note on the existence of alternatives for debt management and the need for a careful determination of the merits and dilemmas of each of those alternatives is discussed.

To this end, first a broad overview of the deterioration of the fiscal balances in the Turkish economy throughout the globalization process of 1990s is provided. Next, I discuss some of the key elements in the conventional fiscal sustainability programs and highlight their limitations. Finally, the consequences of the current program on the Turkish economy are discussed along with possible alternatives.

The Turkish experience in the 1990s: deterioration of the fiscal balance and the IMF stabilization program

The structural adjustment program of 1980 marks the start of Turkish integration with the world economy. This initial step was followed by trade liberalization in 1984, the liberalization of the capital account in 1989 and recognition of the full convertibility of the Turkish Lira in 1990. Thus, the Turkish economy has functioned under the conditions of a fully open, globalized economy throughout the 1990s. As in any other developing economy that has gone through these phases of the liberalization/globalization process, the main motives behind the integration with the evolving world financial system were to increase saving, credit supply and investment, attain a reduction in the national interest rate bringing it closer to the international level, and restore growth and stability. Yet, after more than a decade, we observe that the results turned out to be completely opposite to the expectations.

A major consequence of capital account liberalization in developing countries has been greater exposure to speculative attacks and sudden outflows of short-term capital. With the eradication of the government's ability to use independent monetary, exchange rate and interest rate policies as major macro-policy instruments, these economies have been forced into cycles of speculative capital-led growth and trapped with high real interest rates, appreciated currency and persistent balance of payment difficulties.[9] Figure 8.1 displays the growth cycles of the Turkish economy, each boom followed by a bust triggered by major external crises throughout the 1990s.[10]

At a first glance, Figure 8.1 reveals that the Turkish growth experience throughout 1990s has been on a fluctuating trend, starting at 7.9 percent in 1990, decreasing to 1.1 percent in 1991 and even reaching −5.5 percent during the crisis of 1994. Correlated with output fluctuation are the cyclical variations of consumption and investment. The level of public expenditure, that declined 20 percent in 1988 for instance, did not recover until 1996–1997. Further, private investment was not on a sustainable path. The peak of private capital accumulation in 1993 at 38.8 percent was immediately followed by the contraction of 1994, when it plummeted to a rate of −9.6 percent growth. With the exception of year 2000, both public and

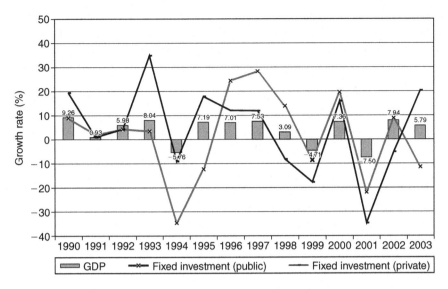

Figure 8.1 Real annual rate of growth (GDP, Fixed Private Investment, Fixed Public Investment), 1990–2003.

private investment have been shrinking with considerably high rates for the last four years. Thus, one can easily agree that the overall expansion of both private and public capital accumulation could not be sustained throughout the 1990s.

Such observations have been concurrent with the deteriorating fiscal panorama of the Turkish economy throughout the decade. As a sign of vulnerability, the public sector borrowing requirement (PSBR) stood around 10 percent on average between 1990 and 1999 and continued to rise thereafter reaching to 16.4 percent in 2001. The explanation is that, while government revenues increased to 24.2 percent of GDP in 1999 from an initial level of 14.2 percent of GDP in 1990, the ratio of public expenditures rose to 35.9 percent from a level of 17.2 percent during the same period. Nevertheless, with the advent of full-fledged financial liberalization, the government had the opportunity of bypassing much of its liquidity constraint problems. The circumstances of the world economy implied that international finance was repressed, and financing of the PSBR relied exclusively on the issues of GDIs to the internal market – especially to the domestic banking sector. In 1989, just before the liberalization of the capital account was completed, domestic debt was only 6 percent of GDP. It then grew rapidly and had reached 29.3 percent of GDP by 1999 and to 54.8 percent by 2002. Meanwhile, interest payments on the outstanding debt stock became progressively the largest item on the expenditure side of the public accounts. The real interest rate on GDIs remained above

20 percent during the decade. Fiscal authorities were trapped to such extent that the targeted expenditures on interest on outstanding debt could not be controlled by the end of the decade. As a ratio to GDP, interest payments on outstanding (domestic) debt reached to 18.8 percent in 2002. Table 8.1 depicts a summary of the deterioration of the fiscal balances throughout the 1990s.

Soon the public sector was caught in a *Ponzi-finance* scheme, concerned uniquely with short-term management of debt.[11] In this regard, the central budget lost its instrumental role in the development of social infrastructure and the achievement of long-term growth. Budgeting has rather become trapped by the dictates of debt-rollover under a borrowing scheme with very high interest rates. In this vein, the fiscal debt management not only acted as an income transfer mechanism to rentier classes, but it has also significantly constrained the social role of the state. The share of public investment on education in government's consolidated budget decreased from its level of 13.2 percent in 1990 to 7.9 percent in 1999, while the share of interest payments increased to 56.6 percent from 24.6 percent in the same period.

It would be extraordinary if investment could actually increase in the context of this structural adjustment program. High rates of interest have attracted short-term foreign capital into the Turkish economic system. Such inflows, on the one hand, enabled financing of the accelerated expenditures of the public sector, and also provided a relaxation of the items of aggregate demand, reducing cost of imports and enlarging the volume of consumption. However, the simultaneous appreciation of the Lira and the rising current-account deficits signaled and sudden drainage of the funds brought the end of each of these mini growth cycles.

In sum, the post-1990 liberalization period signals an environment where accumulation, distribution and growth patterns depend exclusively on the movements of speculative, short-term capital, stimulated by a combination of high real interest rates and an appreciated Lira. This macro policy mix means that the pressure on PSBR has experienced short-term relief, but the economy has become addicted to short-term foreign finance to generate growth. Figure 8.2 depicts the financial arbitrage that the Turkish economy has been offering to the world financial markets since mid-1992. As the figure reveals, in order to sustain the economic performance, Turkey had to offer real interest rates as high as 100 percent in January 1996, 60 percent in December 1998 and 80 percent in March 2001.

After a decade of volatile growth, persistently high rates of inflation, deteriorated fiscal performance, and rapidly increasing debt burden, Turkey initiated the last round of the continuous chain of stabilization attempts in December 1999. Closely backed and supervised by the IMF, the program utterly relied on a nominally pegged exchange rate system for disinflation and a targeted set of austerity measures and structural reforms to restore fiscal balance. Yet, just eleven months after launching the

Table 8.1 Deterioration in fiscal balances, Turkey (1990–2003)

	1990	1995	1999	2000	2001	2002	2003
As a ratio to GNP (%)							
Current account balance	-1.7	-1.4	-0.7	-4.8	2.4	-1.0	-2.9
Public disposable income	13.4	9.6	6.7	7.8	3.4	6.5	7.0
Public savings	3.4	0.1	-6.6	-4.6	-9.7	-6.2	-5.4
Public investment	8.6	3.8	6.6	6.9	5.6	6.3	4.5
Public Sector Borrowing Requirement (PSBR)	7.4	5.0	15.5	11.8	16.4	12.8	8.7
Budget balance	-3.0	-4.0	-11.9	-10.6	-16.2	-14.3	-11.2
Outstanding debt							
Domestic	14.4	17.3	29.3	29.0	69.2	54.8	56.4
Foreign	25.6	29.9	27.6	30.4	48.6	42.6	27.0
Interest expenditures on the Accumulated Stock of Domestic Debt	2.5	6.0	12.7	15.0	22.2	18.8	14.8
Non-interest government expenditures	13.7	21.8	22.4	20.9	22.0	23.3	22.8
Macroeconomic prices							
Annual inflation rate (WPI)[a]	48.6	64.9	66.5	32.1	88.1	31.2	13.9
Nominal depreciation of the TL/US$	22.9	53.5	61.0	23.2	114.2	9.4	-9.8
Nominal interest rate on GDIs[b]	52.8	124.2	100.9	34.7	98.5	64.9	44.4
Share in consolidated budget (%)							
Health	4.7	3.3	4.1	2.5	2.3	2.7	3.5
Education	13.2	10.2	7.9	7.2	6.4	7.6	9.7
Interest payment on debt	24.6	40.8	56.6	61.3	79.8	67.9	64.7

Sources: SPO Main Economic Indicators; Undersecretariat of Foreign Trade and Treasury Main Economic Indicators.

Notes
a Change in whole sale prices, end-of-year values.
b Weighted average of interest on government debt instruments (GDIs).

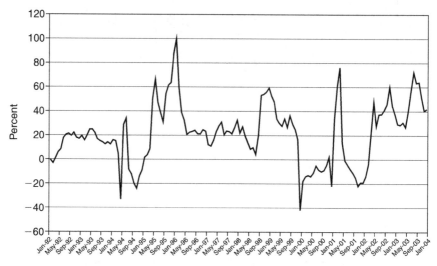

Figure 8.2 Speculative arbitrage on interest rate and depreciation (source: Figure 2, Yeldan (2004)).

Note

* This financial arbitrage can be calculated as the end result of an operation that converts initially the foreign exchange into Turkish Liras at the rate e, and after earning the rate of interest R offered in the domestic asset markets, is re-converted back to the foreign currency at the prevailing foreign exchange rate.

Algebraically, this net arbitrage gain is calculated as

$$\left[\frac{1+R}{1+\varepsilon} - 1 \right] \times 100 \text{ where } \varepsilon \text{ is the depreciation rate}$$

program, Turkey went through the first sign of a severe financial crisis in November 2000 and experienced the major strike in February 2001. Government soon surrendered, floated the exchange rate and effectively declared the end of the program. The stock market and the Lira went into a downward spiral and GDP shrank by 7.6 percent in 2001, the worst performance of the Turkish economy since Word War II, leading to increasing unemployment.[12]

In response to the crisis, and in order to reinvigorate the now-stalled free market reforms, a new *Stand-by* agreement was signed with the IMF. The 2001 TPSE incorporates a whole set of issues concerning the financial sector, the public sector, agriculture and social security, yet the main motivation behind the agreement has been the reduction of fiscal repression in the commodity and asset markets. This in turn, is claimed to be the result of high cost of servicing of public debt, whose net value reached 90.9 percent of GDP in 2001. Thus, the program primarily aimed at providing a signal of confidence to the domestic and international community, suggesting that the Turkish fiscal authorities have achieved the proper mix of stabilization measures. The primary surplus is identified as the crucial indicator of this confidence game. According to the program's offi-cially stated rationale, as the non-interest expenditures of the public sector are reduced and the primary-surplus target of 6.5 percent of GDP is attained, the real interest rate would fall, private consumption and investment would be stimulated and growth would be fuelled. In the meantime, projections by the fiscal authority forecast a reduction in the outstanding net stock of debt as a ratio to GDP. Specifically, the formally stated targets are 69.4 percent of GDP for 2004 and 63.9 percent of GDP for 2006.

However, the foreign debt of the public sector has reached $63.4 billion by the end of 2003 and the public domestic debt is recorded to be $133.3 billion at the same time. These figures were $56.8 billion and $91.7 billion respectively in 2002. Besides, interest costs on debt continue to impose a significant burden under the new program. A comparison of the interest costs as a ratio to aggregate tax revenues shows the evident anomaly in the Turkish fiscal planning exercise: interest expenditures as a ratio to tax rev-enues were recorded to be 103.7 percent in 2001 and 77.1 percent in 2002. Under the crisis management targets, interest expenditures were fixed as 88.1 percent of the tax revenue in 2000 and 109 percent in 2001. In 2004, it is anticipated that the target of interest expenditures will reach to 74.3 percent of the total tax revenue.

All in all, it seems that while the public sector has committed to a fiscal policy of facilitating a smooth roll-over of the government's debt through primary fiscal surpluses, it fails to suggest any realistic measure and decrease the burden of interest expenditures on the public disposable income. This seems to result from a lack of understanding with regard to debt dynamics. Therefore, it becomes important to discuss the concept of fiscal sustainability, the theoretical basis and the relevant elements of the conventional fiscal programming model, currently applied in Turkey as well as a sizeable number of developing economies under the auspices of the IMF. This discussion is also important to elaborate on fiscal policy alternatives of which would allow more rational debt management, public expenditure on infrastructure, investment patterns and growth.

The IMF's conventional vision of fiscal sustainability and solvency

The theoretical literature emphasizes the intertemporal budget constraint as well as the flow budget constraint of the government and focus on fiscal policy alternatives differentiating the ones that can be continued into distant future without threatening government solvency. Yet, on the level of empirical policy analysis, the term fiscal sustainability remains highly controversial and the controversy reveals itself in the various studies where each author develops its own definition of fiscal sustainability and derives conclusions accordingly.

The analytical dimension starts with a current period flow budget constraint of the government. In its simplest form, for a closed economy that is exempt from monetary treatment, this constraint can be written as:

$$B_{t+1} = (1 + r_t)B_t + D_t \tag{1}$$

where B_t is the outstanding debt stock, r_t is the interest rate in the current period on the accumulated stock of debt, and D_t is the deficit (current period expenditures net of the current period revenues of the government). The current debt stock can be written

$$B_t = -\sum_{j=0}^{\infty} \frac{1}{\prod_{k=0}^{j}(1 + r_{t+k})} D_{t+j} + \lim_{T \to \infty} \frac{1}{\prod_{k=0}^{T}(1 + r_{t+k})} B_{t+T+1} \tag{2}$$

According to Equation (2), it is possible for the government to rollover its debt each period in full, borrowing continuously to cover both the principal and the interest payments. Under those conditions the present value of the terminal debt stock (second term in Equation (2)) becomes positive. However, the only way for the government to run this Ponzi debt scheme is that at least one of the lenders in the economy runs a Ponzi credit scheme. However, under the conventional theory, this would violate the necessary transversality condition in the lender's optimization problem. So, a government attempting to play a Ponzi game will not find any rational individual willing to hold its liabilities. Therefore, a sustainable fiscal policy implies that the current value of debt stock, B_t, equates to the present value of the future primary surpluses.[13]

However, given the analytical properties of the present value budget constraint (PVBC) approach, the policy implications derived turn out to be quite impractical. The PVBC does not rule out either large deficits or high debt-to-GDP ratios; it simply constrains the government debt to grow no faster than the interest rate in the economy. So, for instance, a growing economy with a relatively low interest rate, the debt stock could be tending to zero asymptotically, but would still be regarded as unsustainable. Moreover, permanent primary deficits are incompatible whereas permanent overall deficits are compatible with the PVBC.[14] Moreover, there are far too many ways in which fiscal policies can comply with a budget constraint encompassing infinite periods, and for practical purposes the PVBC approach turns out to be not that useful.

Thus, rather than using the *impractical* PVBC approach, policy advisers rely mostly on methods that depend on practical indicators and usually set a constant debt-to-GDP ratio as a benchmark state for sustainable fiscal policies. It is then, frequently the primary deficit (surplus) that is used as the key macroeconomic policy variable indicating a sustainable fiscal policy. If the primary target generates a constant, rather than ever increasing debt-to-GDP ratio, given the projection on the real interest rate and the growth rate of the economy, then debt is considered sustainable. For its exclusive reliance on a limited set of macroeconomic indicators, the method is referred to as the "accounting approach."

It is a broad version of this accounting approach that is followed by the IMF, in gauging whether a fiscal position is sustainable. The following steps are taken sequentially:[15] (i) based on the macro-data of the country under consideration, a projection with a five-year horizon is made assuming that the current fiscal policy is continued; this is regarded as the benchmark scenario; (ii) from this projection, debt dynamics are generated and sustainability is assessed; it is possible that different criteria are used for sustainability, but an increasing debt ratio is regarded as a cause for concern; (iii) if the debt dynamics are indicated as unsustainable, an alternative scenario is prepared, making necessary corrections on fiscal policy variables which will typically define a stable path over the medium-term. Attention is usually focused on the adjustment of the primary balance required to meet the debt target and the fiscal measure that can generate the adjustment.

Equation (3) is a specific version of this accounting approach used by the Turkish fiscal authority on the Public Debt Management Report, as reported by the Undersecretariat of Treasury, February 2004.

$$b_t = d_t - m_t - pri_t + \left[\frac{(1 + r_t^d)}{(1 + g_t)} \right] b_{t-1}^d + \left[\frac{(1 + r_t^f)}{(1 + g_t)} \right] (1 + \Delta rer_t) b_{t-1}^f \qquad (3)$$

where b_t gives the ratio of the net stock of public debt to GDP, b_t^d representing the domestic, b_t^f representing its foreign components. d_t stands for the primary deficit as a ratio to GDP, r_t^d gives the interest rate on the Turkish Lira denominated and r_t^f gives the real interest rate on the foreign currency denominated portion of the public debt; m_t and pri_t represent seigniorage and privatization revenues, respectively; g_t is the real growth rate of the economy and Δrer_t is the change in the real exchange rate (*TL/$*). According to Equation (3), given the projection on revenues from seigniorage and privatization, the debt-to-GDP ratio, b_t, will be lower; (i) the lower the real interest rates, r_t^d and r_t^f, (ii) the higher the growth rate, g_t, of the economy, (iii) the greater the appreciation of the real exchange rate.

Based for the most part on a version of Equation (3), many researchers and financial rating agencies routinely conduct a series of programming exercises to monitor the Turkish fiscal sustainability and its debt burden in the short-to-medium run.[16] However, as observed in Equation (3), in an open economy subject to inflationary pressures, with a floating exchange rate regime, and with the interest rate determined by international market conditions, the only policy tool left for the government to control the pace of debt-rollover is the primary surplus. However, note that the stock of public debt for the next period as a ratio to GDP, b_t is still endogenous since the growth rate of the economy is endogenous and the international market determines the values of the real exchange rate and the expenditure on interest payments.[17]

Thus, such exercises are doomed to be restricted to a partial-adjustment framework, and often do not go beyond an accounting check between the projected real rate of growth of GDP, the interest rate, the exchange rate and the primary surplus ratio. In fact, the crucial critique of this partial adjustment framework is that they take no account of the general-equilibrium effects of the fiscal policy itself on the macroeconomy at large, through interest rates, saving–investment gap, and the current account balance. To analyze such effects, one would ideally use an economic model that explicitly relates the fiscal policy variables to (presumably) endogenous variables such as the interest rate, wages, production, private and public expenditures on consumption and investment and the foreign trade.

Agénor (2001) further summarizes the limitations of this accounting approach: (i) the *a priori* assumption that a sustainable fiscal policy should maintain the debt-to-GDP ratio constant or decreasing is arbitrary, (ii) the framework lacks a simultaneous determination of the crucial variables it depends on, (iii) the framework focuses on a static flow-budget constraint based on a limited set of macro-variables without checking for their joint feasibility. Furthermore, the approach does not consider any effects of the possible reduction in public expenditure on social infrastructure, education and health on the growth performance and the income distribution of the economy as a whole, (iv) the lender's role and its effects are not explicit.

Public sector performance under the program

One may very well ask what have been the effects of the IMF program based on the accounting approach described above. Table 8.2 summarizes the basic macroeconomic targets and the key macroeconomic prices generated via the application of Equation (3) to the Turkish macroeconomy, under the projected values for the variables that take place in the equation. Table 8.3, on the other hand, depicts the key variables of fiscal balances and dynamics of debt under the fiscal programming environment of 2001–2003. At a first glance, what is the most striking about Table 8.2 is that the program aims to reduce inflation to 12 percent in 2004 and 8 percent in 2005. Yet, the program also foresees an *ex-ante* nominal interest rate of 32.4 percent for 2004 and 27.4 percent for 2005, which solve for *ex-ante* real interest rates of 18.2 percent for 2004 and 18 percent for 2005 and 2006. In other words, the program *targets* that the Turkish economy will be working with very high real interest rates in the upcoming years. In fact, the realized real rate of interest on GDIs during the successful implementation of the program remained considerably high and did not display any tendency to fall. Table 8.3 indicates that the level of the real interest rate stood around an average of 22 percent during 2001–2003. In that sense, the fiscal austerity

Table 8.2 The IMF program: macro variables and price targets

	2001	*2002*	*2003*	*2004*	*2005*	*2006*
Macro variables						
GNP growth rate	−8.5	3.0	5.0	5.0	5.0	5.0
Public sector primary balance	5.7	6.5	6.5	6.5	6.5	6.3
Debt stock of the public sector/ GNP (%)	92.2	81.3	73.3	69.4	66.5	63.9
Macro Prices						
Inflation	68.5	35.0	20.0	12.0	8.0	5.0
Nominal interest rate on domestic debt	99.7	69.9	46.0	32.4	27.4	23.9
Ex-ante real interest rate on domestic debt	18.5	25.6	21.7	18.2	18.0	18.0

Source: Report on Public Debt Management, Undersecretariat of Treasury, April 2003.

Table 8.3 Fiscal balances and dynamics of debt under the program (2001–2003)

	2001	*2002*	*2003*
Real rate of growth (%)			
GNP	−7.6	7.8	5.8
Public consumption	−8.6	5.4	−2.4
Public investment	−22.0	14.5	−11.5
Inflation (%)	68.5	29.7	18.4
Real interest rate on GDI's* (%)	18.5	25.6	21.7
Debt dynamics			
Public sector total debt stock ($ billion)	123.58	148.49	202.71
Domestic	84.86	91.69	139.26
Foreign	38.73	56.80	66.36
Total net public debt/GNP	90.90	78.60	70.50
Domestic debt/GNP	52.80	46.20	48.30
Foreign debt/GNP	38.20	32.40	22.20
Composition of public debt (%)			
Domestic	68.66	61.75	68.70
Foreign	31.34	38.25	32.74
As a ratio to the GNP (%)			
Budget Balance	−16.2	−14.3	−11.2
Consolidated budget interest costs	23.0	19.0	16.0
PSBR	16.4	12.6	8.7
Primary surplus/GNP	6.8	4.3	5.3

Sources: SPO Main Economic Indicators; Undersecretariat of Foreign Trade and Treasury Main Economic Indicators.

Note
*Weighted average of annual interest on government debt instruments (GDIs) deflated by WPI

program may have been successful in transforming Turkey into one of the foremost emerging markets, but it is definitely not decreasing the premium that the Turkish economy has been transferring to the world financial markets and furthermore, it does not suggest any realistic measures to decrease the burden of interest spending on the public disposable income.

Table 8.4 further provides the repayment schedule for public foreign debt, discriminating the total and the portion that is to be paid to the IMF. Accordingly, the total cost of borrowing from the IMF in terms of capital repayments and interest costs reached $11.1 billion between 1999 and 2003. Total repayment of public foreign debt is planned to reach $48.5 billion, and $25.2 billion are programmed to be paid to the IMF between 2005 and 2008.

Turkey is planning to face this debt burden via drastic cuts in the non-interest fiscal expenditures, thereby maintaining a primary surplus that reaches 6.5 percent of GNP for the public sector as a whole. In order to reach this courageous objective together with the objectives with respect to the ratios of debt stock to GNP, it is stated in a series of *Letters of Intent* to the IMF that the nominal rate of increase in non-interest fiscal expenditures will be bounded by the nominal rate of growth of GNP. Yet, no significant reduction in the debt burden has been observed. According to our view, with a schedule of repayment on the foreign portion of the public debt as in Table 8.4, it gives no sign of serious reduction in the near future. Rather, a more close attention to Table 8.3 will indicate that the Turkish fiscal authority has been continuing to finance its repayments in foreign debt by more reliance on financing options from the internal market. The share of domestic component of public debt was 68.66 percent in the crisis year of 2001. Although it decreased to 61.75 percent in 2002, it increased back to 68.7 percent in 2003. As a ratio to GNP, public domestic debt increased to 48.3 percent in 2003 from its level of 46.2 percent in 2002, while in the same period ratio of public sector foreign debt stock to GNP ratio decreased by 10 percent.[18]

Further inspection of current macroeconomic conditions under the austerity program reveals ever-worsening balance-of-payments statistics as

Table 8.4 Schedule on repayments of foreign debt (billion dollars)

	2005	2006	2007	2008
Repayments on total foreign debt				
Capital	10.4	15.8	6.2	5.7
Interest	3.5	2.8	2.3	1.8
Total	13.9	18.6	8.5	7.5
Repayments to the IMF				
Capital	7.5	10.9	0.62	
Interest	0.63	0.21	0.08	
Total	8.13	11.11	0.7	

Source: Report on Public Debt Management, Undersecretariat of Treasury, February 2004.

a reflection of the exchange rate appreciation, which is needed to secure the inflows of foreign capital on which the whole growth performance of the economy depends. In 2003, the finance account of the BOP displayed a surplus of $5.9 billion. In contrast, the same account showed a surplus of $1.2 billion in 2002. If the unrecorded foreign-exchange funds of $4.9 billion, which are displayed under the "net errors and omissions" column in the formal accounts, we reach a total sum of $10.8 billion of liquid flows into the Turkish economic system in 2003. The magnitude is on the tenfold order of magnitude compared to 2002, and obviously reveals the scenario behind the much-celebrated growth performance in 2003 and the fragility behind the sources of Turkish growth. The current-account deficit as a ratio to GNP reached 2.9 percent in 2003. It further widened by $5 billion over the first three months of 2004. Instrumental behind this deficit is the surge in the trade deficit, which ran up to more than $5.1 billion over the same period. As the rapid growth in current-account deficit in 2003 continues in 2004, the vulnerability of the Turkish economy keeps increasing, threatening both the objective of debt rollover and the objective of achieving favorable growth rates.

The IMF-led austerity program seems to be successful in achieving its target of creating a budget with a primary surplus, but the success has come at a heavy cost in terms of public services forgone. In the first five months of 2004, interest payments on public debt constituted 77 percent of total tax revenues. The Turkish macro-episode during the course of the program indicates that the room for maneuver in policymaking and public service provision has been severely curtailed, and that the economy has basically been left to the interest of foreign capital in achieving its debt rollover.

Concluding remarks

This study attempts to show that the current consensus that developing economies should maintain high primary surplus-to-GNP ratios cannot be considered as the only scientific alternative for constructing successful fiscal policies. Making use of the Turkish experience under the structural adjustment program, it is possible to show that a fiscal policy that depends solely on attaining pre-determined levels of necessary primary surpluses may be unable to achieve a successful debt rollover together with generating a sustained growth path. The theoretical dimension of the program depends on an accounting-exercise framework, which does not go beyond a partial check amongst a limited set of macro-variables of the economy. In this sense, it neither answers the question of how the economy, under conditions of fiscal repression, will be able to generate plausible rates of growth nor does it takes into account the adverse effect on the economy's potential to generate growth through its constrained transfers of public social spending.

Yet, the macro and fiscal balances of the Turkish economy during the successful implementation of the program disclose that the primary surplus cannot be the only variable to achieve a set of targets that are dependent on a number of macro-variables whose values are determined by the dynamics of the economy. Such observations highlight the importance of building up a model framework, which accounts for stock-flow interactions, and which describes production, public and private-sector expenditures on consumption and investment, savings and asset accumulation, interest rate determination, foreign-sector and fiscal balances, as well as debt dynamics. In a series of studies that are utilizing a general equilibrium framework, Voyvoda and Yeldan (2003, 2004) investigate the effects of the current IMF-led austerity program for the Turkish economy. These studies also assess fiscal policy alternatives of debt management, of public expenditures on the productive factors of the economy, and of economic growth and the welfare of future generations. Constructed under a range of settings, it has been possible to show that the program targets are relatively sensitive to (exogenous) growth shocks, and although the current fiscal program based on the primary-surplus objective succeeds in constraining the explosive dynamics of debt accumulation, the path of aggregate public debt as a ratio to GNP displays a significant degree of inertia and would be brought down only gradually and slowly. A similar result has been highlighted by Agénor *et al.* (2004). Furthermore, taking into consideration the effects of fiscal policy on the determination of the level of strategic macro-variables in the economy at large, it is possible to show that policies of fiscal austerity are fraught with serious tradeoffs between growth and fiscal targets. Such results call for further analysis of fiscal reform to secure that the domestic risk premium falls and interest rates come down. According to Voyvoda and Yeldan (2004), alternative public expenditure programs based on various (compound) taxation schemes, and with the objective of recovering public funds for education and for social infrastructure, are likely to produce superior results.

Notes

1   I am grateful to Erinç Yeldan for his contributions to developing the ideas in this study. I also benefited from discussions with the participants of the HESA Lecture in Department of Economics, University of Utah. I thank all for their valuable suggestions and comments. All usual caveats, of course, do apply.

2   This literature also extends into the context of developed economies. Among the recent studies that discuss the fiscal sustainability in the United States are Trehan and Walsh (1991), and Hakkio and Rush (1991). Chalk and Hemming (2000) focus on fiscal sustainability in the OECD countries and come up with rather mixed results. After the much debated "Stability and Growth Pact" and "Maastricht Treaty," which fix the maximum reference values for the public deficit and the public debt, the budget discipline in the European Union and its candidate countries has been a matter of increasing concern. See Buti, Franco and Ongena (1998), Arestis and Sawyer (this volume) and Buiter and Grafe (2002) for a discussion. The circumstances of fiscal policy in developing countries, not surprisingly, have received the highest attention from both academia and the international organizations such as the International Monetary Fund

(IMF) and the World Bank. A few to mention are Buiter and Patel (1997) on India, Gerson and Nellor (1997) on the Philippines and Agénor (2001) on Ghana and Turkey.

3 Structural adjustment program has recently become a rather fashionable term to describe these liberalization *cum* stabilization packages sponsored by the IMF.

4 Miller and Russek (1997) find that in general, debt-financed expenditures do not appear to affect growth, whereas the portion allocated to re-generation of productive factors, such as education, has a positive sign. Mendoza, Milesi-Feretti, and Asea (1997) report that the effects of revenue increases of the public sector on growth depend on the way that they are financed. In their study, capital income taxation has a positive effect on the growth rate whereas labor income taxation has a negative effect. See Ahn and Hemmings (2000) for a recent survey of the effect of fiscal policy on economic growth.

5 At the time of writing (June 2004), the government authorities were deliberating on a new three-year *Stand-by* agreement to reallocate the portion of foreign debt held by the IMF, to be put in operation after 2005.

6 The amount of IMF funds that have been officially approved for assistance to Turkish economy between 1999 and 2004 is $31.9 billion, of which $29.2 billion have been realized. Of the total amount of $20.4 billion until year 2003, $13.3 billion were used by the Treasury in budgetary finance of its domestic debt management.

7 Grunberg (1998) elaborates more on the transfer of welfare from the most needy stratums of society to wealthier classes, and by this mechanism, government's inability to perform its social duties.

8 See, e.g., the *Public Debt Management Report* by the Undersecretariat of Treasury, February 2004.

9 Adelman and Yeldan (2000) discuss the elimination of independent macroeconomic policies under external liberalization. Grabel (1995) shows that the growth performance of developing economies tends more and more to follow speculation-led patterns. In the context of the Turkish economy, Yeldan (2004); Boratav, Yeldan and Köse (2000), and Ekinci (1998) discuss how the central bank lost its control over the exchange rate and the interest rate policies, and how these variables effectively turned into *exogenous* parameters, usually set under the chaotic conditions of international finance capital.

10 Note the "coincidence" of each boom turning into a negative growth with major external crises: Mexico in 1994; Russia and Brazil in 1998–1999; Argentina in 2001.

11 See Akyüz and Boratav (2002); Boratav, Yeldan and Köse (2002); Ertuğrul and Selçuk (2001); Metin-Özcan, Voyvoda and Yeldan (2001), and Cizre-Sakallığlu and Yeldan (2000) for a thorough overview of the post-1990 Turkish macroeconomic history. For the deterioration of fiscal balances refer to San (2002); Özatay (2000); Türel (1999), and Selçuk and Rantanen (1996).

12 The underlying elements of the disinflation program and the crisis are discussed in detail in Akyüz and Boratav (2002); Alper and Öniş (2003); Ertuğrul and Yeldan (2003); Ertuğrul and Selçuk (2002), and Yeldan (2002).

13 Or, in more formal terms, the second term in Equation (2) tends to zero in the limit.

14 See for instance, Perotti, Strauch and von Hagen (1997) on this issue.

15 See, e.g., Chalk and Hemming (2000) and Agénor and Montiel (1999, chapter 13). The IMF's official programming model, known as the "Polak model," has recently celebrated its fortieth anniversary. See Polak (1997).

16 In one such study, Agénor (2001) reports that with an output growth rate of 5 percent, a real interest rate of 12 percent, and an inflation rate of 5 percent, a primary surplus of 3.5 percent of GNP would be needed to stabilize the Turkish

debt-to-GNP ratio at 60 percent. More recently, Keyder (2003) carried out a similar exercise and, using detailed fiscal data, concluded that Turkey's debt would come out to be sustainable on the condition that the real interest rate be reduced to 15 percent or less. Noting that at the time of her writing (March, 2003), the weighted-average real interest rate was around 25 percent, Keyder recommended strict continuation of the austerity policies programmed. In addition, various financial institutions and rating agencies carried out similar exercises almost on a monthly basis in their close monitoring of the Turkish fiscal stance. In those exercises, various combinations of low and high rates of growth and real interest rates are contrasted to a "plausible" benchmark scenario, and the resultant debt-to-GNP ratio is reported. See also IMF (2000), and World Bank (2000).

17 See Vernengo (this volume) for more on the endogeneity of fiscal crises in open economies.

18 Note that in 2003, the Lira has appreciated by some 9.8 percent against the US dollar, while the CPI inflation has been 13.9 percent. The nominal appreciation of the Turkish Lira has created the illusion that the ratio of foreign debt to GNP has fallen significantly. Any "corrective" depreciation of the Lira in the short-to-medium run would however propel this ratio toward much higher levels, and thus reveal the true nature of the Turkish foreign-debt dynamics.

References

Adelman, Irma and Yeldan, Erinc (2000), "Is this the End of Economic Development?" *Structural Change and Economic Dynamics*, 11(1–2), July, pp. 95–109.

Agénor, Pierre-Richard (2001), "Fiscal Policy, Public Debt Sustainability, and Solvency," Lecture notes, World Bank, available online at: www1.worldbank.org/wbiep/macro-program/agenor/agenor_lectures.htm.

Agénor, Pierre-Richard and Peter J. Montiel (1999), *Development Macroeconomics*, Second edition, Princeton, New Jersey: Princeton University Press.

Agénor, Pierre-Richard, H. Jensen, M. Vergis and Erinc Yeldan (2004), "Disinflation, Fiscal Sustainability, and Labor Market Adjustment in Turkey," processed.

Ahn, Sanghoon and Philip Hemmings (2000), "Policy Influences on Economic Growth in OECD Countries: an Evaluation of Evidence," OECD Economics Department Working Papers, No. 246, June.

Akyüz, Yılmaz and Boratav, Korkut (2002), "The Making of the Turkish Crisis," UNCTAD, Geneva, available online at: www.bagimsizsosyalbilimciler.org/yazilar/AkyuzBoratav.htm.

Alper, C. Emre and Ziya Öniş (2003), "Emerging Market Crises and the IMF: Rethinking the Role of the IMF in the Light of Turkey's 2000–2001 Financial Crises," *Canadian Journal of Development Studies*, 24(2), pp. 255–72.

Auerbach, Alan (2003), "Fiscal Policy, Past and Present," *NBER Working Papers*, No. 10023, October.

Barro, Robert J. (1991), "Economic Growth in a Cross Section of Countries," *Quarterly Journal of Economics*, 106(2), May, pp. 407–43.

Boratav, Korkut; Erinc Yeldan and Ahmet Köse (2002), "Globalization, Distribution and Social Policy: Turkey: 1980–1998," in *External Liberalization and Social Policy*, edited by Lance Taylor, London and New York: Oxford University Press.

Buiter, Willem H. and Clemens Grafe (2002), "Reforming EMU's Fiscal Policy

Rules: Some Suggestions for Enhancing Fiscal Sustainability and Macro-economic Stability in an Enlarged EU," processed.

Buiter, Willem H. and Urjit R. Patel (1992), "Debt, Deficits and Inflation: An Application to the Public Finances of India," *Journal of Public Economics*, 47(2), March, pp. 171–205.

Buti, Marco, Daniele Franco and Hedwig Ongena (1998), "Fiscal Discipline and Flexibility in the EMU," *Oxford Review of Economic Policy*, 14(3), Autumn, pp. 81–97.

Chalk, Nigel and Richard Hemming (2000), "Assessing Fiscal Sustainability in Theory and Practice," International Monetary Fund Working Papers, WP/00/81, April.

Cizre-Sakallıoğlu, Ümit and Erinc Yeldan (2000), "Politics, Society and Financial Liberalization: Turkey in the 1990s," *Development and Change*, 31(1), March, pp. 481–508.

Easterly, William and Sergio Rebelo (1993), "Fiscal Policy and Economic Growth: an Empirical Investigation," *Journal of Monetary Economics*, 32(3), December, pp. 417–58.

Ekinci, Nazim K. (1998), "Türkiye Ekonomisinde Gelişmenin Dinamikleri ve Kriz," *Toplum ve Bilim*, Vol. 77, pp. 7–27.

Ertuğrul, Ahmet and Faruk Selçuk (2001), "A Brief History of the Turkish Economy, 1990–2000," *Russian and East European Finance and Trade*, 37(6), November–December, pp. 6–30.

Ertuğrul, Ahmet and Faruk Selçuk (2002), "Turkish Economy: 1980–2001" in *Inflation and Disinflation in Turkey*, edited by Aykut Kibritcioglu, Libby Rittenberg and Faruk Selçuk, Aldershot, UK: Ashgate.

Ertuğrul, Ahmet and Erinc Yeldan (2003), "On the Structural Weaknesses of the Post-1999 Turkish Disinflation Program," *Turkish Studies Quarterly*, 4(2), pp. 53–67.

Fischer, Stanley (1993), "The Role of Macroeconomic Factors in Growth," *Journal of Monetary Economics*, 32(3), December, pp. 485–512.

Gerson, Philip and David C.N. Nellor (1997), "Philippine Fiscal Policy: Sustainability, Growth and Savings" in *Macroeconomic Issues Facing ASEAN Countries*, edited by John Hicklin, David Robinson and Anoop Singh, Washington, DC: International Monetary Fund.

Grabel, Ilene (1995), "Speculation-Led Economic Development: A Post-Keynesian Interpretation of Financial Liberalization Programmes in The Third World," *International Review of Applied Economics*, 9(2), pp. 127–49.

Grunberg, Isabelle (1998), "Double Jeopardy: Globalization, Liberalization and the Fiscal Squeeze," *World Development*, 26(4), April, pp. 591–605.

Hakkio, Craig S. and Mark Rush (1991), "Is the Budget Deficit Too Large?," *Economic Inquiry*, 29(3), July, pp. 429–45.

International Monetary Fund (2000), *Turkey: Selected Issues and Statistical Appendix*, Country Report No. 00/14, Washington, DC: International Monetary Fund, February.

Mendoza Enrique G., Gian Maria Milesi-Ferretti and Patrick Asea (1997), "On the Effectiveness of Tax Policy in Altering Long-Run Growth," *Journal of Public Economics*, 66(1), October, pp. 99–126.

Metin-Özcan, Kivilcim, Ebru Voyvoda and Erinc Yeldan (2001), "Dynamics of Macroeconomic Adjustment in a Globalized Developing Economy: Growth,

Accumulation and Distribution, Turkey 1969–1998," *Canadian Journal of Development Studies* 22(1), 219–53.

Miller, Stephen M. and Frank S. Russek (1997), "Fiscal Structures and Economic Growth at the State and Local Level," *Public Finance Review*, 25(2), March, pp. 213–37.

Özatay, Fatih (2000), "The 1994 Currency Crisis in Turkey," *Journal of Policy Reform*, 3(4), pp. 327–52.

Perotti, Roberto, Rolf Strauch and Jurgen von Hagen (1997), "Sustainability of Public Finances," Centre for Economic Policy Research, CEPR Discussion Papers, No. 1781, November.

Polak, Jacques J. (1997), "The IMF Monetary Model at Forty," IMF Working Papers, WP/97/49, Washington, D.C.: International Monetary Fund, April.

San, E. (2002), *Sustainability of Fiscal Policy: The Case of Turkey*, Unpublished MS Thesis, Middle East Technical University.

Selçuk, Faruk and Anjaritta Rantanen (1996), *Türkiye'de Kamu Harcamaları ve İç Borç Stoku Üzerine Gözlemler ve Mali Disiplin Üzerine Öneriler*, İstanbul, TUSIAD Publications.

Trehan, Barat and Carl E. Walsh (1991), "Testing Intertemporal Budget Constraint: Theory and Applications to U.S. Federal Budget and Current Account Deficits," *Journal of Money, Credit and Banking*, 23(2), May, pp. 206–23.

Türel, Oktar (1999), "Restructuring the Public Sector in Post-1980 Turkey: An Assessment," Middle East Technical University, ERC Working Papers, No. 99/6.

Republic of Turkey, Prime Ministry: Undersecretariat of Treasury (2004), *Public Debt Management Report*, February, available online at: www.treasury.gov.tr/duyuru/basin2004/PDMreport-Feb2004.pdf.

Republic of Turkey, Prime Ministry: Undersecretariat of Treasury (2003), *Public Debt Management Report*, April, available online at: www.treasury.gov.tr/duyuru/basin/PDMreport-April2003.pdf.

Voyvoda, Ebru and Erinc Yeldan (2003), "Managing Turkish Debt: An OLG Investigation of the IMF's Fiscal Programming Model for Turkey," processed.

Voyvoda, Ebru and Yeldan, Erinc (2004), "IMF Programs, Fiscal Policy and Growth: Investigation of Macroeconomic Alternatives in an OLG Model of Growth for Turkey," *Comparative Economic Studies*, forthcoming.

World Bank (2000), "Turkey – Country Economic Memorandum – Structural Reforms for Sustainable Growth, Vol. I and II," Report No. 20657-TU, September, Washington, DC: World Bank.

Yeldan, Erinc (2002), "On the IMF-directed Disinflation Program in Turkey: A Program for Stabilization and Austerity or a Recipe for Impoverishment and Financial Chaos?" in *The Ravages of Neo-Liberalism: Economy, Society and Gender in Turkey*, edited by Nesecan Balkan and Sungur Savran, Huntington, NY: Nova Science.

Yeldan, Erinc (2004), "Credibility or Neoliberal Global Remedies? From Speculative-led Growth to IMF-led Crisis in Turkey," processed.

Part III

Fiscal policy for our grandchildren

9 Paradox of thrift and budget in a simple Keynesian growth model

Per Gunnar Berglund[1]

Introduction

The "paradox of thrift" says that attempts to increase saving, by reducing spending and aggregate demand, may lower output and national income so much that the actual *ex post* savings end up being smaller than at the outset. The companion "paradox of the budget," as proposed by William Vickrey,[2] holds the same lesson for the government, namely, that attempts to reduce budget deficits by cutting back on spending may induce lower private spending, sluggish growth and erode the tax base to such an extent that the deficit ends up bigger than it was at the outset. These paradoxes are traditionally held to be short-run phenomena whose logic calls for active counter-cyclical measures on the part of the government.

In recent years "supply-side" economists have proposed that lowered taxes and a bigger deficit may induce so much additional growth in the tax base that it ends up "paying for itself" in the long run. These ideas have been advanced under the banner of "dynamic scoring." The underlying argument is a long-run one, and thus quite different from the traditional Keynesian tale, which is based on cyclical, short-run considerations. There are however important parallels that are worthwhile exploring. This paper addresses from a Keynesian point of view the possibility of a long-run paradox of thrift and budget. A model is developed that generates both these phenomena when calibrated by empirically relevant parameter values.

The paper consists of two parts. The first part discusses the various theoretical considerations that are involved in the idea of a long-run paradox of thrift. This discussion is held on an informal level, so as to be digestible also for the non-technical economist. The chief purpose of this part is to indicate how various theoretical strands can be made to converge to a model that displays both the paradox of thrift and budget. The second part of the paper moves from the abstract plane of this general outline to the nitty-gritty of hands-on formulation of a simple dynamic macroeconomic model along these general lines. This part of the paper involves a fair amount of technicalities, so is addressed more to the model-builder than to the general reader.

Part 1   Paradox of thrift and budget

The traditional short-run paradox of thrift

The paradox of thrift is, of course, a main ingredient of Keynesian macro-economics. As Keynesian economics gradually fell out of favor with the economics profession throughout the 1970s and 1980s, the textbook presentation of the paradox became watered down. Most macroeconomics textbooks still make mention of it, but they typically provide no analytical framework in which its results can be generated as a modeling exercise.[3] Standard IS-LM presentations, in which consumption expenditures are a function of income (and possibly the interest rate) and investment outlays are a function of the interest rate, fail to generate the paradox proper. In fact, if the LM schedule is upward-sloping, so that there is some amount of "crowding out" in the model, a cut in government spending or some other budget consolidation measures, will generate a downturn in domestic product, national income and consumer spending, but also – highly unreal-istically – an upswing in investment spending, which partially offsets the negative impact of the policy program.

In order for the paradox to obtain in a model, it is essential that an accelerator-type mechanism be included in the investment function, so that any changes in current income, output and capacity utilization will have repercussions upon investment activity as well as consumption expenditure. It is essential to keep the response parameters – the sum of the marginal propensities to consume and invest out of primary income – within bounds, to maintain stability and get reasonably sized multipliers.[4] A lagged investment response makes the system likely to cycle, as shown by the many different multiplier-accelerator models following upon Harrod's, Lundberg's and Samuelson's pioneering work in the 1930s.[5] These are all well-known if not well-understood findings, and there is little to add to them here.

The paradox of the budget

One interesting and little noted phenomenon, which occurs in the class of models capable of generating a paradox of thrift, is its companion paradox, which we may call the *paradox of the budget*. This paradox says that an increase in government spending, when it has worked its way through the multiplier-accelerator mechanisms, may result in a sufficiently large increase in output and income to boost tax revenues *more* than the initial expenditure increase. In other words, the government budget deficit would be smaller *ex post* in response to a larger deficit *ex ante*. The precise mathematical criteria for this paradox to obtain will depend upon how the model is structured, but in terms of a standard multiplier-accelerator model with simultaneous investment response, the government-spending multiplier must be greater than the inverse of the marginal tax rate (net of transfer payments).

In modern economies the "macro" marginal tax rate typically ranges from (perhaps) 0.5 to 0.9, depending primarily on how extensive the welfare-state arrangements are in the respective countries. These seemingly high figures result in part from the fact that transfer payments to the unemployed and to other low-income groups are reduced whenever economic activity picks up, so that the expenditure side of the budget also becomes endogenous. Inverting these figures we have 1.1 as the lower figure corresponding to the big-government case (e.g., Denmark), and 2.0 as the higher figure corresponding to a small-government case (e.g., United States).

These back-of-the-envelope calculations indicate that it does not take a lot for an economy to qualify for a paradox of the budget. A government-spending multiplier, including accelerator effects on investment, in excess of 1.1 is highly likely to obtain, so it is a fair conjecture that the economies of countries like Denmark, or for that matter most European countries, operate under a paradox of the budget.[6] It is actually not unlikely that the multiplier runs well in excess of 2.0, which would make virtually all countries qualify for the paradox. While it is true that the regular consumption multiplier, which works its way through disposable income (income net of taxes and transfers), will be small in a high-tax economy, there are good reasons to expect that the effect that runs through the investment channel will be considerably bigger.

Some accelerator considerations

One reason why one should think so is the long-run implications of various sizes of these multipliers. If the capital–output ratio varies with counter-cyclical swings around an average level of four, which is a plausible number, then each dollar increase in domestic product will be associated with four dollars' worth of capital formation, reckoned net of economic depreciation.[7] Turning this ratio upside down, each dollar increase in capital stock will be associated with 25 cents' worth of output growth. These are long-run relationships, of course, around which short-run marginal propensities may vary. But they do indicate that in order for the capital–output ratio to remain intact over the long run, the average impact on net investment from one dollar's worth of output growth is four dollars (or whatever the relevant capital–output ratio dictates). To obtain a multiplier value of four, one must assume a corresponding "marginal propensity to invest" of 0.8, since one dollar of autonomous spending, e.g., government expenditures, would then result in $1/(1 - 0.8) =$ five dollars' worth of total output increase, of which four dollars are investment and the remaining dollar is the one that was injected in the first place (supposing, of course, that the injection consisted of consumption expenditures).[8]

We carried out this very simple example on the assumption that the capital–output ratio is stable in the long run, and we also disregarded a host of complexities that arise in a more complete macroeconomic model. One could advance a variable capital–output ratio along more neoclassical lines as one reason for doubt, amongst many others relating to feedback mechanisms that are likely to arise in a more detailed and complex model. But even so, it seems difficult to find arguments that make it probable that the sizeable investment effect would be offset or weakened to an extent sufficient to render the paradox of the budget ineffectual.

For example, if the capital–output ratio is liable to change secularly over time, then one could take differentials and recast the whole argument in "marginal" terms, by which token the marginal or incremental capital–output ratio takes the place of the average ratio we used in our simple argument. It becomes evident that, unless one makes extreme assumptions about the value of said marginal capital–output ratio, the argument stands up very well. In fact the marginal ratio must fall well below half the average ratio in order to upset the paradox of the budget.

The contention is that it is not improbable that traditional Keynesian expansionary fiscal policies may result in a *smaller* budget deficit. This is a possibility that merits serious consideration, not least as concerns about the budget deficit are often advanced as a reason not to engage in stimulus. It is a matter of course that this issue, considering its scope and complexity, cannot be settled here and now, but given that rough preliminary calculations of this sort provide good support for the likelihood of the existence of a paradox of the budget, we should at least point to, and endeavor to explore, the possibility.

Dynamic scoring and the "supply" side

The paradox of the budget relates in some degree to the recent discussions amongst economists and policymakers about so-called dynamic scoring of the budget. The principle of dynamic scoring is probably uncontroversial in the economics profession. Surely the impact of the budget on the economy should be assessed along with the economy's impact on the budget. Causality clearly runs both ways, and making use of that fact in forecasting budgets and calibrating fiscal policy would seem to make good sense.

The problem is that, even though most economists would agree that there should be some form of dynamic scoring, there is no general agreement about *how* to do it. As every economist is painfully aware, the profession is divided on the core question of what should be considered the right way of modeling an economy, and this disagreement carries over to the debate on dynamic scoring, and manifests itself in discord on the choice of scoring models. Most would advocate the use of some variety of supply-side models, in which the possibility of outgrowing the deficit, as it were, hinges on optimistic assumptions about the elasticities of labor supply and similar mechanisms. The rationale behind using a supply-side model is that such models are presumed to better reflect the long-run or "natural" growth path of the economy, i.e., the trend around which cyclical variations occur.

Many Keynesian economists have been accustomed to thinking along similar lines, and therefore typically have little faith in the proposition that fiscal expansion could "pay for itself" through increased growth. Most Keynesians would probably agree, however, that short-run deviations from the "natural" path could be corrected, at any rate in part, by properly designed fiscal policies. The skepticism concerning the long-run possibilities is typically based on pessimistic, or at any rate less sanguine, opinions about labor-supply elasticities than those of "supply-side" economists.

Recent developments of productivity growth have again shown that there is little reason to believe that it is constant, or even that it can be considered a given trend around which pro-cyclical variations take place along the lines of Okun's Law.[9] Economists were as befuddled by the acceleration of productivity in the mid-1990s as they were by its slowdown in the early 1970s. Yet it remains a commonly held view that long-run changes in the over-the-cycles average rate of productivity growth are somehow "exogenous." Explanations are typically cast in terms of technological progress that is presumed to exogenously "shift the production function," to use a common phrase.

We shall leave aside the question of whether the terminology of labeling an unexplained accounting residual "technology" is helpful or relevant. The interesting question is whether changes in the productivity trend should be looked upon as "exogenous" or somehow "induced" or "endogenous."

Demand-driven productivity growth

Over the decades, a number of economists, notably Kaldor amongst the Keynesians, but also modern "new" growth theorists,[10] have advanced the idea that long-run productivity growth is induced by economic factors, not just "exogenous." Opinions differ about what those factors are, and about the transmission mechanisms through which they operate.

Numerous theories of "endogenous growth" have been advanced to challenge within a neoclassical framework the idea of "exogenous" technical progress. While interesting on a theoretical level, these schemes share a common weakness in that they rely on newly introduced concepts of human capital, social capital, *et hoc genus omne*. These imaginative concepts do not readily lend themselves to empirical measurement and inclusion in econometric models, with the unfortunate consequence that theories based on these concepts are difficult to assess empirically.

From the Keynesian point of view, the central question is whether aggregate demand, in some way or another, is capable of affecting enduringly the pace of productivity growth. The Kaldor–Verdoorn Law figures prominently in this context, although it is primarily an observed empirical regularity for which many more or less *ad hoc* explanations have been given, mostly in terms of learning by doing or increasing returns to scale.[11]

It has hardly ever been noticed that a system characterized by (1) a reasonably stable long-term capital–output ratio, (2) short-term labor hoarding causing pro-cyclical movements in labor productivity, and (3) a standard accelerator-type investment function in which investment is driven by capacity utilization, will also display "pro-structural" labor productivity movements in the sense that the growth rate of labor productivity will be positively related to the level of capacity utilization. If these assumptions are relevant, then that may be sufficient[12] to secure that higher aggregate demand induces not only higher capacity utilization in the present, but also faster productivity growth and faster output growth in the long run.

Along these lines, admittedly very briefly sketched here, we can find another type of argument in support of "dynamic scoring" or the paradox of the budget. In contrast to the traditional short-term Keynesian argument underpinning the paradox, we have here an argument that pertains to the long run, but where short-term factors drive the long run. In other words, there is a systematic element of interaction between the short run and the long run in this kind of model. The two are not divorced or dichotomized, as is traditionally the case both in neoclassical and Keynesian models.

The approach also differs from the "supply-side" type of argument, which looks at factor-supply elasticities with respect to taxes (take-home wages) as well as other, similar factors that are considered to be relevant, in order to find arguments *pro* or *contra* dynamic-scoring effects and self-closing budget deficits. The idea we have advanced here is concerned with explaining the development of factor productivity rather than factor supplies, and in particular with linking it to the state of aggregate demand and current output and employment.

Relation between the short run and long run

Short-run Keynesian models, some properties of which were discussed initially, may explain variations of output, employment as well as a host of other relevant macroeconomic variables, around their "benchmark" levels, however defined. Typically benchmarks would result from some filtering exercise, whether by the simple Hodrick-Prescott or some more complex multivariable (e.g., Kalman) filtering method. Capital and other stocks could also be employed to define relevant benchmarks through fixed or time-varying (filtered) stock-flow ratios. The model featured in the second part of this paper introduces accounting-based "floating benchmarks" based on the notion of maintaining the structural composition of the economy intact, namely, that all proportions remain constant in nominal terms.

A common feature of short-run Keynesian models is that they do not link the deviations from benchmark level to other state variables cumulating over time, but simply leave them unexplained. Longer-run models, whether Keynesian or neoclassical, typically do not explain much. A statement that growth is going to occur "naturally" at a particular pace determined by some simplistic decomposition (e.g., the sum of population growth and productivity growth, both exogenous) does not really add much in terms of analytical insights. Almost all interesting issues, and all the modeling excitement, show up in the interaction between the short run and the long run, or in the stories told about how the short runs cumulate into long runs.

The laws of motion of the system need to be specified, and in order to identify partial or global steady states one might benefit from assessing the "grand ratios" of the system. We have already mentioned one such grand ratio, the capital–output ratio. From the point of view of fiscal policy the other relevant ratio would seem to be the public debt-to-GDP ratio. The ordinary national-accounting identities for stocks of assets state that, in a closed system, the private-sector wealth is defined by the capital stock plus the government debt. More precisely, the concept of government debt should be defined along the lines of a system with a capital budget, so that non-financial assets owned by government are deducted from the net financial debt. It is clear that government debt wedges in between private wealth and national wealth, the latter being given by the value of the capital stock, reflecting the principle that the ultimate wealth of the nation consists of non-financial ("real") capital only.[13]

Standard specifications of the consumption function include a "wealth effect" to account for the effect upon consumption expenditures resulting from changes in households' net worth. The other main channel is disposable income.[14] Most models of this sort are however not based on the idea that the stock of household wealth stands in some specific long-run proportion to consumption expenditures. This, in our opinion, may obscure the theoretical situation and at worst result in biased econometric results.

The typical approach involves assuming that households optimize over their "life cycle" a program of consumption and saving under an intertemporal budget constraint and with a certain objective (utility) function, and certain expectations about future income paths.[15] The result is a time-path of desired wealth relative to income, implying also paths of desired consumption and saving. Consumer theorists have noted that part of the wealth should take the form of human capital, or more precisely of the discounted present value of expected future labor income, but since this magnitude cannot be directly observed and measured, assumptions are made to the effect that current labor income is a good proxy. This is standard procedure and therefore rarely called into question. But there may be some reason to doubt whether it is the best way to proceed.

As an alternative approach, one might use non-human capital as a proxy for all wealth, human and non-human capital inclusive, assuming stable proportions between the two kinds. On this approach, one should expect a long-term stable overall wealth-to-spending ratio, subject to secular drift due to changing demographics and other slow-moving factors. In this model, wealth alone will be used as explanatory variable for long-run consumption, with a certain spending-to-wealth ratio predicted by theory. Cyclical deviations can then be grafted onto the long-run model by making deviations in consumption from its long-run level dependent on deviations of current income from its long-run level.

Furthermore, given that the historical record shows a great deal of instability in asset prices and therefore in capital gains and losses on assets, but much less so in volume accumulation of assets (investment and saving), it would seem worthwhile to decompose changes in wealth into a volume and a (real) price component, and then proceed to cumulate these over time, into one investment- (or saving-) based component and one component based on (real) holding gains.[16] The asymmetric pattern of variability in the two dimensions would imply that the propensity to spend out of the fickle holding-gains component be considerably smaller than the propensity to spend out of the relatively solid investment/saving component. It is not unlikely that this approach could imply surprises also about the estimated marginal propensity to consume from disposable income.

In any case, the two grand ratios of the private wealth-to-spending ratio and the overall economy-wide capital–output ratio can easily be combined to generate a model where the long-run level of domestic product is a function of the size of the government debt.[17] The bottom line of these models is a message that bears resemblance of the recently proposed "fiscal theory of the price level."[18] According to this theory, the general price level is a function of the size of the government debt. The papers on the fiscal theory are generally overloaded with strained and headachy mathematical arguments, but they boil down to that the size of the public debt is the chief determinant of the price level. Adjustment is typically, but not always, assumed to be frictionless and instantaneous so that there are no repercussions on output and employment. A highly neoclassical story coupled with a functional-finance tale of the public debt – an interesting hybrid!

Facing these ideas, the Keynesian economist must feel inclined to throw some sand into the wheels of adjustment, in order to have slower movements in prices and larger deviations in output and employment resulting from changes in the public debt. Taken to its extreme point, one would have no price changes and thus solely output and employment adjusting to changes in aggregate demand brought about by a bigger public debt. The contention is that the fiscal theory of the price level, just like the theory of functional finance, rests on the central idea that it is the public debt that drives the economy, and not the other way round. Or, at the very least, there is considerable interaction between the two. Both theories have in common that government debt drives nominal GDP through wealth effects, and the chief difference is whether it is prices or volumes that adjust when nominal GDP changes.

Conclusion of Part 1

In this non-technical part of the paper, we have endeavored to weave a tapestry of theoretical issues and ideas that may be useful in assessing whether real-world economies are subject to a long-run paradox of thrift or paradox of the budget. Recent discussions about "dynamic scoring" have revived interest in this topic, which has been dormant for decades. It is to be hoped that this revival will spur research resulting in some relevant and workable synthesis. As we have argued above, we believe that a theory of that kind can be patched together by borrowing from several strands, including standard short-run Keynesian models, life-cycle type consumption models, Harrodian growth models, Okun-type labor hoarding models, as well as functional finance and the fiscal theory of the price level. This may sound like a frightful hotchpotch, but with a savvy chef stirring it up, it could nevertheless turn out to be appetizing.

Part 2   A dynamic Keynesian model

Introduction

This second part of the paper devises a small, yet (at any rate in some restricted sense of the word) "complete" macroeconomic model. The purpose of the exercise is to illustrate how the principles and ideas that were discussed in the first part might be applied in practice to create the kind of synthesis model there envisaged. The model is a dynamic growth model, which generates trajectories of national-accounts main aggregates (net domestic product, private and government consumption, net capital formation); of national income, tax revenues and private disposable income; of capital stocks, government debt and private wealth; and of employment, wages and prices.

There are two main building blocks: the supply block and the demand block. The supply block consists of two sub-modules, namely, the Okun–Verdoorn module and the Phillips Curve module. The demand side has at its core a straightforward Keynesian multiplier–accelerator system. The stock-adjustment accelerator mechanism also plays a core role in the Okun–Verdoorn module. The blocks and modules interact with one another by "importing" inputs from the rest of the model, processing them, and then "exporting" output to the rest of the model, along the following lines:

The Okun–Verdoorn module imports from the rest of the model the actual growth rate, as well as the inflation rate, of output (domestic product), and it exports to the rest of the model the growth rates of benchmark ("potential") output, of capital stock, and of actual and benchmark ("equilibrium") employment. The Phillips Curve module imports the growth rates of actual and benchmark ("trend") productivity, and of actual and benchmark output; it exports the actual and benchmark inflation rates of prices and money wages, three flavors of real wage growth rates (actual, benchmark and "desired," the latter reflecting the "wage claims" or "wage aspirations" of workers), and also actual and benchmark unit labor cost.

It is worth noticing that the consolidated supply block, including both sub-modules, imports only one variable from the rest of the model, namely, the actual output growth rate. Hence, in order to "drive" and close the model, we must devise a mechanism that generates and furnishes that missing input. This is the role of the demand block; it exports the output growth rate. On the other hand, the demand block makes use of inputs from the supply block, namely, the growth rate of benchmark or potential output and the actual inflation rate.

The model has two separate (but not logically independent!) mechanisms for capital formation: one on the demand side and one on the supply side. It is important that these two mechanisms be equivalent, lest the model will be over-determined and logically self-contradictory. The main point of repeating the same mechanisms in two places is to maintain a tidy separation of the demand and supply blocks, with only a bare minimum of interface communication between the two. By this token it will be easy to, e.g., switch-off the demand block and run the supply block as an independent unit, with exogenously imposed trajectories of actual output growth. Conversely, one might switch-off the supply block and run the Keynesian multiplier core of the demand block by itself, feeding it exogenous, filtered data on potential output. The build of the model facilitates this.

Another point worth observing is that the modules of the supply block are hierarchical. The Phillips Curve cannot function without inputs from the Okun–Verdoorn module, and can therefore be described as a "secondary" module; the Okun–Verdoorn unit, on the other hand, is the "primary" module, and can be run independently of the Phillips Curve. In other words, the supply block can be run with the Phillips Curve switched-off, but it cannot be run with the Okun–Verdoorn module switched-off. In a more complex model, similar module hierarchies would be built on the demand side as well, but in this simple model, the demand side consists of one module only.

In the traditional literature on growth models, the ordinary Keynesian macroeconomic aggregates and the related accounting identities are typically suppressed. It is a fair guess that this is due in large part to the perceived problem of converting standard macroeconomic demand models to logarithmic growth rates. One of the novelties of our system is that we have based the demand system on modern chain-index-based macroeconomic accounting.[19] It is well known amongst macroeconomic model-builders that, since the relatively recent adoption of chain-index formulae by statistical agencies producing national accounts, the usual national accounting aggregates are no longer additive in volume terms ("constant dollars"). For example, the traditional textbook identity $Y \equiv C + I + G$ still holds in nominal terms, but in volume terms a re-basing discrepancy creeps in and disrupts the equality. This has the unfortunate consequence of disabling the use of accounting identities for Keynesian-type feedback loops, thus removing the very keystone of macroeconomic modeling.[20]

The remedy we propose, and which should be logically obvious, consists of recasting the identities in terms of "contributions to growth" for volumes, and "contributions to inflation" for prices. These contributions are additive by construction; the contributions to domestic-product growth, for example, add up by definition to the growth rate of domestic product. To give an example of what this might look like, consider recasting the ordinary textbook Keynesian consumption function in terms of these concepts. Instead of having "real consumption" as a function of "real disposable income," we would now have the "consumption contribution to domestic-product growth" as a function of the "disposable-income contribution to national-income growth." Since in a closed economy the growth rate of national income must be identically equal to the growth rate of domestic product, we can link the two and proceed with the usual multiplier calculations by virtue of the feedback loop running through this identity.[21]

Note that nothing needs to be changed in terms of the structure of the model; only the variables entered into the equations are different, and have a different interpretation. Another intriguing possibility, which we must leave unexplored in this paper, would be to exploit the property that "contributions to inflation," too, are additive by construction, and model the propagation of price shocks using multiplier techniques analogous to those employed in the volume dimension. One more observation: Whereas ordinary "constant prices" time-series are non-stationary (trended) and typically co-integrated, and therefore call for de-trending and other, related econometric considerations, the "contributions to growth" are typically stationary (if not martingales), so are more amenable to direct econometric analysis, without pre-cooking.

Notation

Having thus described the broad principles of the modeling system, we can proceed to address the specifics. In order to do so, we need a system of

notation. The reader might at first find our system cumbersome and difficult to penetrate. We must urge patience, since the notation has been
developed with great care and serves its purpose very well. A certain level
of complexity is unavoidable due to the fact that even so small and simple
a model as the one featured in this paper involves a substantial number of
variables and parameters. But it is also desirable to have a notation system
that permits expansion to larger and more complex modeling systems. Our
system is designed to accommodate such expansion.[22] It is worth spending
a little time and effort understanding it.

The general nomenclature for model variables is:

$$_n Z_\tau^{k,m}, \quad Z \in Z; k, n \in K, \Lambda, \Xi; m \in M \tag{1}$$

The symbol Z denotes the type of variable (nominal value, volume,
price level, contribution to growth, etc.). The variable type is surrounded
by no less than four superscripts and subscripts. The subscript (τ) is simply
a continuous-time index (taking the value zero at the "initial" point). The
first superscript (k) indicates the economic category to which the variable
belongs (private consumption, domestic product, capital stock, labor services, etc.). The second superscript (m) gives what we may call the "flavor"
of the variable, i.e. whether it is an actual value, a filtered ("structural,"
"underlying," "potential") benchmark, or a gap between the actual value
and the benchmark, and so on. The pre-subscript (n), finally, appears only
in ratio-type variables, and designates the economic class to which the
renormalization (denominator) variable belongs; for instance, we have
$n = Y$ for variables expressed relative to the domestic product.

We have assigned to each index, whether variable, subscript or superscript, index sets denoted by uppercase Greek letters. It will be seen that
the variable type Z belongs to the index set Z, superscript k and pre-
subscript n belong to the same index sets, namely, K, Λ, and Ξ, and superscript m belongs to index set M. Table 9.1 provides a summary tableau of
these index sets, with further references to a series of explanatory tables

Table 9.1 Indices and index sets

Index	Explanation	Index set	Refer to
Z	Type of variable	$\zeta = \{B, C, F, G, H, P, Q, R, S, V, W\}$	Table 2 & 3
k, n	National accounts (stocks of assets)	$\kappa = \{K, W, D\}$	Table 4
k, n	National accounts (flows of funds)	$\Lambda = \{C, I, G, Y, T, B, YD, S\}$	Table 4
k, n	National accounts (stock-flow links)	$\Psi = \{I, S, B\} \subset \Lambda$	Table 4
k, n	Labor services	$\Xi = \{L\}$	Table 4
m	Flavor	$M = \{\alpha, \beta, \gamma, \delta, \epsilon, \phi\}$	Table 5

Table 9.2 Types of variables: primary definitions

Value of Z	Explanation	Symbol	Primary definition
$Z = B$	Real value	$_nB_\tau^{k,m}$	$_nB_\tau^{k,m} \equiv \dfrac{V_\tau^{k,m}}{P_\tau^{n,m}}$
$Z = C$	Unit cost	$_nC_\tau^{k,m}$	$_nC_\tau^{k,m} \equiv \dfrac{V_\tau^{k,m}}{Q_\tau^{n,m}}$
$Z = F$	Contribution to inflation	$_n\dot{f}_\tau^{k,m}$	$_n\dot{f}_\tau^{k,m} \equiv {}_nW_\tau^{k,m} \cdot \dot{p}_\tau^{\kappa,m}$
$Z = G$	Contribution to volume growth	$_n\dot{g}_\tau^{k,m}$	$_n\dot{g}_\tau^{k,m} \equiv {}_nW_\tau^{k,m} \cdot \dot{q}_\tau^{\kappa,m}$
$Z = H$	Contribution to nominal value growth	$_n\dot{h}_\tau^{k,m}$	$_n\dot{h}_\tau^{k,m} \equiv {}_nW_\tau^{k,m} \cdot \dot{v}_\tau^{\kappa,m}$
$Z = P$	Inflation rate	$\dot{p}_\tau^{k,m}$	Basic unit
$Z = Q$	Volume	$Q_\tau^{k,m}$	$Q_\tau^{k,m} \equiv \dfrac{V_\tau^{k,m}}{P_\tau^{k,m}}$
$Z = V$	Nominal value	$V_\tau^{k,m}$	Basic unit
$Z = R$	Relative price level	$_nR_\tau^{k,m}$	$_nR_\tau^{k,m} \equiv \dfrac{P_\tau^{k,m}}{P_\tau^{n,m}}$
$Z = S$	Relative volume	$_nS_\tau^{k,m}$	$_nS_\tau^{k,m} \equiv \dfrac{Q_\tau^{k,m}}{Q_\tau^{n,m}}$
$Z = W$	Relative nominal value	$_nW_\tau^{k,m}$	$_nW_\tau^{k,m} \equiv \dfrac{V_\tau^{k,m}}{V_\tau^{n,m}}$

(Tables 9.1 to 9.5) to be found in the right-hand column. The table also includes a supplementary index set, Ψ, which is a subset of Λ.

The elements of index set Z are detailed in Table 9.2, which shows primary definitions, and Table 9.3, which shows implied (derived) definitions of the variables. Lowercase symbols will be used to denote natural logarithms of the corresponding uppercase ones, namely, $_nz_\tau^{k,m} \equiv \ln(_nZ_\tau^{k,m})$. A single dot surmounting the symbol denotes a first time-derivative, namely, $_n\dot{Z}_\tau^{k,m} \equiv d(_nZ_\tau^{k,m})/d\tau$ for plain time-derivatives, and $_n\dot{z}_\tau^{k,m} \equiv d(_nz_\tau^{k,m})/d\tau$ for logarithmic time-derivatives (instantaneous growth rates). Similarly, double dots will denote second time-derivatives, namely, $_n\ddot{z}_\tau^{k,m} \equiv d^2(_nz_\tau^{k,m})/d\tau^2$.

The two basic categories of observables are levels of nominal values and rates of price inflation, i.e., growth rates of price levels. Price levels can be obtained from inflation rates by assuming an initial price level to definitize the index-number series,[23] then integrating the rate of inflation over time, and finally exponentiating the integral, as shown in the right-hand column of the "$Z = P$" row of Table 9.3. Volumes can then be calculated "implicitly," namely, by deflating the nominal value with the price level, as shown in the "$Z = Q$" row of the same table.

Table 9.3 Types of variables: implied definitions

Value of Z	Explanation	Symbol	Implied definition
$Z = B$	Real value growth rate	$_n\dot{b}_\tau^{k,m}$	$_n\dot{b}_\tau^{k,m} \equiv \dot{v}_\tau^{k,m} - \dot{p}_\tau^{n,m}$
$Z = C$	Unit cost growth rate	$_n\dot{c}_\tau^{k,m}$	$_n\dot{c}_\tau^{k,m} \equiv \dot{v}_\tau^{k,m} - \dot{q}_\tau^{n,m}$
$Z = P$	Price level	$P_\tau^{k,m}$	$P_\tau^{k,m} \equiv \exp\left(p_0^{k,m} + \int_0^\tau \dot{p}_u^{k,m} \mathrm{d}u\right)$
$Z = Q$	Volume growth rate	$\dot{q}_\tau^{k,m}$	$\dot{q}_\tau^{k,m} \equiv \dot{v}_\tau^{k,m} - \dot{p}_\tau^{\kappa,m}$
$Z = V$	Nominal value growth rate	$\dot{v}_\tau^{k,m}$	$\dot{v}_\tau^{k,m} \equiv \dfrac{\mathrm{d}(\ln V_\tau^{k,m})}{\mathrm{d}\tau}$
$Z = R$	Relative inflation rate	$_n\dot{r}_\tau^{k,m}$	$_n\dot{r}_\tau^{k,m} \equiv \dot{p}_\tau^{k,m} - \dot{p}_\tau^{n,m}$
$Z = S$	Relative volume growth rate	$_n\dot{s}_\tau^{k,m}$	$_n\dot{s}_\tau^{k,m} \equiv \dot{q}_\tau^{k,m} - \dot{q}_\tau^{n,m}$
$Z = W$	Relative nominal value growth rate	$_n\dot{w}_\tau^{k,m}$	$_n\dot{w}_\tau^{k,m} \equiv \dot{v}_\tau^{k,m} - \dot{v}_\tau^{n,m}$

Table 9.4 specifies and explains the index sets K, Λ, and Ξ, to which the superscript k and the pre-subscript n pertain. The index set K consists of national accounts aggregate stocks of assets, namely, capital stock (K), private net worth (W), and government debt (D), and the index set Λ of national accounts aggregate flows, namely, private consumption (C), domestic net investment (I), government consumption (G), and so on. Note also that the index set Ψ, as defined in Table 9.1, consists of a subset of the national accounts flows Λ, namely those flows which accumulate to stocks, or "stock-building flows" for short. Finally, we have the index set Ξ, which contains only one element, namely, the flow labor services (L).

Table 9.4 First superscripts (k) and pre-subscripts (n)

Value of k or n	Explanation
K	National accounts aggregates (stocks)
K	Capital stock/national net worth
W	Private net worth
D	Government debt[1]
Λ	National accounts aggregates (flows)
C	Private consumption
I	Domestic net investment
G	Government consumption
Y	Net domestic product/net national income
T	Government net transfer balance[2]
B	Government budget deficit (government net saving with negative sign)
YD	Private disposable income
S	Private saving
Ξ	Employment
L	Employment

Notes
1 Defined as government net worth with negative sign.
2 Defined as taxes minus transfers and interest payments.

Table 9.5 lists superscript *m*, and its index set M relating to "flavors" of variables. Lowercase Greek symbols are used here, α denoting "actual" values, β "benchmarks," γ "gaps" (between actual and benchmarks), and δ "desired" values, which are benchmark-type notional equilibrium values

Table 9.5 Second superscripts (*m*)

Value of m	Explanation	Example
α	Actual value	$_n\dot{z}_\tau^{k,\alpha}$
β	Benchmark	$_n\dot{z}_\tau^{k,\beta}$
γ	Gap (actual over benchmark)	$_n\dot{z}_\tau^{k,\gamma} \equiv {}_n\dot{z}_\tau^{k,\alpha} - {}_n\dot{z}_\tau^{k,\beta}$
δ	Desired value	$_n\dot{z}_\tau^{k,\delta}$
ε	Gap (desired over benchmark)	$_n\dot{z}_\tau^{k,\epsilon} \equiv {}_n\dot{z}_\tau^{k,\delta} - {}_n\dot{z}_\tau^{k,\beta}$
φ	Gap (desired over actual)	$_n\dot{z}_\tau^{k,\phi} \equiv {}_n\dot{z}_\tau^{k,\delta} - {}_n\dot{z}_\tau^{k,\alpha}$

Table 9.6 Model parameters

Parameter	Explanation	Derived
α	Okun-Verdoorn equation intercept	$\alpha \equiv -(\kappa - \lambda\mu)q_0^{Y,\gamma}$
β	"Verdoorn effect" on labor productivity	$\beta \equiv \kappa - \lambda\mu$
γ	"Okun effect" on labor productivity	–
δ	Wage Phillips Curve: intercept	$\delta \equiv \epsilon(\dot{p}_0^{L,\beta} - q_0^{Y,\gamma})$
ε	Wage Phillips Curve: long-run slope	$\epsilon \equiv \omega(\rho\mu + \xi - \gamma)$
φ	Wage Phillips Curve: short-run slope	$\phi \equiv \psi\mu$
π	Price Phillips Curve: intercept	$\pi \equiv \delta - \alpha$
ρ	Price Phillips Curve: long-run slope	$\rho \equiv \epsilon - \beta$
σ	Price Phillips Curve: short-run slope	$\sigma \equiv \phi + \xi - \gamma$
η	Benchmark output equation: intercept	$\eta \equiv \dot{q}_0^{L,\beta} - \kappa q_0^{Y,\gamma}$
ν	Employment function: intercept	$\nu \equiv (\dot{q}_0^{L,\beta} - \lambda\mu q_0^{Y,\gamma})$
κ	Adjustment speed, capital stock	–
λ	Adjustment speed, employment trend	–
μ	Short-run elasticity of employment with respect to capacity utilization	–
ρ	Short-run elasticity of real wage claims with respect to employment	–
ω	Adjustment speed, money-wage trend	–
ξ	Short-run elasticity of the mark-up with respect to capacity utilization	–
ψ	Short-run elasticity of nominal wages with respect to employment	–
θ	Marginal tax rate	–
χ	Marginal propensity to consume from disposable income	–
ζ	Marginal propensity to consume from private wealth	–

Notes
1 Defined as government net worth with negative sign.
2 Defined as taxes minus transfers and interest payments.

of price variables. Further, ϵ and ϕ denotes gaps between "desired" and "benchmark" values, and between "desired" and "actual" values, respectively.

Table 9.6, lastly, explains the model parameters, for which lowercase Greek symbols will be used. (There is no index set relating to parameters.) In this particular model, all parameters will be treated as constants, so carry no time index. In a more sophisticated model, however, parameters would be made time-varying and stochastic.

Let us also, before closing the notation section, provide a sequence of examples to illustrate how the notation system works. The actual nominal value, price level and volume of private consumption will read $V_\tau^{C,\alpha}$, $P_\tau^{C,\alpha}$ and $Q_\tau^{C,\alpha}$, respectively; the actual volume growth rate, $\dot{q}_\tau^{C,\alpha}$, and the actual rate of price inflation, $\dot{p}_\tau^{C,\alpha}$. The nominal value of private consumption relative to domestic product (i.e., the nominal share) will read $_YW_\tau^C$; and the actual relative price, $_YR_\tau^{C,\alpha}$, and the actual relative volume, $_YS_\tau^{C,\alpha}$.[24] The actual contribution to output growth from private consumption will read $_Y\dot{g}_\tau^{C,\alpha}$; the actual contribution to inflation, $_Y\dot{f}_\tau^{C,\alpha}$.

Some general model assumptions and accounting elaborations

Our model is simple and constructing a simple model inevitably involves making a host of simplifying assumptions. We have tried our best to keep them as few as possible, and to avoid making them overly restrictive.

The most basic limitations derive from the scope of the model itself. It pertains to a closed economy, and it has no monetary policy module. To open the economy for cross-border trade and capital transactions, and to equip it with a monetary-policy module is obviously desirable. Yet this is a simplification we shall have to live with unless we want a considerably more complex model.

All relative-price changes have been assumed away, except for the relative price of labor *vis-à-vis* all other goods, i.e., the real wage, which is free to vary. In formal terms we have, for all $k \in K$, Λ,[25] that

$$\dot{p}_\tau^{k,\alpha} = \dot{p}_\tau^{K,\alpha} \tag{2}$$

which implies that

$$_K\dot{f}_\tau^{k,\gamma} \equiv {}_KW_\tau^k(\dot{p}_\tau^{k,\alpha} - \dot{p}_\tau^{K,\alpha}) = 0 \tag{3}$$

The more specific assumptions in respect of equations and parameters will be addressed as we go along. Before we conclude this section, and move on to discuss the supply and demand blocks, let us say a few more words on some general accounting structures.

All variables in the model will be normalized to capital stock, which is a convenient accounting trick by which to secure straightforward stock-flow consistency.[26] This assumption implies that K will be the typical pre-subscript indicating this renormalization. As will be seen in the section on the demand block, the accumulation equations are extraordinarily simple. The loss is in terms of intuitive interpretation, since all flows must be thought of in terms of "shares of capital stock" or "relative to capital stock" rather than the more straightforward "shares of domestic product" or "relative to output."

The concept of a filtered trend variable has many different labels in the literature, e.g., "structural," "underlying" or "potential" values. We will typically use the neutral term "benchmark" for any and all of these. As was mentioned in the first part of the paper, our demand block features "floating benchmarks," which are somewhat different from the benchmarks typically used in macroeconomic modeling. The most important of the *differentiae* is that our floating benchmarks are given directly by the accounting system, so there is no need for making assumptions about the shape and scope of the smoothing window, as in univariate (e.g. Hodrick-Prescott) filtering, or the signal-to-noise ratio, as in multivariate (e.g., Kalman) filtering.

The floating benchmarks are defined as the nominal share of capital stock multiplied by the rate of growth of capital stock. Formally we have, for all $k \in K, \Lambda$, that

$$_K \dot{g}_\tau^{k,\beta} \equiv {}_K W_\tau^k \cdot \dot{q}_\tau^{K,\alpha} \tag{4}$$

Note also that $_K W_\tau^K \equiv 1$, which implies that $\dot{q}_\tau^{K,\alpha} \equiv \dot{q}_\tau^{K,\beta}$, or, equivalently that $\dot{q}_\tau^{K,\gamma} \equiv 0$. Actual and benchmark growth rates of capital stock are therefore interchangeable.

Simple manipulation of the Divisia index shows that by defining the benchmarks as we have done here, we can quickly extract the first time-derivative of nominal weights as follows:

$$_K \dot{W}_\tau^k \equiv {}_K W_\tau^k \cdot {}_K \dot{w}_\tau^k \equiv {}_K W_\tau^k (\dot{v}_\tau^{k,\alpha} - \dot{v}_\tau^{K,\alpha}) \equiv {}_K W_\tau^k ((\dot{p}_\tau^{k,\alpha} - \dot{p}_\tau^{K,\alpha}) + (\dot{q}_\tau^{k,\alpha} - \dot{q}_\tau^{K,\alpha}))$$
$$\equiv ({}_K \dot{f}_\tau^{k,\alpha} - {}_K \dot{f}_\tau^{k,\beta}) + ({}_K \dot{g}_\tau^{k,\alpha} - {}_K \dot{g}_\tau^{k,\beta}) \equiv {}_K \dot{f}_\tau^{k,\gamma} + {}_K \dot{g}_\tau^{k,\gamma} \tag{5}$$

where $_K \dot{g}_\tau^{k,\gamma} \equiv {}_K \dot{g}_\tau^{k,\alpha} - {}_K \dot{g}_\tau^{k,\beta}$, as explained in Table 9.6. Since $_K \dot{f}_\tau^{k,\gamma} = 0$, as per Equation (3) above, the result boils down to the still simpler $_K \dot{W}_\tau^k = {}_K \dot{g}_\tau^{k,\gamma}$. In other words, the gaps between actual and benchmark contributions to capital stock growth are equal to the change in nominal weights, which describe the proportions of the economy. It is now easy to understand the meaning of these accounting-based "floating benchmarks." They are "benchmarks" in that they portray an economy where nominal proportions remain constant. Proportions cannot change except by deviations from the benchmarks. Such "gaps" between actual and benchmark contributions to growth will cause the benchmarks themselves to adjust, so that at each instant, they reflect the current nominal proportions of the economy. It is in this sense that they are "floating"; they continuously adjust so as to incorporate structural change in the proportions of the economy.

Our modeling philosophy also transpires from this. "Shocks," whether or not they are propagated and amplified by multiplier mechanisms, always imply changes in the structure or proportions of the economy. Volume shocks, which are the only shocks we can consider in a model where relative-price changes have been ruled out by assumption, contribute to changes in the structure of the economy; in the absence of shocks, the economy moves along in parallel lines, as it were, retaining its structure. Now, these "shocks," while typically exogenous, can also be endogenized in the form of stock-to-flow feedback mechanisms, as is the case with the "wealth effect" on private consumption in our model. Shocks, in other words, need not be symmetric and random; in fact in a larger, disaggregated system, structural changes induced by innovations and new technology can be modeled using systematically biased shocks, and a similar strategy can be taken to deal with secular changes in consumer tastes and spending patterns.

The supply block

Our journey through the model starts out with the supply block, which consists of two sub-modules: the Okun–Verdoorn module and the Phillips curve. The function of the Okun–Verdoorn module is to generate trajectories for labor productivity, employment, capital stock and benchmark ("potential") output. Labor productivity and employment appear in three different guises or "flavors," namely, actual values, benchmarks and gaps (meaning the excess of actual values over benchmarks). The module imports from the rest of the model the growth rate of actual output, which is generated in the demand block, or which, if the demand block is switched-off, can be fed into the module as exogenous data.

The theoretical backdrop of the Okun–Verdoorn module is well captured by the two names of Okun and Verdoorn.[27] Okun's 1962 paper on the concept and measurement of potential output features three different models, the two most familiar of which relate the "Okun gap" between actual and potential output to the unemployment rate. The third model is a log-linear model, which relates the gap to the level of employment; it is this model that we have drawn upon and incorporated into ours. In this version "Okun's Law" must be reformulated as a cyclical, short-run elasticity of the output gap with respect to the employment gap; the numerical estimates should be of the same order of magnitude as the ordinary rule-of-thumb, namely, between 2 and 3.

As to Verdoorn, his 1949 paper features a model in which the growth rate of employment is a linear function of the growth rate of capital stock. It is a straightforward extension of his model to add an accelerator-type investment function linking the growth rate of capital stock to the Okun-type output gap.[28] It is important to understand that the "Verdoorn effects" of our model, namely, that secular labor productivity growth is a function of the level of capacity utilization, do not result directly from assumptions to this effect; they are implied by other relationships and emerge as an indirect result from combining "Okun's Law" with an accelerator-type investment function. Briefly expressed, it is the pro-cyclical variations in labor productivity that cumulate into the long-run "pro-structural" Verdoorn relationship. In this respect, the Okun and Verdoorn effects are intrinsically linked, the former being the more fundamental of the two.

The task of the Phillips Curve module is to process inputs from the Okun–Verdoorn module, namely, the growth rates of actual and benchmark output, employment and labor productivity (actual output being obtained indirectly, via the Okun–Verdoorn module, from the demand block) into inflation rates of actual and benchmark money wages and prices, as well as growth rates of real wages, unit labor costs, and the wage share of national income.

Our Phillips Curve inflation model is of the "conflicting-claims" variety, which is to say that the acceleration of money wages depends on the "claims gap" between wage aspirations (here called "desired" wages) and actual wages.[29] Formulating the model in terms of a Marshallian "excess-price" gap rather than a Walrasian "excess-quantity" gap is mainly a matter of convenience; it is typically not very difficult to establish duality between the two modes of expression. In our model, the "desired" real-wage level depends cyclically on the current state of employment, namely, the employment gap between actual and benchmark employment, and structurally on the benchmark rate of labor-productivity growth, by simply assuming a long-term stable income distribution.[30]

With time-varying, gradually adapting benchmark employment, we obtain a "pro-structural" steady-state relationship between capacity utilization (employment) and money-wage inflation. That is to say, higher capacity utilization likely entails a higher "underlying" long-run rate of money-wage increases.[31] Depending on the degree of "pro-structural" variations in labor productivity, price inflation could be either pro- or counter-structural or simply independent of capacity utilization.

The Okun–Verdoorn model

The Okun–Verdoorn model is based on four model assumptions; three of which take the form of behavioral assumptions, and one concerning the filtering of benchmark output-to-capital ratios. The behavioral assumptions are captured in the following three equations:

$$\hat{q}_\tau^{K,\alpha} = \kappa \hat{q}_\tau^{Y,\gamma} \qquad \text{Accelerator investment function} \qquad (6)$$

$$\ddot{q}_\tau^{L,\beta} = \lambda \dot{q}_\tau^{L,\gamma} \qquad \text{Adjustment of benchmark employment growth} \qquad (7)$$

$$\dot{q}_\tau^{L,\gamma} = \mu \dot{q}_\tau^{Y,\gamma} \qquad \text{Okun equation (employment cycle)} \qquad (8)$$

Accelerator investment function: This investment function is a straight-forward "neoclassical synthesis" stock-adjustment equation, in which the rate of growth of capital stock depends on the size of the gap between actual and benchmark (potential) output. It should be noted that it makes little difference whether this equation is formulated in our terms or in the more traditional terms of a gap between "desired" and "actual" capital stock; all it takes is to link "desired" stock to actual output and "actual" stock to benchmark output. In order to provide for secular drift in the output–capital ratio, we have moved the function up one step, from the first derivative to the second. Empirical work indicates that it is reasonable to expect the speed-of-adjustment parameter (κ) to lie somewhere in the neighborhood of 0.15 to 0.20.[32]

Adjustment of benchmark employment growth: This equation governs the degree of "persistence" or "partial hysteresis" in the labor-supply dynamics of the model. A positive adjustment coefficient λ means that the equilibrium level of employment adjusts in response to the state of the labor market, so that high employment implies more workers flowing into the labor market, which speeds up potential-employment growth. Various mechanisms can be alluded to in support of this idea, including immigration, women joining the labor force, and discouraged workers coming back to look for work when the job market improves.[33]

Okun equation: This equation reflects Okun's Law, albeit turned on its head. The elasticity parameter of our model (μ) is the inverse of the elasticity usually quoted in Okun's Law; typical estimates of μ might therefore range from about 0.5 to 0.7.

Let us now proceed to some model analysis, and more specifically to deriving the reduced-form "Okun–Verdoorn equation," which combines the Okun effect and the Verdoorn effect, and which constitutes the bottom line of this module. For the long-term Verdoorn component we can then write:

$$L_K \ddot{s}_\tau^{Y,\beta} \equiv \ddot{q}_\tau^{Y,\beta} - \ddot{q}_\tau^{L,\beta} \equiv \left({}_K \ddot{s}_\tau^{Y,\beta} + \ddot{q}_\tau^K\right) - \ddot{q}_\tau^{L,\beta} = {}_K \ddot{s}_\tau^{Y,\beta} + \kappa\lambda \dot{q}_\tau^{L,\gamma} = {}_K \ddot{s}_\tau^{Y,\beta} + \kappa \dot{q}_\tau^{Y,\gamma}$$
$$- \lambda\mu \dot{q}_\tau^{Y,\gamma} = {}_K \ddot{s}_\tau^{Y,\beta} + (\kappa - \lambda\mu) \dot{q}_\tau^{Y,\gamma} \tag{9}$$

Now introduce the fourth assumption, namely, that the filtering of structural variables over any significant sample period must satisfy the condition

$$E[{}_K \ddot{s}_\tau^{Y,\beta}] \equiv \frac{1}{\tau}\int_0^\tau {}_K \ddot{s}_u^{Y,\beta} d\mu = 0 \tag{10}$$

where E[.] is the expectations operator. What this means is simply that we permit secular drift in the benchmark output–capital ratio, but we do not permit secular acceleration. On this assumption the integral in question reads:

$$_L\dot{s}_\tau^{Y,\beta} \equiv {}_L\dot{s}_0^{Y,\beta} + \int_0^\tau {}_L\ddot{s}_u^{Y,\beta}du = \int_0^\tau {}_K\ddot{s}_u^{Y,\beta}du + (\kappa - \lambda\mu)\int_0^\tau \dot{q}_\tau^{Y,\gamma}du$$

$$= (\kappa - \lambda\mu)(q_\tau^{Y,\gamma} - q_0^{Y,\gamma}) = \alpha + \beta q_\tau^{Y,\gamma} \tag{11}$$

The Verdoorn component, thus, boils down to a linear "pro-structural" relationship between the output gap (between actual and benchmark output, also known as capacity utilization) and the underlying growth rate of labor productivity. Thus, the more demand pressure there is in the economy, the higher will be the rate of productivity growth. The relationship is not just cyclical but long term. As to the coefficients, rough estimates for various industrialized countries indicate that the slope parameter for the "Verdoorn effect" (β) might lie in the interval from zero to about 0.2.

The Okun component models the cyclical deviations in labor productivity growth from the underlying trend as given by the Verdoorn component. The derivation is straightforward:

$$_L\dot{s}_\tau^{Y,\gamma} \equiv (\dot{q}_\tau^{Y,\gamma} - \dot{q}_\tau^{L,\gamma}) = \dot{q}_\tau^{Y,\gamma} - \mu\dot{q}_\tau^{Y,\gamma} = (1 - \mu)\dot{q}_\tau^{Y,\gamma} = \gamma\dot{q}_\tau^{Y,\gamma} \tag{12}$$

Cyclical labor productivity, thus, is simply a constant times the output gap. The constant, which gauges the "Okun effect" of the model, is given as one minus the inverse of the traditionally stated Okun elasticity, which in practice would render a figure of about 0.3 to 0.7.[34]

The reduced-form "Okun–Verdoorn equation" obtains by simply adding the Okun component to the previously derived Verdoorn component, i.e., by grafting on the cycle to the underlying long-term or "structural" relationship. The resulting equation, which is suitable for econometric estimation, reads:

$$_L\dot{s}_\tau^{Y,\alpha} \equiv {}_L\dot{s}_\tau^{Y,\beta} + {}_L\dot{s}_\tau^{Y,\gamma} = \alpha + \beta q_\tau^{Y,\gamma} + \gamma\dot{q}_\tau^{Y,\gamma} \tag{13}$$

An intriguing aspect of this model is that the benchmark employment speed-of-adjustment parameter λ, which corresponds to the *ad hoc* smoothing parameters (signal-to-noise ratios) used in the literature on the time-varying NAIRU, can be obtained indirectly from estimates of the investment function and the Okun–Verdoorn equation. Combining $\beta \equiv \kappa - \lambda\mu$ and $\gamma \equiv 1 - \mu$ we get $\lambda \equiv (\kappa - \beta)/(1 - \gamma)$, where κ is obtained from the investment equation, and β and γ from the Okun–Verdoorn equation. In other words, there is no need for direct estimation of λ; its value is implied by the other parameters of the model.

We noted above that the Okun–Verdoorn module exports the growth rates of actual employment and benchmark (potential) output to the rest of the model. It may be of interest, therefore, to derive from the above model the two relevant equations. Starting with benchmark output, we have:

$$\dot{q}_\tau^{Y,\beta} \equiv \dot{q}_\tau^{L,\beta} + {}_L\dot{s}_\tau^{Y,\beta} = \left(\dot{q}_0^{L,\beta} + \int_0^\tau \ddot{q}_u^{L,\beta}du\right) + (\alpha + \beta q_\tau^{Y,\gamma}) = \dot{q}_0^{L,\beta} + \lambda\mu\int_0^\tau \dot{q}_u^{Y,\gamma}du$$

$$- (\kappa - \lambda\mu)q_0^{Y,\gamma} + (\kappa - \lambda\mu)q_\tau^{Y,\gamma} = \dot{q}_0^{L,\beta} + \lambda\mu(q_\tau^{Y,\gamma} - q_0^{Y,\gamma}) + (\kappa - \lambda\mu)$$
$$(q_\tau^{Y,\gamma} - q_0^{Y,\gamma}) = \eta + \kappa q_\tau^{Y,\gamma} \tag{14}$$

Benchmark output growth, thus, is a simple linear function of the output gap. The slope parameter (κ) is simply the speed-of-adjustment coefficient of the investment function. A 10-percent output gap may therefore be expected to speed up potential-output growth by about $1\frac{1}{2}$ to 2 percentage points. η is the intercept constant, as defined in Table 9.6.

Turning to the employment function, we have:

$$\dot{q}_\tau^{L,\alpha} \equiv \dot{q}_\tau^{L,\beta} + \dot{q}_\tau^{L,\gamma} = \left(\dot{q}_0^{L,\beta} + \int_0^\tau \ddot{q}_u^{L,\beta}du\right) + \mu\dot{q}_\tau^{Y,\gamma} = \dot{q}_0^{L,\beta} + \lambda\mu(q_\tau^{Y,\gamma} - q_0^{Y,\gamma})$$

$$+ \mu\dot{q}_\tau^{Y,\gamma} = \nu + \lambda\mu q_\tau^{Y,\gamma} + \mu\dot{q}_\tau^{Y,\gamma} \tag{15}$$

Not surprisingly, this equation has the same linear first-order differential form as the Okun–Verdoorn equation. The cyclical effect is taken directly from the Okun equation, with the Okun elasticity as its slope parameter; the benchmark effect also depends on the benchmark-employment speed-of-adjustment coefficient.

The Phillips Curve

The Philips Curve inflation model is based on five very straightforward assumptions, expressed by the following five equations:

$$\dot{p}_\tau^{L,\gamma} = \psi\dot{q}_\tau^{L,\gamma} \qquad \text{Money-wage cycle} \tag{16}$$

$$\dot{p}_\tau^{Y,\gamma} = \gamma\dot{c}_\tau^{L,\gamma} + \xi\dot{q}_\tau^{Y,\gamma} \quad \text{Mark-up cycle} \tag{17}$$

$$\gamma\dot{r}_\tau^{L,\epsilon} = \rho\dot{q}_\tau^{L,\gamma} \qquad \text{Real-wage-claims cycle} \tag{18}$$

$$\ddot{p}_\tau^{L,\beta} = \omega \cdot \gamma\dot{r}_\tau^{L,\phi} \qquad \text{Adjustment of underlying money-wage trend} \tag{19}$$

$$\gamma\dot{r}_\tau^{L,\beta} = {}_L\dot{s}_\tau^{Y,\beta} \qquad \text{Steady-state income distribution} \tag{20}$$

Money-wage cycle: This equation describes the cyclical deviations of the rate of increase of money wages from the underlying benchmark trend.

The elasticity coefficient (ψ) is likely to take a slightly negative value reflecting the pattern that a cyclical upswing tends to create jobs that are paid less than the trend average. Another way of thinking about the same phenomenon is that relatively high-paid career jobs are also relatively stable jobs, and thus less susceptible to cyclical variations. A reasonable guess about the elasticity might be somewhere between -0.3 and zero.

Mark-up cycle: Mark-ups of prices over costs are clearly pro-cyclical. In this equation the excess of the output price level over unit labor cost is specified as a simple elasticity response to the output gap – all this, of course, written up in terms of growth rates. Empirically, the elasticity in question might lie in the region of 0.3 to 0.5.[35]

Real-wage-claims cycle: This equation shows the response of workers' wage aspirations (namely, "desired" real wages) to cyclical changes in the state of employment. Clearly an employment upswing should induce higher real-wage claims, so the response elasticity (ρ) must be positive. How steep the slope of the curve actually is remains an open question; the author feels inclined to guess a value around 2.

Adjustment of underlying money-wage trend: This equation shows how money wages accelerate in response to a "claims gap," where desired real-wages exceed actual real wages. The speed-of-adjustment coefficient (ω) will depend on a host of institutional and other factors, notably the average duration of "staggered" wage contracts.[36] It is likely that this adaptation is rather sluggish; a vague guess is that ω might lie between 0.2 and 0.6.

Steady-state income distribution: This equation merely reflects the hypothesis that in the long run, real wages tend to increase along with labor productivity so as to keep the wage share of national income constant. While empirically relevant, this is a rather crude assumption from the theoretical point of view. In a more sophisticated model one could refine the story by involving real interest rates, profit margins, etc., so as to provide more of an actual "explanation" of the forces underlying the empirical stylized fact. Our model only involves one such refinement, namely the role of taxation in the drama of "functional" income distribution.

To capture in a simplified way the supply-side effects of changes in the rate of taxation, we modify the equation so as to reflect the increased distributive tension arising from heavier taxation, and the lowering of take-home real wages that it entails. If we assume that the tax rate (relative to income) is ramped-up linearly by a total of 100Δ percentage points in the time interval $\tau = [a, b]$, we can express this ramp as follows:

$$_Y\dot{r}_\tau^{L,\beta} = {}_L\dot{s}_\tau^{Y,\beta} - \frac{\Delta}{c - a}, \quad a < \tau < c \tag{21}$$

In effect, ramping up taxes, while keeping aggregate demand going by e.g. traditional "tax-and-spend" policies, means that take-home real wages will be eroded, and this erosion will intensify the level of distributive conflict (in model terms, increase the "claims gap" between "desired" and actual real wages) and therefore lead to somewhat faster inflation. This mechanism provides a "cost-push" explanation of some observed phenomena, e.g., the acceleration of inflation during the 1960s and early 1970s, prior to the oil shock.[37]

Let us now turn to a brief model analysis. Using the Okun equation, it is easy to rewrite the money-wage cycle in terms of the output gap rather than the employment gap:

$$\dot{p}_\tau^{L,\gamma} = \psi \dot{q}_\tau^{L,\gamma} = \psi \mu \dot{q}_\tau^{Y,\gamma} = \phi \dot{q}_\tau^{Y,\gamma} \tag{22}$$

Substitution of this result and the Okun component (of the Okun–Verdoorn equation) permits us to re-express also the unit-labor-cost cycle in terms of the output gap:

$$_Y\dot{c}_\tau^{L,\gamma} \equiv \dot{p}_\tau^{L,\gamma} - {}_L\dot{s}_\tau^{Y,\gamma} = \phi \dot{q}_\tau^{Y,\gamma} - \gamma \dot{q}_\tau^{Y,\gamma} = (\phi - \gamma)\dot{q}_\tau^{Y,\gamma} \tag{23}$$

This leads, sequentially, to the mark-up cycle, the real-wage cycle, and to the wage-share cycle, all of which can be rewritten as functions of the output gap:

$$\dot{p}_\tau^{Y,\gamma} = {}_Y\dot{c}_\tau^{L,\gamma} + \xi \dot{q}_\tau^{Y,\gamma} = (\phi - \gamma)\dot{q}_\tau^{Y,\gamma} + \xi \dot{q}_\tau^{Y,\gamma} = (\phi - \gamma + \xi)\dot{q}_\tau^{Y,\gamma} \tag{24}$$

$$_Y\dot{r}_\tau^{L,\gamma} \equiv \dot{p}_\tau^{L,\gamma} - \dot{p}_\tau^{Y,\gamma} = \phi \dot{q}_\tau^{Y,\gamma} - (\phi - \gamma + \xi)\dot{q}_\tau^{Y,\gamma} = (\gamma - \xi)\dot{q}_\tau^{Y,\gamma} \tag{25}$$

$$_Y\dot{w}_\tau^{L,\gamma} \equiv {}_Y\dot{r}_\tau^{L,\gamma} - {}_L\dot{s}_\tau^{Y,\gamma} = (\gamma - \xi)\dot{q}_\tau^{Y,\gamma} - \gamma \dot{q}_\tau^{Y,\gamma} = -\xi \dot{q}_\tau^{Y,\gamma} \tag{26}$$

Furthermore, we can substitute the Okun equation into the real-wage-claims cycle to obtain:

$$_Y\dot{r}_\tau^{L,\epsilon} = \rho \dot{q}_\tau^{L,\gamma} = \rho \mu \dot{q}_\tau^{Y,\gamma} \tag{27}$$

Again invoking the Verdoorn component of the Okun–Verdoorn equation, we can re-express the steady-state income distribution:

$$_Y\dot{r}_\tau^{L,\beta} = {}_L\dot{s}_\tau^{Y,\beta} = \alpha + \beta q_\tau^{Y,\gamma} \tag{28}$$

For actual real wages and real-wage claims we then have, respectively:

$$_Y\dot{r}_\tau^{L,\alpha} \equiv {}_Y\dot{r}_\tau^{L,\beta} + {}_Y\dot{r}_\tau^{L,\gamma} = \alpha + \beta q_\tau^{Y,\gamma} + (\gamma - \xi)\dot{q}_\tau^{Y,\gamma} \tag{29}$$

$$_Y\dot{r}_\tau^{L,\delta} \equiv {}_Y\dot{r}_\tau^{L,\beta} + {}_Y\dot{r}_\tau^{L,\epsilon} = \alpha + \beta q_\tau^{Y,\gamma} + \rho \mu \dot{q}_\tau^{Y,\gamma} \tag{30}$$

This enables us to reformulate the real-wage-claims gap as:

$$\gamma \dot{r}_\tau^{L,\phi} = (\alpha + \beta q_\tau^{Y,\gamma} + \rho\mu \dot{q}_\tau^{Y,\gamma}) - (\alpha + \beta q_\tau^{Y,\gamma} + (\gamma - \xi)\dot{q}_\tau^{Y,\gamma})$$
$$= (\rho\mu + \xi - \gamma)\dot{q}_\tau^{Y,\gamma} \tag{31}$$

The wage-trend-adjustment equation, finally, can be written:

$$\dot{p}_\tau^{L,\beta} = \omega \cdot {}_\gamma \dot{r}_\tau^{L,\phi} = \omega \, (\rho\mu + \xi - \gamma)\dot{q}_\tau^{Y,\gamma} = \epsilon \dot{q}_\tau^{Y,\gamma} \tag{32}$$

Integration of the wage-trend-adjustment equation yields:

$$\dot{p}_\tau^{L,\beta} = \dot{p}_0^{L,\beta} + \int_0^\tau \ddot{p}_u^{L,\beta}du = \dot{p}_0^{L,\beta} + \int_0^\tau \epsilon\dot{q}_u^{Y,\gamma}du = \dot{p}_0^{L,\beta} + \epsilon(q_\tau^{Y,\gamma} - q_0^{Y,\gamma})$$
$$= \delta + \epsilon q_\tau^{Y,\gamma} \tag{33}$$

Combining the short- and long-run components we can write:

$$\dot{p}_\tau^{L,\alpha} \equiv \dot{p}_\tau^{L,\beta} + \dot{p}_\tau^{L,\gamma} = \delta + \epsilon q_\tau^{Y,\gamma} + \phi\dot{q}_\tau^{Y,\gamma} \tag{34}$$

which is the bottom line of our derivations, namely, the estimable reduced-form "Wage Phillips Curve" equation. Note the direct parallel to the Okun–Verdoorn productivity equation! Again we have a linear first-order differential with one long-term or "structural" slope parameter (ϵ), and one short-run cyclical elasticity (ϕ).

It will also be of interest to derive an equation for the output price dynamics, namely, a "Price Phillips Curve." Combining the Wage Phillips Curve, the Verdoorn component of the Okun–Verdoorn equation, and the real-wage cycle equation, we have:

$$\dot{p}_\tau^{Y,\alpha} \equiv \dot{p}_\tau^{L,\alpha} - (\dot{p}_\tau^{L,\alpha} - \dot{p}_\tau^{Y,\alpha}) \equiv \dot{p}_\tau^{L,\alpha} - {}_\gamma \dot{r}_\tau^{L,\alpha} = (\delta + \epsilon q_\tau^{Y,\gamma} + \phi\dot{q}_\tau^{Y,\gamma})$$
$$- (\alpha + \beta q_\tau^{Y,\gamma} + (\gamma - \xi)\dot{q}_\tau^{Y,\gamma}) = (\delta - \alpha) + (\epsilon - \beta)q_\tau^{Y,\gamma} + (\phi + \xi - \gamma)\dot{q}_\tau^{Y,\gamma}$$
$$= \pi + \rho q_\tau^{Y,\gamma} + \sigma\dot{q}_\tau^{Y,\gamma} \tag{35}$$

The pattern thus repeats itself. This equation, too, is a linear first-order differential, i.e. the very same functional form that we have seen three times already. Money-wage and price inflation both depend upon the level and the changes in "capacity utilization" (the output gap). It is a fair guess that the cyclical coefficients (ϕ and σ) will turn out to be negative in both cases, σ considerably more so than ϕ, thus indicating counter-cyclical wage and price patterns. As to the structural or trend coefficients (ϵ and ρ), the wage curve is probably sloping upward ($\epsilon > 0$), although it is hard to tell *a priori* how steep it might be. It is anybody's guess whether the price curve has any significant positive slope at all; it is very likely to be somewhat flatter than the wage curve, but it could also go below zero into the downward-sloping territory.

Summary of the supply block

To summarize Okun–Verdoorn and Phillips Curve modules, let us just restate the two central reduced-form equations of each model – four equations all in all, and they are all of the same linear first-order differential form. In the Okun–Verdoorn module, we have the Okun–Verdoorn equation, which expresses labor-productivity growth in terms of both the level and the changes in capacity utilization. The employment function shows actual employment growth as a function of the level and changes in capacity utilization. The Phillips Curve comes in two variants: The wage curve describes the rate of increase of money wages as a function of the level and changes in capacity utilization; the price curve models the rate of output price inflation as a function of the same independent variables. The four equations are reproduced here for convenience:

$$_L\dot{s}_\tau^{Y,\alpha} = \alpha + \beta q_\tau^{Y,\gamma} + \gamma \dot{q}_\tau^{Y,\gamma} \qquad \text{Okun–Verdoorn equation} \qquad (36)$$

$$\dot{q}_\tau^{L,\alpha} = \nu + \lambda\mu q_\tau^{Y,\gamma} + \mu\dot{q}_\tau^{Y,\gamma} \qquad \text{Employment function} \qquad (37)$$

$$\dot{p}_\tau^{L,\alpha} = \delta + \epsilon q_\tau^{Y,\gamma} + \phi\dot{q}_\tau^{Y,\gamma} \qquad \text{Wage Phillips Curve} \qquad (38)$$

$$\dot{p}_\tau^{Y,\alpha} = \pi + \rho q_\tau^{Y,\gamma} + \sigma\dot{q}_\tau^{Y,\gamma} \qquad \text{Price Phillips Curve} \qquad (39)$$

Reduced-form differential equations on the same form as the above four can be derived also for unit labor costs, for the wage share of national income, and for real wages. We will leave those derivations as exercises for the interested reader, and instead turn to the demand block.

The demand block

The demand block consists of a stock-flow consistent Keynesian multiplier model, which generates trajectories for a selection of national-accounts stock and flow aggregates. Despite its appearance, the model is actually very simple; it little more than a "Keynesian cross" or 45-degree-diagram model, with the implications of saving, investment and public debt accumulation drawn out by means of stock-flow accounting. Two feedback effects from stocks to flows have been added, in the form of an accelerator-type investment function[38] (capital stock impacts the investment flow) and a wealth effect in the consumption function (private net worth impacts private consumption).

The rationale behind this particular design is to provide a model that fulfils the following requirements: (1) it must generate the actual domestic product trajectory needed as input in the supply block; (2) it must permit fiscal-policy analysis and therefore include government expenditures and taxation along standard Keynesian lines; (3) it must be stock-flow consistent and account for the accumulation of financial and nonfinancial stocks of assets; (4) it must permit behavioral feedback loops from stocks to flows, e.g. the wealth effect on consumption spending. We have aimed at finding the simplest possible blueprint given these constraints and requirements. The point is to provide a basic model as a starting-point from which one might proceed to build more complex contraptions. Starting at the Rube Goldberg level may not be advisable.

The demand block uses as inputs from the supply block the growth rate of benchmark (potential) output, and the rate of inflation, which is assumed to be common for all stock and flow variables except the flow of labor services. The demand block can be run independently of the supply block, i.e., the supply block of the model can be switched-off, provided that the two mentioned variables are fed into the model as exogenous data. One can also run the model with the Okun–Verdoorn block "on," but the Phillips Curve "off," in which case the non-wage inflation rate (but not potential output) must be specified exogenously.

The main novelty, and also, we suspect, the chief source of bewilderment on the part of the reader, is the Divisia-type contributions-to-growth accounting featured in this model. The comforting message is that behind this unusual casting lurks nothing revolutionary or even unusual. We are dealing with the same old Keynesian textbook story; it only looks different when recast in terms of contributions to growth instead of the ordinary "real" levels.

Much like in the supply block, the dynamics of the model may fruitfully be subdivided into short-term or cyclical dynamics on the one hand, and long-term or structural dynamics on the other. In this respect, the model is fully in line with the traditional approach of the "neoclassical synthesis," which has two distinct systems for the short run and the long run. Yet our system is different from the "synthesis" in one crucial respect. Whereas the "synthesis" *dichotomizes* the short run and the long run, so that the one can be analyzed independently of the other, our system does not permit such partitioning. In our system the long-run analysis is intertwined with the short-run analysis; there is no presumption of orthogonality between the two. Our short runs cumulate into our long run, and our long run feeds back into our short runs.

The long-run dynamics of our system, which may be seen as the "backbone" of the model, are governed by the interaction of two "grand ratios," namely, the capital–output ratio and the private wealth-to-spending ratio, with the fiscal-policy instruments of government spending and taxation. Let us, for the purpose of quick explanation, make a brief excursion from our ordinary and more complex notation system, to consider briefly and somewhat informally the basic principles of the steady-state properties of the "grand-ratios" model.[39]

Let A denote private demand (consumption and investment), G government spending, Y domestic product, K capital stock, W private net worth, and D government debt – all renormalized by capital stock. Let $A = \alpha W$ depict the steady-state wealth-to-spending relationship, and $K = \beta Y$ the steady-state output–capital relationship. Substituting this into the identities $Y \equiv A + G$ and $W \equiv K + D$ and solving for Y, we obtain the following steady-state relationship between output, government spending and debt:

$$Y = \frac{1}{1 - \alpha\beta} (\alpha D + G) \tag{40}$$

Setting, for the sake of illustration, $\alpha = 0.2$ and $\beta = 4$, we have $Y = D + 5G$. Thus, on the basis of the exceedingly simple assumptions we have made, the steady state level of output becomes a simple linear function of government spending and debt (all relative to capital stock). The economy is driven, functional-finance style, by government spending and debt. The same basic approach underpins our demand-block model, although some layers of complexity have been added, e.g., by subdividing private demand into consumption and investment spending, by allowing the capital–output ratio to drift over time, by grafting cyclical swings to the structural benchmarks, and by using the Divisia-type growth-accounting system.

The short-run deviations from benchmark values – the "cyclical swings" – form a Keynesian multiplier system, with feedback loops running through the basic macroeconomic accounting identities. The multiplier system is linear and therefore easiest to express in matrix form. When the dynamics of the system is included, however, the resulting system of differential equations becomes non-linear. The non-linearities are by no means severe, but will nevertheless make analytical "pencil-and-paper" work quite complicated. The best way to proceed with the analysis of the properties of the system is through computer-based Monte Carlo simulation exercises, in which one may also consider making the parameters stochastic.[40]

Additional notation

It will be convenient to express the demand model in matrix and vector notation. In order to do so, we must risk straining the reader's patience by introducing some additional notation for the purpose. We will use a bold typeface to designate matrices and vectors, as is customary.

First let us define three vectors, consisting, respectively, of national-accounts asset stocks (index set K, see Table 9.4), of national-accounts income and expenditure flows (index set Λ), and of national-accounts stock-building flows (index set Ψ, which is a subset of Λ):

$$_n\mathbf{Z}_\tau^{K,m} \equiv [_nZ_\tau^{K,m} \quad _nZ_\tau^{W,m} \quad _nZ_\tau^{D,m}]^\mathrm{T} \tag{41}$$

$$_n\mathbf{Z}_\tau^{\Lambda,m} \equiv \left[_nZ_\tau^{C,m} \quad _nZ_\tau^{L,m} \quad _nZ_\tau^{G,m} \quad _nZ_\tau^{Y,m} \quad _nZ_\tau^{T,m} \quad _nZ_\tau^{B,m} \quad _nZ_\tau^{YD,m} \right.$$
$$\left. _nZ_\tau^{S,m} \right]^{\mathrm{T}} \tag{42}$$

$$_n\mathbf{Z}_\tau^{\Psi,m} \equiv \left[_nZ_\tau^{L,m} \quad _nZ_\tau^{S,m} \quad _nZ_\tau^{B,m} \right]^{\mathrm{T}} \tag{43}$$

where superscript $[.]^{\mathrm{T}}$ denotes the matrix transposition operator.

Second let us introduce bars over the "m" superscript to designate model intercepts or "shocks." A single bar, namely, $\bar{m}$, will denote the Keynesian-multiplier intercept, and double bars, namely, $\bar{\bar{m}}$, the autonomous part of the intercept – if the intercept is induced by the extra-multiplier components of the model.

Third, introduce the following notation for the multidimensional array (or "cube") of partial derivatives projecting contributions to volume growth into themselves:

$$\Gamma_{k,m,n,\tau}^{k',m',n',\tau'} \equiv \left[\frac{\partial\left(_{n'}\dot{g}_{\tau'}^{k',m'}\right)}{\partial\left(_n\dot{g}_\tau^{k,m}\right)} \right] \tag{44}$$

where the bracketed partial derivative is the typical element of the cube.

Model assumptions and some analysis

In our model, the Γ-array will materialize as the following matrix, defined with respect to the index sets $k, k', n, n' \in \mathrm{K}, \Lambda; m, m' \in \mathrm{M}$

$$\Gamma_{\Lambda,\gamma,K,\tau}^{\Lambda,\gamma,K,\tau} = \begin{bmatrix} 0 & 0 & 0 & 0 & 0 & 0 & \chi & 0 \\ 0 & 0 & 0 & \kappa\cdot_\gamma W_\tau^K & 0 & 0 & 0 & 0 \\ 0 & 0 & 0 & 0 & 0 & 0 & 0 & 0 \\ 1 & 1 & 1 & 0 & 0 & 0 & 0 & 0 \\ 0 & 0 & 0 & \theta & 0 & 0 & 0 & 0 \\ 0 & 0 & 1 & 0 & -1 & 0 & 0 & 0 \\ 0 & 0 & 0 & 1 & -1 & 0 & 0 & 0 \\ -1 & 0 & 0 & 0 & 0 & 0 & 1 & 0 \end{bmatrix} \tag{45}$$

Using the vector notation we just introduced, we can write the core Keynesian multiplier system as follows:

$$_K\dot{\mathbf{g}}_\tau^{\Lambda,\gamma} = \Gamma_{\Lambda,\gamma,K,\tau}^{\Lambda,\gamma,K,\tau} \cdot {}_K\dot{\mathbf{g}}_\tau^{\Lambda,\gamma} + {}_K\dot{\mathbf{g}}_\tau^{\Lambda,\bar{\gamma}} \tag{46}$$

In three places we find the 8×1 vector of gap contributions to growth (i.e., the difference between actual and benchmark contributions to growth). The first right-hand side term makes it clear that the Γ-matrix serves to project the **g** vector into itself, in a Keynesian feedback loop. Observe that the last right-hand side term is the intercept vector, as indicated by the bar over the second superscript γ.

The solution of this system reads (provided, of course, that the inverse exists):

$$_K\dot{\mathbf{g}}_\tau^{\Lambda,\gamma} = [\mathbf{I}_\Lambda - \Gamma_{\Lambda,\gamma,K,\tau}^{\Lambda,\gamma,K,\tau}]^{-1} \cdot {}_K\dot{\mathbf{g}}_\tau^{\Lambda,\bar{\gamma}} \tag{47}$$

where $\mathbf{I}_\Lambda$ is an identity matrix of the same dimension as the number of elements in the index set Λ (eight in this model), and where the $[.]^{-1}$ superscript is the matrix inversion operator. This expression is just a standard "matrix multiplier," a standard tool in input-output analysis as well as in other macroeconomic analysis.

The Γ-matrix, which constitutes the very core of the system, calls for some commentary. This matrix is a powerful tool, which incorporates not only the key national accounting identities, but also the central behavioral assumptions of the system. Let us therefore walk through the matrix row by row.

The top row is the short-run consumption function, with χ denoting the "marginal propensity to consume" from disposable income (column 7); there are no other factors behind consumption. The second row shows the investment function, with $\kappa \cdot {}_Y W_\tau^K$ denoting the Hicksian super-multiplier "marginal propensity to invest," as related to the output gap (column 4).[41] The third row pertains to government spending, and is occupied by zeros indicating its exogeneity in the model. The fourth row pertains to output (domestic product), and it shows the familiar accounting identity $Y \equiv C + I + G$,[42] as indicated by the ones occupying the first (consumption), second (investment) and third (government spending) columns respectively.

The fifth row is the tax revenue row; θ is the traditional "marginal macro" tax rate defined net of transfer payments. Row number six relates to the budget deficit, which is defined by government spending (column 3) minus tax revenues (column 5), as indicated by the one and the minus one, respectively. The next last row refers to disposable income, defined by national income (=domestic product in a closed economy, column 4) minus taxes (column 5). Lastly, we have the saving row, defined by disposable income (column 7) minus consumption (column 1).

Evidently this type of matrix is a very convenient way of compactly assembling the behavioral and the accounting relationships in respect of the multiplier core of a Keynesian macroeconomic model. Our model is of course very crude – it is just a simple three-sector "Keynesian cross" model. Larger feedback matrices can be devised for more detailed and sophisticated systems, including systems based on fully articulated social accounting matrices.[43]

Extracting growth rates and levels

After solving the multiplier core, we can proceed to extract a substantial amount of national-accounts information from it. First recall our assumption that all (non-wage) relative prices are constant, namely,

$$_K\dot{\mathbf{f}}_\tau^{\Lambda,\gamma} = 0 \tag{48}$$

On this assumption the Divisia growth-accounting identity

$$_K\dot{\mathbf{W}}_\tau^\Lambda \equiv {}_K\dot{\mathbf{h}}_\tau^{\Lambda,\gamma} \equiv {}_K\dot{\mathbf{f}}_\tau^{\Lambda,\gamma} + {}_K\dot{\mathbf{g}}_\tau^{\Lambda,\gamma} \tag{49}$$

boils down to

$$_K\dot{\mathbf{W}}_\tau^\Lambda \equiv {}_K\dot{\mathbf{h}}_\tau^{\Lambda,\gamma} = {}_K\dot{\mathbf{g}}_\tau^{\Lambda,\gamma} \tag{50}$$

In other words, the changes in flow weights (nominal shares) are obtained directly from the solution of the flow matrix multiplier system. The next step will be to cumulate these changes in weights to levels of weights, which is done by integration:

$$_K\mathbf{W}_\tau^\Lambda \equiv {}_K\mathbf{W}_0^\Lambda + \int_0^\tau {}_K\dot{\mathbf{W}}_u^\Lambda \cdot du \tag{51}$$

We may also recall that our "floating benchmarks" are defined by:

$$_K\dot{\mathbf{g}}_\tau^{\Lambda,\beta} \equiv {}_K\mathbf{W}_\tau^\Lambda \cdot \dot{q}_\tau^{K,\alpha} \tag{52}$$

and that the actual contributions to growth can be calculated by adding the gaps as obtained from the multiplier core to the benchmarks:

$$_K\dot{\mathbf{g}}_\tau^{\Lambda,\alpha} \equiv {}_K\dot{\mathbf{g}}_\tau^{\Lambda,\beta} + {}_K\dot{\mathbf{g}}_\tau^{\Lambda,\gamma} \tag{53}$$

Further consider the definition of the actual contributions to growth:

$$_K\dot{\mathbf{g}}_\tau^{\Lambda,\alpha} \equiv [_K\mathbf{W}_\tau^\Lambda]^D \cdot \dot{\mathbf{q}}_\tau^{\Lambda,\alpha} \tag{54}$$

where superscript $[.]^D$ denotes the matrix diagonalization operator. Solving this system yields the vector of volume growth rates:[44]

$$\dot{\mathbf{q}}_\tau^{\Lambda,\alpha} \equiv [_K\mathbf{W}_\tau^\Lambda]^{D,-1} \cdot {}_K\dot{\mathbf{g}}_\tau^{\Lambda,\alpha} \tag{55}$$

where $[.]^{D,-1}$ indicates diagonalization and inversion of the matrix, in that order.

Under our simplifying assumption of constant relative prices, we have $\dot{\mathbf{p}}_\tau^{\Lambda,\alpha} = \dot{p}_\tau^{Y,\alpha}$, as imported from the supply block of the model. We can use this to extract nominal-value growth rates:

$$\dot{\mathbf{v}}_\tau^{\Lambda,\alpha} \equiv \dot{\mathbf{p}}_\tau^{\Lambda,\alpha} + \dot{\mathbf{q}}_\tau^{\Lambda,\alpha} \tag{56}$$

Integration then yields the log nominal values:

$$\mathbf{v}_\tau^{\Lambda,\alpha} \equiv \mathbf{v}_0^{\Lambda,\alpha} + \int_0^\tau \dot{\mathbf{v}}_u^{\Lambda,\alpha} \cdot du \qquad (57)$$

and nominal-value levels are finally reached by exponentiation:

$$\mathbf{v}_\tau^{\Lambda,\alpha} \equiv \exp(\mathbf{v}_\tau^{\Lambda,\alpha}) \qquad (58)$$

where exp(.) is the exponential function. Similarly, integration of price inflation yields logarithmic price levels:

$$\mathbf{p}_\tau^{\Lambda,\alpha} \equiv \mathbf{p}_0^{\Lambda,\alpha} + \int_0^\tau \dot{\mathbf{p}}_u^{\Lambda,\alpha} \cdot du \qquad (59)$$

Price levels then obtain by exponentiation:

$$\mathbf{P}_\tau^{\Lambda,\alpha} \equiv \exp(\mathbf{p}_\tau^{\Lambda,\alpha}) \qquad (60)$$

Volumes, finally, are best obtained not by integration and exponentiation of growth rates, but by deflation of nominal values. The reason for this is that volumes, but not prices, sometimes take on negative values. The deflation expression reads:

$$\mathbf{Q}_\tau^{\Lambda,\alpha} \equiv [\mathbf{P}_\tau^{\Lambda,\alpha}]^{D,-1} \cdot \mathbf{V}_\tau^{\Lambda,\alpha} \qquad (61)$$

We have now showed that the information in the core matrix multiplier system, supplemented only by inflation rates (imported either from the supply block or as exogenous data) and some initial conditions of no economic significance (they only serve to definitize index numbers) is sufficient to recover both growth rates and levels of all components involved in the system. In particular, the actual output growth rate can be computed and exported to the supply block.

It is worth observing that the connection between the demand and supply block does not involve any simultaneous feedbacks. The benchmark output growth rate, exported from the supply block to the demand block, is a "state variable," whereas the actual output growth rate, exported from the demand block to the supply block, is a "rate," not a level. The demand side gets started, so to speak, by assuming an initial condition for the benchmark output growth rate. On this basis it can generate a first value for the actual growth rate for the next "tick" of time. The supply block receives this information and cranks out a new value for the benchmark output growth rate, and so on. The interaction is sequential, not simultaneous, and it is so by virtue of the "dimensional" difference between actual and benchmark output from the modeling point of view. The actual economic dimension of the two is of course the same (they are both flows).

Moreover, the actual price inflation rates exported from the supply block to the demand block are all precisely equal to the "floating benchmark" price inflation rates that would obtain had they been calculated independently in the demand block of a fully specified demand system. The assumption of constant relative prices is therefore crucial to avoid simultaneity in the interaction between the Phillips Curve and the demand block. The picture would also be vastly complicated by the concurrence of two different benchmarking systems. Future developments of this modeling system should therefore probably focus on the demand block, and develop pricing mechanics and dynamics that can supersede the present Phillips Curve specifications. Again the present situation is an outcome of starting with the supply block and then working out a suitable demand block that can "drive" the supply side.

Stock-flow accounting relations

Thanks to the renormalization of all variables by capital stock, the stock-flow accounting linkages are exceedingly simple. First let us note that the growth rate of any asset is defined by the ratio of the nominal value of the investment (or saving) flowing into the asset and the nominal value of the asset stock itself. In our notation this reads:

$$\dot{\mathbf{q}}_\tau^{K,\alpha} \equiv [\mathbf{V}_\tau^{K,\alpha}]^{D,-1} \cdot \mathbf{V}_\tau^{\Psi,\alpha} \tag{62}$$

We can now substitute this into the definition of the stock contributions to volume growth, to obtain:

$$_K \dot{\mathbf{g}}_\tau^{K,\alpha} \equiv {}_K\mathbf{W}_\tau^K \cdot \dot{\mathbf{q}}_\tau^{K,\alpha} \equiv (V_\tau^{K,\alpha})^{-1} \cdot \mathbf{V}_\tau^{K,\alpha} \cdot \dot{\mathbf{q}}_\tau^{K,\alpha} \equiv (V_\tau^{K,\alpha})^{-1} \cdot \mathbf{V}_\tau^{\Psi,\alpha} \equiv {}_K\mathbf{W}_\tau^\Psi \tag{63}$$

Taking derivatives with respect to time yields the second-order time derivative, which is the core equation for our stock-flow linkages.

$$_K \ddot{\mathbf{g}}_\tau^{K,\alpha} \equiv {}_K\dot{\mathbf{W}}_\tau^\Psi \tag{64}$$

The right-hand side is taken direct from the solution of the matrix multiplier system, and it is then straightforward to integrate to stock contributions to growth:

$$_K \dot{\mathbf{g}}_\tau^{K,\alpha} \equiv {}_K\dot{\mathbf{g}}_0^{K,\alpha} + \int_0^\tau {}_K\ddot{\mathbf{g}}_\tau^{K,\alpha} \cdot du \equiv {}_K\mathbf{W}_\tau^\Psi - {}_K\mathbf{W}_0^\Psi \tag{65}$$

Asset-stock contributions-to-growth benchmarks are defined by:

$$_K \dot{\mathbf{g}}_\tau^{K,\beta} \equiv {}_K\mathbf{W}_\tau^K \cdot \dot{q}_\tau^{K,\alpha} \tag{66}$$

We can therefore calculate the gap contributions to growth for asset stocks as:

$$_K\dot{\mathbf{g}}_\tau^{K,\gamma} \equiv {}_K\dot{\mathbf{g}}_\tau^{K,\alpha} - {}_K\dot{\mathbf{g}}_\tau^{K,\beta} \tag{67}$$

Asset-stock changes in weights are defined by:

$$_K\dot{\mathbf{W}}_\tau^K \equiv {}_K\dot{\mathbf{h}}_\tau^{K,\gamma} \equiv {}_K\dot{\mathbf{f}}_\tau^{K,\gamma} + {}_K\dot{\mathbf{g}}_\tau^{K,\gamma} \tag{68}$$

This however reduces to:

$$_K\dot{\mathbf{W}}_\tau^K \equiv {}_K\dot{\mathbf{h}}_\tau^{K,\gamma} = {}_K\dot{\mathbf{g}}_\tau^{K,\gamma} \tag{69}$$

owing to our fixed-relative-price assumption, which for asset stocks reads:

$$_K\dot{\mathbf{f}}_u^{K,\gamma} = 0 \tag{70}$$

Weight changes in asset stocks are thus obtained indirectly, by subtracting from the actual contributions to growth (as obtained via the above stock-flow accounting links) the independently computed benchmark contributions to growth. Weight levels can now be computed by straightforward integration:

$$_K\mathbf{W}_\tau^K \equiv {}_K\mathbf{W}_0^K + \int_0^\tau {}_K\dot{\mathbf{W}}_u^K \cdot \mathrm{d}u \tag{71}$$

Having obtained these weights, we can proceed to extract volume growth rates and nominal values along the same lines as were shown for flows in the previous section.[45]

Stock-flow behavioral feedback and other intercept amendments

The only feedback effect in our model is the "wealth effect" running from private wealth to private consumption. Recast in terms of contribution to growth gaps, we can write this effect as follows:

$$_K\dot{g}_\tau^{C,\bar{\gamma}} = \zeta \cdot {}_K\dot{g}_\tau^{Y,\gamma} + {}_K\dot{g}_\tau^{C,\bar{\bar{\gamma}}} \tag{72}$$

The intercept of the gap contributions to growth in the flow of private consumption is thereby linked to the gap asset-stock contributions to growth in private wealth, the "marginal propensity to consume from wealth" being given by the parameter ζ. Note that the former intercept (denoted by a single bar over the γ superscript) has now been endogenized, and the exogenous part of the flow intercept is replaced by another intercept (denoted by a double bar over the γ) on the right-hand side.

In order to provide for (endogenous) changes in the benchmark output-to-capital ratio, we need to amend the investment function by including in its intercept the following term:

$$_K\dot{g}_\tau^{I,\tilde{\gamma}} = -\kappa \cdot {}_K\dot{s}_\tau^{Y,\beta} + {}_K\dot{g}_\tau^{I,\bar{\tilde{\gamma}}} \tag{73}$$

Again the "double-bar" variable replaces the "single-bar" variable as the autonomous component, as the (single-bar) multiplier intercept is now endogenized, namely, made dependent on changes in the benchmark output-to-capital ratio.

Another intercept adjustment that we may want to consider is to ramp the tax rate up or down. Let $_Y\dot{W}_\tau^{\bar{T}}$ denote the policy-induced rate of increase in the nominal tax-to-income ratio. The corresponding change in the tax-to-capital-stock ratio $_K\dot{W}_\tau^{\bar{T}}$, which enters into the intercept, can then be calculated as follows:

$$_K\dot{W}_\tau^{\bar{T}} \equiv {}_KW_\tau^Y \cdot {}_Y\dot{W}_\tau^{\bar{T}} \tag{74}$$

Note that the cyclical part of this derivative is excluded by definition, since it falls outside the scope of the "policy-induced" changes, which must be exogenous. Now, if we again use the linear ramp for the tax rate, raising it by 100Δ percentage points in the time interval $\tau = [a, b]$, we can write:

$$_K\dot{W}_\tau^{\bar{T}} = {}_KW_\tau^Y \cdot \frac{\Delta}{c-a}, a < \tau < c \tag{75}$$

Inserting this into the multiplier intercept, we have:

$$_K\dot{g}_\tau^{T,\tilde{\gamma}} = {}_K\dot{W}_\tau^{\bar{T}} + {}_K\dot{g}_\tau^{T,\bar{\tilde{\gamma}}} = {}_KW_\tau^Y \cdot \frac{\Delta}{c-a}, + {}_K\dot{g}_\tau^{T,\tilde{\gamma}}, a < \tau < c \tag{76}$$

where the "double-bar" term is introduced to provide a vehicle for stochastic shocks and other "truly exogenous" mechanisms.

To incorporate these amendments into the core model, arrange them in the following vector:

$$_K\dot{\mathbf{g}}_\tau^{\Lambda,\tilde{\gamma}} = \begin{bmatrix} \zeta \cdot {}_K\dot{g}_\tau^{W,\gamma} - \kappa \cdot {}_K\dot{s}_\tau^{Y,\beta} & 0 & 0 & {}_KW_\tau^Y \cdot \dfrac{\Delta}{c-a} & 0 & 0 & 0 \end{bmatrix}^{\mathrm{T}} \tag{77}$$

The tilde indicates the endogenized part of the intercept. This maneuver permits us to write the intercept vector of the multiplier core as:

$$_K\dot{\mathbf{g}}_\tau^{\Lambda,\tilde{\gamma}} \equiv {}_K\dot{\mathbf{g}}_\tau^{\Lambda,\tilde{\gamma}} + {}_K\dot{\mathbf{g}}_\tau^{\Lambda,\bar{\tilde{\gamma}}} \tag{78}$$

In this expression, the "double-bar" vector includes the "true" intercepts, i.e. after removing the stock-dependent component.

Summary of demand block

We have reached the point where we can summarize the demand block. It turns out that most of what we have seen is merely algebraic footwork that serves to illuminate the functioning of the Divisia-type accounting system. The behavioral core is very simple, and can be expressed by a couple of compressed equations. The solution of the core multiplier system reads:

$$_K\dot{\mathbf{g}}_\tau^{\Lambda,\gamma} = [\mathbf{I}_\Lambda - \Gamma_{\Lambda,\gamma,K,\tau}^{\Lambda,\gamma,K,\tau}]^{-1} \cdot (_K\dot{\mathbf{g}}_\tau^{\Lambda,\bar{\gamma}} + _K\dot{\mathbf{g}}_\tau^{\Lambda,\bar{\bar{\gamma}}}) \tag{79}$$

The core component is the behavioral and accounting relations matrix:

$$\Gamma_{\Lambda,\gamma,K,\tau}^{\Lambda,\gamma,K,\tau} = \begin{bmatrix} 0 & 0 & 0 & 0 & 0 & 0 & \chi & 0 \\ 0 & 0 & 0 & \kappa\cdot_Y W_\tau^K & 0 & 0 & 0 & 0 \\ 0 & 0 & 0 & 0 & 0 & 0 & 0 & 0 \\ 1 & 1 & 1 & 0 & 0 & 0 & 0 & 0 \\ 0 & 0 & 0 & \theta & 0 & 0 & 0 & 0 \\ 0 & 0 & 1 & 0 & -1 & 0 & 0 & 0 \\ 0 & 0 & 0 & 1 & -1 & 0 & 0 & 0 \\ -1 & 0 & 0 & 0 & 0 & 0 & 1 & 0 \end{bmatrix} \tag{80}$$

The intercept feedback vector reads:

$$_K\dot{\mathbf{g}}_\tau^{\Lambda,\bar{\gamma}} = [\zeta\cdot_K\dot{g}_\tau^{W,\gamma} - \kappa\cdot_K\dot{s}_\tau^{Y,\beta} \quad 0 \quad 0 \quad _K W_\tau^Y\cdot\frac{\Delta}{c-a} \quad 0 \quad 0 \quad 0]^\mathrm{T} \tag{81}$$

The intercept vector $_K\dot{\mathbf{g}}_\tau^{\Lambda,\bar{\gamma}}$ should be set to zero except for the component in respect of government spending, which is the sole exogenous variable in our highly simplified system.

As to parameter values, the marginal propensity to consume (MPC) out of income (χ) might reasonably lie in the region between zero and 0.3. These values will strike the reader as low compared to typical estimates, which are in the order of 0.5. One must bear in mind that our parameter pertains to the "contribution to growth" defined in respect of capital stock, which is a concept that is likely to produce a lower MPC figure. But the main culprit behind the low parameter range is our specification of the consumption function, which was discussed in the first part of the paper.[46]

The "accelerator coefficient" (κ), which feeds into the Hicksian super-multiplier "marginal propensity to invest" (MPI, a time-varying parameter in our system), might be positioned in the region from 0.15 to 0.20.[47] With an overall nominal output–capital ratio of 4, this translates to a MPI of 0.60 to 0.80. Clearly the inverse of this is sizeable, thus indicating multiplier effects that are well into the region that produces a paradox of thrift and budget, even if the MPC should be as low as zero.[48]

The "macro marginal" tax rate (θ), finally, will be different for different economies, depending on the size of the government. It should be emphasized that this rate is defined so as to include the taxes and other compulsory fees levied and the transfers paid out by government. This definition implies that θ is considerably higher than the average level of taxation in the economy, mainly for two reasons: Firstly it is a "marginal" rate and thus higher than the average rate in a system of progressive taxation, which most countries have. Secondly, the inclusion of transfer payments will make it reflect also the counter-cyclicality, i.e., the "macro marginal" effect, of unemployment benefits and other social assistance that is being paid out to alleviate cyclically related hardship. In a "big government" country with an extensive "welfare state," θ might reach values of perhaps 0.6 to 0.9, whereas in a "small government" country, with limited social protection, it will likely stay in the region of 0.4 to 0.6.

Let us conclude this summary by pointing to a particularly noteworthy feature of our modeling system, namely that the size of the system is immaterial; the same equations apply for a system of any size. Introducing sub-sectors or more detailed breakdowns by types of income or expenditure flows will make the system bigger, but nevertheless follow the same general approach that we have outlined here. Obviously a larger system would have more components and therefore a higher-dimensional **g**-vector and Γ-matrix, but the very same principles would still hold. All simultaneous "multiplier" feedbacks must still be specified, along with the relevant accounting identities, in the Γ-matrix, and all flow-to-stock feedbacks must be channeled through the intercept **g** vector. It does not matter whether the behavioral parameters are time-varying or stochastic; all it takes is to let the computer invert the matrix and solve out the multipliers for each "step" or "tick" of time in simulations.

Conclusion

"Supply-side" economists have argued that tax cuts, while leading to a bigger deficit in the short run, might stimulate growth and therefore boost tax revenues to such an extent that they become self-financing over time. This paper has analyzed this long-run rendition of the traditional Keynesian "paradox of thrift" or "paradox of the budget" in some detail.

The "paradox of thrift" relates to private saving behavior. It says that increased thriftiness, i.e., an attempt on the part of private consumers to save more, will depress consumption spending and this will reduce capacity utilization. The reduction in capacity utilization will in its turn reduce investment spending. But in a closed economy, investment and saving must be equal, and a reduction in investment must therefore be accompanied by a reduction in saving. Hence, at the end of the day, society as a whole will save less not more for being thriftier.

We have pointed also to the possibility of a corresponding "paradox of the budget" pertaining to government finances. In this version, it is the government that initially attempts to get thriftier, i.e. to consolidate its budget through expenditure cutbacks or increased taxes. But these measures will reduce private incomes, and if direct spending on goods and services is cut, it will also directly reduce capacity utilization. The reduction of private incomes is likely to lead to reduced consumption spending, reduced capacity utilization, and to a lower national income than would have obtained otherwise. The reduction in direct spending has the same effect, only that it is much stronger. Now, if the reduction in activity and income is large enough, the government may end up losing tax revenue, and facing increased expenditures for unemployment and social protection, to an extent that outweighs the initial consolidation gains. We then face a "paradox of the budget."

Evidently the conditions for a paradox of the budget to obtain are somewhat stricter than for the paradox of thrift. In both cases, however, it is a necessary condition that capacity utilization is free to vary, so that changes in aggregate demand, whether brought about by changes in private propensities to save and spend or by government intervention though fiscal policies, will have an impact on output and employment, and not just on the price level. Now for the paradox of thrift to obtain, it is only necessary that investment be positively related to changes in capacity utilization. For the paradox of the budget to obtain, however, the total response in income to a change in the fiscal policy stance must be greater than the "macro marginal" tax rate, i.e., the combination of revenue increases and expenditure decreases induced by a one-dollar expansion of national income.

These conditions hold generally, so are relevant both for the traditional short-run and the newly proposed long-run versions of the twin paradoxes. The long run, however, must be defined so as not to permit unidirectional, secular changes in "capacity utilization." This is where the explanatory problems start. For how does one reconcile the short-run paradoxes, which clearly hinge on the assumption of variable capacity utilization, with the long-run versions, which cannot involve such changes?

The solution must lie in keeping capacity utilization free to vary in the short run, but making it a mean-reverting process in the long run, either by having actual output adjusting toward its potential level, or by having potential output adjusting toward the actual level (or some mix of the two). Whereas the traditional "neoclassical synthesis" model relies on the former alternative, our alternative strategy takes the latter route. Even so, long-run considerations must involve supply conditions such as the state of the labor market, the development of labor productivity, and any inflationary "speed limits." We have endeavored to design a simple model of the supply side of the economy, which takes into account all these considerations in that it models actual and potential employment growth, labor productivity growth, and wage and price inflation. This model can then be driven by a simple Keynesian demand-side model, reinforced with accumulation rules for stocks of assets.

Most of the paper is devoted to the discussion and technical description of that model. The system, while based on a host of simplifying and limiting assumptions that serve to keep its level of complexity at a minimum, involves a fair number of equations specifying the accounting relationships between the variables as well as their dynamic laws of motion. Considerable space has been devoted to walking the reader through this system, yet the exposition is limited in that it does not systematically analyze the properties and characteristics of the dynamical system.

However, it is in the nature of multi-dimensional dynamical systems at this level of complexity that virtually any combination of empirical trajectories can be generated, or reproduced, by the appropriate choice of parameter values. This can be a difficult task, in which one must combine econometric results with a stiff dose of intuition and common sense. We have hinted at some broadly "reasonable" values for the parameters of the system, which should suffice to get the model up and running. Detailed study of the model properties will take a fair amount of sensitivity analysis based on Monte Carlo simulation. Since econometric estimates of the behavioral relationships will inevitably include margins of error, it is wise to design a simulation model so that it permits randomization of the parameters. Adding stochastic elements to the model will of course render Monte Carlo techniques appropriate for analysis of its properties.

Notwithstanding the fact that "cyclical" deviations from benchmark trend are included in all components of the model, it is not an inherently cyclical model. That is to say, cycles do not tend to occur endogenously at normal parameter values (although parameter constellations can be "tweaked" so as to generate cycles) by the inner workings of the system; they rather arise through cyclical variations in the exogenous parameters. This in effect translates to that the model economy is viewed as inherently "stable" and that any cyclical fluctuations arise from economic policy programs. Since there is no monetary policy module in the model, "policy" means fiscal policy. It is not difficult to design and incorporate into the model a ruled-based endogenous fiscal policy program, and if this program is "out of phase" with the rest of the model, it is highly likely to generate cyclical patterns. This, of course, would reflect the traditional "timing problem" of counter-cyclical fiscal policy.[49] For those who are strongly wedded to the idea of the inherent cyclicality of capitalist economies, rescue can be found in (e.g.) incorporating a lag into the investment function. Amendments of this kind are perhaps best thought of as adding "fine dynamics" to the relatively crude structure of our model. They are obviously not the only refinement that could be made in a more detailed model.

The agenda for future work is obviously extensive. We already indicated quite a few areas as we went along, and will briefly reiterate them here. Firstly, the model needs a monetary-policy block. This could take the form of a simple Taylor-rule type mechanism, which determines one "policy rate" of interest that rules the roost so far as rates of interest and profits are concerned.[50] A more sophisticated solution would be to develop a "Tobinesque" portfolio-choice module, in which asset prices and rates of return can be jointly determined.[51] This option involves the development of a sizeable stock-flow consistent accounting system, preferably of the fully articulated social accounting matrix (SAM) variety. In particular, the producer sector of the economy must be subdivided into financial and nonfinancial producers, and assets must be broken down by type, at a minimum into money, equity, bonds and nonfinancial assets. Unfortunately, the introduction of breakdowns like these in several dimensions will create an avalanche of permutations, and a model designed to account for them all must quickly become unwieldy if not altogether unmanageable.

Another area of work involves relaxing our assumption of fixed relative prices. The most important relative price is probably that between stocks of assets on the one hand and flows of output and income on the other. A simple solution, to parallel a Taylor rule for monetary policy, would be to base asset prices on (expected) real rates of interest and flows of property incomes, using some discounting mechanism. One would then retain the assumption of fixed relative prices between assets and also between flows of output and income. The sophisticated alternative would be to let the above "Tobin" module determine the asset prices, thus allowing relative prices to vary in between assets. As we observed earlier, releasing the relative prices of flows of output and income would require scrapping our Phillips Curve and putting in its place another inflation mechanism. The natural way to do this is to elaborate our very telegraphic national-accounting system to properly incorporate the income side of the accounts. By this token, we can take the matrix-multiplier route to modeling cyclical movements in labor compensation, producers' operating surplus and "indirect" taxes on products. We can then use a modified version of the conflicting claims model to obtain the secular movements in benchmark "contributions to inflation."

A third area of work is to open the model economy for foreign trade. The simple solution here consists of adding exports and imports to the accounting structure, and also introducing a distinction between domestic product and national income. The matrix-multiplier model would thus become somewhat larger but basically the same. On the supply side, one would presumably want to incorporate the effects of changing terms of trade, as we noted before, but one must recognize that letting the relative price between imports and exports vary may have awkward implications for the demand side of the model, since these prices appear in the accounting structure. In the sophisticated open-economy modeling approach, on the other hand, one might start off by constructing a closed two-country model, where the "home" country exchanges goods, services and financial assets with the "foreign" country.[52] The design of a full-fledged model of this kind would parallel the comprehensive closed-economy model, only that every component of the accounting system would appear in two different "flavors," namely, "domestic" and "foreign," as would every agent. This effectively quadruples the number of relationships to be modeled (if the system has two different currencies, the number increases eightfold!). Unwieldiness is bound to become a severe problem in this kind of model.

Fourth, given the aforementioned omission of a monetary policy block, the policy levers are very few in our system, in fact there are only two: government spending and the tax rate. It would clearly be useful to introduce a number of different tax rates, and to separate out the transfer payments. The detail to which such breakdown can meaningfully be taken will depend on the detail of the accounting system. Given that our model has a very simplistic accounting framework, there may not be scope for extensive breakdown. However, if the accounting system were amended so as to include the income side, as we suggested above, then it would be meaningful and indeed necessary to account separately for indirect taxes. It would also be possible and useful to distinguish between taxation of labor and capital income. Taxes on assets and wealth can also be included; in fact this is fully possible already in our model. A more detailed system of stock accounting would permit different taxation of different types of wealth.

Lastly, our model is purely oriented toward simulation. It might be of interest for certain purposes (policy evaluation comes to mind) to extend the model by specifying a set of objective functions that assign values to the paths generated by the model. On this basis one can carry out dynamic optimization exercises, e.g. to find policy programs that maximize some weighted combination of social objectives. One can also force private agents to observe "intertemporal consistency" in their decision-making and derive time-varying parameters from the solution of this optimization problem. Clearly there are a number of more or less interesting possibilities in this regard.

Notes

1 I would like to thank Alan Isaac, James Rock, Max Sawicky, Lance Taylor, Matias Vernengo, and the participants in the EEA conference session for helpful comments on various vintages of this paper. All errors are mine.

2 See Vickrey (1992), pp. 308–9.

3 The treatment in Blanchard (2003) is a rare, albeit still imperfect, exception to this rule.

4 Hicks (1950) launched the "super-multiplier" combining the consumption and investment feedback channels.

5 Refer to Harrod (1936, 1939), Lundberg (1937), and Samuelson (1939a, 1939b). I am indebted to Matias Vernengo for pointing to Harrod's *Trade Cycle*.

6 There are many further complications that need to be considered, not least relating to cross-border trade and investment in the open economy. In this

paper we will restrict our discussion to the closed-economy case, and this limitation should be borne in mind when considering the applicability to open, real-world economies.

7 According to available data for the United States economy (for the period 1947–2001; US Bureau of Economic Analysis, National Income and Product Accounts, and Stocks of Assets Tables), the ratio between the stock of produced assets (including housing, consumer durables, and inventories) valued at current cost, and net domestic product valued at current prices varied counter-cyclically around a virtually trendless average of 3.90. The lowest reading was 3.52 in (in 1966) and the highest, 4.51 (in 1980).

8 The figures here are broadly consistent with some of the latest available empirical estimates, e.g., of the "standard model" in Roberts (2003). It is important to recognize that investment behavior is dominated by the impact of changes in capacity utilization, although the "neoclassical" component of capital user cost also seems to have some impact.

The literature on investment behavior is too extensive to review in detail in this paper. Several comprehensive survey articles exist, the most recent one being Chirinko (1993), which the reader may want to consult for further references to the literature in the field. Earlier surveys include Jorgenson (1971), Klein (1974), and Eisner (1978). Landmark studies since the seminal work by Clark (1917) and Keynes (1936), include Chenery (1952), Meyer and Kuh (1957), Eisner and Strotz (1963), Jorgenson (1963), Brainard and Tobin (1968), Tobin (1969), Hayashi (1982), Abel and Blanchard (1983, 1986), Fazzari, Hubbard and Petersen (1988), and Bernanke and Gertler (1988).

9 Refer to Okun (1962).

10 Refer to Kaldor (1957, 1966, 1970), Kaldor and Mirrlees (1962), Romer (1986, 1990, 1994), Rebelo (1991). For a recent overview of endogenous growth theory, see Seiter (2004).

11 Refer to Kaldor (1966), Verdoorn (1949), Young (1928), Arrow (1962).

12 We must also, of course, suppose that there is some elasticity in the supply of input factors with respect to demand, i.e. that there is scope for "capacity utilization" to change. For an interesting and powerful argument for flexibility in utilization rates, refer to Braun and Evans (1998).

13 This also involves the long-debated issue of "Ricardian equivalence," and whether government debt should at all be regarded as private wealth (Barro 1974, Buchanan 1976). We will adhere to the traditional approach of treating government debt as private wealth, which we believe is relevant for our analysis. Barro's "equivalence theorem" results from a considerable list of restrictive assumptions, including absence of uncertainty about the future, full employment, lump-sum taxation and that government expenditures are unproductive – none of which can be safely assumed to obtain in reality.

Barro himself (1981) contends that "direct" government expenditures (i.e., purchases of goods and services), are not subject to "equivalence." Feldstein (1988) drops the assumption of certainty about future incomes, and concludes that the "neutrality" result no longer holds. Arestis and Sawyer (in this volume) make some pertinent observations on what happens to Barro's "equivalence theorem" when the assumption of full employment (or fixed capacity utilization) is dropped.

14 For review of relevant theory and recent empirical estimates, refer to Poterba (2000), Boone *et al.* (2001); Palumbo and Maki (2001); Davis and Palumbo (2001); Palumbo, Rudd and Whelan (2002); Bertaut (2002); Juster *et al.* (2004); Barrell and Davis (2004). Parker and Gourinchas (2002) provide a state-of-the art econometric exercise on the life-cycle theme.

It is interesting to note that Barrell and Davis (op. cit.), who distinguish between financial and non-financial wealth in their estimates of the wealth effect on consumption, consistently find that changes in financial wealth have a smaller impact on consumption than do changes in non-financial wealth. Given the higher price volatility of financial wealth, and equity in particular, this is in line with our prior suspicions.

Juster *et al.* (op. cit.) go still further and attempt to separate out capital gains on equity. Contrary to what one might expect, they find that the wealth effect related to equity is greater than for other types of wealth. Their framework, however, is at variance with the traditional life-cycle approach in that they consider the twin *flows* of saving and holding gains, which jointly account for the value changes in net worth, as independent variables. In the life-cycle theory, of course, it is the *stock* of net worth that constitutes the independent variable, and, as we suggest in this paper, the stock of net worth can be decomposed into a cumulated saving and a cumulated holding gains component.

The cited findings about wealth effects from financial wealth can be called into question also on the grounds that current national-accounting conventions do not adequately account for reinvested earnings – a problem addressed in detail by Dalsgaard *et al.* (2000). This conceptual problem becomes acute in the decomposition of changes in the value of equity into a saving and a holding gains component; the bulk of reinvested earnings will register as holding gains rather than saving in the equity holders' accounts. It is anybody's guess how an adjustment of the saving flows for reinvested earnings would affect the estimates of wealth effects from equity; the impact on overall financial wealth would be similar but mitigated by the presence of non-equity wealth in the aggregates.

15 Refer to Modigliani and Brumberg (1954), Ando and Modigliani (1963); Modigliani (1986).

16 The model featured in the second part of this paper simplifies this away; holding gains are assumed to be "neutral," namely, nominal holding gains will correspond to the general rate of inflation, and real holding gains will be zero.

17 Refer to Vickrey (1993, 1994, 1997).

18 The fiscal theory of the price level was originally proposed by Sims (1994) and Woodford (1995). For further expositions and explorations, refer to Carlstrom and Fuerst (2000), Christiano and Fitzgerald (2000), Cochrane (1998, 2003), Kocherlakota and Phelan (1999), McCallum (1998), and Woodford (1996, 2001). For a critical view, refer to Buiter (1998).

19 The theoretical "ideal" chain-index formula is the Divisia index, which runs in continuous time and is continuously "re-based" using current expenditure shares as weights. For empirical application, discrete approximations to the Divisia formula must be found, since data always comes in discrete-time format. The most common formulae are the (chained) Laspeyres, Paasche, Törnqvist, and Fisher index. The Törnqvist and Fisher formulae are preferable from a theoretical point of view, since they provide second-order approximations to the (exact) Divisia index; Laspeyres and Paasche give only first-order approximations.

For a survey article on Divisia index numbers, refer to Hulten (1973); for current methods of handling chain indices in macroeconomic models, see Renfro (1998), Lasky (1998), Witte (1998), Varvares *et al.* (1998), Bachman *et al.* (1998), and Whelan (2002, 2003).

20 Unless, of course, one is prepared to somehow allocate the discrepancy between the two sides of the identity, a procedure that might seem to do little or no harm if the gap is small. This method falls apart as the discrepancy gets bigger, which it is likely to do over longer time spans and particularly under conditions of large relative price movements and rapid structural change.

However, the chief argument against the method is not that it is impractical, but that it is theoretically unsound. Chain indices, and indeed index numbers in general, are inherently multiplicative and the very idea of adding index numbers is fundamentally flawed.

The problem, thus, is not that macroeconomists have found out that chain indices are not additive so do not conform to the models of received doctrine, but that received doctrine – the traditional macroeconomic models using additive identities in constant prices that is – is based on flawed concepts.

21 This approach is in line with standard contributions-to-growth decompositions published by most statistical agencies, and increasingly featured in their main publications and news releases in respect of national accounts statistics. Eurostat's press releases, for example, include the tables "Contributions of expenditure components to variations in GDP" and "Contributions by gross value added to by industry to variation in GDP"; US Bureau of Economic Analysis include as the second table in their main National Income and Product Accounts news releases "Contributions to percentage change in real Gross Domestic Product."

Kohli (2003), using the Törnqvist index formula, shows how these additive decompositions in growth-rate terms can be converted back into levels to form a multiplicative decomposition of GDP. This decomposition approach is of course perfectly familiar to growth accountants; it is only its application to the expenditure side of the accounts that might come across as unfamiliar.

22 The main exception is the parameter notation, which we decided to keep simple in spite of the fact that it must be abandoned for a bigger model. We have developed appropriate parameter notation for large models, but it is simply too cumbersome to be worthwhile for our present purposes.

23 Typically this "initial" price level is set to unity for the "reference year" of comparison, so as to render implicit "constant-dollars" estimates of volumes.

24 The floating benchmark technique implies that we do not need to distinguish between "flavors" of nominal weights in this paper; thus the m index has been dropped for the W variables.

25 Note that the index set Ξ has been excluded; there is no assumption of constant real wages.

26 This renormalization is a standard approach in Keynesian growth modeling; for several examples, see Lance Taylor (2004).

27 Refer to Okun (1962) and Verdoorn (1949). A simpler version of the Okun–Verdoorn model featured in this section model was developed in collaboration with Matias Vernengo; refer to Berglund and Vernengo (2001).

28 Verdoorn's original model actually includes an investment function, which however is peculiarly ill-suited for his analysis. While not immediately obvious, it is not difficult to extract "Verdoorn's Law," which relates productivity growth to output growth, as a partial elasticity from our model. The traditional rule of thumb, based on cross-sectional estimates limited to the manufacturing sector, has been to set this elasticity to about 0.5. There is however no reason to expect this particular figure to obtain from our model (nor from Verdoorn's own for that matter!); the time-series elasticity is a *partial* one and simulation output will reflect the confluence of several factors. For this reason it is better to formulate the "Verdoorn effect" (rather than the "Law") in terms of the "Verdoorn coefficient" of our reduced-form model; more on this shortly.

29 For literature in this tradition, refer to Jackson, Turner and Wilkinson (1972), Rowthorn (1977), Carvalho (1993), Lance Taylor (2004).

30 The long-term shares of labor and capital income can be disrupted, though, by changes in the level of taxation.

31 This property is consistent with the "Old" Phillips Curve, as originally con-

ceived by Phillips (1958) and Samuelson and Solow (1960). However, the short-run movements around the long-run steady-state curve – the "Phillips loops" – move in the opposite direction compared to Phillips's observations. The empirical performance of our Phillips Curve remains an open question. Under all circumstances, amendments must be made to account for changes in import prices, terms of trade and other "supply shocks." Typically these shocks explain the lion's share of the variation in inflation rates, implying that the demand side plays a secondary role in the process.

32 See, e.g., Roberts (2003).

33 The model is also broadly compatible with recent "time-varying NAIRU" models of inflation and labor supply; see, e.g., Gordon (1997, 1998); Staiger, Stock and Watson (1997, 2001); Richardson *et al.* (2000).

34 It will be seen that the traditional Okun elasticity is in fact a "multiplier," namely, $1/(1 - \mu)$, and it may therefore be convenient to refer to it as the "Okun multiplier" and reserve the term "Okun elasticity" or "Okun coefficient" for our parameter μ.

35 Unfortunately, there appears to be no recent survey articles available on the state of the art of mark-up estimation. The bulk of existing work on the cyclical variations of the mark-up focuses on the so-called marginal mark-up of output price over marginal cost, and empirical estimates are generally confined to the manufacturing sector. Seminal papers in this literature are Hall (1988) and Rotemberg and Woodford (1991). Martins and Scarpetta (1999, 2002) provide disaggregate estimates for the US manufacturing industries and for the G5 countries, respectively; Haskel, Martin and Small (1995) applies the Hall (op. cit.) approach using UK manufacturing data. The weight of this evidence is that mark-ups, thus defined, tend to move counter-cyclically.

Given the substantial differences in market and production conditions, there are reasons to doubt whether these findings for the manufacturing sector will carry over to the service sector and other parts of the economy as well. Moreover, as Puty (2004) emphasizes, it is fully possible to have counter-cyclical movements in the marginal mark-up and pro-cyclical movements in the average mark-up at the same time. What counts in our context is, of course, the average mark-up. It is well nigh impossible to reconcile a counter-cyclical average mark-up with the indisputably pro-cyclical patterns of the share of operating surplus (the "profit share") in domestic product.

The literature on the mark-up also ties in with the age-old and seemingly never-ending debate on the cyclicality of real wages. This discourse goes back at least to Dunlop (1938) and Tarshis (1939) critique of Keynes (1936) assumption of a negative short-period relationship between the level of output and the level of wages grounded in competitive pricing and diminishing returns. The debate was no doubt energized by Keynes' own doubts expressed in his reply to Dunlop and Tarshis (Keynes, 1939).

This debate has continued over the decades and has maintained enough vigor for Fischer (1988) to make it a central theme of his general survey article on "Recent Developments in Macroeconomics." Fischer contends there that "real wage changes are, if at all, only mildly procyclical" (p. 312), although he also notes that the empirical literature is somewhat inconclusive. Empirical work in clear support of counter-cyclical real wages is a scarce commodity; Neftci (1978) is one example.

The interest in studying marginal mark-ups typically derives from prior notions about how the degree of competitiveness – and imperfect competition in particular – might affect the overall working of the macroeconomy. Similarly, studies of the cyclicality of real wages are often driven by an interest in finding out whether business cycles are driven by changes on the "supply" side or the "demand" side; theories of real business cycles here stand against traditional Keynesian theories. In our view, the obsession with theoretical paradigms is not only exaggerated but also harmful in that it distorts the focus of research. The above-noted lack of empirical work on such a central factor as the average mark-up and the profit share provides an excellent illustration of the lacuna left by such preoccupation.

We note, finally, that combining the cyclical changes in the average mark-up with the changes in labor productivity enables us to determine the cyclical variations in real wages by simple accounting. It is peculiar to say the least that one hardly finds any mention of this relationship in the literature on real-wage and mark-up cyclicality.

36 Refer to John B. Taylor (1979, 1980, 1998).
37 The oil shock itself, like any price movements adverse to the nation's terms of trade, can actually be modeled along the same lines, by treating changes in the terms of trade as a form of "taxation." The main difference is that the terms of trade are typically beyond the control of the national government, and that the loss in real private income resulting from a deterioration of the terms of trade is also a loss of real national income. In the case of increased taxation, the private sector faces a worsening of its terms of trade, but the nation as a whole does not. Looking at taxation in terms of "interior terms of trade" between the private and public sector adds another dimension to the analysis of fiscal policy. Obviously our model is a closed-economy model so does not incorporate the external terms-of-trade mechanisms.
38 This function is equivalent to the one included in the supply block, as it must be in order to avoid over-determination.
39 The "grand-ratios" model is a formalization of ideas formulated by Vickrey (1993, 1994, 1997), and foreshadowed by Godley and Cripps (1983). A simple version of the model can be found in Berglund (2003).
40 We have constructed a simulation model of the system, but space and time constraints forces us to leave the simulation-based study of system properties for another occasion.
41 Notice that in our model, the nominal capital–output ratio enters multiplicatively into the marginal propensity to invest. Since this ratio is time varying, the whole matrix will be time varying and must be continuously inverted. In practice, where discrete steps must be defined for simulations, one instructs the computer to invert the matrix for each step of the simulation.

The appearance of a time varying "marginal propensity" in the Keynesian feedback matrix was an accidental (and admittedly somewhat inelegant) consequence of building the supply system first, and then proceeding to find a demand system to drive the supply side. More specifically, it is the specification of the investment function in the Okun–Verdoorn block that is the culprit.

Models that incorporate into the Keynesian block income distribution as well as "augmented" (in the growth-accounting sense) factor-input flows are currently under development. These extensions of the demand side will call for revisions of the supply block; in particular, the income-distribution mechanisms devised in our Phillips Curve must be dropped. The Okun–Verdoorn employment dynamics can be retained, but only for "unaugmented" factor inputs; the gap between "augmented" and "unaugmented" factors (the "factor productivities" in the growth-accounting sense) thus obtaining residually.
42 The identity has been recast, of course, in terms of additive Divisia chain-index contributions to growth, to adhere to modern national accounting principles.
43 An accounting system is "fully articulated" if it shows all transactions on a "from-whom-to-whom" basis, so that both the creditor and the debtor parties can be identified and the flows of funds traced in a manner analogous to the

commodity flows of an input-output matrix. In order to project a social accounting matrix (SAM) into itself, along Keynesian multiplier lines, the matrix must first be "flattened," i.e., converted to a long vector where the columns of the matrix are stacked on top of one another (or the rows one after the other).

If the SAM is large, these flattened vectors will be very large, and the resulting feedback matrix spanned up by two such vectors will be still larger; its number of elements will be the square of the number of elements in the vectors. For example, a ten-account (10×10) SAM will have 100 entries, implying that the flattened column and row vectors will be of dimension 100×1 and 1×100, respectively. The feedback matrix will have $100 \times 100 = 10,000$ entries, most of which, luckily, will be identically equal to zero.

44 The "solution" amounts to dividing the actual contributions to growth by the respective weights; it is only because division is not defined in matrix algebra that we must diagonalize, invert and then pre-multiply – a simple operation made cumbersome!

45 Just follow the steps from Equation 52 to Equation 60, substituting the index set K for Λ.

46 Cf. the section on the "Relation between the short run and long run."

47 Cf. the "Okun–Verdoorn model" section of the supply block above.

48 Of course, the stability of the Hicksian super-multiplier requires that the sum of the MPI and the (post-tax) MPC be less than unity, which, provided that the accounting identities are entered correctly, is tantamount to the Γ-matrix being invertible.

49 For an interesting proposal of how to get around the timing problem, see Seidman and Lewis' paper in this volume.

50 Refer to John B. Taylor (1993, 1995).

51 Refer to Brainard and Tobin (1968); Tobin (1969, 1982); Frankel (1985, 1995).

52 For a pioneering attempt along these lines, see Lance Taylor (2004), Chapter 10.

References

Abel, Andrew B. and Olivier J. Blanchard (1983), "An Intertemporal Model of Saving and Investment," *Econometrica*, 51(3), May, pp. 675–92.

Abel, Andrew B. and Olivier J. Blanchard (1986), "The Present Value of Profits and Cyclical Movements in Investment," *Econometrica*, 54(2), March, pp. 249–74.

Ando, Albert and Franco Modigliani (1963), "The 'Life Cycle' Hypothesis of Saving: Aggregate Implications and Tests," *American Economic Review*, 53(1), March, pp. 55–84.

Arrow, Kenneth J. (1962), "The Economic Implications of Learning by Doing," *Review of Economic Studies*, 29(3), June, pp. 155–73.

Bachman, Daniel, Peter Jaquette, Kurt Karl, and Pasquale Rocco (1998), "The WEFA U.S. Macro Model with Chain-Weighted GDP," *Journal of Economic and Social Measurement*, 24(2), pp. 143–55.

Barro, Robert J. (1974), "Are Government Bonds Net Wealth?" *Journal of Political Economy*, 82(6), November–December, pp. 1095–117.

Barro, Robert J. (1981), "Output Effects of Government Purchases," *Journal of Political Economy*, 89(6), December, pp. 1086–121.

Berglund, Per Gunnar (2003), "Equality and Enterprise: Can Functional Finance

Offer a New Historical Compromise?" in *Reinventing Functional Finance*, edited by Edward J. Nell and Mathew Forstater, Cheltenham, UK: Edward Elgar, pp. 243–65.

Berglund, Per Gunnar and Matias Vernengo (2001), "The 'New Economy' and the 'New Economics': Okun and Verdoorn Effects in the United States 1961–1998," Center for Economic Policy Analysis, New School for Social Research.

Bernanke, Ben S. and Mark Gertler (1989), "Agency Costs, Net Worth, and Business Fluctuations," *American Economic Review*, 79(1), March, pp. 14–31.

Bertaut, Carol C. (2002), "Equity Prices, Household Wealth, and Consumption Growth in Foreign Industrial Countries: Wealth Effects in the 1990s," Board of Governors of the Federal Reserve System, *International Finance Discussion Papers*, No. 2002-724, April.

Blanchard, Olivier J. (2003), *Macroeconomics*, Third edition, London: Prentice Hall.

Boone, Laurence, Nathalie Girouard, and Isabelle Wanner (2001), "Financial Market Liberalisation, Wealth and Consumption," OECD Economics Department Working Papers, No. 308, ECO/WKP(2001)34, September.

Brainard, William C. and James Tobin (1968), "Pitfalls in Financial Model-Building," *American Economic Review*, 58(2), May, pp. 99–122.

Braun, R. Anton and Charles L. Evans (1998), Seasonal Solow Residuals and Christmas: A Case for Labor Hoarding and Increasing Returns," *Journal of Money, Credit and Banking*, 30(3), Part 1, August, pp. 306–30.

Buchanan, James M. (1976), "Barro on the Ricardian Equivalence Theorem," *Journal of Political Economy*, 84(2), April, pp. 337–42.

Buiter, Willem H. (2002), "The Fiscal Theory of the Price Level: A Critique," *Economic Journal*, 112(481), July, pp. 459–80.

Carlstrom, Charles T. and Timothy S. Fuerst (2000), "The Fiscal Theory of the Price Level," *Federal Reserve Bank of Cleveland Economic Review*, 36(1), 1st Quarter, pp. 22–32.

Carvalho, Fernando J. Cardim (1993), "Strato-Inflation and High Inflation: The Brazilian Experience," *Cambridge Journal of Economics*, 17(1), March, pp. 63–78.

Chenery, Hollis B. (1952), "Overcapacity and the Acceleration Principle," *Econometrica*, 20(1), January, pp. 1–28.

Chirinko, Robert S. (1993), "Business Fixed Investment Spending: Modeling Strategies, Empirical Results, and Policy Implications," *Journal of Economic Literature*, 31(4), December, pp. 1875–911.

Christiano, Lawrence J. and Terry J. Fitzgerald (2000), "Understanding the Fiscal Theory of the Price Level," *Federal Reserve Bank of Cleveland Economic Review*, 36(2), 2nd Quarter, pp. 1–37.

Clark, J. Maurice (1917), "Business Acceleration and the Law of Demand: A Technical Factor in Economic Cycles," *Journal of Political Economy*, 25(3), March, pp. 217–35.

Cochrane, John C. (1998), "A Frictionless View of US Inflation," *NBER Working Papers*, No. 6646, July.

Cochrane, John C. (2003), "Money as Stock," Graduate School of Business, University of Chicago, June.

Dalsgaard, Esben, Christoffer Eff, and Annette Thomsen (2000), "Reinvested

Earnings in the National Accounts," *Review of Income and Wealth*, 46(4), December, pp. 401–19.

Davis, Morris A. and Michael G. Palumbo (2001), "A Primer on the Economics and Time Series Econometrics of Wealth Effects," *Finance and Economics Discussion Series*, 2001-9, Washington: Board of Governors of the Federal Reserve System, January.

Dunlop, John T. (1938), "The Movement of Real and Money Wage Rates," *Economic Journal*, 48(191), September, pp. 413–34.

Eisner, Robert (1978), *Factors in Business Investment*, Cambridge, Mass.: National Bureau of Economic Research.

Eisner, Robert and Robert H. Strotz (1963), "Determinants of Business Investment," Research Study Two in *Impacts of Monetary Policy*, prepared for the Commission on Money and Credit, Englewood Cliffs: Prentice-Hall, pp. 59–337.

Fazzari, Steven M., R. Glenn Hubbard, and Bruce C. Petersen (1988), "Financing Constraints and Corporate Investment," *Brookings Papers on Economic Activity*, 1988(1), pp. 141–206.

Feldstein, Martin (1988), "The Effects of Fiscal Policies When Incomes Are Uncertain: A Contradiction to Ricardian Equivalence," *American Economic Review*, 78(1), March, pp. 14–23.

Fischer, Stanley (1988), "Recent Developments in Macroeconomics," *Economic Journal*, 98(391), June, pp. 294–339.

Frankel, Jeffrey A. (1985), "Portfolio Crowding Out, Empirically Estimated," *Quarterly Journal of Economics*, 100, Supplement, pp. 1041–65.

Frankel, Jeffrey A. (1995), *Financial Markets and Monetary Policy*, Cambridge, Mass.: MIT Press.

Godley, Wynne and Francis Cripps (1983), *Macroeconomics*, Oxford, UK: Oxford University Press.

Gordon, Robert J. (1997), "The Time-Varying NAIRU and its Implications for Economic Policy," *Journal of Economic Perspectives*, 11(1), Winter, pp. 11–32.

Gordon, Robert J. (1998), "Foundations of the Goldilocks Economy: Supply Shocks and the Time-Varying NAIRU," *Brookings Papers on Economic Activity*, No. 2, pp. 297–346.

Hall, Robert E. (1988), "The Relation between Price and Marginal Cost in U.S. Industry," *Journal of Political Economy*, 96(5), October, pp. 921–47.

Harrod, Roy F. (1936), *The Trade Cycle: An Essay*, Oxford: Clarendon Press.

Harrod, Roy F. (1939), "An Essay in Dynamic Theory," *Economic Journal*, 49(193), March, pp. 14–33.

Haskel, Jonathan, Christopher Martin, and Ian Small (1995), "Price, Marginal Cost and the Business Cycle," *Oxford Bulletin of Economics and Statistics*, 57(1), February, pp. 25–41.

Hayashi, Fumio (1982), "Tobin's Marginal *q* and Average *q*: A Neoclassical Interpretation," *Econometrica*, 50(1), January, pp. 213–24.

Hicks, John R. (1950), *A Contribution to the Theory of the Trade Cycle*, Oxford: Clarendon Press.

Hulten, Charles R. (1973), "Divisia Index Numbers," *Econometrica*, 41(6), November, pp. 1017–25.

Jackson, Dudley, H.A. Turner, and Frank Wilkinson (1972), "Do Trade Unions

Cause Inflation? Two Studies: With a Theoretical Introduction and Policy Conclusion," *University of Cambridge Department of Applied Economics Occasional Papers*, No. 36, Cambridge, UK: Cambridge University Press.

Jorgenson, Dale W. (1963), "Capital Theory and Investment Behavior," *American Economic Review*, 53(2), May, pp. 247–59.

Jorgenson, Dale W. (1971), "Econometric Studies of Investment Behavior: A Survey," *Journal of Economic Literature*, 9(4), December, pp. 1111–47.

Juster, F. Thomas, Joseph P. Lupton, James P. Smith, and Frank Stafford (2004), "The Decline in Household Saving and the Wealth Effect," Board of Governors of the Federal Reserve System, Finance and Economics Discussion Series, No. 2004-32, June.

Kaldor, Nicholas (1957), "A Model of Economic Growth," *Economic Journal*, 67(268), December, pp. 591–624.

Kaldor, Nicholas (1966), *Causes of the Slow Rate of Economic Growth of the United Kingdom*, Cambridge: Cambridge University Press.

Kaldor, Nicholas (1970), "The Case for Regional Policies," *Scottish Journal of Political Economy*, 17(3), November, pp. 337–48.

Kaldor, Nicholas and James A. Mirrlees (1962), "A New Model of Economic Growth," *Review of Economic Studies*, 29(3), June, pp. 174–92.

Keynes, John Maynard (1936), *The General Theory of Employment, Interest and Money*, London: Macmillan.

Keynes, John Maynard (1939), "Relative Movements of Real Wages and Output," *Economic Journal*, 49(193), March, pp. 34–51.

Klein, Lawrence R. (1974), "Issues in Econometric Studies of Investment Behavior," *Journal of Economic Literature*, 12(1), March, pp. 43–9.

Kocherlakota, Narayana R. and Christopher Phelan (1999), "Explaining the Fiscal Theory of the Price Level," *Federal Reserve Bank of Minneapolis Quarterly Review*, 23(4), Fall, pp. 14–23.

Kohli, Ulrich (2003), "GDP Growth Accounting: A National Income Function Approach," *Review of Income and Wealth*, 49(1), March, pp. 23–34.

Lasky, Mark J. (1998), "Chain-type Data and Macro Model Properties: The DRI/McGraw-Hill Experience," *Journal of Economic and Social Measurement*, 24(2), pp. 83–108.

Lundberg, Erik (1937), *Studies in the Theory of Economic Expansion*, London: P.S. King.

Martins, Joaquim Oliveira and Stefano Scarpetta (1999), "The Levels and Cyclical Behaviour Across Countries and Market Structures," *OECD Economics Department Working Papers*, No. 213, ECO/WKP(99)5, May.

Martins, Joaquim Oliveira and Stefano Scarpetta (2002), "Estimation of the Cyclical Behaviour of Mark-Ups: A Technical Note," *OECD Economic Studies*, No. 34, pp. 173–88.

McCallum, Bennett T. (1998), "Indeterminacy, Bubbles, and the Fiscal Theory of Price Level Determination," *NBER Working Papers*, No. 6456, March.

Meyer, John R. and Edwin Kuh (1957), *The Investment Decision: An Empirical Study*, Cambridge, Mass.: Harvard University Press.

Modigliani, Franco (1986), "Life Cycle, Individual Thrift, and the Wealth of Nations," *American Economic Review*, 76(3), June, pp. 297–313.

Modigliani, Franco and Richard E. Brumberg (1954), "Utility Analysis and the Consumption Function: An Interpretation of Cross-Section Data," in *Post-*

Keynesian Economics, edited by Kenneth H. Kurihara, New Brunswick, NJ, Rutgers University Press.

Neftci, Salih N. (1978), "A Time-Series Analysis of the Real Wages–Employment Relationship," *Journal of Political Economy*, 86(2), Part 1, April, pp. 281–91.

Okun, Arthur M. (1962), "Potential GNP: Its Measurement and Significance," in "Full Employment Potential and Fiscal Policy," *American Statistical Association 1962 Proceedings of the Business and Economics Section*, Washington, D.C.: American Statistical Association, pp. 98–104.

Palumbo, Michael G. and Dean R. Maki (2001), "Disentangling the Wealth Effect: A Cohort Analysis of Household Saving in the 1990s," Finance and Economics Discussion Series, 2001-21, Washington: Board of Governors of the Federal Reserve System, April.

Palumbo, Michael G., Jeremy Rudd, and Karl Whelan (2002), "On the Relationships between Real Consumption, Income, and Wealth," *Finance and Economics Discussion Series*, 2002-38, Washington: Board of Governors of the Federal Reserve System, August.

Phillips, A. William (1958), "The Relation between Unemployment and the Rate of Change of Money Wage Rates in the United Kingdom, 1861–1957," *Economica*, New Series, 25(100), November, pp. 283–99.

Poterba, James M. (2000), "Stock Market Wealth and Consumption," *Journal of Economic Perspectives*, 14(2), Spring, pp. 99–118.

Puty, Claudio C.B. (2004), "Sectoral Mark-ups in US Manufacturing 1958–1996," Doctoral Dissertation, New School for Social Research.

Rebelo, Sergio (1991), "Long-Run Policy Analysis and Long-Run Growth," *Journal of Political Economy*, 99(3), June, pp. 500–21.

Renfro, Charles G. (1998), "Macroeconometric Models and Changes in Measurement Concepts: An Overview," *Journal of Economic and Social Measurement*, 24(2), p. 63–82.

Richardson, Pete, Laurence Boone, Claude Giorno, Mara Meacci, David Rae, and David Turner (2000), "The Concept, Policy Use and Measurement of Structural Unemployment: Estimating a Time-Varying NAIRU Across 21 OECD Countries," *OECD Economics Department Working Papers*, No. 250, ECO/WKP(2000)23, Organisation for Economic Co-operation and Development, June.

Roberts, John M. (2003), "Modeling Aggregate Investment: A Fundamentalist Approach," Board of Governors of the Federal Reserve System, Finance and Economics Discussion Series, No. 2003-48, September.

Romer, Paul M. (1986), "Increasing Returns and Long-Run Growth," *Journal of Political Economy*, 94(5), October, pp. 1002–37.

Romer, Paul M. (1990), "Endogenous Technical Change," *Journal of Political Economy*, 98(5), Part 2, October, S71–S102.

Romer, Paul M. (1994), "The Origins of Endogenous Growth," *Journal of Economic Perspectives*, 8(1), Winter, pp. 3–22.

Rotemberg, Julio J. and Michael Woodford (1991), "Markups and the Business Cycle," in *NBER Macroeconomics Annual 1991*, Cambridge and London: MIT Press, pp. 63–129.

Rowthorn, Robert E. (1977), "Conflict, Inflation and Money," *Cambridge Journal of Economics*, 1(3), September, pp. 215–39.

Samuelson, Paul A. (1939*a*), "Interactions between the Multiplier Analysis and the

Principle of Acceleration," *The Review of Economic Statistics*, 21(2), May, pp. 75–8.

Samuelson, Paul A. (1939*b*), "A Synthesis of the Principle of Acceleration and the Multiplier," *The Journal of Political Economy*, 47(6), December, pp. 786–97.

Samuelson, Paul A. and Robert M. Solow (1960), "Analytical Aspects of Anti-Inflation Policy," *American Economic Review*, 50(2), May, pp. 177–94.

Seiter, Stephan (2004), "Endogenous Growth; One Phenomenon: Two Interpretations," in *Growth Theory and Growth Policy*, edited by Harald Hagemann and Stephan Seiter, London and New York: Routledge, pp. 27–39.

Sims, Christopher A. (1994), "Simple Model for Study of the Determination of the Price Level and the Interaction of Monetary and Fiscal Policy," *Economic Theory*, 4(3), pp. 381–99.

Staiger, Douglas, James H. Stock, and Mark W. Watson (1997), "The NAIRU, Unemployment and Monetary Policy," *Journal of Economic Perspectives*, 11(1), Winter, pp. 33–49.

Staiger, Douglas, James H. Stock, and Mark W. Watson (2001), "Prices, Wages and the U.S. NAIRU in the 1990s," *NBER Working Papers*, No. 8320, June.

Tarshis, Lorie (1939), "Changes in Real and Money Wages," *Economic Journal*, 49(193), March, pp. 150–4.

Taylor, John B. (1979), "Estimation and Control of a Macroeconomic Model with Rational Expectations," *Econometrica*, 47(5), September, pp. 1267–86.

Taylor, John B. (1980), "Aggregate Dynamics and Staggered Contracts," *Journal of Political Economy*, 88(1), February, pp. 1–23.

Taylor, John B. (1993), "Discretion versus Policy Rules in Practice," *Carnegie-Rochester Conference Series on Public Policy*, 39(0), December, pp. 195–214.

Taylor, John B. (1995), "The Monetary Transmission Mechanism: An Empirical Framework," *Journal of Economic Perspectives*, 9(4), Autumn, pp. 11–26.

Taylor, John B. (1998), "Staggered Price and Wage Setting in the Economy," *NBER Working Papers*, No. 6754, October.

Taylor, Lance (2004), *Reconstructing Macroeconomics: Structuralist Proposals and Critiques of the Mainstream*, Cambridge, Mass.: Harvard University Press.

Tobin, James (1969), "A General Equilibrium Approach to Monetary Theory," *Journal of Money, Credit and Banking*, 1(1), February, pp. 15–29.

Tobin, James (1982), "Money and Finance in the Macroeconomic Process," *Journal of Money, Credit and Banking*, 14(2), May, pp. 171–204.

Varvares, Chris, Joel Prakken, and Lisa Guirl (1998), "Macro Modeling with Chain-Type GDP," *Journal of Economic and Social Measurement*, 24(2), pp. 123–42.

Verdoorn, P. Johannes (1949), "On the Factors Determining the Growth of Labour Productivity," in *Italian Economic Papers*, Vol. II, edited by Luigi L. Pasinetti, Oxford: Oxford University Press, 1993, pp. 59–68.

Vickrey, William S. (1992), "Meaningfully Defining Deficits and Debt," *American Economic Review*, 82(2), May, pp. 305–10.

Vickrey, William S. (1993), "Necessary and Optimum Debt," in *Public Economics: Selected Papers by William Vickrey*, edited by Richard Arnott *et al.*, Cambridge, UK: Cambridge University Press, 1994, pp. 421–31.

Vickrey, William S. (1994), "Why Not Chock-Full Employment?" *Atlantic Economic Journal*, March, 22(1), pp. 39–45.

Vickrey, William S. (1997), "A Trans-Keynesian Manifesto (Thoughts about an

Asset-Based Macroeconomics)," *Journal of Post Keynesian Economics*, Summer, 19(4), pp. 495–510.

Whelan, Karl (2002), "A Guide to U.S. Chain Aggregated NIPA Data," Whelan, Karl, *Review of Income and Wealth*, 48(2), June, pp. 217–33.

Whelan, Karl (2003), "A Two-Sector Approach to Modeling U.S. NIPA Data," *Journal of Money, Credit, and Banking*, 35(4), August, pp. 627–56.

Witte, Willard E. (1998), "Price Determination in the Indiana Econometric Model of the U.S.," *Journal of Economic and Social Measurement*, 24(2), pp. 109–22.

Woodford, Michael (1995), "Price-Level Determinacy without Control of a Monetary Aggregate," *Carnegie-Rochester Conference Series on Public Policy*, 43(0), December, pp. 1–46.

Woodford, Michael (2001), "Fiscal Requirements for Price Stability," (Money, Banking and Credit Lecture), *Journal of Money, Credit and Banking*, 33(3), August, pp. 669–728.

Young, Allyn A. (1928), "Increasing Returns and Economic Progress," *Economic Journal*, 38(152), December, pp. 527–42.

10 Budget deficits, unemployment and economic growth

A cross-section time-series analysis

Robert Eisner

I have reported on a large number of occasions that properly measured, inflation-adjusted and cyclically adjusted public budget deficits have been associated with more rapid subsequent growth in real GNP or GDP and with reductions in unemployment.[1] I have confirmed these findings repeatedly with time-series beginning in 1955 for the United States. I now have OECD historical data for 19 countries – Australia, Austria, Belgium, Canada, Denmark, Finland, France, Germany, Greece, Ireland, Italy, Japan, the Netherlands, Norway, Portugal, Spain, Sweden, the United Kingdom, and the United States – over the 26-year period from 1970 to 1995. The data are associated with *Fiscal Positions and Business Cycles* (OECD, 1997), from the Economics Department of OECD, Paris. I utilize these data to test and estimate more widely, with sets of pooled time-series and cross-section regressions, relations previously explored for the United States.

The model

In previous work with US data I have estimated relations in which changes in unemployment and in real GDP (or real GNP) were functions of previous values of the real or inflation-adjusted and cyclically adjusted budget deficit (labeled *PAHED*, the price-adjusted, high-employment deficit), changes in the real monetary base, and the real exchange rate. This deficit was thought to increase aggregate demand both by increasing after-tax income and liquidity and by increasing perceived wealth of holders of public debt. Changes in the real monetary base were considered the best available measure of an exogenous monetary role in affecting aggregate demand. The real exchange rate was expected to relate negatively to aggregate demand; a higher exchange rate would increase US imports and reduce exports.

Lacking data on the monetary base for countries other than the United States, I take no explicit account of monetary variables, although they may be reflected in values of the real exchange rate. I have also modified my earlier formulations to capture the possible, special direct effect on unemployment and real GDP of changes in current government expenditures for goods and services. Data were not available as to net government financial liabilities for Greece, Ireland and Portugal; I was therefore unable to calculate price effects, as explained below, and construct inflation-adjusted deficits for these countries. The initial autoregressive relations I estimated were therefore:

$$UNRCH_{it} = b_{0u} + b_{1u}BDQPA_{it}(-1) + b_{2u}DGEPC_{it} + b_{3u}ERR_{it}(-1)$$
$$+ u_{itu} \tag{1}$$

$$GDPVGR_{it} = b_{0g} + b_{1g}BDQPA_{it}(-1) + b_{2g}DGEPC_{it} + b_{3g}ERR_{it}(-1)$$
$$+ u_{itg}, \quad i = 1 \text{ to } 16, t = 72 \text{ to } 95 \tag{2}$$

UNRCH denotes the change in the unemployment rate, *BDQPA* is the inflation-and-cyclically adjusted deficit as a percentage of potential output, and *ERR* is the real exchange rate. The precise definitions of these variables will be discussed shortly. Appendix Table 1 provides a summary overview of the notation. Subscripts *i* and *t* are country and year indexes, respectively. These relations were estimated as pooled time-series for all countries (with "fixed effects," i.e., a dummy variable for each country), as pooled cross-sections (with dummy variables for each year, taking on values of 1 for observations of that year and zero for all other years), and as "overall" regressions, entailing variance and covariance of observations for all countries in all years around the overall mean (calculated by using the common constant terms, b_{0u} and b_{0g}, instead of the separate constants for each country entailed by the "fixed effects" of the time-series relation). First and second-degree autoregressive terms were introduced to eliminate serial correlation in the residuals; the autoregressive terms generally brought the Durbin–Watson statistics close to values of 2.0. The lagged terms of the autoregressive relations reduced our set of observations to those beginning no earlier than 1972. Further reducing our available sample, for a number of countries necessary data were not available for the early years.

I also estimated time-series relations for each of the 19 countries. Then, noting the particular impact of US budget deficits, I estimated pooled time-series and cross-section relations that included the US budget deficit as an argument for all countries, both alone and with own-country deficits.

The data

The series have been put together largely from INTERLINK, the OECD Secretariat's world economic model. They are described briefly in *Fiscal Positions and Business Cycles*. The series utilized are as follows:

a.   *UNRCH* = the change (first difference) in the rate of unemployment, *UNR*, which is taken from INTERLINK.

b.   *GDPVGR* = percentage rate of growth of real GDP, constructed from the INTERLINK series *GDPV*, which denotes "gross domestic product (market prices) volume."

c.   *BDQPA* = the inflation-and-cyclically-adjusted budget deficit as a percentage of the nominal value of potential output.

BDQPA was calculated using *NLGQA*, defined in INTERLINK as "net lending, government, cyclically adjusted, % potential GDP," or $100 \cdot NLGA/GDPTR$, where *NLGA* is cyclically adjusted net lending and *GDPTR* is potential GDP.[2] In turn, $NLGA = YRGA - YPGA - CAPOG$, where *YRGA* and *YPGA* are, respectively, current government receipts and payments, cyclically adjusted, and *CAPOG* is net capital outlays of government. Current payments are thus augmented by net capital outlays.

The measure of the deficit relevant to the impact on aggregate demand with which we are concerned, however, should include all outlays. We should thus further augment payments by the value of government consumption of fixed capital, *CFKG*. Except for the United States, I have therefore, for those countries where the series was available, added *CFKG* to outlays. Operationally, this meant subtracting *CFKGPC*, or *CFKG* as a percentage of potential output, from *NLGQA* to get our measure of the cyclically adjusted budget surplus as a percentage of potential GDP. Alternatively it meant, after the adjustment for inflation explained below, subtracting *CFKGPC* from the value of net lending as a percentage of potential output after inflation and cyclical adjustment, to arrive at *BSQPA*, the price-and-cyclically-adjusted budget surplus as a percentage of potential GDP.

This subtraction of *CFKGPC* was not possible, however, for France and the United Kingdom, where *CFKG* was not available. Inspection of the series for the United States indicated that the measure of net lending corresponded pretty much to the US figures for the budget surplus and no subtraction was made either, therefore, for the United States.

The inflation adjustment consisted of adding to the cyclically adjusted budget surplus series what I dub as *PE*, the price effect, which equals the reduction in the real value of outstanding debt due to inflation, or what may be called the inflation tax. This is calculated by multiplying the average of debt at the end of the year and the end of the previous year by the rate of inflation in the GDP implicit price deflator during the year. I calculated the implicit price deflator, *GDPP*, as $100 \cdot GDP/GDPV$, where *GDP* is given by INTERLINK as the value of gross domestic product at market prices and *GDPV* is gross domestic product (market prices) volume, as already noted. The price effect is thus calculated as:

$$PE = \frac{GNFL + GNFL(-1)}{GDPP + GDPP(-1)} \cdot (GDPP - GDPP(-1))$$

$$= \left(GDPP(-1) \cdot \frac{(GNFL + GNFL(-1))/2}{GDPP + GDPP(-1)/2} \right) \cdot \frac{GDPP - GDPP(-1)}{GDPP(-1)}$$

where *GNFL*, taken from INTERLINK, is net financial liabilities of government. As a percentage of potential output we have:

$$PEPC = 100 \cdot PE/GDPTR$$

Thus, the total, cyclically-and-price-adjusted surplus as a percentage of potential GDP is then defined as:

$$BSQPA = NLGQA + PEPC - CFKGPC$$

where *CFKGPC* is taken to equal zero for France, Greece, Portugal, the United Kingdom and the United States. Our final deficit series, *BDQPA*, are simply the negatives of those surplus series.

d. *ERRN* = the normalized real exchange rate. INTERLINK offers *EXCH*, the nominal exchange rate for each country in US dollars per unit of the local currency. For all countries other than the United States, I converted these to real rates by multiplying by the ratio of the local GDP implicit price deflator, *GDPP*, to the implicit price deflator for the United States, thus deriving *ERR*. For the United States, I took *ERR* for the years 1973 to 1995 from the index of the real "multilateral trade-weighted value of the US dollar."[3] For the years 1970 to 1972, for which a real index is not available, I took the nominal index, which almost exactly equaled the real index in 1973. I then normalized all of these at unity for 1992 by dividing the unnormalized series, *ERR*, for each country by its value of *ERR* for 1992.

e. *DGEPC* = the change in government spending for goods and services as a percentage of the value of potential output. I defined *GE*, government expenditures, as the sum of *CG*, the value of government consumption, and *IG*, the value of government fixed investment, both taken from INTERLINK.

The findings

Changes in unemployment

As shown in Table 10.1, the unemployment rate increased 0.304 percent per year on average in the 287 observations in our panel of observations including own-country price-and-cyclically-adjusted deficits. The time-series regression, reported in column (2), indicates that the price effect or inflation tax, as well as the cyclically adjusted deficit without the price effect, was related significantly and negatively to subsequent changes in the rate of unemployment. The coefficient of the price effect variable,

Table 10.1 Changes in unemployment rates as function of lagged inflation-and-cyclically adjusted budget deficits or separate cyclically-adjusted budget deficits and inflation tax, lagged real exchange rates, and current changes in government expenditures for goods and services

(1) $UNRCH_{it} = b_{0u} + b_{1u}BDQPA_{it}(-1) + b_{2u} DGEPC_{it} + b_{3u}ERR_{it}(-1) + u_{itu}$

(2) $UNRCH_{it} = b_{0u} + b_{1qu}BDQA_{it}(-1) + b_{ipu}BDPE(-1) + b_{2u}DGEPC_{it} + b_{3u}$
$ERR_{it}(-1) + u_{itu}$
$i = 1$ to 16, $t = 1972$ to 1995

Regression coefficients, standard errors and probability levels

Variable (1)	Time-series (2)	Time-series (3)	Cross-sections (4)	Overall (5)
Constants (Mean of *UNRCH* equals 0.304)	Fixed effects	Fixed effects	Fixed effects and year dummies	−0.137 (0.238) 0.5647
BDQPA(−1)	–	−0.124 (0.033) 0.0002	−0.117 (0.031) 0.0002	−0.099 (0.029) 0.0007
BDQA(−1)	−0.115 (0.036) 0.001	–	–	–
BDPE(−1)	−0.155 (0.062) 0.014	–	–	–
DGEPC	−0.173 (0.085) 0.044	−0.178 (0.085) 0.036	−0.219 (0.084) 0.010	−0.121 (0.081) 0.137
ERRN(−1)	1.475 (0.427) 0.001	1.441 (0.425) 0.001	0.947 (0.502) 0.060	0.857 (0.284) 0.003
AR(1)	0.795 (0.057)	0.801 (0.057)	0.713 (0.060)	0.834 (0.055)
AR(2)	−0.453 (0.057)	−0.454 (0.057)	−0.377 (0.061)	−0.439 (0.056)
Adjusted R^2	0.476	0.477	0.601	0.475
Durbin–Watson statistic	2.12	2.11	2.11	2.08
Total observations	287	287	287	287

$BDPE(-1)$, did not differ significantly, however, from the coefficient of the cyclically adjusted deficit, $BDQA(-1)$, without the price effect. It was appropriate therefore to combine the two in the inflation-and-cyclically-adjusted budget deficits $BDQPA(-1)$. In both the time-series and cross-sections, as may be noted in columns (3) and (4), larger inflation-and-cyclically-adjusted deficits were associated significantly with lesser subsequent increases or greater subsequent reductions in unemployment.

Our formulation does not generate a long run or permanent relation;

clearly, large enough deficits cannot cause unemployment rates to decline at a constant arithmetic rate forever. The estimated coefficients of $BDQPA(-1)$, for both the time-series and the cross-sections, do indicate, however, that on average, one percentage point more of deficit as a ratio of potential GDP was associated with some 0.12 percentage points less of unemployment the following year.

To the extent that higher deficits were embodied in increases in government expenditures for goods and services, there appeared to be further reductions in unemployment or in the rate at which it was increasing. Each percentage point of increase in the ratio of government expenditures to potential GDP, $DGEPC$, was associated, in both the time-series and the cross-sections, with about 0.2 percentage points less of unemployment during the current year.

And higher real exchange rates, $ERRN(-1)$, particularly in the time-series, were associated with greater subsequent unemployment. Each ten-percentage-point higher exchange rate was associated with 0.14 percentage points more of unemployment the following year in the time-series and 0.09 percentage points more in the cross-sections.

The pooled time-series indicate covariance over time, that is, the extent to which, if an independent variable was higher in a given year than its mean over all the years, the dependent variable was higher. They offer information, for example, as to what happened to unemployment rates when our adjusted deficits went down: the rate of increase of unemployment went up! Pooled cross-sections abstract from changes over time and offer information as to the extent to which unemployment rates were higher in countries that had lower deficits. It turns out that the time-series and cross-section estimates of the relation between unemployment and deficits are consistent.

Current increases in government expenditures for goods and services seemed to have a slightly greater impact in reducing unemployment in the cross-sections, but the difference with the time-series coefficient was not significant. The lagged real exchange rate had a lower coefficient in the cross-section and one that was no longer sharply significant, although it was also not significantly less than the time-series coefficient. It should be recalled, though, that the real exchange rates, derived from the dollars that could be bought for a unit of local currency adjusted by the ratio of the local GDP deflator to that of the United States, were normalized to equal unity in the year 1992. Thus, the differences in exchange rates across countries reflected only the differences in other years, particularly years distant from 1992, resulting from different trends in real exchange rates over time.

Both the pooled time-series and the pooled cross-sections, while yielding estimates which fit my priors as to sign, offer coefficients that are of considerably lesser magnitude, where comparable, to those that I have derived in previous analyses of US data. And indeed, they mask considerable differences among the individual time-series regressions of the 16 countries, shown in Table 10.2.

Table 10.2 Changes in unemployment rate, UNRCH, as function of lagged inflation-and-cyclically-adjusted budget deficits, lagged real exchange rates, and current changes in government expenditures for goods and services: individual country and pooled time series

(1) $UNRCH_{it} = b_{0u} + b_{1u}BDQPA_{it}(-1) + b_{2u}DGEPC_{it} + b_{3u}ERR_{it}(-1) + u_{tiu}$ $i = 1$ to 16, $t = 1972$ to 1995

| Country (1) | Regression coefficients and probability levels | | | Other statistics | | | |
	BDQPA(−1) (2)	DGEPC (3)	ERRN(−1) (4)	Adj. R² (5)	D-W (6)	Mean of UNRCH (7)	No. of obs. (8)
Australia	0.285 / 0.342	2.451 / 0.108	16.671 / 0.114	0.725	2.63	0.213	7
Austria	−0.508 / 0.022	−0.715 / 0.088	1.676 / 0.070	0.068	2.08	0.174	12
Belgium	0.092 / 0.332	0.235 / 0.631	2.299 / 0.287	0.554	2.14	0.373	19
Canada	−0.282 / 0.225	0.468 / 0.478	1.716 / 0.711	0.305	2.15	0.180	22
Denmark	−0.032 / 0.881	0.105 / 0.711	2.068 / 0.278	0.482	1.18	−0.012	12
Finland	0.061 / 0.508	−0.308 / 0.036	7.293 / 0.002	0.866	1.98	0.749	20
France	0.060 / 0.759	0.454 / 0.447	−0.404 / 0.789	−0.066	1.85	0.423	21
Germany	0.001 / 0.996	−0.024 / 0.942	−0.015 / 0.994	0.285	1.91	0.381	22
Italy	−0.060 / 0.464	−0.511 / 0.047	−0.729 / 0.511	0.196	2.09	0.383	21
Japan	0.022 / 0.429	0.071 / 0.599	0.010 / 0.979	−0.014	1.79	0.063	20
Netherlands	−0.102 / 0.395	−0.545 / 0.291	1.718 / 0.404	0.566	1.63	0.160	19
Norway	−0.171 / 0.018	0.028 / 0.868	2.927 / 0.054	0.738	2.376	0.125	12
Spain	−0.661 / 0.000	−0.320 / 0.049	2.173 / 0.101	0.921	2.15	0.914	16
Sweden	0.046 / 0.440	−0.251 / 0.157	4.913 / 0.002	0.633	2.04	0.238	22
United Kingdom	−0.178 / 0.097	−0.448 / 0.110	2.421 / 0.199	0.646	1.78	0.278	22
United States	−0.534 / 0.003	0.216 / 0.763	1.207 / 0.172	0.371	2.14	0.033	22
Pooled time-series	−0.124 / 0.0002	−0.178 / 0.036	1.441 / 0.001	0.477	2.11	0.304	287

The properly adjusted deficit here, as in my earlier work, would appear to have a major impact in the case of the United States. Its coefficient of $BDQPA(-1)$ was a highly significant -0.534, very considerably greater in absolute value than the coefficient of -0.124 for the pooled time-series. Similarly, the absolute values of the coefficients of $BDQPA(-1)$ were high for Austria and for Spain. But for other countries they are not, at any high probability level, significantly negative, and in several cases they have perverse, positive signs.

The coefficients of the other variables also differ considerably across countries. The United States yielded a perverse, positive sign for increases in government expenditures for goods and services. France, which I would have anticipated, in view of what I take to be deleterious effects on employment of maintaining "le franc fort," in fact had non-significant or perversely negative coefficients of $ERRN(-1)$, as did Germany and Italy. I cannot say how much these differences or anomalies relate to imperfections in the data, important omitted variables whose impact is different in different countries, different underlying structural relations in different countries or, indeed, misspecification for all countries of the essentially reduced-form relation that we are estimating.

In earlier work for earlier years (Eisner and Pieper, 1985, 1986) with only the seven largest OECD economies – Canada, France, Germany, Italy, Japan, the United Kingdom and the United States – I noted that the US budget deficit appeared considerably more relevant in other countries than their own deficits. The relatively larger role of the US deficit in the US economy would seem to confirm the desirability of following up on these earlier findings. Results are dramatic.

In examining the possible impact of the US inflation-and-cyclically-adjusted deficit we are able to utilize data for all 19 countries. As shown in column (2) of Table 10.3, the coefficient in the pooled time-series of $USBDQPA(-1)$, the lagged US deficit, is a highly significant and substantial -0.229, considerably larger (absolutely) than the -0.124 for own-country deficits shown in Table 10.1.

The cross-section and overall regression coefficients are as substantial or more so, -0.249 and -0.317, respectively, but with substantial standard errors as well.

What is striking is that even when all of the own-country deficits are included, the US budget deficit remains highly significant, with a coefficient of -0.169 in the time-series. The coefficient of the own-country deficits is nevertheless little reduced in absolute size; it was a highly significant -0.106 in the time-series and an even more substantial and more significant -0.117 in the cross-sections.

In the pooled regressions for all 19 countries with the US budget deficit alone, increases in government expenditures were associated significantly with lesser unemployment and higher real exchange rates were associated significantly with higher subsequent unemployment. The coefficients on

Table 10.3 Changes in unemployment rates as function of US and own-country lagged inflation-and-cyclically-adjusted budget deficits or separate cyclically adjusted budget deficits and inflation tax, lagged real exchange rates, and current changes in government expenditures for goods and services

(1) $UNRCH_{it} = b_{0u} + b_{1u,us} USBDQPA_{it}(-1) + b_{1u,oc} BDQPA_{it}(-1) + b_{2it} DGEPC_{it} + b_{3it} ERR_{it}(-1) + u_{it}$
$i = 1$ to 16 or 19, $t = 1972$ to 1995

Variable (1)	Regression coefficients, standard errors and probability levels					
	Time-series (2)	Time-series (3)	Cross-sections (4)	Cross-sections (5)	Overall (6)	Overall (7)
Mean of *UNRCH* or Constant	0.326 (1.057)	0.304 (1.094)	0.326 (1.057)	0.304 (1.094)	0.204 (0.289) 0.4803	0.530 (0.418) 0.2058
USBDQPA(−1)	−0.229 (0.043) 0.0000	−0.169 (0.055) 0.002	−0.249 (0.162) 0.125	−0.427 (0.248) 0.087	−0.317 (0.170) 0.063	−0.456 (0.263) 0.085
BDQPA(−1)	—	−0.106 (0.032) 0.0010	—	−0.117 (0.031) 0.0002	—	−0.091 (0.026) 0.0007
DGEPC	−0.154 (0.064) 0.016	−0.212 (0.084) 0.012	−0.178 (0.061) 0.004	−0.219 (0.084) 0.010	−0.147 (0.060) 0.014	−0.156 (0.080) 0.054
ERRN(−1)	1.620 (0.372) 0.0000	1.649 (0.415) 0.0001	1.304 (0.456) 0.004	0.947 (0.502) 0.060	0.503 (0.244) 0.040	0.632 (0.279) 0.024
AR(1)	0.702 (0.048)	0.793 (0.056)	0.651 (0.050)	0.713 (0.060)	0.687 (0.049)	0.754 (0.059)
AR(2)	−0.431 (0.048)	−0.485 (0.056)	−0.344 (0.051)	−0.377 (0.061)	−0.317 (0.050)	−0.348 (0.060)
Adj. R^2	0.424	0.492	0.552	0.601	0.552	0.600
D–W	2.11	2.16	2.04	2.11	2.03	2.07
Total obs.	409	287	409	287	409	287

government expenditures differed little among the regressions, ranging from about -0.15 to -0.18, suggesting that a one-percentage-point increase in the proportion of government expenditures is associated with a reduction of up to almost 0.2 percent in the rate of increase of unemployment. And higher real exchange rates are associated with subsequently greater increases in unemployment, significantly in all regressions, with the highest coefficients, 1.62 and 1.30, in the time-series and cross-sections respectively.

In regressions with both the US and own-country deficits, the coefficients of $DGEPC$, the change in government expenditures proportion, were again substantially and significantly negative, ranging from -0.156 to -0.219. And real exchange rates were again associated with subsequently greater increases in unemployment, most importantly in the time-series, where the coefficient of $ERRN(-1)$ was a highly significant 1.649.

The adjusted R^2 in the time-series with both budget deficit variables was 0.492, as against 0.477 with the own-country deficits alone (shown in Table 10.1) and 0.424 with only the US deficit. In the cross-sections, the corresponding values of the adjusted R^2 were 0.601 with the own-country deficits, 0.601 again with both deficit variables but only 0.552 with just the US deficit. In the overall regressions, adjusted R^2 was 0.600 with both deficit variables, 0.475 with only the own-country deficits, and 0.552 with only the US deficit. It would appear that generally the explanation of changes in unemployment is improved by inclusion of a separate US deficit variable in addition to the own-country deficit variable.

Growth in real GDP

Employment may certainly be expected to correlate positively with output. We should therefore expect relations of deficits to growth in real GDP $(GDPVGR)$ similar to those with unemployment – but of course, with opposite signs. And that is indeed what we observe in the growth Tables 10.4 to 10.6, which are analogous to the unemployment Tables 10.1 to 10.3.

As shown in Table 10.4, real GDP grew on average 2.25 percent per year in our 287-observation sample. Both the lagged cyclically adjusted deficit, $BDQA(-1)$ and the current price effect, $BDPE$, were again explanatory in the pooled time-series, the latter, however, at a probability level of only 0.095. Combining the two variables in the inflation-and-cyclically-adjusted deficit, $BDQPA(-1)$ was again in order and yielded a significantly positive coefficient of 0.167; each percentage point more of deficit was thus associated with 0.167 percentage points more of growth in the following year. The cross-sections yielded a somewhat higher and even more significant coefficient of 0.210. This value, about double the absolute value of the corresponding coefficient in the unemployment regression of Table 10.1, would seem consistent with Okun's Law formulations, which

Table 10.4 Growth in real GDP as function of lagged inflation-and-cyclically-adjusted budget deficits or separate cyclically adjusted budget deficits and inflation tax, lagged real exchange rates, and current changes in government expenditures for goods and services

(1) $GDPVGR_{it} = b_{0g} + b_{1g}BDQPA_{it}(-1) + b_{2g}DGEPC_{it} + b_{3g}ERR_{it}(-1) + u_{itg}$

(2) $GDPVGR_{it} = b_{0u} + b_{1qg}BDQA_{it}(-1) + b_{ipg}BDPE(-1) + b_{2g}DGEPC_{it} + b_{3g}$
$ERR_{it}(-1) + u_{itg}$
$i = 1$ to 16, $t = 1972$ to 1995

Variable (1)	Regression coefficients, standard errors and probability levels			
	Time-series (2)	Time-series (3)	Cross-sections (4)	Overall (5)
Constant (Mean of *GDPVGR* equals 2.252)	Fixed Effects	Fixed effects	Fixed effects and year dummies	−0.137 (0.238) 0.5647
BDQPA(−1)	–	0.167 (0.069) 0.016	0.210 (0.066) 0.002	0.145 (0.055) 0.010
BDQA(−1)	0.157 (0.071) 0.028	–	–	–
BDPE(−1)	0.230 (0.137) 0.095	–	–	–
DGEPC	0.442 (0.234) 0.060	0.462 (0.232) 0.048	0.431 (0.218) 0.049	0.387 (0.207) 0.063
ERRN(−1)	−2.835 (0.863) 0.001	−2.739 (0.847) 0.001	−0.635 (1.102) 0.565	−0.556 (0.562) 0.323
AR(1)	0.342 (0.059)	0.347 (0.059)	0.352 0.063	0.398 (0.061)
AR(2)	−0.188 (0.058)	−0.189 0.057	−0.173 (0.062)	−0.130 (0.061)
Adjusted R^2	0.170	0.172	0.357	0.356
Durbin–Watson stat.	1.927	1.927	1.867	1.850
Total observations	287	287	287	287

argue that each percentage point of unemployment is associated with the loss of about 2 percentage points of output.

Increases in government expenditures are associated positively with increases in real GDP but at probability levels hovering around 0.05 and 0.06. Lagged real exchange rates were most significantly related to GDP in the time-series but not in the cross-sections or overall regressions. Again, the cross-section variance in *ERRN* is muted by the definition of that variable as identically equal to unity in 1992 for all countries. The time-series suggest though that each ten-percentage-point increase in the real exchange rate is associated with a subsequent drag of 0.27 percentage points on the growth in real output.

Again, the pooling of the time-series masks very considerable differences among the different countries. As may be noted in Table 10.5, in 7 of 16 cases the coefficients of $BDQPA(-1)$ are, perversely, negative. The ratio is the same for the change in government expenditures, $DGEPC$, although the identity of the "perverse countries" is not entirely the same. The ratio with regard to exchange rates is somewhat better; 11 out of 16 countries have the "right" negative sign.

Table 10.6 confirms the major role in other countries of the US budget deficit. It was significantly related to subsequent growth in real GDP in all regressions and even added significantly where own-country budget deficits, including that of the United States, were also among the regressors. Changes in government expenditures had larger and more significant coefficients in these regressions that included the US deficit as a separate regressor, but the coefficients of the real exchange rate variable were little affected. Comparing Table 10.6 and Table 10. 4, we see that coefficients of determination (adjusted R^2) were lower in regressions with the US deficit than in those with own-country deficits, but were higher when both the US and own-country deficits were included.

Summary and conclusion

Pooled time-series and cross-section regressions of observations from 1970 to 1995 for up to 19 OECD countries have confirmed basic hypotheses of the relation of inflation-and-cyclically-adjusted deficits to subsequent changes in unemployment and real GDP. The deficit coefficients were significantly negative for unemployment and positive for GDP in the pooled relations even though they were rarely significant and not infrequently of the wrong sign in individual country regressions. The absolute sizes of the coefficients were markedly less than those in the US regression.[4]

The US deficit variable turned up with highly significant coefficients, even when included along with all of the own-country deficit variables. US deficits would appear to help the rest of the world; possibly their stimulative effect on the US economy spills over. When US deficits come down, the rest of the world would appear to suffer; perhaps there is something to the old adage that when the United States economy develops a cold, the rest of the world develops pneumonia.

Coefficients of other variables also had "correct" signs in the pooled regressions. Increases in government expenditures for goods and services were associated with current reductions in the rate of increase of unemployment and current increases in the rate of growth of real GDP. Higher real exchange rates were associated with subsequently greater unemployment and lesser growth in GDP.

Table 10.5 Growth in real GDP as function of lagged inflation-and-cyclically-adjusted budget deficits, lagged real exchange rates, and current changes in government expenditures for goods and services: individual country and pooled time series

(1) $GDPVGR_{it} = b_{0g} + b_{1g}BDQPA_{it}(-1) + b_{2g}DGEPC_{it} + b_{3g}ERR_{it}(-1) + u_{itg}$
$i = 1$ to 16, $t = 1972$ to 1995

| Country (1) | Regression coefficients and probability levels | | | Other statistics | | | |
	BDQPA(-1) (2)	DGEPC (3)	ERRN(-1) (4)	Adj. R^2 (5)	D–W (6)	Mean of GDPVGR (7)	No. of obs. (8)
Australia	-0.268 0.797	-6.462 0.476	-14.717 0.631	0.083	1.83	2.375	6
Austria	1.033 0.254	1.374 0.548	-1.609 0.643	-0.160	1.74	2.340	12
Belgium	-0.303 0.142	-1.249 0.241	5.070 0.164	-0.004	1.76	1.808	19
Canada	0.513 0.352	-1.368 0.404	5.979 0.596	-0.013	2.07	2.763	22
Denmark	0.421 0.053	-0.102 0.862	-3.348 0.081	0.616	2.00	2.097	12
Finland	-0.210 0.452	0.457 0.390	-13.326 0.022	0.612	2.06	2.032	20
France	-0.987 0.011	-1.425 0.175	2.675 0.262	-0.030	1.80	2.064	21
Germany	-0.245 0.654	2.798 0.023	4.475 0.431	0.228	1.62	2.449	22

Italy	0.613 0.031	1.346 0.065	−6.905 0.022	0.260	1.42	2.207	21
Japan	−0.240 0.495	−0.048 0.949	4.677 0.222	0.393	2.20	3.287	20
Netherlands	−0.089 0.736	0.916 0.454	−3.756 0.207	0.096	1.59	2.078	19
Norway	0.663 0.001	1.360 0.070	−12.452 0.006	0.764	1.88	2.833	12
Spain	0.527 0.121	1.227 0.100	−4.358 0.187	0.456	1.86	2.297	16
Sweden	0.000 0.997	0.269 0.544	−8.171 0.004	0.439	2.26	1.525	22
United Kingdom	0.218 0.270	−0.784 0.286	−7.292 0.042	0.174	1.19	1.718	22
United States	0.624 0.091	0.063 0.970	−2.071 0.310	0.053	1.95	2.432	22
Pooled time-series	0.167 0.016	0.462 0.048	−2.739 0.001	0.172	1.93	2.252	287

Table 10.6 Growth in real GDP as function of US and own-country lagged inflation-and-cyclically-adjusted budget deficits or separate cyclically adjusted budget deficits and inflation tax, lagged real exchange rates, and current changes in government expenditures for goods and services

(1) $GDPVGR_{it} = b_{0g} + b_{1g,us}USBDQPA_{it}(-1) + b_{1g,oc}BDQPA(-1) + b_{2g}DGEPC_{it} + b_{3g}ERR_{it}(-1) + u_{itg}$
$i = 1$ to 16 or 19, $t = 1972$ to 1995

Variable (1)	Regression coefficients, standard errors and probability levels					
	Time-series (2)	Time-series (3)	Cross-sections (4)	Cross-sections (5)	Overall (6)	Overall (7)
Mean of *GDPVGR* or Constant	2.414 (2.168)	2.252 (2.053)	2.414 (2.168)	2.252 (2.053)	1.040 (0.663) 0.1179	0.213 (0.887) 0.8107
USBDQPA(−1)	0.215 (0.090) 0.017	0.200 (0.119) 0.094	1.168 (0.338) 0.001	1.726 (0.514) 0.001	1.589 (0.382) 0.0000	2.006 (0.542) 0.0003
BDQPA(−1)	—	0.153 (0.070) 0.029	—	0.186 (0.067) 0.006	—	0.129 (0.056) 0.022
DGEPC	0.714 (0.172) 0.0000	0.523 (0.233) 0.026	0.721 (0.162) 0.0000	0.558 (0.214) 0.010	0.659 (0.162) 0.0001	0.525 (0.203) 0.010
ERRN(−1)	−2.650 (0.737) 0.0004	−2.789 (0.846) 0.001	−1.187 (0.990) 0.231	−0.217 (1.106) 0.845	−0.096 (0.530) 0.856	−0.486 (0.576) 0.400
AR(1)	0.234 (0.048)	0.351 (0.059)	0.250 (0.051)	0.397 (0.063)	0.328 (0.051)	0.440 (0.060)
AR(2)	−0.190 (0.049)	−0.187 (0.058)	−0.141 (0.051)	−0.167 (0.061)	−0.078 (0.050)	−0.126 (0.059)
Adj. R^2	0.168	0.178	0.342	0.387	0.314	0.391
D–W	1.84	1.94	1.93	1.97	1.91	1.95
Total obs.	409	287	409	287	409	287

It would not appear reasonable to place much confidence in the values of estimated parameters from these pooled data. Our regressions are essentially reduced-form approximations to whatever perhaps varying structural relations exist in different countries. The comparability and quality of the data are doubtful; there are likely substantial errors in variables.

The time-series and cross-section estimates, given these frailties though, are remarkably consistent. And analysis of the pooled series has here permitted statistically significant confirmation, not always available in limited data of individual countries, of important aggregative relations.

Table 1 Sources and definitions of variables

Symbol	Explanation	Source/definition
i	Country index	
t	Time index	
UNR	Unemployment rate	INTERLINK
UNRCH	Change (first difference) in the rate of unemployment	$UNRCH = UNR - UNR(-1)$
GDPVGR	Percentage rate of growth of real GDP	$GDPVGR = (GDPV - GDPV(-1))/GDPV(-1)$
GDPV	Gross domestic product (market prices), volume	INTERLINK
YRGA	Current government receipts, cyclically adjusted, nominal value	INTERLINK
YPGA	Current government payments, cyclically adjusted, nominal value	INTERLINK
CAPOG	Net capital outlays of government, nominal value	INTERLINK
NLGA	Cyclically adjusted net lending, nominal value	INTERLINK $NLGA = YRGA - YPGA - CAPOG$
GDPTR	Potential GDP, nominal value	INTERLINK
NLGQA	Net lending, government, cyclically adjusted, percentage of potential GDP	$NLGQA = 100 \cdot NLGA/GDPTR$
CFKG	Government consumption of fixed capital, nominal value	INTERLINK
CFKGPC	Government consumption of fixed capital, percentage of potential GDP	$CFKGPC = 100 \cdot CFKG/GDPTR$
BSQPA	Inflation-and-cyclically-adjusted budget surplus, percentage of potential GDP	$BSQPA = NLGQA + PEPC - CFKGPC$
BDQPA	Inflation-and-cyclically-adjusted budget deficit, percentage of potential GDP	$BDQPA = -BSQPA$
BDQA	Cyclically adjusted deficit, without the price effect, percentage of potential GDP	$BDQA = BDQPA + PEPC$
USBDQPA	Price-and-cyclically-adjusted budget deficit, percentage of potential GDP, United States	$BDQPA(US, t)$

GDP	Value of gross domestic product at market prices (nominal GDP)	INTERLINK
GDPP	GDP implicit price deflator	$GDPP = 100 \cdot GDP/GDPV$
GNFL	Net financial liabilities of government, nominal value	INTERLINK
PE	Price effect on budget surplus ("inflation tax") *	$PE = \dfrac{GNFL + GNFL(-1)}{GDPP + GDPP(-1)} \cdot$

$$(GDPP - GDPP(-1)) =$$

$$\left(GDPP(-1) \cdot \frac{(GNFL + GNFL(-1))/2}{GDPP + GDPP(-1)/2} \right)$$

$$\cdot \frac{GDPP - GDPP(-1)}{GDPP(-1)}$$

PEPC	Price effect on budget surplus, percentage of potential GDP	$PEPC = 100 \cdot PE/GDPTR$
BDPE	Price effect on budget deficit ("inflation tax")	$BDPE = -PEPC$
EXCH	Nominal exchange rate, US dollars per unit of local currency	
ERR	Real exchange rate	$ERR(i,t) = GDPP(i,t)/GDPP(US,t) \cdot EXCH(i,t)$
ERRN	Normalized real exchange rate	$ERRN(i,t) = ERR(i,t)/ERR(i,1992)$
CG	Government consumption, nominal value	INTERLINK
IG	Government fixed investment, nominal value	INTERLINK
GE	Government expenditures for goods and services, nominal value	$GE = CG + IG$
GEPC	Government expenditures for goods and services, percentage of potential GDP	$GEPC = 100 \cdot GE/GDPTR$
DGEPC	Change in government spending for goods and services, percentage of potential GDP	$DGEPC = GEPC - GEPC(-1)$

Note
*Price effect = (Initial price level × Real period-average net financial liabilities) × Rate of inflation where: Real period-average net financial liabilities = Nominal period-average net financial liabilities/Period-average price level.

Notes

1 See Eisner (1986, 1989, 1994*a*, 1994*b*, and 1995) and Eisner and Pieper (1984 and 1988), for example. In Eisner and Pieper (1985 and in a revised French version in 1986), I have examined some of these relations in time-series for the seven large OECD economies: Canada, France, Germany, Italy, Japan, the United Kingdom and the United States.
2 Potential GDP or potential output, as noted in *Fiscal Positions and Business Cycles* (OECD, 1997, p. 6), estimated with a production function approach "using a two-factor constant-returns-to-scale Cobb–Douglas production function ... [and] depends on potential employment, the actual capital stock and trend-labor efficiency."
3 *Economic Report of the President, February 1997*, Table B-108, p. 422.
4 This was true both for coefficients reported in this paper and for those found in previous work of the author with quarterly and with annual US data.

References

Eisner, Robert (1986), *How Real is the Federal Deficit?* New York: Macmillan, Free Press; London: Collier Macmillan.

Eisner, Robert (1989), "Budget Deficits: Rhetoric and Reality," *Journal of Economic Perspectives*, 3(2), Spring, pp. 73–93.

Eisner, Robert (1994), "National Saving and Budget Deficits," *Review of Economics and Statistics*, 76(1), February, pp. 181–6.

Eisner, Robert (1994), *The Misunderstood Economy: What Counts and How to Count It*, Boston: Harvard Business School Press.

Eisner, Robert (1995), "US National Saving and Budget Deficits," in *Macroeconomic Policy after the Conservative Era: Studies in Investment, Saving and Finance*, edited by Gerald A. Epstein and Herbert M. Gintis, Cambridge, New York and Melbourne: Cambridge University Press, pp. 109–42.

Eisner, Robert and Paul J. Pieper (1984), "A New View of the Federal Debt and Budget Deficits," *American Economic Review*, 74(1), March, pp. 11–29.

Eisner, Robert and Paul J. Pieper (1985), "Measurement and Effects of Government Debt and Deficits," in *Economic Policy and National Accounting in Inflationary Conditions*, Proceedings of an international conference in Dorga/Bergamo, Italy in January 1984, edited by J. Mortensen; in *Studies in Banking and Finance*, Vol. 2, edited by Bertrand Jacquillat, Arnold W. Sametz, Marshall Sarnat and Giorgio P. Szego, 1985, pp. 115–44.

Eisner, Robert and Paul J. Pieper (1986), "Dette et déficit gouvernementaux: mesures et effets," *Annales d'Économie et de Statistique*, 0(3), July–September, pp. 27–52. Updated and revised version of Eisner and Pieper (1985). In French.

Eisner, Robert and Paul J. Pieper (1988), "Deficits, Monetary Policy, and Real Economic Activity," in *The Economics of Public Debt*, edited by Kenneth J. Arrow and Michael J. Boskin, New York: St. Martin's Press, pp. 3–38.

OECD (1997), *Fiscal Positions and Business Cycles*, Paris: Organisation for Economic Co-operation and Development.

11 Public spending and public debt in the euro area

Alfred Greiner, Uwe Koeller, and Willi Semmler[1]

Introduction

In recent years, we have seen a shift in paradigm with respect to the efficacy of fiscal policy. Economists have become increasingly skeptical about whether short-run fiscal policy and Keynesian stabilization policy has any immediate stabilization effects. The traditional Keynesian macroeconomic policy was to undertake tax reductions and spending increases to cushion recessions. Cushioning recessions through automatic stabilizers is however still favored by most macroeconomists. Yet because of the uncertainty about the immediate effects of short-run fiscal policy, economists have become hesitant about fiscal policy – beyond its function as automatic stabilizer – as a means to stabilizing the business cycle.

Over the past couple of decades, most countries have shown high fiscal deficits and debts, and the scope for fiscal policy has become very narrow. Because of this, as well as the above-mentioned uncertainty about the expansionary effects of fiscal policy, monetary policy is frequently preferred to fiscal policy for discretionary measures. Monetary policy, it is often argued, is likely to have a more direct effect on economic activity. Fiscal policy is nowadays seen as a less viable stabilization tool, in particular for countries where high public deficits and debt prevail. In the view of some economists, fiscal policy is relegated today to setting the right incentives for private agents, and to providing the right infrastructure for long-run economic growth.

Especially in the Euro-area countries, issues of fiscal policy and public debt have gained importance amongst economists and politicians since the 1990s. Most of the OECD countries have shown chronic government deficits since the mid-1970s, which has led to an increase in their debt-to-GDP ratios. Looking at time-series data, the increase in public debt in the 1970s was mainly related to the two oil crises. In addition, the efforts, on the part of the governments of the EU member states, to preserve the welfare state in times of recession, caused a rise in public deficits and debt until the mid-1990s.[2] Since then, however, the efforts to reduce the public debt in preparation of the 1999 start of the European Monetary Union

(EMU) have produced declining deficits. It is only recently, in the recession of 2001–2003, that the deficit has again begun to increase for some countries, notably Germany and France.

In the academic debate on the deficit and debt of the Euro-area countries, it has been argued that fiscal policy is threatening to become unsustainable, and that it is no longer an effective instrument in stabilizing the macroeconomy. The crucial issue is that of sustainability. This paper is concerned with formal econometric procedures that allow testing for the sustainability of fiscal policy. What we are concerned with here is not the short-run violation of the Stability and Growth Pact of the EMU, but rather the long-run sustainability of the member countries' fiscal policy.

Empirical studies that help to clarify whether governments follow the intertemporal budget constraint or not are indeed desirable. For the United States there exist numerous studies starting with the paper by Hamilton and Flavin (1986). In this paper they propose a framework for analyzing whether governments can run a Ponzi scheme or not, and apply the test to US time-series data. They find sustainability of fiscal policy in the United States. Other papers followed, which investigated this issue for the United States, as well as for other countries, but reached partly different conclusions (see, e.g., Kremers, 1988; Wilcox, 1989, or Trehan and Walsh, 1991, and Greiner and Semmler, 1999). However, the testing methods employed in these papers have been criticized by Bohn (1995, 1998) on the grounds that they make assumptions about future states of nature that are difficult to estimate from a single set of observed time-series data. In a recent paper, Bohn (1998) proposes a new test that is not open to this criticism. In this paper we extend the approach by Bohn and apply it to some Euro-area countries.

The remainder of this paper is organized as follows. The next section studies empirically the sustainability of fiscal policy in four Euro-area countries (France, Germany, Italy and Portugal), as well as in the United States. The third section investigates the connection between public debt and public investment; the fourth section explores whether the relationship between deficit and macroeconomic performance might be nonlinear. The fifth section concludes the paper. An appendix gives a brief sketch of the theoretical background of our sustainability test.

Sustainability of fiscal policy in selected Euro countries

Bohn (1995, 1998) introduced a sustainability test, which helps to explore whether a given time-series of government debt is sustainable by analyzing whether the primary-deficit-to-GDP ratio is a positive linear function of the debt-to-GDP ratio. If this holds, a given fiscal policy is said to be sustainable.[3] The reasoning behind this approach is that if a government raises the primary surplus when the public debt ratio increases, then it takes corrective action. This implies that the initial rise in the debt-to-GDP ratio should be compensated and, as a consequence, that the ratio should remain bounded.

We perform this test for a selection of countries in the European Monetary Union (EMU), namely those which have been recently characterized by high deficits or by a high debt ratio and which have violated the Maastricht criteria. The countries in question are Germany, France, Italy and Portugal. We also include the United States for reasons of comparison. The main idea is to estimate the following equation:

$$s_t = \rho b_t + \phi^T \mathbf{V}_t + \epsilon_t \tag{1}$$

where s_t and b_t are the primary surplus and debt ratio, respectively; $\mathbf{V}_t$ is a vector which consists of the number 1 and of other factors related to the primary surplus, and ϵ_t is an error term which is independent and identically distributed (i.i.d.).

As concerns the other variables contained in $\mathbf{V}_t$, which are assumed to affect the primary surplus, we include the net interest payments on public debt relative to GDP (*Int*), and a variable reflecting the business cycle (*YVAR*). *YVAR* is calculated by applying the Hodrick–Prescott filter twice on the GDP series. Further, the social-surplus ratio (*Soc*) is subtracted from the primary-surplus ratio and is considered as exogenous in order to catch possible effects of transfers between the social insurance system and the government.

In addition, we decided that it would be more reasonable to include the lagged debt ratio b_{t-1} instead of the contemporaneous b_t, although theory says that the response of the surplus on higher debt should be immediate. We do this because interest payments on debt and repayment of the debt occur in later periods.

Summarizing our discussion, the equation to be estimated is as follows:

$$s_t = \phi_0 + \rho b_{t-1} + \phi_1 Soc_t + \phi_2 Int_t + \phi_3 YVAR_t + \epsilon_t \tag{2}$$

Estimating (2) with ordinary least squares (OLS) may give biased standard errors and *t*-statistics because of possible heteroskedasticity and autocorrelation in the residuals. Therefore, we calculate heteroskedasticity and autocorrelation-consistent *t*-statistics to get robust estimates (see White, 1980; Newey and West, 1987). As to the data, we use OECD *Economic Outlook Statistics and Projections*. We use the data set corresponding to the June 2003 issue of the OECD *Economic Outlook*.

France

Figure 11.1 shows that the French debt ratio has been growing most of the time and that it increased very fast at the beginning of the 1990s. Until the

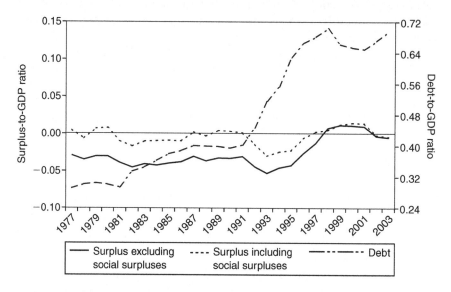

Figure 11.1 Primary surplus-to-GDP and debt-to-GDP ratio for France (1977–2003).

mid-1990s, France experienced deficits (net of the social surplus) that implied a further increase of the already-high debt ratio.

The primary deficit displays a different trend. Relatively low deficits, and in some cases primary surpluses, generated only a moderate growth of the debt ratio. The recession in the early 1990s caused higher deficits and reduced social surpluses, and thus created higher debt ratios. In face of the Maastricht criteria, France strengthened its fiscal discipline and reduced the debt ratio. Since the last recession, at the beginning of 2001, the fiscal situation worsened and the debt ratio started growing again.

Equation (2) is estimated for the entire sample period. We obtain the following result (with standard errors in parenthesis):

$$s_t = -\ 0.012 + \ 0.077b_{t-1} - 0.913Soc_t - 1.256Int_t - 0.048YVAR_t$$
$$\quad\ (0.02)\quad (0.042)\qquad (0.298)\qquad (0.753)\qquad (0.187) \qquad\qquad (3)$$

The parameter of interest ρ is positive and significant at the 10 percent level (t-statistic = 1.812), indicating that overall, French fiscal policy has followed a sustainable path. As one can observe, corrective measures were taken in response to an increase in the debt ratio in the previous period. The good fit of the model is displayed by a high R^2 of 0.749. The Durbin-Watson (DW) statistic is 1.063. The ϕ_1-parameter shows a negative response of the social surplus to debt. This might be interpreted as high social surpluses weakening the fiscal discipline and lowering the deficit.

The positive sign of the ϕ_2-parameter indicates the efforts on the part of the government to run surpluses to pay the debt service.

The cyclical variable is insignificant at all usual levels, which might be due to the fact that the French business cycle was following the German business cycle – because of the fixed European exchange rate system and also because of the Bundesbank interest rate policy.

In conclusion, the hypothesis of an overall sustainable fiscal policy cannot be rejected for France. Next, we look at Germany.

Germany

As Figure 11.2 shows, at the beginning of the mid-1970s the German government was confronted with high debt ratios accompanied with permanent primary deficits. In the mid-1970s, the debt ratio increases very rapidly due to the oil shock, which also caused a recession with a rise of the unemployment rate. This fact is highlighted in Figure 11.2 by the solid line for debt-to-GDP ratio and the dotted lines for the primary surplus. The second sharp increase of the debt ratio was caused by the German unification and began in the early nineties as the GDP growth rates slowed down.

Next, we explore if the test procedure agrees with our presumptions. For Equation (4) we get the following estimates:

$$s_t = -\ 0.002 + 0.148b_{t-1} - 0.068Soc_t - 2.552Int_t - 0.240YVAR_t$$
$$(0.005)\ \ (0.043)\phantom{b_{t-1}}\ \ (0.255)\ \ (0.670)\ \ (0.060) \tag{4}$$

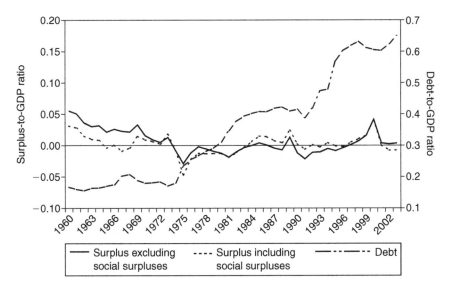

Figure 11.2 Primary surplus-to-GDP and debt-to-GDP ratio for Germany (1960–2003).

The p-coefficient of 0.148 is significant at all levels and indicates a strong positive response of the primary surplus to a higher debt in the previous period. The same effect is observed for the net-interest-payment and the business-cycle variable; the coefficients are both highly significant. But we found no significant positive effect of the social surplus on the primary surplus. The good fit of the data is reflected in the relatively high R^2 of 0.642 and a DW statistic of 1.181, although still other variables must be brought into the model in order to explain the remaining structure of the residuals.

As in the case of France, our estimation suggests that Germany follows a sustainable fiscal policy. In all estimations, the primary surplus ratio increases with a rising debt ratio, suggesting that the intertemporal budget constraint is being met.

Italy

Since the mid-eighties, Italy has shown a fast-growing debt ratio accompanied by a permanent primary deficit. Faced with the criteria for joining the EMU in 1999, her fiscal policy changed course. The Italian government reduced the deficit, and subsequently, at the beginning of the nineties, ran a surplus, which policy brought to a halt the growth of the public debt ratio. Although the debt criteria could not be fulfilled at the start of the EMU, Italy joined the EMU in 1999. The trends of Italian fiscal policy are shown in Figure 11.3.

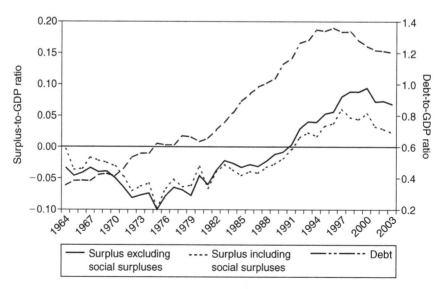

Figure 11.3 Primary surplus-to-GDP and debt-to-GDP ratio for Italy (1964–2003).

The fiscal consolidation efforts in response to higher debt ratios are seen when we estimate Equation (2). The result obtained is as follows:

$$s_t = -\ 0.122 + 0.163b_{t-1} - 0.531Soc_t - 0.525Int_t - 0.128YVAR_t$$
$$\quad\ (0.013)\ \ (0.023)\qquad (0.274)\qquad (0.131)\qquad (0.024) \qquad\qquad (5)$$

The response parameter ρ is 0.163 and significant at all levels (t-statistic = 6.956), meaning that the conjecture of a sustainable fiscal policy holds in spite of the extraordinarily high initial debt ratio. The other estimates are all significantly different from zero; only the social-surplus effect (t-statistic = −1,933) is insignificant at the 5 percent level but significant at the 10 percent level. Finally, the R^2 reaches 0.911 and the DW-statistic is 1.071. The latter suggests that there might still be some structure in the residual, which our framework fails to uncover.

The estimates confirm our results above. The Italian fiscal policy leans toward sustainability in the long run in spite of the initial high debt-to-income ratio.

Portugal

Another candidate for testing the sustainability of fiscal policy is Portugal, which has also been in the news for violating the Maastricht criteria. The situation in Portugal differs from Italy in that Portugal's indebtedness is relatively low; as shown in Figure 11.4, she suffered from persistent deficits

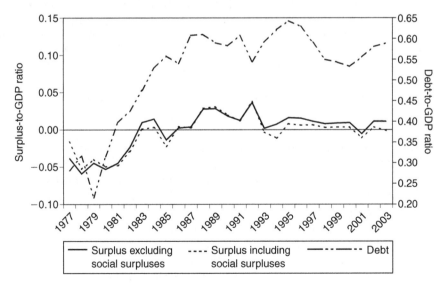

Figure 11.4 Primary surplus-to-GDP and debt-to-GDP ratio for Portugal (1977–2003).

mainly in the last few years. The main difference compared to the other countries is that Portugal's net interest payments affect her budget in an extreme way; although the primary surplus is near zero over most of the sample period, the debt service generates a deficit.

The estimation of Equation (2) for Portugal gives the following results:

$$s_t = -\ 0.083 + 0.164b_{t-1} - 0.314Soc_t - 0.014Int_t - 0.051YVAR_t$$
$$\quad\ (0.012)\ (0.025)\qquad (0.364)\qquad (0.093)\qquad (0.014)\qquad\qquad (6)$$

The main parameter ρ, with a value of 0.164, is positive and significant at all usual levels (t-statistic = 6.547). The same holds for the constant and the business cycle variable. Yet, the latter shows a negative sign, which means if the economy is growing, the surplus will be reduced. As in the case of France, the business cycle upswing has a negative effect also on the surplus, although in the case of France, it was not significantly different from zero. The remaining variables, namely the social surplus and the interest payments, do not have a significant effect on the primary surplus. The R^2 value of 0.861 and the DW statistic of 1.812 indicate that the data is very well represented by Equation (2).

United States

Finally we will look at the fiscal policy trends of the United States. Many authors have focused their attention on the sustainability of fiscal policy in the US. This issue is back in the news due to the current deficit caused by the Iraq war, as well as the tax cuts that were enacted with a view to stimulating the US economy. We first consider the graph of the time-series of US debt and primary-surplus ratios and the scatter plot of these two variables.

Estimating Equation (2) for the US we get:

$$s_t = -\ 0.056 + 0.165b_{t-1} - 0.600Soc_t - 1.617Int_t - 0.138YVAR_t$$
$$\quad\ (0.017)\ (0.035)\qquad (0.266)\qquad (0.381)\qquad (0.036)\qquad\qquad (7)$$

All coefficients are highly significant, and ρ is positive, so that sustainability cannot be rejected. As our regression shows, the US government tried to compensate the additional debt by running a higher surplus a year later. Interestingly, the business-cycle coefficient is negative. As in the case of Portugal, a growing economy will reduce the surplus. Also, if a social surplus is produced, the surplus will be reduced, meaning that the government will take advantage of the good social position and reduce its efforts to run a surplus elsewhere. Our conjecture of a low R^2 and a poor DW statistic is verified; they take values of 0.375 and 0.656 respectively.

The poor quality of our estimation remains and suggests that one might include other variables to properly model the outliers in these time-series.

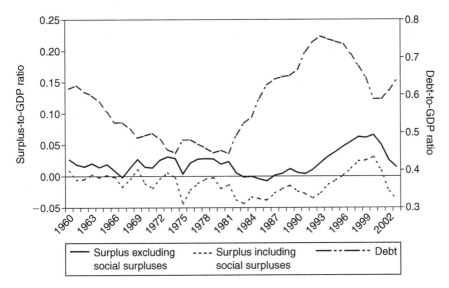

Figure 11.5 Primary surplus-to-GDP and debt-to-GDP ratio for the United States (1960–2003).

Yet all parameters are significant and the ρ's have the expected sign. Finally, even though we use another dataset and also include some additional components in the framework, our findings seem to verify Bohn's results when he characterized US fiscal policy as sustainable.

Effects of government debt on public investment

In the previous section we presented evidence that the countries under consideration raise the primary surplus as a result of a rising debt-to-GDP ratio. One possible way to achieve an increase in the primary surplus is to reduce public spending. If one looks at government spending in OECD countries during the 1990s, one can observe in many of these countries a significant decline in public investment. This holds true both for the ratio of public investment to GDP and for the ratio of public investment to overall public spending. For countries that joined the EMU, the need to comply with the Maastricht criteria could be a possible explanation of this reduction. But that argument does not, of course, apply to the other countries. One might conjecture, therefore, that public investment was reduced in order to achieve a higher primary surplus, which guarantees sustainability of the public debt.

To gain further evidence, econometric studies should be performed. One analysis dealing with this subject is the one undertaken by Heinemann (2002), in which panel studies were estimated with 16 OECD countries for the period 1980–1999. The dependent variable is the ratio of public investment to GDP in one specification, and the ratio of public investment relative to total government expenditures in another specification. They are explained by a number of variables, which are considered to be the driving forces behind public investment. In order to avoid bias in the results, the study also takes into account business-cycle effects and the impact of the privatization process.

The empirical estimations show that the debt-to-GDP ratio is significant in both specifications. This lends support to the idea that the decline of public investment in the 1990s resulted from the growing debt ratios between the 1970s and the 1990s. A further result is that the privatization process does not seem to play a role in explaining declining public investment. The assumption that the privatization process in the 1990s, which could be considered as an explanation for the reduction of public investment, does not turn out to be valid. Finally, a dummy variable capturing the effect of the qualification for the EMU in 1997 also did not turn out to be significant; thus, the requirement of the deficit limit in the Maastricht treaty does not offer an explanation for the decline in public investment.

Next, we consider the time-series of public investment and public debt in a single European country, namely Germany, from 1970 to 2000. As to public investment, denoted by $i_{p,t}$, we consider it in real (deflated) terms. We have also eliminated the trend in this time-series by following the standard macroeconometric approach as suggested, (e.g.) by King *et al.* (1988), or Campbell (1994). That is, we assume that the log of real public investment follows a linear time trend, i.e., $\ln(i_{p,t}) = a_1 + a_2 \cdot t$, with t denoting time, and estimate that equation with OLS. The detrended variable then is given by

$$\bar{i}_{p,t} \equiv \frac{\ln(i_{p,t}) - (\hat{a}_1 + \hat{a}_2 \cdot t)}{\hat{a}_1 + \hat{a}_2 \cdot t} \tag{8}$$

with $\hat{a}_1$ and $\hat{a}_2$ designating the OLS estimates for a_1 and a_2.

First, we look at the correlation between public investment and lagged ratios of public debt to GDP, b_{t-i}. The correlation coefficients are given in Table 11.1.

Table 11.1 shows that in Germany, public investment and public debt are negatively correlated and independent of the length of the time lag. This is as expected, and it suggests that public investment declines as public debt rises, as could be observed also in the panel study mentioned above.

To get further insights into this relationship we perform Granger causality tests. We do so because we want to find out whether higher debt ratios lead to less public investment, where the causality is to be understood in the sense of Granger. To perform this test the following general equation is estimated:

Table 11.1 Correlation between detrended real public investment and lagged debt ratios

	b_{t-1}	b_{t-2}	b_{t-3}	b_{t-4}
Correlation coefficient	−0.008	−0.07	−0.081	−0.04

$$y_t = c + \alpha_1 y_{t-1} + \ldots + \alpha_p y_{t-p} + \beta_1 x_{t-1} + \ldots + \beta_p x_{t-p} + \eta_t \tag{9}$$

with c being a constant and η_t a stochastic error term. If the null hypothesis

$$H_0: \beta_1 = \ldots = \beta_p = 0$$

can be rejected, then the variable x has a statistically significant effect on y. In our case, we tested whether the public-debt-to-GDP ratio exerts a negative influence on detrended public investment $\bar{i}_{p,t}$. In this test we set $p = 3$ and $p = 5$. We do so because we think that three and five years are a reasonable and long-enough time lag over which public debt affects public investment.

Estimating Equation (9) with $p = 3$ yields a value for the F-test statistic of 3.38 and the 5 percent critical value is 3.16. This implies that the hypothesis H_0 can be rejected at the 5 percent significance level. The same holds for $p = 5$. In this case, we get an F-test statistic of 3.09, which exceeds the 5 percent critical value given by 2.85 so that the hypothesis that public debt does not affect public investment can be rejected.

These results indicate that higher debt ratios are likely to lead to less public investment. The reason for this outcome can be seen in the fact that higher public debt implies higher debt service in the future, in particular higher interest payments, which reduces the scope for other types of public spending. Obviously, public investment is that part of public spending which can be reduced most easily because public investment does not have lobbies. In a way, we may speak of an "internal crowding out" implying that public investment is crowded-out by non-productive public spending such as interest payments on the public debt.

Nonlinear relationship of deficit spending and macroeconomic performance

An important issue concerning the efficacy of fiscal policy is whether deficit spending has an expansionary or contractionary effect on GDP. In particular, we will study to what extent the effect of deficit spending on GDP depends on the level of the debt-to-GDP ratio. There may exist a threshold debt-to-GDP ratio, below which deficit spending is expansionary and above which deficit spending may be ineffective or even contractionary. That is, we want to test whether the effects of the public deficit on detrended real GDP differ according as to whether the debt ratio is low or high. The detrended variable as computed in Greiner, Gong and Semmler (2001) is given by

$$\tilde{y} \equiv \frac{\ln(GDP) - (\hat{a} + \hat{b} \cdot t)}{\hat{a} + \hat{b} \cdot t} \tag{10}$$

with $\hat{a}$ and $\hat{b}$ denoting the OLS estimates for a and b.

To gain insight into the relation between public debt, public deficit, and GDP, we estimate a nonlinear equation, which assumes that the effect of public deficit on detrended GDP depends on the debt-to-GDP ratio. This is done by assuming that the coefficient giving the impact of public deficit on detrended GDP is a function of the debt-to-GDP ratio. As to the latter function we assume a polynomial of the third order. More concretely, we estimate the following equation:

$$\tilde{y}_t = \alpha + \beta \tilde{y}_{t-1} + \theta(b_t)d_t \tag{11}$$

with

$$\theta(b_t) = \theta_0 + \theta_1 b_t + \theta_2 b_t^2 + \theta_3 b_t^3 \tag{12}$$

Equations (11) and (12) state that detrended GDP depends on its own lagged value and on the deficit ratio d_t, where the effect of the deficit ratio is assumed to be affected by the debt ratio b_t. If $\theta(b_t)$ is positive, the deficit ratio has a positive impact on detrended GDP; if it is negative; the reverse holds. Further, since $\theta(\cdot)$ depends on the debt ratio, the effect of the deficit ratio on detrended GDP also depends on the debt ratio.

Table 11.2 shows the results of estimating (11) for a pooled data set with nonlinear least squares.[4]

Figure 11.6 gives the curve of θ_t and of b_t, showing a negative relation for a wide range of b_t. This implies that the public deficit-to-GDP ratio has a negative impact on the detrended GDP if the ratio of the public debt to

Table 11.2 Results from estimating equation (11) for a pooled data set with non-linear least squares

Parameter	Value	Std. Deviation
α	0.00012	0.00012
β	0.775	0.044
θ_0	0.015	0.026
θ_1	−0.112	0.129
θ_2	0.169	0.189
θ_3	−0.075	0.084

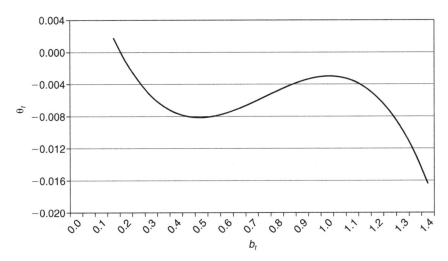

Figure 11.6 Non-linear output response to fiscal stimulus: impact coefficient plotted against debt-to-GDP ratio (θ_t vs. b_t).

GDP passes a certain threshold. In fact, in our estimation, if the debt-to-GDP ratio is smaller than roughly 20 percent, an increase in the public deficit-to-GDP ratio has a positive impact on detrended GDP. Thus deficit spending is expansionary as Keynesian macroeconomic theory predicts. Yet as our nonlinear regression also shows, the expansionary effect may be reversed if the debt-to-GDP level is already very high. This is a result for public debt that can also be found for private debt and its impact on economic growth, for the latter see Grüne, Semmler and Sieveking (2004).

Conclusion

This paper has analyzed current issues with respect to fiscal policy, in particular, the question of whether fiscal policy is sustainable, in selected Euro-area countries. We have focused on those Euro-area countries which are characterized by a high debt ratio, or which have recently violated the 3-percent Maastricht deficit criteria. Our study is a follow-up on an approach that Bohn (1998) developed to study sustainability of fiscal policy in the United States. Theoretically, we could establish that if the government primary-surplus-to-GDP ratio increases linearly with a rising ratio of public debt to GDP, then the fiscal policy is sustainable for dynamically efficient economies.

Our empirical results suggest that fiscal policies in the countries under consideration are sustainable in spite of temporary violations of the 3-percent rule defined by the Stability and Growth Pact. The reason for the sustainability of fiscal policy in the long run is that governments take corrective actions in the face of rising debt ratios, by increasing the primary-surplus ratio. This, however, implies that the intertemporal budget constraint of the government, which should be fulfilled in the distant future as time approaches infinity, has immediate implications for the current-period budget constraint.

Yet the compliance with the intertemporal budget constraint implies that, with a rising public debt ratio, either public spending must decrease or tax revenues must increase. Looking at the Euro-area countries one can observe that it was not a rise in tax revenue, but a decline in public spending, which generated the primary surpluses. As to the component of public spending that has been reduced the most, it can be seen that in many countries public investment has been decreased. In practice, public investment is likely to be the variable that is easiest to reduce. Thus, the decline of public investment can be explained as the result of a rising public debt, which, indeed, can be observed empirically (see, e.g., Gong, Greiner and Semmler, 2001, or Heinemann, 2002). By this token, high debt-to-GDP ratios may have negative repercussions on the long-run growth rates of economies.[5]

Finally, we have shown that the controversy on whether deficit spending has an expansionary or contractionary effect on GDP can be properly answered by applying a nonlinear test of deficit spending and GDP, whereby the effect is likely to be impacted by a threshold of the public debt-to-GDP ratio. Below a certain debt-to-GDP ratio, spending is expansionary, but above that threshold deficit spending may be ineffective or even contractionary.

Appendix: Sustainability of public debt

Public debt is "sustainable" when the following equation holds:

$$\lim_{t \to \infty} e^{-rt} B(t) = 0 \tag{13}$$

where r denotes the (constant) interest rate, and $B(t)$ the level of public debt at time t. The equation is usually referred to as the no-Ponzi-game condition (see, e.g., Blanchard and Fischer, 1989, chapter 2).

We assume a deterministic economy in continuous time, in which the primary surplus of the government relative to GDP depends on the debt-to-GDP ratio and on a constant, i.e.

$$\frac{T(t) - G(t)}{Y(t)} = \phi + \rho \cdot \frac{B(t)}{Y(t)} \tag{14}$$

with $T(t)$ designating tax revenue at time t, $G(t)$ public spending exclusive of interest payments at time t, $Y(t)$ GDP at time t, $B(t)$ public debt at time t and ϕ, ρ are constants. All variables are real numbers.

Using (14), the differential equation describing the evolution of public debt can be written as

$$\dot{B}(t) = r \cdot B(t) + G(t) - T(t) = (r - \rho) B(t) - \phi \cdot Y(t) \qquad (15)$$

where $\dot{B}(t)$ denotes the time-derivative of the debt level. Solving this differential equation and multiplying both sides by $e^{-\rho t}$ gives

$$e^{-\rho t} B(t) = \left(\frac{\phi}{r - \gamma - \rho} \right) Y(0) e^{(\gamma - \rho)t} + e^{-\rho t} C_1 \qquad (16)$$

with $B(0) > 0$ standing for debt at time $t = 0$, which is assumed to be strictly positive; γ is the constant growth rate of GDP, and C_1 a constant given by $C_1 = B(0) - Y(0)\phi/(r - \gamma - \rho)$. Assuming that $r > \gamma$, which holds in dynamically efficient economies and which is also realistic (see Abel *et al.*, 1989), Equation (16) shows that $\rho > 0$ guarantees that the intertemporal budget constraint is met.

Notes

1 We want to thank Professor Alan Isaac for helpful comments on an earlier version of the paper.
2 In Germany, the unification of East and West Germany gave rise to an increase in the debt-to-GDP ratio, from about 44 percent in 1990 to roughly 58 percent in 1995.
3 In the appendix we demonstrate this for an economy with a constant interest rate and a constant growth rate.
4 For the details of the subsequent test with pooled data of Euro-area countries, see Greiner, Gong and Semmler (2001).
5 For details, see Greiner, Semmler and Gong (2004), Chapter 6.

References

Abel, Andrew B., N. Gregory Mankiw, Lawrence H. Summers, and Richard J. Zeckhauser (1989), "Assessing Dynamic Efficiency: Theory and Evidence," *Review of Economic Studies*, 56(1), January, pp. 1–19.
Blanchard, Olivier J. and Stanley Fischer (1989), *Lectures on Macroeconomics*, Cambridge, Massachusetts: MIT Press.
Bohn, Henning (1995), "The Sustainability of Budget Deficits in a Stochastic Economy," *Journal of Money, Credit and Banking*, 27(1), February, pp. 257–71.
Bohn, Henning (1998), "The Behavior of U.S. Public Debt and Deficits," *Quarterly Journal of Economics*, 113(3), August, pp. 949–63.
Campbell, John Y. (1994), "Inspecting the Mechanism: An Analytical Approach to the Stochastic Growth Model," *Journal of Monetary Economics*," 33(3), June, pp. 463–506.
Greiner, Alfred, Gang Gong, and Willi Semmler (2001), "Growth Effects of Fiscal Policy and Debt Sustainability in the EU," *Empirica*, 28(1), pp. 3–19.

Greiner, Alfred, Gang Gong, and Willi Semmler (2004), *The Forces of Economic Growth: A Time Series Perspective*, Princeton University Press (forthcoming).

Grüne, Lars, Willi Semmler, and Malte Sieveking (2004), "Creditworthiness and Threshold in a Credit Market Model with Multiple Equilibria," *Economic Theory* (forthcoming).

Heinemann, Friedrich (2002), "Factor Mobility, Government Debt and the Decline in Public Investment," *ZEW Discussion Paper*, No. 02-19. Available online at: ftp://ftp.zew.de/pub/zew-docs/dp/dp0219.pdf.

King, Robert G., Charles I. Plosser, and Sergio T. Rebelo (1988), "Production, Growth and Business Cycles I: the Basic Neo-Classical Model," *Journal of Monetary Economics*, 21(2/3), March/May, pp. 195–232.

Newey, Whitney K. and Kenneth D. West (1987), "A Simple, Positive Semi-Definite, Heteroskedasticity and Autocorrelation Consistent Covariance Matrix," *Econometrica*, 55(3), May, pp. 703–8.

White, Halbert (1980), "A Heteroskedasticity-Consistent Covariance Matrix Estimator and a Direct Test for Heteroskedasticity," *Econometrica*, 48(4), May, pp. 817–38.

12 Varieties of fiscal stimulus

A conflicting claims analysis

Alan G. Isaac[1]

Introduction

This paper develops a Post Keynesian model of the effects of fiscal policy on a growing economy. The theoretical model integrates the core Post Keynesian model of inflation (the conflicting-claims approach) with a specific characterization of endogenous monetary policy (a Taylor rule). The policy objective is to determine how varieties of fiscal policy affect growth, unemployment, and the distribution of income.

In conflicting-claims economies, inflation emerges when the target claims of workers and firms exceed total income. At the level of the firm, a shortfall of the current price of output from the target price leads to price increases. Thus, in contrast with the neoclassical tradition but in alignment with some of the New Keynesian literature, the conflicting-claims model emphasizes the price-setting activities of firms. Price-setting behavior, subject to costs of adjustment, emerges as one of the important determinants of the evolution of the economy.[2]

While the price setting of individual firms is the proximate source of aggregate inflation, a macroeconomic description must not neglect the behavior of the monetary authority. Post Keynesians have consistently recognized that monetary policy responds endogenously to the economic environment, which substantially complicates the characterization of economic causality. Despite the general Post Keynesian emphasis on the fundamental importance of endogenous money, however, the bulk of the conflicting-claims literature avoids explicit consideration of the monetary aspects of macroeconomic adjustment. This paper adopts a popular, simple characterization of that endogeneity: a "Taylor rule." Taylor (1993) proposed that the federal-funds rate should move with inflation and against the GDP gap. Monetary policy discussions often treat Taylor rules as a descriptively plausible and prescriptively appropriate characterization of monetary policy.

This paper contributes to the literature on the role of aggregate demand in a growing economy (Harrod, 1939; Rose, 1966; Marglin, 1984) and to the conflicting-claims literature (Goodwin, 1967; Rowthorn, 1977). The paper models a growing, conflicting-claims economy with endogenous monetary policy. It then applies this model to the analysis of various fiscal policies.

The next section lays out the model. Post Keynesian influences are evident in the savings function and the conflicting-claims formulation of price adjustment. Monetary considerations are introduced by means of a simple Taylor-rule characterization of monetary policy. The subsequent two sections explore the implications of various forms of fiscal policy, and the final section concludes.

Growth with unemployment

Let N^s be the available supply of labor hours. Technological progress augments this to an effective labor supply of AN^s, where A indexes the level of technological progress. Let K be the aggregate capital stock, and define the relative factor supply n^s by

$$n^s = AN^s/K \tag{1}$$

Natural and warranted growth rates

Let g_{AN} be the growth rate of the effective labor supply and g_K be the rate of capital accumulation. Then we can characterize the growth rate of n^s by

$$g_{n^s} = g_{AN} - g_K \tag{2}$$

Here g_{AN} denotes the natural rate of growth (i.e., the growth rate of the effective labor supply), and g_K denotes the warranted rate of growth (i.e., the actual saving rate, which determines the rate of capital accumulation). So n^s rises or falls as the natural rate of growth is greater than or less than the warranted rate of growth. In a steady state, the warranted rate of growth equals the natural rate of growth: $g_K = g_{AN}$. Exogenous growth models, this paper included, generally treat the natural rate of growth as given. Attention then turns to the determinants of the warranted growth rate.

A common reference point for models of a growing economy is the basic Solow (1956) model, in which $g_K = \sigma(n^s)$.[3] The dynamics of the Solow model are therefore given by

$$g_{n^s} = g_{AN} - \sigma(n^s) \tag{3}$$

Under the usual assumption that $\sigma(\cdot)$ is strictly increasing, a steady state in this Solow model is stable and unique.[4]

Models in the tradition of Keynes differ from those in the neoclassical tradition by specifically allowing that aggregate demand deficiencies can produce persistent involuntary unemployment. An economy experiences unemployment when the available supply of labor hours is greater than the amount of labor demanded: $N^s > N$, where N is the actual input of labor hours into the production process. In terms of relative factor supplies and inputs, we rewrite this as $n^s > n$, where

$$n = AN/K \tag{4}$$

We may interpret $n = AN/K$ as the labor intensity of production or as the rate of capacity utilization. In standard fashion, the output–capital ratio (y) is determined by the rate of capacity utilization:

$$y = y(n) \tag{5}$$

Goods market equilibrium

To economists in the Keynesian tradition, Equation (3) looks strikingly odd for two related reasons: it links saving to potential rather than actual employment, and it ignores the need to explicitly link saving and investment. While the link between saving and potential income (and thereby to potential employment) is harmless given continuous full employment, it is noxious in the presence of persistent unemployment. Post Keynesian growth models link saving to actual income and actual employment.[5] We will therefore replace the Solow saving function: thereby saving will be determined by actual earnings rather than by full-employment earnings. We also allow for an influence of income distribution on saving behavior: incorporating the standard Post Keynesian recognition of a lower saving rate among wage earners, saving decreasing in labor's share of income, which for given n we index by the cost of labor, ω.[6] Finally, the tax rate (τ) and the national-income-share of government consumption expenditure (g^c) both influence aggregate saving. The resulting saving function is $\sigma(n, \omega, \tau, g^c)$, where $\sigma_n > 0$, $\sigma_\omega < 0$, $\sigma_\tau > 0$, and $\sigma_{g^c} < 0$. (The response $\sigma_\tau > 0$ embodies the assumption that private saving is reduced by less than the increase in public saving.) The evolution of the potential labor intensity of production is therefore determined as follows:

$$g_{n^s} = g_{AN} - \sigma(n, \omega, \tau, g^c) \tag{6}$$

Replacing (3) by (6) allows for the possibility of unemployment. Labor hired for production may be less than the aggregate supply of labor ($N < N^s$), so saving should respond to actual earnings rather than potential earnings. The evolution of the relative factor supply (i.e., the potential labor intensity of production) is determined by the actual level of saving, not the level of saving that would obtain at full employment. To give this a more traditional phrasing, we can say that at any given n, unemployment rises or falls as the natural rate exceeds or falls short of the warranted rate of growth.

Our next model ingredient is a traditional specification of goods-market equilibrium. The Solow specification of capital accumulation as $g_K = \sigma(\cdot)$ suppresses any difficulties in equilibrating the desired accumulation of equity by households and the desired level of investment by firms.[7] In the tradition of Kalecki and Keynes, we include (7) as our explicit characterization goods market equilibrium.[8]

$$\kappa(i - \pi, g^i) = \sigma(n, \omega, \tau, g^c) \tag{7}$$

The function $\kappa(\cdot)$ represents the desired rate of growth of the capital stock, where i is the nominal interest rate, π is the rate of inflation, and g^i the share of government investment in national income. The behavioral response to the cost of borrowing $(r = i - \pi)$ is negative, $\kappa_r < 0$, and government can contribute to capital formation, $\kappa_{gi} > 0$. Equation (7) is a standard representation of goods-market equilibrium, aside from the Post Keynesian functional specifications.

As Keynes (1936) noted, it is not evident that (7) can be satisfied at $n = n^s$ for a positive nominal rate of interest. In addition, once the monetary nature of the economy is recognized, the interaction between the goods and assets markets becomes an important concern. Specifically, given π and the standard dependence of money demand on income and the nominal interest rate, there may be no interest rate compatible with simultaneous clearing of the goods and money markets at the full-employment level of income. This is particularly true once we allow for sticky prices, a stylized fact of advanced capitalist economies (Romer, 2000; Wolman, 2000).

Price adjustment

Price adjustment takes place in an economy with price rigidities: firms experience increasing costs in the speed of price increases.[9] The resulting price dynamics are given the conflicting-claims representation of Equation (8). Firms initiate price increases when the cost of labor (ω) is high or when capacity utilization (n) is high. In the aggregate, this manifests as inflation (π).

$$\pi = \pi(n, \omega), \quad \pi_n, \pi_\omega > 0 \tag{8}$$

The price-setting behavior of firms is decentralized, so that price adjustments that may prove pointless in the aggregate are nevertheless individually rational.

Monetary authority

The final ingredient of the model is interest rate determination. Neoclassical models traditionally treat the money supply as exogenous, although the strong empirical evidence against this exogeneity has been slowly changing the mainstream characterization of the money-supply process (Romer, 2000). Formal Marxian macroeconomic models often neglect the financial sector altogether. The Post Keynesian tradition, in contrast, has persistently and more realistically stressed the endogeneity of the money supply and the reliance of the monetary authority on interest rate instruments (Hewitson, 1995).

Acknowledging endogeneity of the money supply does not close the question as to whether the monetary authority uses an interest rate or a money supply instrument. However, many authors suggest an interest rate instrument characterization of the monetary-policy reaction function. This characterization of the monetary authority seems aligned with actual central bank behavior.[10] This paper therefore models the monetary authority as controlling an interest rate instrument, which it adjusts in response to prevailing economic conditions. Specifically, the monetary authority adjusts the interest rate in response to inflation and unemployment, in line with standard Taylor-rule characterizations of central bank behavior.

$$i = i(\pi, n/n^s) \text{ where } i_\pi, i_\lambda > 0 \tag{9}$$

(Here $\lambda = n/n^s$.) Higher inflation leads to contractionary monetary policy, in the form of higher interest rates. This corresponds to the observation of Goodfriend (1993) that the monetary authority often builds an inflation premium into its interest rate instrument. In addition, higher unemployment (lower n/n^s) leads to monetary easing in the form of lower interest rates. This corresponds to Goodfriend's observation that in the United States the monetary authority "routinely lowers the funds rate in response to cyclical downturns and raises it in cyclical expansions." A fairly standard monetary policy result obtains: for economic stability it is important that the monetary authority react strongly – or in Goodfriend's parlance, aggressively – to the rate of inflation. This also proves to be an important component of stabilization policy.

Model summary

For convenience of reference, Table 12.1 summarizes the model.

Table 12.1 A conflicting-claims model with endogenous money

(6)	Growth dynamics	$g_{n^s} = g_{AN} - \sigma(n, \omega, \tau, g^c)$	$\sigma_n > 0$
(7)	Goods market equilibrium	$\kappa(i - \pi, g^i) = \sigma(n, \omega, \tau, g^c)$	$\kappa_r < 0$
(8)	Price adjustment	$\pi = \pi(n, \omega)$	$\pi_n > 0$
(9)	Monetary policy	$i = i(\pi, n/n^s)$	$i_\pi, i_\lambda > 0$

Equilibrium

This section characterizes equilibrium in our conflicting-claims economy. We find that the Taylor-rule parameters influence macroeconomic outcomes, influencing the distribution of income and the steady-state unemployment rate. To keep the development simple, we will ignore the wage-negotiation process, treating ω as exogenous.[11]

Combining (8) with (9) yields (10).

$$i = i[\pi(n, \omega), n/n^s] \tag{10}$$

Since this equation characterizes monetary policy, we follow Taylor (1995) in referring to its graph as the MP curve. The slope of the MP curve is positive.[12] An increase in employment reduces the pressure on the monetary authority to ease; it also indirectly increases inflation, thereby directly increasing the pressure on the monetary authority to tighten.

Combining (8) with (7) yields (11):

$$\kappa[i - \pi(n, \omega), g^i] = \sigma(n, \omega, \tau, g^c) \tag{11}$$

Since this equation is a fairly traditional representation of goods-market equilibrium, we will refer to its graph as the IS curve. The slope is indeterminate. An increase in the interest rate reduces desired investment.

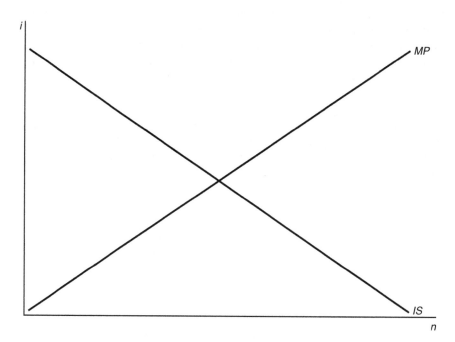

Figure 12.1 Temporary equilibrium.

Equilibrium can be restored by higher inflation, which offsets increases in the interest rate, or by reduced saving. A decrease in n produces reduced saving, but it also reduces price pressures: the relative size of these effects determines the slope.[13] For ease of exposition, we treat the case when the slope of the IS curve is negative. (All that is needed for the analysis that follows is satisfaction of the familiar requirement that the IS slope does not exceed the MP slope, which can always be assured by the monetary authority.) A negative slope means that the indirect response of desired investment to a reduction in unemployment does not exceed the direct effect on savings.

Figure 12.1 graphs (11) and (10) in (i, n) space (for a given level of n^s). The IS curve is familiar, and the Taylor-rule characterization of monetary policy replaces the traditional LM curve. As Goodfriend (1993, p. 5) notes, use of an interest rate instrument effectively sets "money to the side, since at any point in time money demand is accommodated at the going interest rate." However, as Post Keynesian structuralists have emphasized, this does not imply a horizontal MP curve, since the monetary authority responds to current economic conditions. The slope of the MP curve represents the responsiveness of monetary policy to inflation and unemployment.

When the natural growth rate and warranted growth rate differ, the economy does not rest at the temporary equilibrium represented by the intersection in Figure 12.1. To see why, reconsider the growth dynamics embodied in (6). If the natural rate of growth exceeds the warranted rate of growth, so that capital formation does not keep up with the growth of effective labor, then n^s rises. Movements in capacity utilization affect inflation and unemployment, leading to shifts in the MP curve.

The key question for stability is whether increases in n^s increase the warranted rate of growth. More formally, (6) implies that a steady state will be stable if

$$-\sigma_n n_{n^s} < 0 \tag{12}$$

Since desired saving is increasing in income and therefore in employment, $\sigma_n > 0$. Therefore stability requires $dn/dn^s > 0$.

An increase in n^s means greater unemployment at each value of n, which leads to a cut in interest rates. In the IS-MP diagrams of Figure 2, this is represented by a downward shift in the MP curve to MP'. This increases n and thereby increases the warranted rate of growth. The economy is stable.[14]

This highlights the importance of monetary policy for economic stability. The response of monetary policy to unemployment is also a crucial determinant of stability. For example, a simple interest rate peg destabilizes this economy. Since the slope and shifts of the MP curve are determined by the policy rule adopted by the monetary authorities,

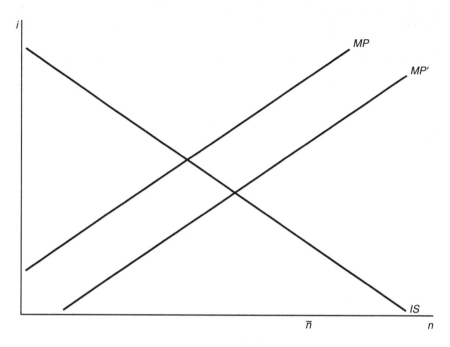

Figure 12.2 Adjustment dynamics.

monetary policy is a crucial determinant of stability in this conflicting-claims economy.

To recapitulate, if n is low then saving is low and capital formation is inadequate. As a result, labor becomes increasingly abundant relative to capital: n^s increases. The rise in unemployment shifts our MP curve down: interest rates are lower at each n because unemployment is higher at each n. Lower nominal interest rates provide a needed stimulus to the economy, raising n. Such an adjustment process is obviously stable.

In this setting, the monetary policy rule is also an important determinant of long-run unemployment. To see this, begin by reconsidering the growth dynamics embodied in (6). Long-run capacity utilization, $\bar{n}$, is the level that equates the natural and warranted growth rates. This long-run relationship is represented by (13).

$$\sigma(\bar{n}, \omega, \tau, g^c) = g_{AN} \tag{13}$$

Once we have determined the long-run rate of capacity utilization, $\bar{n}$, we can use our IS-MP model to determine the long-run interest rate, $\bar{\imath}$, and the long-run relative factor intensity of the economy, $\bar{n}^s$. (Unemployment is, of course, determined by $\bar{n}/\bar{n}^s$.) The long-run role of the goods and assets markets can be represented by Equations (14) and (15), which determine $\bar{i}$ and $\bar{n}^s$ for any given $\bar{n}$.

$$\kappa[\bar{i} - \pi(\bar{n}, \omega), g^i] = \sigma(\bar{n}, \omega, \tau, g^c) \tag{14}$$

$$\bar{i} = i[\pi(\bar{n}, \omega), \bar{n}/\bar{n}^s] \tag{15}$$

A change in monetary policy to respond more aggressively to inflation can be represented as an upward shift of the MP curve. This raises unemployment (lowers n) in the short run, but it also has a long-run effect. Higher interest rates discourage private investment, which produces higher unemployment even in the long run.[15]

Varieties of fiscal policy

This section explores how fiscal policy changes unemployment and the distribution of income. We consider the following varieties of fiscal policy: an increase in government consumption characterized as a simple demand expansion (an increase in g^c), and an increase in government real investment in capital formation (an increase in g^i).

Government consumption

The short-run effects of an increase in government consumption are familiar: we get an upward shift in the IS curve, a reduction in unemployment, and a contractionary response by the monetary authority (higher i). This IS-curve shift is shown in Figure 12.3. Along an upward-sloping MP curve, we know that i is higher, but π is also higher, so the short-run effects on the rate on capital formation depend on the aggressiveness of the monetary authority's response to inflation.

The long-run effects are interesting. In the long run, private saving must offset the effects of government consumption to restore equality between the warranted and natural growth rates. So in the long run, we must have a rise in n. (The increase in $\bar{n}$ must be such that $d\bar{n}/dg^c = -\sigma_g/\sigma_n > 0$.)

Does this mean a fall in unemployment? Not necessarily. To see this, recall that investment depends on $r = i - \pi$, so that in the long run we must restore $i - \pi$ to its original steady-state value. If monetary policy responds aggressively to inflation ($i_\pi > 1$), then a constant real interest rate at a higher inflation rate implies that the monetary authority has eased somewhat in response to higher steady-state unemployment. An increase in government consumption can increase unemployment in the long run. This is the case illustrated in Figure 12.3.

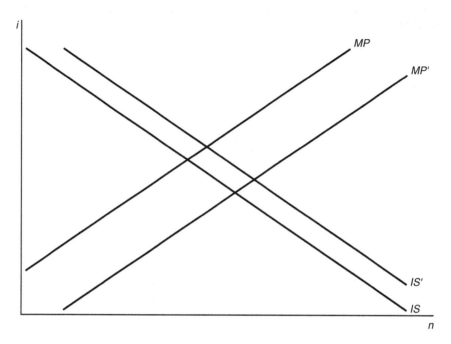

Figure 12.3 Effects of an increase in government consumption (g^c).

Government investment

Our next fiscal policy experiment is an increase in government investment expenditure. That is, instead of a change in g^c, we increase g^i, which produces an exogenous increase in κ (a shift of the investment function). In our IS-MP framework, the initial effect is again familiar. Indeed it is unchanged from our previous experiment: the IS curve shifts up, and we get an increase in i and n.

The subsequent dynamics are quite different, however, as shown in Figure 12.4. Since we have raised the warranted rate of growth above the natural rate, the unemployment rate will fall and (in response) interest rates will rise over time. This is represented by an upward shift of the MP curve.

In the long run, the warranted rate returns to equality with the natural rate of growth, and n returns to its pre-shock level. However, the increased capital accumulation has also changed the relative factor supplies: n^s has fallen. The real rate of interest has risen, crowding out private investment one-for-one with the increase due to new government investment. The inflation rate is unchanged, but the interest rate is higher, reflecting the response of the monetary authority, to lower unemployment. That is, an increase in government investment lowers unemployment, even in the long run.

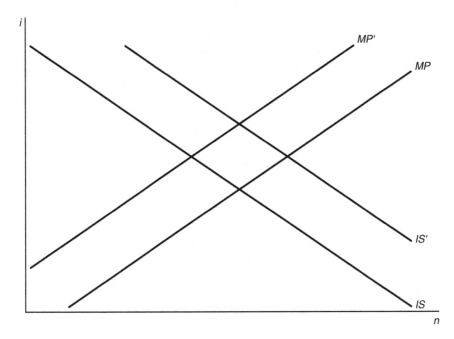

Figure 12.4 Effects of an increase in government investment (g^i).

Income distribution

Finally, we briefly explore the effects of policies targeting the distribution of income, here characterized by an increase in the cost of labor (ω). In the short run, firms respond by raising prices, which encourages interest rate increases by the monetary authority. This is an upward shift of the MP curve. At the same time, the distributional shift toward wage earners reduces saving. This produces an upward shift of the IS curve. The short-run effect on employment depends on the sensitivity of private investment to the interest rate and on the aggressiveness of monetary policy. The long-run effect depends on the monetary policy stance. In the long run saving must rise again to restore the equality between the warranted and natural growth rates, so $\bar{n}$ must rise. The interest rate and inflation rate must therefore be higher in the new steady state. If monetary policy responds aggressively to inflation, then steady-state unemployment must rise. This suggests that redistribution policies will be most successful when supported by an accommodating monetary policy.

Conclusion

This paper explores the short-run and long-run importance of a variety of fiscal policies in a conflicting-claims model of a growing economy with endogenous monetary policy. It extends the existing conflicting-claims literature by incorporating a Taylor-rule characterization of monetary policy in a growing economy with variable factor utilization rates. Fiscal policy is shown to influence unemployment in the long run as well as in the short run. Increases in government investment lower long-run unemployment, but the effects of increased government consumption depend on the monetary policy stance. Neither policy affects long-run growth rates in this model: to raise long-run growth rates, fiscal policy must invest directly in increasing the rate of technological change (e.g., through R&D subsidies).

Directions for future research are suggested by the limitations of the present paper. In particular, the long-run growth rate remains exogenous in the model considered. One natural extension is to explore the ability of fiscal policy to affect the long-run growth rate when technological innovation responds to the state of the economy. The unemployment results of the present paper should prove robust to such extensions. Another important possibility to explore is whether direct government investment in R&D can promote technological change. This raises the possibility that a specific variety of fiscal policy can influence not only output and unemployment, but even long-run growth rates in the macroeconomy.

Notes

1 Thanks to Per Gunnar Berglund for many helpful comments.
2 Isaac (1991) shows that the conflicting claims characterization of price adjustment is compatible with the characterization of inflation as the result of a gap between capitalists' desired and actual profit share, as introduced in Desai's (1973) first modification of the Goodwin (1967) growth cycle model. Also see Rowthorn (1977), Flaschel and Krüger (1984), Dutt (1987), and Lavoie (1992, pp. 391–421). In many settings, a constant desired profit share implies a constant desired mark-up over unit costs (Weintraub, 1959; Harris, 1978; Naish, 1990). Short-run variability and long-run constancy of the mark-up has found empirical support in studies on the stability of the wage share (Klein, 1989).
3 Depreciation is suppressed for presentational convenience.
4 Note that we have chosen the state variable to be AN^s/K, not K/AN^s. For $g_{AN} > 0$, existence is assured if $\sigma: \mathfrak{R}_+ \to \mathfrak{R}_+$ is bijective (although much weaker conditions suffice). In the Solow model, $\sigma(n^s) = \bar{\sigma} y(n^s)$, where $\bar{\sigma}$ is the constant saving rate, $y = Y/K$, and Y is aggregate output as determined by the first degree homogeneous production function $Y = F(AN^s, K)$. Thus stability of the steady state is equivalent to a positive marginal product of labor ($y' > 0$), since $d(dn/dt)/dn = n\bar{\sigma} y'$ at a steady state.
5 Rose (1966) offers an extensive discussion of this in his seminal paper on Keynesian growth models. He shows that $\sigma(n)$ offers a fairly general specification of saving behavior: for example, the saving specification of Kaldor (1966) can be transformed to this form in a Keynesian setting. In a setting with sales constraints, many Post Keynesians will nevertheless want to adopt a saving function of the form $\sigma(n, \omega)$, where $\omega = W/AP$ is the real wage per effective unit of labor (and therefore, given n, determines the wage share).
6 Here $\omega = W/AP$, where W is the nominal wage and P is the price level. Rose

(1966) calls W/A the wage unit, so we could call ω the real wage unit, but we instead we will call it the cost of labor. The wage share is $WN/PY = \omega\, NA/Y = \omega$ n/y. Ruling out increasing returns to scale, $n/y(n)$ is increasing in n, so the wage share is increasing in n and in ω. In the special case $Y = AN$, ω equals the wage share (but there is no role for capital).

7 For example, a dependence of desired investment on the profit rate R – so that $g_K(R) = \sigma(n^s)$ in temporary equilibrium – would generally require the profit rate to adjust independently of the labor intensity of production. In the Solow model, however, this is not possible. The Solow model's assumption of competitive markets implies $R = y - y'n^s$ in equilibrium, where y and y' depend on n^s.

8 The investment function $\kappa(i - \pi,\ g^i)$ is subject to many variants, the most popular of which are the inclusion of an accelerator or capacity-utilization effect (Bhaduri and Marglin, 1990) and the "Wicksellian" replacement of the interest rate argument with the gap between the profit rate and the real interest rate (Rose, 1966; Malinvaud, 1982). Modest accelerator effects are empirically important but do not affect our results and are therefore neglected in this presentation. (A strong accelerator effect could change the sign of the slope of the IS curve (7).) "Wicksellian" formulations of investment demand are intended to capture in a stylized fashion the role of expected profitability in the investment decision. For simplicity of presentation, this paper has followed the Keynesian tradition of suppressing these influences except in discussions of volatility of the IS curve (Robinson, 1970). Adopting a Wicksellian formulation would affect the slope of the IS curve: if sales constraints mean that the profit rate is increasing in n, this might cause the IS curve to slope upward (e.g., if price adjustment is very insensitive to the profit gap). Otherwise it has no effect on the points made in this paper.

   Note that since investment behavior focuses on the *rate* of additions to the capital stock, which is a natural scaling in a growing economy, capital stock augmentations do not of themselves increase unemployment. Contrast with Palley (1996).

9 A more explicit characterization of such costs can be found in Goldstein's (1985) treatment of the links between relative prices and market share. Also, see Brayton and Tinsley (1996) for a discussion of links between the target price and input costs.

10 Many authors have argued that US monetary policy is best characterized in terms of a federal funds rate policy instrument (Taylor, 1993; Romer, 2000). Goodfriend (1993) and Broadhaus (1995) have argued that this is true even when this rate has been targeted indirectly via manipulation of the discount rate or borrowed reserves. Cook (1989) has argued that even during the October 1979 – October 1982 period most federal-funds-rate changes reflected judgmental actions of the Fed. Note that, by combining full accommodation of money-demand shocks while still incorporating the policy reactions of the central bank to economic conditions, Taylor rules can be seen as finding a crude middle ground between the accommodationist and structuralist descriptions of the money supply process (Fontana, 2003).

11 Allowing ω to depend on unemployment, as in efficiency wage models, is a straightforward extension.

12 The MP slope is $di/dn|_{MP} = i_\pi \pi_n + i_\lambda/n_s > 0$.

13 The IS slope is $di/dn|_{IS} = (\sigma_n + \kappa_r \pi_n)/\kappa_r$ and so depends on $\sigma_n + \kappa_r\, \pi_n$.

14 From the IS-MP model we find the responses to a change in n^s:

$$\begin{bmatrix} \kappa_r & -(\kappa_r \pi_n + \sigma_n) \\ 1 & -(i_\pi \pi_n + i_\lambda/n^s) \end{bmatrix} \begin{bmatrix} di \\ dn \end{bmatrix} = \begin{bmatrix} 0 \\ -(i_\lambda \lambda/n^s)dn^s \end{bmatrix}$$

So we conclude that $n_n^s = i_\lambda \lambda/(n^s \Delta)$, where $\Delta = (\sigma_n/\kappa_r + \pi_n) - (i_\pi \pi_n + i_\lambda/n^s)$ is the difference between the IS slope and the MP slope. Since $i_\lambda > 0$, stability requires $\Delta < 0$: the slope of the MP curve must exceed that of the IS curve. Satisfaction of the condition can always be assured by the monetary authority.

15 We have found that monetary policy influences the level of unemployment in the long run as well as the short run. Of course the analysis up to this point maintains the exogeneity of the cost of labor, but evidently this result is easily generalized to an efficiency wage environment – say, where $\omega = \omega(n/n^s)$. Phillips curve models are more problematic and can produce quite different conclusions: they render long-run effects on the unemployment rate impossible in many mainstream, Marxian, and even Post Keynesian macromodels.

References

Bhaduri, Amit and Stephen Marglin (1990), "Unemployment and the Real Wage: The Economic Basis for Contesting Political Ideologies," *Cambridge Journal of Economics* 14(4), December, pp. 375–93.

Brayton, Flint and Peter A. Tinsley (1996), "A Guide to FRB/US: A Macroeconomic Model of the United States," *Finance and Economics Discussion Series*, No. 1996-42, Divisions of Research and Statistics and Monetary Affairs, Washington, DC: Board of Governors of the Federal Reserve System.

Broadhaus, J. Alfred (1995), "Reflections on Monetary Policy," *Federal Reserve Bank of Richmond Economic Quarterly*, 81(2), Spring, pp. 1–11.

Cook, Timothy (1989), "Determinants of the Federal Funds Rate: 1979–1982," *Federal Reserve Bank of Richmond Economic Review*, 75(1), January/February, pp. 3–19.

Desai, Meghnad (1973), "Growth Cycles and Inflation in a Model of the Class Struggle," *Journal of Economic Theory*, 6(6), December, pp. 527–45.

Dutt, Amitava Krishna (1987), "Alternative Closures Again: A Comment on 'Growth, Distribution and Inflation'," *Cambridge Journal of Economics*, 11(1), March, pp. 75–82.

Fontana, Giuseppe (2003), "Post Keynesian Approaches to Endogenous Money: A Time Framework Explanation," *Review of Political Economy*, 15(3), July, pp. 291–314.

Goldstein, Jonathan P. (1985), "The Cyclical Profit Squeeze: A Marxian Microfoundation," *Review of Radical Political Economics*, 17(1/2), Spring/Summer, pp. 103–28.

Goodfriend, Marvin (1993), "Interest Rate Policy and the Inflation Scare Problem: 1979–1993," *Federal Reserve Bank of Richmond Economic Quarterly*, 79(1), Winter, pp. 1–24.

Goodwin, Richard M. (1967), "A Growth Cycle Model," in *Socialism, Capitalism, and Economic Growth*, edited by Charles H. Feinstein, Cambridge: Cambridge University Press.

Harris, Donald J. (1978), *Capital Accumulation and Income Distribution*, Stanford, CA: Stanford University Press.

Harrod, Roy F. (1939), "An Essay in Dynamic Theory," *Economic Journal*, 49(193), March, pp. 14–33.

Hewitson, Gillian (1995), "Post-Keynesian Monetary Theory: Some Issues," *Journal of Economic Surveys*, 9(3), pp. 285–310.

Isaac, Alan G. (1991), "Economic Stabilization and Money Supply Endogeneity in a Conflicting Claims Environment," *Journal of Post Keynesian Economics*, 14(1), Fall, pp. 93–110.

Kaldor, Nicholas (1966), "Marginal Productivity and the Macro-Economic Theories of Distribution: Comment on Samuelson and Modigliani," *Review of Economic Studies*, 33(4), October, pp. 309–19.

Keynes, John Maynard (1936), *The General Theory of Employment, Interest and Money*. New York: Harcourt Brace Jovanovich, First Harbinger Edition, 1964.

Klein, Lawrence R. (1989), "The Restructuring of the American Economy," in *Inflation and Income Distribution in Capitalist Crisis*, edited by Jan A. Kregel, New York: New York University Press, pp. 25–45.

Lavoie, Marc (1992), *Foundations of Post-Keynesian Economic Analysis*, Bookfield, VT: Edward Elgar.

Malinvaud, Edmond (1982), "Wages and Unemployment," *Economic Journal*, 92(1), March, pp. 1–12.

Marglin, Stephen A. (1984), "Growth, Distribution, and Inflation: A Centennial Synthesis," *Cambridge Journal of Economics*, 8(2), June, pp. 115–44.

Naish, Howard F. (1990), "The Near Optimality of Mark-up Pricing," *Economic Inquiry* 28(3), July, pp. 555–85.

Palley, Thomas I. (1996), "Aggregate Demand in a Reconstruction of Growth Theory: The Macro Foundations of Economic Growth," *Review of Political Economy*, 8(1), January, pp. 23–35.

Robinson, Joan (1970), "Quantity Theories Old and New," *Journal of Money, Credit and Banking*, 2(4), November, pp. 504–12.

Romer, David (2000), "Keynesian Macroeconomics Without the LM Curve," *Journal of Economic Perspectives*, 14(2), Spring, pp. 149–69.

Rose, Hugh (1966), "Unemployment in a Theory of Growth," *International Economic Review*, 7(3), September, pp. 260–82.

Rowthorn, Robert E. (1977), "Conflict, Inflation and Money," *Cambridge Journal of Economics*, 1(3), September, pp. 215–39.

Solow, Robert M. (1956), "A Contribution to the Theory of Economic Growth," *Quarterly Journal of Economics*, 70(1), February, pp. 65–94.

Taylor, John B. (1993), "Discretion versus Policy Rules in Practice," *Carnegie-Rochester Conference Series on Public Policy*, 39(0), December, pp. 195–214.

Taylor, John B. (1995), "The Monetary Transmission Mechanism: An Empirical Framework," *Journal of Economic Perspectives*, 9(4), Fall, pp. 11–26.

Weintraub, Sidney (1959), *A General Theory of the Price Level, Output, Income Distribution, and Economic Growth*, Philadelphia, PA: Chilton Co.

Wolman, Alexander L. (2000), "The Frequency and Costs of Individual Price Adjustment," *Federal Reserve Bank of Richmond Economic Quarterly*, 86(4), Fall, pp. 1–22.

Part IV

What are the questions?

13 The political economy of the deficit

Roundtable session

Barbara R. Bergmann, Jeffrey A. Frankel,
William A. Niskanen, and Laurence S. Seidman;
with an introduction by Per Gunnar Berglund
and Matias Vernengo

Introduction

The political views on the effects of fiscal deficits have changed over the years. The Great Depression marked a period of transition from sound finance to Keynesian principles, as enshrined in the Kennedy–Johnson tax cut of the mid-1960s. The 1960s were the culmination of the prosperity of the post-World War II period, known as the Golden Age of capitalism. Rates of growth in the Western World were the highest on record, unemployment rates were historically low, and although great inequalities still existed, the gap between the rich and poor narrowed, both within and between countries. This period can be seen in the Western World, in part, as the result of a tacit accord between social classes, according to which progressive taxation financed an expanding Welfare State and a set of social rights, which in turn translated in a relatively low degree of social confrontation.

The tacit social agreement was a fragile one. The stagflation of the 1970s was the straw that broke the camel's back. The increasing social tensions of the 1960s, associated, in the United States, with civil rights and the Vietnam War, led to a change in the social balance that supported the tacit agreement. Prior to this period, wages had increased hand in hand with productivity. While full employment and expanding social benefits gave workers the upper hand in wage bargaining, the brisk pace of investment in new technology, of rationalization and automation, provided a countervailing force that kept inflation in check.

In the late 1960s, all this began to change. Steadily rising taxes; an unanticipated slowdown of productivity; shock increases in raw-materials prices; a weaker dollar following upon the breakdown of the Bretton Woods system – all these factors combined to unleash the vicious wage-price spiral, and to bring about the hitherto-unseen combination of economic stagnation and rising inflation. Discontent and social tensions rose as distributive conflict over the proverbial "pie" intensified. By the mid-1970s, the days of the tacit accord were definitely over.

After a quarter century of secular reduction, the government debt-to-GDP ratio reached its nadir in the early 1970s. Significant budget deficits reappeared along with the stagnation and became endemic as inflationary forces and increasingly restrictive monetary policies pushed interest rates ever higher. Moreover, the escalating inflation and interest rates meant significant losses for those holding financial assets, particularly government bills and bonds. The preparedness, on the part of the wealthier classes, to foot the bill for the Welfare State under the new terms was then greatly diminished.

A fiscal revolt became visible in America during the 1970s. Proposition 13 in California, which greatly reduced property taxes, was one of the landmarks of the movement, which culminated with Reagan's tax cuts. A theoretical revolution was also taking place that would eventually justify the new reinvigorated resistance to taxes among the wealthy. Politically the tax revolt was justified under the banner of "supply-side economics" (later referred to as "voodoo economics" by Bush senior). The accumulated deficits of the Reagan era, and the backlash against Keynesian ideas and policies, meant that during the recession of the early 1990s monetary policy was seen as the only effective instrument to combat the downturn. Fiscal policy was all but dead.

Further, the Keynesian belief in the positive effects of deficits, at least in the short run, was turned upside down in some circles. The argument was that fiscal consolidation could be expansionary provided that the cuts in government spending led to a perception of permanently lower taxes. That is, if the government decides to spend less, then taxpayers would have to pay less in the future and, realizing this, they would increase both consumption and investment in the present. If the increase in consumption and investment were large enough to outweigh the decrease in government spending, then higher levels of current activity and income would result. The recent American experience with fiscal consolidation during the Clinton years, and the relative prosperity that ensued, led many to believe that the Treasury and Fed exchange of fiscal adjustment for lower rates of interest was the prime mover behind the Clintonian expansion.

However, reasonable estimates of the effects of deficits on interest rates cast serious doubt on whether the exceptional growth of the late 1990s was caused chiefly by fiscal consolidation. Further, it is worth noticing that accurate measures of fiscal consolidation must be adjusted for the impact of cyclical fluctuations in the economy. Appropriately adjusted measures show that a good deal of the increase in revenue was caused by the economic expansion, not least by colossal capital gains made on booming asset markets. Hence, the deficit reduction during the Clinton presidency was in large part a consequence of the economic boom itself. Also, as is now clear, a good part of the boom was the result of an inflated bubble in the stock market. Increasing debt and unrealistic expectations about future earnings, rather than the perspective of permanently lower taxes, fueled the surge in consumption and investment. The reversal of the boom is then related to the frustration of expectations, with lower than expected earnings, and with high and perhaps unsustainable levels of indebtedness.

The 2000 recession and the three rounds of tax cuts implemented by George W. Bush had at least two important effects. First, they made explicit the paradoxical switch on fiscal positions between Democrats and Republicans. It is clear that the first Bush tax cut was not directly related to the objective of stimulating the economy, since it was a campaign promise that preceded the actual recession. However, the following tax cuts were defended as instruments against the recession in Keynesian fashion. Democrats, on the other hand, have been stalwart defenders of balanced budgets and "fiscal responsibility." Al Gore famously argued for balanced budgets even in face of recessions during the 2000 campaign, sounding more like a Hoover Republican than an Eisenhower one, as Bill Clinton was sometimes referred to.

More importantly, the 2000 recession brought fiscal policy back to the fore. It was clear that with interest rates at historical lows, the only effective way to counteract the recession was fiscal activism. This, however, does not mean that there is a renewed consensus on fiscal matters. It seems clear, though, that the majority of economists and politicians would agree with the old Keynesian canon that fiscal policy is effective in the short run. We are not suggesting that there is consensus on the effectiveness of Bush's tax cuts, which mainly targeted the wealthy. It seems reasonable, however, to suppose that alternative expansionary fiscal packages would have been more effective in providing short-run stimulus to the economy.

The effects of fiscal policy in the long run are far more contentious, and the issues at stake cannot be more important. One of the main sticking points is the long-run sustainability of government finances. It appears that most economists agree that the ratio of government debt to GDP must somehow be stabilized in the long run. There is, however, little agreement about the level at which to stabilize it.

Some argue that there exists a ceiling beyond which it would be unwise to push the debt ratio for fear of jeopardizing the government's creditworthiness and risking the specter of "State bankruptcy." Another line of argument is that an, in some sense, excessive government debt implies losing the option of using fiscal policy, namely, actively raising the deficit, as a means to combat recessions. A third story is concerned about the effects of government debt on long-term interest rates, and the potential for the interest burden "crowding out" other, more socially beneficial, expenditures. Although all these arguments emanate in the same conclusion, namely that government debt should be limited relatively to GDP, opinions differ widely on the adequate size of the debt ratio.

In contrast to this, economists in the "functional finance" tradition argue that a high debt-to-GDP ratio, at any rate as long as the borrowing is done internally in the country's own currency, does not imply any appreciable risk for "State bankruptcy." Nor does it limit the scope for active, counter-cyclical policy measures in any relevant sense. Moreover, it is argued that wealth effects – through which public debt fuels private spending – tend to spontaneously establish a certain level to which the debt-to-GDP ratio converges in the long run. In this view, therefore, the debt problem takes care of itself in the long run, and there is little cause for concern.

Disagreement tends to be centered on the long-run issues. Diametrically opposed conclusions can be drawn, depending on the analytical perspective taken. The presence – or the absence – of sustained fiscal deficits, as well as their "quality" in terms of their use, may potentially endanger several social rights acquired over long struggles during the twentieth century. At the dawn of the twenty-first century economists and politicians have rediscovered that fiscal policy may still be a means to prosperity. Fiscal responsibility is not about permanent balanced budgets, but about the quality of the deficits, and whether the public debt accumulated is sustainable.

The roundtable that follows, organized during the Meetings of the Eastern Economics Association in Washington, DC, last February, and chaired by one of us, is part of a broader discussion on the effects of the current fiscal policy stance, and the ironic swap between Democrats and Republicans. The views on the switch on fiscal policy are varied, but all hypotheses suggest that short-term political gain and a bit of naiveté or cynicism are involved. More significantly, it is clear that a wide spectrum of the profession – from the liberal to the conservative end – is concerned about Bush's tax policies and hoping for change.

Matias Vernengo

The topic of the roundtable is "The Political Economy of the Deficit." The topic is broad enough to encompass several issues, but the most important from our perspective are the policy consequences of the current fiscal stance, in particular, the results in terms of the limitations and possibilities it opens for social policy. In other words, fiscal policy is crucial for promoting a minimal government, in the conservative-libertarian tradition, as well as projects with a progressive bent that would want to extend the Welfare State. In that respect, the future of Social Security, the possibilities of funding a national health program would be part of the debate. Also, the apparent paradox that Democrats and Republicans have switched sides on fiscal policy is crucially important, and will be discussed.

We have a distinguished panel to discuss these issues. Barbara Bergmann is at American University and emerita from the University of Maryland. She was on the staff of the Kennedy Council of Economic Advisers, and was the President of the Eastern Economic Association. Professor Jeffrey Frankel is the James W. Harpel Professor at the JFK

School of Government at Harvard. He was a member of Clinton's Council of Economic Advisers, and directs the International Finance section of the National Bureau of Economic Research. Dr. William Niskanen, the chairman of the Cato Institute, was acting chairman of Reagan's Council of Economic Advisers, and also taught at Berkeley and UCLA. The final member of our panel is Professor Laurence Seidman, who is the Chaplin Tyler Professor at the University of Delaware. We will start with a general presentation from each panel member in alphabetical order, and then have a general discussion at the end.

Barbara Bergmann

Being invited to this session on fiscal policy caused me to remember my childhood, when I took lessons on fiscal policy from Alvin Hansen at Harvard. In those happy days, the correct size of the deficit was defined as the "full-employment deficit," which was the deficit necessary to bring the economy to full employment. A major question of that day was the size of the multiplier – the amount of GDP that an extra dollar of government expenditure would engender. It was taken to be the reciprocal of the marginal propensity to save and was thought to be somewhere between two and ten.

However, more recent developments bring us to realize that we have to be concerned with what you might call the quality of the deficit, as well as its size. A deficit of a given size can have a different effect depending on how it is incurred. For example, sending money to rich people might not have too big an effect on aggregate demand. I am lucky enough to be married to a rich guy, so the tax refund that President Bush is sending me is going right into my checking account. I doubt I will even increase my stock portfolio as a result. So the multiplier for that bit of the deficit is zero.

Then there is all money going to defense. Presumably what's going to buy replacement helicopters will have a multiplier. But the money that's going to buy fuel from Kuwait for Iraq is going to have a multiplier close to zero. However, that some of that may come back to the United States as either profit or stockholders in Halliburton or – probably more likely – higher salaries for people who work for Halliburton. They probably have enough yachts, so that part of the deficit is not going to do us much good in terms of aggregate demand.

Since the days of Alvin Hansen, the American economy has become much more open. These days, if you give tax cuts to the middle class, they are going to go right down to the store and buy some clothing made in China. That again makes for a low multiplier.

We can think of expenditures, including tax expenditures, which would produce a greater level of aggregate demand than our current deficit does. I would include things like increased spending on mental health, on childcare, on education, on public transport, and so on. So to sum up, the mere size of the deficit is no longer a good measure of the expansionary effect of the government budgetary position. We need to pay attention to the components of government expenditure, and how each component contributes to aggregate demand. We have to do the same for the tax cuts.

Another aspect of fiscal policy is the usefulness of the things that the extra government expenditure buys, as well as the usefulness of what the recipients of a tax cut spend the money on. Keynes said that it was worthwhile in a depression for the government to hire people to dig holes in the ground and fill them up again. But we have a lot of unfilled needs for public goods, and for private goods for people of very low incomes, so we cannot afford to be so cavalier about what kind of expenditures and tax cuts we make when trying to boost aggregate demand.

I would suspect that in the future we are going to have a bigger employment problem than has been true in the immediate past. Many American workers now are competing on the world labor market, and the world labor market is not a very cheery place to compete in, as we all know. I worry that the theory of factor price equalization will come true after all. And if wages here don't fall fast enough toward Mexican or Chinese levels, unemployment will be the result. As jobs are lost, other jobs may very well be created. But they will not be as well paid.

You have to be amazed by the Democrats, who are badmouthing deficits, while the Republicans are saying "Don't worry about it!" In this case the Republicans would be right, if only the deficits were of a better quality – if their expenditures were going for something better than the war in Iraq and if their tax cuts were reductions in the payroll tax.

Alvin Hansen used to say "We owe it to ourselves." Well, that wasn't true even then. The national debt was owed to the rich people who directly or indirectly held the bonds. Now a lot of it is owed to people abroad. But that should not stop us from having a high-quality deficit and a high enough deficit to get us to a reasonable level of employment.

Jeffrey Frankel

My title is "The Bush Budget Bungle," which is not an entirely non-partisan title. I told the organizers of this session that we needed to get someone from the Bush administration to defend the budget, but they tried and tried and couldn't find anybody. I think that is understandable, given how hard it is to do this job of defending the budget. They should have outsourced to Bangalore – should have got someone on a speakerphone, with a good English accent, to defend the budget, since they couldn't find anyone in town to do it.

Proposition 1: When a Republican president comes in, the budget balance plummets. It may sound surprising, but here it is, in Figure 13.1. Ronald Reagan becomes president in 1981 – the budget plummets.

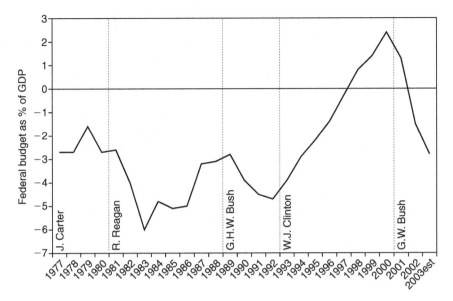

Figure 13.1 Spending and budget balance as % of GDP (Current US$).

George Bush I takes office in 1989 – the budget plummets. George Bush II arrives in 2001– the budget plummets. Now, you might think this pattern was entirely because of Republican tax cuts, and Democrat tax increases. If you fell for the line that the Republican Party is the party of small government, then that's what you would expect. But the striking pattern in budget deficits is not entirely, or even primarily, due to taxes. Figure 13.2 shows federal spending, by presidential term. When a Republican becomes president, spending increases sharply. It was true when Ronald Reagan became president, when George Bush I became President, and when George Bush II became President – 1981, 1989, or 2001.

During the Clinton Administration, 1993–2000, the pattern was just the reverse: falling deficits, consisting in large part of spending falling as a share of GDP. How did it happen during the 1990s, that we were able to eliminate these record budget deficits and achieve a record budget surplus by the year 2000? Obviously the strong growth in the economy played a big role, and the stock market played a big role, but there are some specific policy actions that played a big role as well, and I would like to identify three.

The first important step, to give George Bush, Sr., credit, was the Budget Enforcement Act of 1990, which raised taxes and legislated a combination of spending caps and the PAYGO rule. The PAYGO system (pay-as-you-go) said that anyone proposing future tax cuts or spending increases had to say how they would pay for them. The package probably

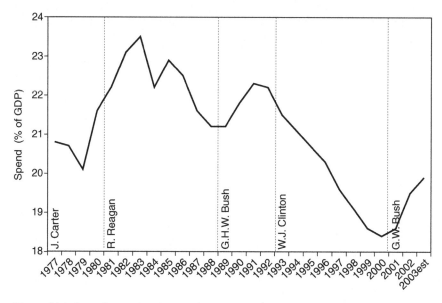

Figure 13.2 Spending as % of GDP (Current US $).

cost Bush the election because it was a reversal of his "no-new-taxes" pledge. But it deserves a lot of credit for putting the economy on a path to a future of declining budget deficits.

In 1993, when Clinton came in, he decided to give top priority to addressing the deficit (thereby postponing some things he had talked about in the election campaign: a middle-class tax cut and investment spending). He renewed the spending caps and the PAYGO system and set a path for tax revenue and government spending such that gradually, in the course of time, as the economy grew, the paths would cross and we would return to a surplus.

The third step that I think was important came when surpluses did emerge in 1998. There was tremendous pressure to spend them – the Republicans in Congress wanted tax cuts; the Democrats (and some Republicans too) had all kinds of projects to spend money on. The White House succeeded in holding the line with the stratagem of "Save Social Security First." In the State of the Union address in 1998, Clinton offered that as a slogan. It generated a bipartisan consensus, which lasted three years, to save the Social Security surplus – not use it to fund the rest of the deficit. You know about the retirement of the baby boom generation. The surpluses were not enough money to pay for it entirely, the upcoming cost of Social Security and Medicare; but the policy was at least "let's save the surpluses until we put Social Security on a firm footing" – no tax cuts, no big spending increases.

What the mechanisms of the 1990s – spending caps, PAYGO, and "save Social Security first" – have in common is budget neutrality as a criterion for future changes relative to the baseline. The strategy comes from the logic that to achieve budget balance we need what I will call Shared Sacrifice. It is the idea that, "I forego my spending increases if you forego your tax cut." The only way one ever gets budget discipline in the long run, is a common spirit along the lines "I would like to get my pork-barrel project funded for my constituents, but I will hold back if everybody else is holding back." The 1990s showed that the principle of shared sacrifice works.

There are other proposed mechanisms to implement the principle of shared sacrifice in a more rigid way: The Gramm–Rudman legislation that was tried in the 1980s, the Balanced Budget Amendment (BBA) that was proposed in the US ten years ago, the Stability and Growth Pact (SGP) in Europe. Those mechanisms are all crude. We rejected the balanced-budget amendment, in large part because governments should have flexibility to run deficits in recessions. The Europeans are having troubles with their SGP. Not only is it not sufficiently flexible, but it lacks any credibility. (In part it lacks credibility because the cost of rigid adherence is sufficiently high that people don't believe governments will abide by it, even sincere responsible governments.) There are proposals for a BBA or SGP that allows cyclical adjustment of the deficit targets, while maintaining a balance of zero on average. But if you allow more flexibility in the form of cyclical adjustment, then you will lose even more credibility: governments will always claim that their budget shortfalls are due to temporary bad luck in the economy. The proposal I like is a formalized version of an institution that Chile now has. The rule is a cyclically adjusted budget surplus of zero (actually 1 percent, in Chile's case); but one appoints an independent fiscal authority or commission of experts, by analogy with the Fed and other independent central banks; they are the ones who have the responsibility for saying what constitutes deviations from potential output, for computing the cyclically adjusted budget, and for announcing whether this year's budget satisfies the rule. The rest of the government still has the responsibility for allocating spending and taxes within the total, as it should in a democracy.

Short of major political reforms that are improbable in the US, I think the shared-sacrifice mechanisms of the 1990s worked pretty well. The problem of course is that they expired in 2001 and that there has been no effort to restore them, at least not from the White House.

I have discussed how we, or Clinton, achieved a surplus. How was Bush able to achieve such big deficits? The 2001 recession helped. And it is always easier to give away money than it is to collect money – that is an important principle of political economy. But there is a third factor, namely the government made predictably overly optimistic forecasts of future budgets. This enabled it to say "Look, we can afford these huge tax cuts." That was part of the mechanism that allowed this fiscal mess to come about. They release their budget forecasts twice a year and, until now, every time they have been forced to admit that last time they were wrong. And then, every time, they have done it again – "they" being both CBO and OMB. (Two qualifications: (1) CBO has little choice but to base its projections on current legislation. (2) The OMB forecast for 2004 is, for the first time, on the pessimistic side, which will allow them for once to say the budget in 2005 came in better than expected.)

When the new Administration came in, in January 2001, it boosted the revenue estimates (OMB raised the predicted share of income going to wages, a subtle way to achieve this effect), helping them claim that we were going to have record surpluses rising as far as the eye could see. In May 2001, they admitted that the surpluses weren't going to be quite as big as they had said, but still claimed substantial surpluses, and still rising. In January 2002, the same thing: that the surplus was small now, but it was still positive and still rising in the future. (This is after the recession and September 11.) Then in August – whoops! – we were in deficit after all, but that was going to go away gradually in the future. And then they continued to, each time, to be forced to revise, as Figure 13.3 shows.

It is surprising that the press went on reporting these forecasts, largely

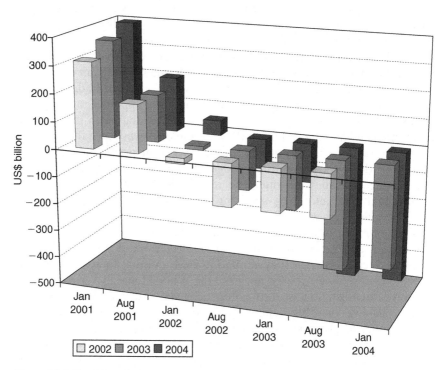

Figure 13.3 Revisions in forecasted annual budget balance.

at face value. Here is what the government is still forecasting. (CBO forecast, since the OMB has decided to stop forecasting at the ten-year horizon.) "Yes, we are going to have deficits for the next few years, but we're on a path to surplus by 2013." That is still overly optimistic, for a lot of reasons.

Some of the original sources of bias in the forecasts have gone away. The original budget forecasts were overly optimistic on the economic assumptions, but that's no longer true – they are now being realistic on their economic assumptions. The current official budget forecast, although they have revised way down and they admit to $2 trillion of budget deficits cumulating over the next ten years, is still way overly optimistic on the revenue side. The trick of making estimated future tax revenue look good through the pretence of sun-setting tax cuts is still there. The administration is still proposing to make the tax cuts permanent, and is proposing new tax cuts after 2009. Also they are not proposing a way of dealing with the Alternative Minimum Tax, which is going to cost, maybe, $700 billion spread over ten years. Various estimates of the cost of those omissions on the tax side are about $2 trillion over the next ten years if you add it up.

The over-optimism on the spending side is, if anything, as bad as ever. They claim that they are going to limit overall spending. But they are going to let military spending grow rapidly, which implies cutting non-defense discretionary spending by 15 percent over the next five years. How could anybody believe that? Just like Ronald Reagan before them, they have never made specific proposals to slash agricultural subsidies or the manned space program or much of anything else; quite the opposite. Also they are not allowing anything in the budget for spending in Iraq or Afghanistan after September 1. They are planning on asking for a supplemental to cover it, which means they are going to pretend to be caught by surprise by the need to continue spending money there. They do have in the budget an estimate of the cost of the Medicare drug benefit program that they supported for votes in the 2004 election; but – notoriously – they suppressed the realistic estimate from the relevant expert, in order to make the budget look artificially good.

If spending rises along with GDP, then the outlook is $1.6 trillion worse than last year's CBO forecast. If it rises in the future at the same rate that it has over the last five years, which is approximately 10 percent a year (7 percent, last year; more than 10 percent in the previous three years), then the outlook for the budget over the next ten years is over $3 trillion worse than what CBO has been forecasting.

But let's be very conservative. Let's assume that real spending increases only along with population, not as a share of GDP; but let's add in a conservative estimate of the Medicare drug cost, and add in the tax corrections. These figures are from a new book of Alice Rivlin and Isabel Sawhill's at Brookings (Rivlin and Sawhill, 2004). Goldman-Sachs has done something pretty similar and gotten the same answer. Far from getting better, the budget deficit as a share of GDP stays approximately as bad as it is today. That is the middle line in Figure 13.4, as opposed to the official upper line. The difference is about $4.6 trillion relative to what is officially forecast. Thus, overall, the forecast is about $6 trillion of debt over the next ten years. That implies a rising ratio of debt to GDP. And of course real interest rates are very low today. If they start rising sharply, we could fall into the sort of explosive debt path with which Argentina is familiar.

Bill Niskanen and I overlapped in the first Reagan Administration. (You may be surprised to hear that I was there. I was on the professional staff of the Council of Economic Advisers in 1982 and 1983, not a politically appointed member as Bill was then and as I was in the Clinton Administration). In 1981 Ronald Reagan complained that he had inherited $1 trillion of national debt. He gave a number of speeches where he said that in terms of $1,000 bills stacked up, the debt would reach 67 miles high. I had thought he also said that if one put the $1,000 bills end to end they would reach the moon. It is a true statistic – but I haven't been able to find in the archives that he said it. I wonder if Bill remembers Reagan saying that. I wish I could find the line about the thousand dollar bills reaching to the moon, because then I could say: "George Bush is going to Mars."

What happened in the 1980s? Reagan did pretty much fiscally what

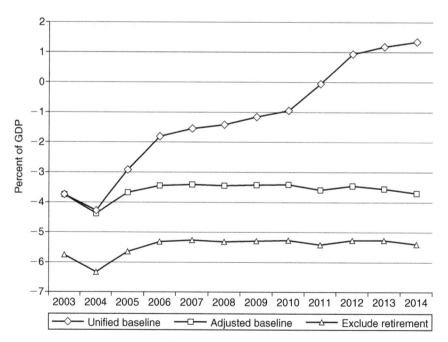

Figure 13.4 Baseline official forecast and alternative estimates as % of GDP, 2003–2004.

Bush is doing, which is to say increase military spending rapidly and cut taxes sharply. Over his first term, and his second term, and the term of the first George Bush, they each added roughly one trillion dollars, so that by the time the Republicans left office in 1993, the national debt was four trillion dollars. In each of their three terms, they added more debt than the previous 39 presidents of the U.S. history had added. But if the second George Bush gets another term, he will add roughly as much to the national debt as did his father *plus* Ronald Reagan *plus* the 39 previous presidents added together.

Those statistics, and everything I have told you so far, do not take into account the fact that they are raiding the Social Security surplus to pay for this. If you take out the Social Security surplus, then that's another $200 billion per year; that is the lower line in Figure 13.3, approximately another 2 percent of GDP. I am also not counting the recent White House proposal to privatise social security or to expand tax-deferred saving accounts, which is another time bomb designed specifically to lose its money outside the reported budget window.

What does this administration think it is doing? What is its goal? If you take literally the name of the Jobs and Growth Act, you might think the goal is to stimulate economic demand during the recession. It had some effect it that direction, but I think it is poorly designed to provide fiscal stimulus for some of the reasons that Barbara Bergmann mentioned. True, you cannot blow $6 trillion without having *some* stimulative effect of the economy and I think it has had that. But it is as if they are trying to minimize the "bang for the buck," to make this as expensive as you possibly can, with as little stimulus as they can possibly get out of it. Partly because it is specifically going to things like eliminating the estate tax in the year 2010, which is not going to do anything for the economy today. It is not designed to boost the economy today.

Clearly some of the features are designed to move towards a tax system that promotes saving. Apparently the goal, eventually, is to reform the corporate income tax or perhaps to abolish taxes on capital altogether. We can argue the pros and cons of that, but I would say that the White House actions have not constituted a sound pro-investment tax reform program, not good public finance economics. One knows what a good tax-reform program looks like: it worries about budget balance, and it tries to avoid driving up interest rates.

Some observers, particularly some economists associated with the University of Chicago, say that what the Bush Administration has in mind is a clever, deliberate political strategy to reduce the size of the government. This is the Starve the Beast theory; if you cut taxes, the government will be forced to cut spending. They say "Congress can't spend money it doesn't have" – evidently never having watched Congress in operation. This is an argument that was trundled out by the first Reagan Administration after two or three years of record deficits, in other words, after the Laffer curve and Ricardian equivalence and the other rationales for big tax cuts had failed to work. They switched to the Starve the Beast theory. Here is one piece of evidence that this wasn't what they had in mind from the beginning. Bill Niskanen got into trouble with the White House in 1981 for saying "don't worry that much about the deficit." At that time, they were still arguing that they needed to eliminate the deficit.

I don't think that it's right, the idea that the Bush White House really wants to cut spending, but supposedly they are just not able to because Congress won't go along. It doesn't make sense. Who is going to cut the spending for them? Do they think the "big spending" Democrats are going to do it? The Republicans haven't even tried to cut spending in any serious way. They only want to talk about cutting spending, not actually to do it.

I have already mentioned what I consider to be the competing altern-ative hypothesis of political economy: the way to establish fiscal discipline is a regime of Shared Sacrifice. "I will give up my pet spending increase or tax cut if you give up yours." Remember, what worked in the 1990s: spending caps and PAYGO. This legislation constituted a mechanism so that a given Congressman felt constrained, that if he gave money away, that is, if he increased spending, he would have to pay for it somewhere else, and his constituency would get mad at the tax increase. That suc-ceeded in restraining spending in the 1990s.

It's quite different from the principle of Starve the Beast. The first is "I will give up the tax cut I want if you give up the spending you want." The second is "I will take the tax cut I want, and in return you give up the spending you want." Which sounds like a more politically plausible route to a deal between factions who disagree?

The Starve the Beast approach says that the way to restrain spending is to create huge deficits so that people worry so much about the national debt that they will come complaining to their Congressman: "I'm worried about raising taxes on my grandchildren." Maybe people might worry about the national debt, about taxes on their grandchildren. But surely they don't worry more about such uncertain prospective future taxes (as in Starve the Beast logic) than they worry about *certain taxes today* (as in Shared Sacrifice logic, under which changes have to be paid for today). Having to pay *today* provides more discipline on spending than some vague idea of having to pay in the distant future. So as a political economy argument, Starve the Beast just doesn't work, if the alternative is the preceding regime. I don't think it even describes the ori-ginal motives behind the Bush Administration fiscal policy. It is an ex post rationalization which it is convenient to use in some circles and not in others.

So what, then, describes their motives? Getting re-elected is the most obvious argument, particularly if you look at how they also abandoned Republican principles on trade policy, agricultural subsidies, and lots of other things. It seems to make sense, that they just want to get re-elected. But people say that Karl Rove is the political genius behind the Bush Administration, and they say that he is out to create a Republican domination of this country well beyond two presidential terms. Well, if so, what is he thinking?

Bush – assuming he is re-elected – can try to put off the fiscal day of reckoning for another four years. But 2008 is when the baby boom generation starts to retire. At that point, the fiscal problem will be so obvious to the financial markets, and even to the electorate, that it will become hard to continue postponing adjustment, no matter how irresponsible they want to be. So that means that, if they do get another term, they will have to deal with the consequences of this, of creating a fiscal crisis. So answering the question of what they think they are doing is difficult, I have to say that I don't know what they are doing, and I worry that they don't know what they are doing either.

Finally, let me say a little about economic effects of the deficits. For you who were here in the previous session, there seems to be a consensus, that in the short run, fiscal expansion is expansionary. But, at the same time, expectations of being on a path of a rising debt-to-GDP ratio in the future could put a lot of pressure on long-term interest rates today, and that in itself is contractionary. The two effects go in opposite directions – the contemporaneous expansionary effect and the contractionary effect via long-term interest rates. In practice it is hard to separate the two out. Actual moves towards fiscal discipline are usually required in order to influence expectations and achieve credibility. Table 13.1 reports regressions for the US and five other countries, where the effects of expected future debt seem to show up in determining long-term real interest rates today.

Table 13.2 is a stylized account of recent fiscal history in this light. It covers four presidential terms, two for Clinton, one for Bush, and a fourth that will be heavily influenced by the Bush legacy of debt whether he is the president again or not. The effects of contemporaneous fiscal stimulus appear in the first Clinton column and the first Bush column. I would say that Clintons' mildly contractionary fiscal policy had a mildly contractionary effect contemporaneously, and Bush's expansionary fiscal policy had a modest positive stimulus contemporaneously.

But now let's talk about expectations, the effects on the economy of expected future fiscal paths, which come through long-term interest rates. They are illustrated in the second and fourth columns. Both Clinton and Bush claimed to be on a good long-term path. Initially it wasn't entirely credible on either part. But Clinton took some concrete steps in 1993, and even in his first term got some credibility benefit. In the second term, when the markets saw that these promises were coming true, interest rates declined, the stock market rose, investment boomed, and the economy grew.

Clinton set goals by the end of the first administration to cut the deficit in his second administration. This became increasingly credible, these claims of fiscal responsibility, so it cut the long-term interest rates (with accommodation from the Fed).

I think that in the second term of Bush, if there is one, or the

Table 13.1 Expected budget deficits and the determination of long-term real interest rates

	US	Germany	France	Italy	Spain	UK
Constant	−0.001	−0.122***	−0.022	−0.081	−0.043*	−0.034
	(0.008)	(0.038)	(0.027)	(0.041)	(0.023)	(0.030)
Inflation	1.00	1.00	1.00	1.00	1.00	1.00
Debt ratio	0.060**	0.182***	0.027	0.109	0.031	0.067
	(0.019)	(0.047)	(0.040)	(0.062)	(0.051)	(0.044)
Expected change	0.144**	0.112***	0.177**	0.324**	0.289***	0.066
in debt ratio	(0.061)	(0.032)	(0.073)	(0.106)	(0.048)	(0.110)
Output gap	0.388**	0.608**	0.252	0.297	0.218	−0.316
	(0.174)	(0.219)	(0.202)	(0.484)	(0.223)	(0.324)
Foreign interest	0.096	1.529***	0.923****	0.390	1.204***	0.815**
rate	(0.122)	(0.327)	(0.241)	(0.446)	(0.145)	(0.348)
N	15	15	15	15	15	15
Adj. R^2	0.32	0.51	0.82	0.77	0.82	0.55
DW	2.24	2.50	2.47	1.70	2.47	1.44

Source: Menzie Chinn and Jeffrey Frankel, October 15, 2003.

Notes
OLS regression using annual data, in levels.
(Newey-West robust standard errors in parentheses.)
Percentage variables defined in decimal form.
N is the number of observations.
Adj. R^2 is the adjusted R-squared.
* (**) [***] denotes significance at the 10% (5%) [1%] level.

Table 13.2 Stylized account of recent fiscal history

	Clinton Administration		Bush Administration	
Effects on growth	1st term 1993–1996	Effects in 2nd term 1997–2000 and beyond	1st term 2001–2004	Effects in 2nd term 2005–2008 and beyond
As, over time, the numbers show the promises of fiscal responsibility		To be increasingly credible		To be less and less credible
(1) Effect of contemporaneous fiscal stance, via demand	Mild contraction	Mild contraction	Positive stimulus	Approx. neutral
+(2) Effect of expected future fiscal path, via long-term interest rates	Mild contraction	Strong positive effect	Mild contraction	Strong positive effect
=Overall impact of fiscal policy on growth	Approx. neutral	Positive	Weakly positive	Strongly negative

Democratic candidate, we are going to see the emergence of the deficit numbers that I gave you, which have not been properly absorbed by the public and the markets. Interest rates are eventually going to go up, and that is going to start to have a negative effect on the economy.

Of the adverse consequences of growing deficits, interest rates are perhaps the most debated. The concern, of course, is crowding out investment and slowing growth. Glenn Hubbard, George Bush's first Council of Economic Advisers chair, responded to interest rate concerns in two forms, one for political audiences, and one for a professional audience. He wrote a proper phrase for the White House: "Interest rates do not move in lockstep with deficits." Superficially that sounded in support of the proposition that there is no connection. We understood that trick right away in academia; deficits aren't the only thing that affects interest rates. Monetary policy does too, for example, but, you know, big deal. It is like saying, "Who wins in a ballgame doesn't move in lockstep with who hits the more homeruns." I guess that's true, but if you hit more homeruns, you are better off! Similarly, bigger deficits mean higher interest rates *other things equal*. As a defense, it is true, but practically empty of content.

Then there is the response Glenn gave for his economist peers. This was a calculation that said, yes, the budget deficit would affect interest rates, but the effect would be small. Though his calculation gave a smaller number than would many others, it was based on a perfectly respectable economic model. Do you know how he got his estimate? He assumed that increased debt causes one-for-one crowding out of investment, and asked what magnitude is that as a fraction of the total capital stock, and what does that do to the marginal product of capital? That is the estimated effect on the real interest rate. In other words, the exercise is to compute what increase in the interest rate you need to accomplish the crowding-out. He got a relatively small number. I don't much care. The reason we are worried in the first place is because of crowding out. If we have a given amount of crowding out, then whether that's accomplished through a small increase in interest rates, or a big increase in interest rates, or a fall in the stock market, or some other channel, I don't really care. It's a crowding out of investment and the trade balance that are the problem.

If the Democrats are trying to pin the blame of the recent recession on Bush, I don't think that's right. Rather it's the next recession that is going to be his fault. I don't know when that will be. But when it comes, we are not going to have the ability to use fiscal policy, to cut taxes, the way they did in 2001. Next time, tax rates will already be low, and the fiscal policy option will be gone.

William Niskanen

My role in this panel is that of a scoundrel who sees things as they are, rather than as they ought to be. I want to share with you two intriguing findings about what drives federal spending. In a prior exploratory article, I found that federal spending as share of GDP from 1981 through 2000 was a *negative* function of federal revenues as a share of GDP (Niskanen, 2002). In a separate article, I found that the rate of increase in real federal spending since World War II was lower in administrations in which at least one of the two houses in Congress were controlled by the other party (Niskanen, 2003). My new paper presents separate estimates of each of these relations.

First let me talk about what has been called the "starve the beast" hypothesis. Over nearly three decades, many conservatives and libertarians have argued that reducing federal tax rates, in addition to an increase in long-term economic growth, would reduce the growth of federal spending by "starving the beast." This position was recently endorsed, for example, by Nobel laureates Milton Friedman and Gary Becker, in separate *Wall Street Journal* columns in 2003 (Becker *et al.*, 2003, Friedman, 2003).

The problem with this hypothesis is that it is *not* consistent with the evidence, at least since 1980. My article presented evidence of the relative level of federal spending over the period 1981 through 2000, where coincidentally the relative level of the burden of federal taxes went in the opposite direction; in other words there was a strong *negative* relation between the relative levels of federal spending and tax revenue. Controlling for the unemployment rate, federal spending during this period increased about one half of one percent of GDP for each percentage point decline in the relative level of federal tax revenues.

What is going on here? The most direct interpretation of this relation is that it represents a "demand curve" for federal spending. Demand for federal spending by current voters declines with the amount of this spending that is financed by current taxes. Future voters will bear the burden of any resulting deficit but are apparently not effectively represented by those making the current fiscal choices.

One implication of this relation is that tax *increases* may be among the most effective policies to reduce the relative level of federal spending. On this issue I would be pleased to be proven wrong.

Second, for the divided government hypothesis, my brief 2003 article presented evidence that the rate of growth of real federal spending in the years after World War II was lower during the administrations in which at least one house of the Congress was controlled by the other party. The only two long periods of fiscal restraint in the sample were during the Eisenhower and Clinton administrations, during which the opposition party controlled the Congress in the last six years of each of these two administrations. Conversely, the only long period of unusual fiscal expansion was the Kennedy–Johnson administration, which brought us both the Great Society and the Vietnam War, with the support of the same party in Congress.

One reason for this condition is that the prospect for major war has been substantially higher under unified government. I recently went back over history and found that American participation in *every* war in which the ground combat lasted for more than a few days – beginning with the War of 1812 to the current war in Iraq – was initiated by a unified government. A more general reason for this effect of unified government is that each party in a divided government has the opportunity to block the most divisive issues proposed by the other party.

My judgment is that our federal government may work better, or less badly, when at least one house of Congress is controlled by a party other than the party of the president. American voters, in their unarticulated collective wisdom, have voted for a divided government for most of the past 50 years. Divided government is not the stuff of which legends are made, but the separation of powers is probably a better protection of our liberties if the presidency and the Congress are controlled by different parties.

I have updated both of these tests. On the "starve-the-beast" hypothesis, the test equation is the spending share of GDP as a function of the federal revenue share of GDP in the *prior* year, the current unemployment rate and a first-order autoregressive term. The other thing that I have done is that I have tested the same relationship for the period 1949 to 1980, to see whether this relationship that I had found for the post-1980 period would also fit the period prior to 1981. It doesn't, as it turns out.

The first conclusion from this test is that both the relative level of federal revenues in the prior year and the unemployment rate had a significant positive effect on the relative level of federal spending in the sample 1949 to 1980. This finding is consistent with the "starve-the-beast" hypothesis during this period.

The more important conclusion, and the more perplexing conclusion in a way, consistent with my prior estimates of this equation, is that there is a strong negative relation between the relative level of federal spending and the relative level of federal revenues in the sample 1981 to 2000. Controlling for the unemployment rate, federal spending during this period increased again about one half of one percent of GDP for each 1-percentage point of relative decline of federal revenues in the prior year. The first three years of the current Bush administration were not in this sample, but they are consistent with this relationship. During the period that conservatives and libertarians promoted the "starve-the-beast" hypothesis, the developing evidence was strongly contrary to this hypothesis.

Finally we are left with a puzzle. Why was the relation between the relative level of federal spending and federal receipts strongly negative in the period 1981 to today, but positive and significant during the period from 1949 to 1980? What happened in federal fiscal policy that might explain this substantial difference in the estimates from these two samples? I do not know. But I suspect that it is the growing influence from the "supply-siders," who have a good case that high marginal tax rates substantially reduce economic growth; their influence undermined the influence of the traditional conservatives' commitment to a balanced budget. This is only a suggestion.

My new test of the divided-government hypothesis does three things. One is that I test these effects year-by-year rather than administration-by-administration, and second, I add the years 1949 through 1952 to the sample, and the third is that I do a formal difference-of-means test to test the significance of the difference between these. What I found is that during periods of unified government, all the way from 1949 to today, the mean rate of growth of real per-capita federal expenditures was 3.8 percent per year, whereas in divided government, the mean annual change in real per-capita federal expenditures was 1.27 percent. So the rate of growth during unified government was basically three times that during divided government. Then doing a difference-of-means test, the difference of the means was 2.53 percent per year, and with a standard deviation of this difference of means of 1.32, I get a t-ratio of roughly 2, so it does look like there is a significant effect.

Again we are left with a puzzle. Much of the annual variance in total federal spending per capita in the short run is due to changes in defense spending. But if most of the variance in defense spending is exogenous, it may be only a coincidence that the largest increases in total real federal spending per capita had been under a unified government, and the lowest increases under a divided government.

My judgment, however, is that a large part of the variance in real defense spending has been a function of domestic political conditions. I find it hard to dismiss the implications of a nearly 200-year pattern in which American participation in *every* war involving more than a few days of ground combat was initiated by and under a unified government. Divided government may have the lowest rate of growth of real federal spending in part because it has been an important constraint on American participation in war.

In conclusion, each of these tests has produced an intriguing finding about federal spending. Each of these tests, however, is a test of a single possible explanation of federal expenditures without controlling for the condition addressed by the other tests, or for other conditions that may also affect federal spending. And each of these tests has left us with a puzzle to which the answer is not apparent, at least to me. My hope is that this presentation has planted some ideas that others may develop.

Laurence Seidman

What I would like to do is set out a way to run fiscal policy both in the short run and in the long run – and to take both into account simultaneously. My position is intermediate between two extremes. One extreme says, "Always worry about budget deficits, every year." The other view is, "Never worry about budget deficits, this year, next year or the year after." In a normal economy over the long run, we want balanced budgets and fiscal discipline, and I will get into the details about how to do that. But when the economy goes into a recession, we want temporary short-run fiscal stimulus. In a recession, run the deficits as a fiscal stimulus, but in normal economies over the long run, have tight fiscal policy and fiscal discipline. If you don't normally have fiscal discipline, you can't run this fiscal stimulus with temporary deficits in the short run that you may need. John Taylor, of the famous Taylor rule, who was on the Council of Economic Advisers in the first Bush administration during the 1991 recession, admitted that it was very difficult then to propose short-term fiscal stimulus, because during the 1980s they had run up such budget deficits, and therefore debt, that people were afraid of it – financial markets were afraid of it – and their hands got tied about using it in the emergency of the recession.

So if you want to use it in the emergency of recession, you need to – I think Larry Summers may have been the one to use this phrase – "reload the fiscal cannon" in good times. When the sun is shining, do Rubinomics or whatever you want to call it, have tight budgets, surpluses if possible, and keep a low debt-to-GDP ratio, so that if we get into trouble in a recession, we can temporarily run deficits and it is acceptable to the public and the financial markets. Let me first talk about the long run. My proposal for the long run is really an old idea. For half a century economists have advocated it. It is the full-employment balanced budget rule. There are some little wrinkles in it, so I will change the acronym to NUBAR, "Normal Unemployment Balanced Budget Rule." Congress should be under a statute (I would not try to put it in the Constitution) that says the following: Each year Congress should enact a budget, a planned budget for the coming fiscal year, that technicians estimate will be balanced next year if next year's unemployment rate is normal. This is the old full-employment balanced budget rule idea, except it avoids the debate on "What is full employment?" I would just say, take normal unemployment, we might define that as the unemployment rate of the last ten years, to get realistic, on average, that is really what happens, and try to avoid a debate about "What is really full employment?" Conceptually, it is exactly the same. It focuses on the planned budget. Technicians, probably at the CBO, would be the ones who would have to sign-off on it. Once you get into the next year, and the economy drops into a recession and the revenues drop, you won't have to do anything because this is about the planned budget, not about the actual budget. So it avoids the danger that we could get into with the old, classical rule of a balanced budget all the time, through which a recession could turn into a depression. But the new rule would put pressure on Congress and the President every time they are planning a budget. To liberals it would say, "You want to raise spending –

fine. But are you willing to raise taxes?" To conservatives it would say, "You want to cut taxes – fine. But you have got to be willing to plan a cut in spending." So it would impose some discipline on the politicians, whether liberal or conservative.

Having a tight fiscal policy has other benefits. In the old days they used to call it the "tight fiscal, easy monetary mix," which would promote long-run economic growth, as Bob Solow, Paul Samuelson and others emphasized. The composition of the pie would be more investment with a low interest rate and less consumption with a tight fiscal policy, so that over time, you would have faster capital accumulation and growth, and improve the standard of living at a faster rate. Another reason for keeping fiscal discipline in normal times is to keep the confidence of financial markets. If financial markets feel that there is no fiscal discipline, as Jeff [Frankel] pointed out, the markets will expect interest rates to rise in the future, so immediately you get a rise in long-term interest rates, and you get harm to investment and capital accumulation in the short run. And you certainly don't want to test out how far you can go with running up your debt-to-GDP ratio. Look at Japan! Whenever some of us say, "Japan needs fiscal stimulus," we quickly are given the argument that their debt-to-GDP ratio has now gone over 100 percent, and everybody is worried – "We can't do it." Well, I think that can be debated, but the practical answer is, "In normal times, get that debt ratio low, have fiscal discipline, so that when you get into trouble and need stimulus, you've got the means to do it."

Now, what about the stimulus in the short run? This is where some economists have gotten pessimistic about whether in practice; can Congress, in a timely and effective manner get the stimulus out? I think we have to push, in our textbooks, in our public debate, for making fiscal stimulus automatic in a recession. Just to quickly sketch it: It should be automatically triggered when the unemployment rate, for example, rises above a given point in a given quarter. Automatically, transfers would be sent out to households. It could be done with purchases or with cash transfers to state governments, but I am going to concentrate on the transfers to households like the $600 tax rebate in 2001, which I think was a step in the right direction. It was too small, it wasn't repeated, but it was a start. The key is to have this pre-enacted, and if our textbooks would spend some time, and our courses, saying that a missing ingredient in current macro policy is that Congress pre-enact a fiscal policy package that would be triggered automatically when the unemployment rate jumps above a threshold and is de-triggered automatically when the unemployment rate comes back down below that threshold, so that it is clearly temporary. This is the key missing ingredient.

The latest evidence suggests that consumption does respond to cash transfers. Not as much as, say, the early Keynesian view that, if you give them $1,000 they will spend $900 immediately, but also that the permanent-income and lifecycle views are overly pessimistic to say that people would spread it out over the rest of their lives. It is something in the middle. Greg Mankiw did a nice review of empirical work in the 2000 AER, which said it is somewhere in between (Mankiw, 2000). If you then look at the numbers and run some simulations, you find that if you would trigger a tax rebate twice as large as the 2001 rebate ($1,200 instead of $600), but you keep repeating it every quarter as long as you are in a high-unemployment-rate period, you could chop roughly a full percentage point off the unemployment rate. That's a lot of jobs, that's a lot of well-being of the people and the economy, which I think would occur.

During this debate, in the last few years, there were very few economists publicly saying, "We need to have this on the books, an automatic policy like this, triggered and de-triggered." Once again, we got to cover that, in the long run, and over the normal economies, you are running tight fiscal discipline. By the way, I think the methods that Jeff [Frankel] emphasized in the nineties, about pay-as-you-go, that anytime you propose a spending increase, you got to propose a tax increase. Anytime you propose a tax cut, you got to propose a matching spending cut. That's exactly right, that's the discipline you want to press on them in normal times, and you also need to have an administration – as Secretary Rubin exemplified – saying to the public, "We are worried about fiscal discipline in normal economy and in the long run. We temporarily want to stimulate, but it is not that we are going to do this on a permanent basis." We haven't had that in this country in the last several years. And we still don't have it coming loud and clear from the economics profession. Part of the economics profession believes monetary policy alone can handle a recession. Well, it can handle some, but not all recessions. So that is my proposal as set out. Stimulus in a recession, but discipline in normal economies and for the long run, and make the stimulus in a recession automatically triggered. Thank you.

Barbara Bergmann

I would like to talk a little bit about the slogan President Clinton chanted in his State of the Union messages: "Save Social Security Now." Those who want to destroy Social Security are pretending it is going to go bankrupt, and they are telling the public they are going to lose their contributions and never get the promised pensions. Clinton made a terrible mistake pretending that Social Security needed saving – his slogan plays right into the hands of the people who want to destroy the public system. By the time the baby boomers retire, there are plenty of relatively minor changes that can be made. We can of course increase taxes, particularly on the part of income not now taxed, and we can reduce scheduled benefits. So I think it is terrible to give the false impression that the Social Security System is like a private insurance company, which does not have the power of increased taxation or the power to cut its obligations.

William Niskanen

I think President Clinton was right. In order to maintain the current promised benefits, payroll taxes have to be increased from 12.4 percent to about 18 percent – that is the level of increase in the payroll taxes that is necessary to meet promised benefits, and that doesn't correct for the several biases in the system against young workers, those who have a shorter expected life, and two-worker families.

Barbara Bergmann

The public has shown itself willing to take hefty tax increases when it is told that the proceeds will go to Social Security.

William Niskanen

That's right, but you would have to increase revenues by the equivalent of a six-percentage-point increase in the payroll tax in order to meet promised benefits. One way or the other the government is either going to have to break promises or it is going to have to have a substantial tax increase to make Social Security sustainable.

Now that is overwhelmed by the problems of Medicare. The Medicare expenditures are going to take something like 12 percent of GDP, up from about 3 or 4 right now, in the next 40 to 50 years. The current estimate is that if we keep the increase in medical expenditures to no more than 1 percent above the growth of GDP, Medicare expenditures will grow up to about 12 percent of GDP. Now I want to warn you, that in the past 40 years, medical-care expenditures have been increasing 3 percent per year faster than GDP, so 1 percent is very optimistic. I think that it is irresponsible to claim that there is "no problem" for Social Security or, for that matter, for Medicare. In the absence of a major reform of these two programs, the only way that these problems are going to be solved is for the government to break promises.

Everybody who has been promoting, in one form or another, a privatization of Social Security would maintain the full benefits for people who are now retired or who are about to retire. There would be no reduction of promised benefits for those who are now retired or about to retire – or for those who choose to stay in the Social Security system. All of these proposals give people an *option* for a private account, maintaining the full benefits of those who have retired or are about to retire.

So I think it is irresponsible to ignore what is a looming crisis. The Ponzi game is over. There is no longer any politically viable way to save Social Security and Medicare.

Jeffrey Frankel

Barbara [Bergmann] is right that it is not bankrupt. We are not going to have to cut Social Security or Medicare benefits to zero. Sometimes people get overly alarmist about it, so that is correct. But that observation doesn't take you very far, and I agree with everything Bill [Niskanen] said. There is a serious problem there. One could have imagined, three years ago, being on a path where we could have got through this with minor adjustments in benefits or taxes. I can't imagine that now. We are looking at more drastic cuts in benefits, breaking promises, together with pretty steep tax increases. If we got started on it right away, then maybe we could have only a moderate breaking of promises and moderate tax increases; but if we put it off much longer, then the necessary adjustment will be more extreme. The idea that we are going to get through it without any adjustment is now, I think, out of the question. Even if the White House were to achieve a fantasy projection of the growth rate, we are not going to get there.

But I have a second question. Barbara [Bergmann], presumably the reason you don't like Clinton's "Save Social Security First" strategy is because you think it has limited the ability to increase domestic spending. But why won't you give us some credit for having for three years held the line against the Republicans, who wanted to give away money in tax breaks? That was the more likely danger, which I can assert with confidence because that's what actually happened the moment Bush II came in.

Barbara Bergmann

Wouldn't a better way to fend off tax cuts be to call attention to the fact that we are the only country that doesn't have national health insurance? That we need more government subsidies for childcare? That we need more housing assistance for working-poor families? More help with college expenses? Part of the reason the Democrats are out of office is that they haven't done enough to educate the public on the nation's needs. The Republican Senate Majority Leader Bill Frist said we can't afford national health insurance. We're the richest country in the world, and we're the only ones who don't have it. How come we can't afford it?

Instead of this "Save Social Security Now" business, we could have told the country what it needs and tried to promote it. That is the most essential thing that the Democrats have to do. The Clinton Administration was traumatized by Hillary Clinton's bungle of national health insurance. But we will never make progress unless we get the public to stop believing that the government is a big bad evil thing that can't do anything good for us. The Democrats' failure to do that is part of the reason that they ended up out of power.

Let me remind Bill Niskanen that the privatization of Social Security would not be free. It would cost, perhaps, $2 trillion of extra money. There has been a suggestion that the way to finance that transition is to borrow it. Guess what? To increase the debt some more!

William Niskanen

It does take some increase in the explicit debt to allow people a private option. But that increase in the explicit debt reduces the implicit debt, which is many times the explicit debt. Our explicit debt that is not owned by the Fed is now about $4 trillion. But the implicit debt for Social Security alone is in the order of $12 trillion. So the privatization or Social Security choice options reduce the implicit debt because people opt out of Social Security, and increase the explicit debt to fund the transition. So it does require an increase in the explicit debt or other taxes or spending cuts, but you should look at the sum of the explicit debt and the implicit debt, and that goes down with this proposal.

Laurence Seidman

If I could just comment here. I am sitting right between Bill [Niskanen] and Barbara [Bergmann] on this, but actually I am right where Jeff Frankel's view is. We got a serious long-term problem with Social Security, but it doesn't mean that you got to go to privatization; it does mean that you need to build-up surpluses. I wrote a book a few years ago called *Funding Social Security: A Strategic Alternative* (Seidman, 1999). One of the best things that we have done is in the 1980s, a commission led by Alan Greenspan, before he went to the Fed, bipartisan, began to build up the Social Security Trust Fund. That is important. By the way, it is real, it is going to be able to be cashed in when we start drawing it down, we need to build it up more, and build it up better, and it is not painless because you have to raise taxes or slow benefit growth in order to do it. We don't have to go to privatization. We have to go to building up in advance, and I think that's what President Clinton meant by saying "Save Social Security First" and transfer some of the funds. Anyway, before I let Barbara [Bergmann] grab this, I want to let her know that I agree with some of what she said earlier.

Barbara Bergmann

The effect of this attempt to prepay Social Security has been nil for Social Security. All it has done is to make the tax system more regressive, by financing the defense budget through the payroll tax. And I disagree that the Trust Fund is a "real" thing. The money collected in the form of extra Social Security taxes has gone over to the Pentagon. All we have out of it now is a fleet of used fighter planes, and that is not going to help us buy bread for the older citizens.

Laurence Seidman

Now this is the beginning to a long debate. I just want to tie this in with what I said earlier. When you have a full-employment balanced budget rule, or normal unemployment-balanced budget rule – and one wrinkle I didn't point out is that we need to separate Social Security and Medicare off-budget; the balanced-budget rule applies to the rest of the budget – Social Security and Medicare need to build-up surpluses – Bill [Niskanen] would say, "Privatize it!" but I don't agree with that – they need to build-up surpluses and pre-fund them. Barbara [Bergmann] you are right. If the rest of the budget is running larger deficits while you are building up the surplus, you are offsetting it. But if you have discipline in the rest of the budget and build-up the surpluses in Social Security and Medicare, then you accomplish something.

Barbara Bergmann

Surpluses in the Social Security account are sent to the Treasury, which in return sends bonds, which we can think of as going into a drawer at the Social Security Agency. If the Agency ever needed to make expenditure that could not be covered by current Social Security taxes, it could get money from Treasury by presenting those bonds to the Treasury and asking for repayment. To make the repayment, the Treasury would have to raise taxes, or lower expenditures, or run a deficit. But it could do these things and send the proceeds to the Social Security Agency whether or not the Agency had bonds in its drawer. So the presence of those bonds has no meaning. The Social Security Trust Fund is fictional.

William Niskanen

I would like the audience to know and remember that we have finally heard something on which Barbara [Bergmann] and I agree! [Audience laughs . . . applause.]

Jeffrey Frankel

We have been listening here to an interesting debate on the question of privatizing Social Security, between Bill Niskanen who is a principled conservative of a libertarian bent, and Barbara Bergmann, who is a principled liberal, and Larry [Seidman] is in the middle. And we could have debates like that about the proper scope of the government when it comes to the environment or inequality or lots of issues, how to pick a balance, an optimal point on the trade-off, between those values versus the desirability of efficiency and laissez faire, efficiency and growth.

But my problem is that, in this country we are not having any kind of optimal trade-off like that. We have a government that is composed, not of honest conservatives, but rather of people who talk the rhetoric of discipline and small government and laissez faire and free trade, and then do exactly the opposite every time they think it will get them votes. We are not on the optimal production possibility frontier between maximizing real growth in GDP and these other objectives. And I think that, if we economists continue to debate as if it is all honest liberal versus honest conservative, then we are missing the picture.

Any time you want to know what an honest conservative position would be, look up Bill Niskanen's numbers. But he is in a minority. The people in the public debate, who push most of the proposals to privatize Social Security, or others like the flat tax, tend to jimmy the numbers. They pretend that we can get something for nothing; they don't depict an honest trade-off.

So we first have to focus attention on the dishonesty and look at the truth of the trade-off, before we can talk about where we want to be on it. Over the last five presidencies, it seems to me, Democrats have actually looked honestly at what the trade-offs are, and Republicans have been in "never-never land."

William Niskanen

I don't know of any Social Security proposal that assumes that there are no costs. There are a variety of tax-cut proposals out there that assume it can be done without cost, but I don't know of any Social Security proposal that assumes that you can do it without costs. There are several proposals out there that would give everybody a default portfolio of 60 percent equity and 40 percent bonds, of a very widespread amount of securities. Only after they have accumulated a good bit in their accounts would they have greater freedom in choosing their portfolios. All proposals also have a safety net. We are proposing 120 percent of whatever is the then poverty line as a safety net. So we have a first line of defense in that we should have a conservative, broadly based portfolio, and then a safety net.

The numbers we are using come from the government, from the Social Security actuaries, so we are not using numbers that are any different than the numbers that go into the Social Security's own calculations.

I blame the Republicans indirectly for the fact that we do not have a substantial Social Security choice proposal in place. In 1998 Clinton had half-a-dozen town meetings around the country to talk about this issue. We had a major White House conference in December of 1998, in which four Cato people participated. He was very close to endorsing a Social Security choice proposal in the State of the Union message in 1999.

What happened in the meantime was the impeachment period, and the Democratic Left made it clear to Clinton that their support in the impeachment hearings was dependent upon him backing away from this

Social Security proposal. So I think that the impeachment process, which was an absurd process and wholly unnecessary, has destroyed the possibility or the probability that we would otherwise have a Social Security reform system in place already.

Matias Vernengo

I would like to intervene at this point, since we are approaching the end, and ask all of you to give a final round of comments on the Democrat/Republican switch on fiscal policy matters.

Laurence Seidman

I think it is sort of who is on offence. In the 1960s, the Democrats were on offence with the Presidency and the Congress; they wanted to raise spending for domestic programs. The Republicans said "If you are going to raise spending, which we don't want you to do, you've got to raise taxes and balance the budget." The Republicans, on defense, preached a balanced budget. The Democrats said "Don't make such a big deal out of deficits." Now, in more recent years, Republicans were on offence, they want to cut taxes, and Democrats say "Alright, if you want to cut taxes, which we don't want you to do, you've got to cut spending, and we've got to have a balanced budget."

Just one other point though: In the short-run stimulus, in these last few years, just to connect to your point, if we have slogans "Deficits matter" or "Deficits don't matter," we are going to really be in trouble. We need to say "In a recession, run deficits. But in normal circumstances, have fiscal discipline." You've got to have that degree of complexity in the message.

Look at the debate in the last two or three years. The problem with the Bush administration's approach is not deficits in the short run. The problem is permanent long-run deficits. And the problem was that tax cuts for the wealthy were a very inefficient and inequitable way to provide stimulus. Both parties agreed to $600 for everybody. But the Bush administration said "For more stimulus, there has to be many more dollars for the upper-income groups," and that was very divisive, very unfair, and very inefficient in terms of the marginal propensity to spend. They could have gotten stimulus that was efficient and equitable, but they went for their own distributional priorities instead.

Jeffrey Frankel

Let me elaborate on my claim that the Republicans and Democrats have switched places regarding responsible economic policy. I am talking about the performance of the actual presidents, not candidates during the campaign, and not Congress. And I am talking about what the presidents actually do, not what they say. My claim is that the pattern is not just Clinton versus Bush, but that it goes back 25 years. The Republicans have become the more irresponsible party, not just on budget deficits, where it is very striking as in the graphs I showed, but also on trade policy, on subsidies for agriculture and other special interests, on attempts to strong-arm the Fed into easier monetary policy. I have heard Bill Niskanen say in the past that Ronald Reagan, and the current President Bush, have been more protectionist – certainly than Bill Clinton – but also than any president in the post-war period. So this is a very general puzzle, why the two parties have switched places. Here is the best I can do at a hypothesis.

If you are out of Washington, and pride yourself on being an "out-of-Washington," and your whole mindset is anti-government and anti-Washington, you fall into the habit of thinking that it is very easy to cut back government – that all you have to do is cut back waste and abuse, give some speeches. It's evil bureaucrats who are expanding government. There doesn't have to be any pain for the public. It is just a matter of standing up to the bureaucrats. But it's not like that. For pork-barrel project, there are people who benefit from it, and can make a good-sounding case, why they deserve it. It is a difficult business to tell people that they can't have their import protection or their pork-barrel project. If you come into office thinking it is easy, you are completely unprepared to make the real compromises, the political trade-offs and the difficult calculations that you have to make. So you give speeches instead. I think that describes Ronald Reagan and that it describes the current President.

Barbara Bergmann

The reversal in rhetoric on the deficit results from truly evil behavior on both sides. On the Republican side is their desire to shovel money to the rich, their desire to increase without rational limit or need the money spent on fancy weapons, and their macho desire to establish permanent American hegemony in the world, starting with an expensive Iraqi adventure. On the Democratic side is their pusillanimous failure to try to explain to the American public that there are times when deficits are helpful (to the extent that they increase aggregate demand when that is needed, which the current deficit does poorly), and times when we would do better to balance the budget, or pay off past debt. Instead they are trying to get political mileage out of accusing the Republicans of a "crime" that the Republicans in olden days falsely propagandized the public to believe should never, ever, be committed. It's a sad spectacle.

William Niskanen

Seldom do I have an opportunity to have the last word, but it is appropriate on this issue. For I believe that the change in the major party positions on fiscal policy has been tactical and temporary, not structural and enduring.

For the past several decades, the Republican perspective on fiscal policy has been shaped primarily by supply-siders who have promoted a politically attractive but inconsistent free-lunch perspective about tax cuts:

1   A reduction of marginal tax rates would significantly increase long-term economic growth, a position that I share and has been confirmed by the accumulation of empirical studies.
2   An increase in the deficit has no significant short-term economic effects (other than on the current account deficit), a position that I may have been the first to defend and has also been confirmed by subsequent empirical studies.
3   A reduction of marginal tax rates would not increase the deficit, a position that is both implausible and inconsistent with the evidence.
4   A reduction of marginal tax rates would increase the deficit, but that is a desirable effect because it would "starve the beast," a position that has not been consistent with the evidence since 1980.

My guess is that most Republican members of Congress would revert to their more traditional position about the deficit (if the president is a Democrat and tax cuts are not on the agenda) as an argument against spending increases; for the most part, this was their position during the Clinton administration.

The recent Democratic position of fiscal policy was also tactical and is probably temporary. "Rubinomics" was clearly an ex post attempt to explain the long boom of the 1990s as the result of some policy that Clinton had proposed and was approved without Republican support; the 1993 tax increase was the only major policy change that met those conditions. From that came a revived Hooveresque claim that tight fiscal policy increases economic growth, primarily by reducing interest rates, although, in fact, interest rates increased until the Republicans won control of Congress in 1994. My guess is that this perspective would not survive the election of a Democratic president because, so far, the spending increases proposed by the Democratic presidential candidates are a good bit larger than the increased revenues from their tax proposals.

The sad fact is that neither party has an institutional commitment to a responsible fiscal policy. My guess is that the federal government will continue to have a substantial deficit until we are disciplined, probably, by a balance of payments crisis.

Matias Vernengo

Let me thank everybody, the panelists and the audience, for an enlightening and entertaining session. Although it is clear that there is no consensus on what optimal fiscal policy should be, in particular regarding the long-term effects of deficits, it seems that a wide range of the profession – from the progressive liberals to the conservative libertarian – would agree that the current fiscal stance is problematic. Irrespective of the electoral results, it is patent that important challenges lie ahead.

References

Becker, Gary S., Edward O. Lazear, and Kevin M. Murphy (2003), "The Double Benefit of Tax Cuts," *Wall Street Journal*, 7 October.

Frankel, Jeffrey A. and Menzie Chinn (2003), "The Euro Area and World Interest Rates," Conference proceedings, Centre for Economic Policy Research, London, processed.

Friedman, Milton (2003), "What Every American Wants," *Wall Street Journal*, 20 January.

Mankiw, N. Gregory (2000), "The Savers-Spenders Theory of Fiscal Policy," *American Economic Review*, 90(2), May, pp. 120–5.

Niskanen, William A. (2002), "Tax Policy: Tax Policy from 1990 to 2001: Comments," in *American Economic Policy in the 1990s*, edited by Jeffrey A. Frankel and Peter R. Orszag, Cambridge, Massachusetts: MIT Press, pp. 184–7.

Niskanen, William A. (2003), "A Case for Divided Government," *Cato Policy Report*, March/April, p. 2.

Rivlin, Alice and Isabel Sawhill (editors) (2004), *Restoring Fiscal Sanity: How to Balance the Budget*, Washington, DC: Brookings Institution Press.

Seidman, Laurence S. (1999), *Funding Social Security: A Strategic Alternative*, Cambridge; New York: Cambridge University Press.

14 The final word on fiscal policy

Interview

Robert Eisner; with an introduction by
Per Gunnar Berglund

Introduction

This interview was the first time I met Robert Eisner. It was in July 1997, on a beautiful day at the scenic campus of Northwestern University in Evanston, Illinois. At the time I was still living in Sweden, and in great conscientious woes about the hackneyed domestic debate on the budget deficit and the national debt. Briefly put, the general notion was that the deficit meant mortgaging our grandchildren and that the country was facing state bankruptcy. In the face of economic depression and double-digit unemployment, the government in 1996 pushed through a budget consolidation of monumental proportions. The minister of finance proudly declared that Sweden would become the "World Champion in Budget Consolidation." And so she did. Objections were not heard, in fact, given the ferocious media campaign, few if any dared questioning anything.

In defiance of these headwinds, I had just published a small, non-academic book on the unemployment problem in Sweden, in which I proposed an expansionary fiscal strategy to overcome the unemployment problem. I had picked up a couple of Eisner's articles in *The American Economic Review*, and thought his arguments about fiscal policy, on the deficit and debt, made a lot of sense. Digging deeper, I found out that Eisner had expressed many if not all of my ideas well before I was even born! I was working at the time with a social and cultural magazine, which also happened to be the only public outlet in the country for dissenting views on fiscal policy. I decided to approach the editor-in-chief about interviewing Eisner. He approved and even stretched his budget to get me a ticket and a hotel room.

Eisner picked me up at the hotel and we drove off to the campus. Small talk. We had lunch together and then went over to his office for the interview. I can't remember ever having met a more cordial man. He had a very particular, disarming warmth about him, radiating the relaxedness of a man at peace with himself. One couldn't help thinking that he seemed satisfied with his life, his career and his accomplishments overall. But there was also something very youthful, curious and playful about this white-haired man. He had a wonderfully nuanced sense of humor, and years and years of this *joie de vivre* seemed to have shaped his face into an everlasting smile, which made him look extraordinarily sympathetic. He had this big, mellow voice that one seems to find only amongst senior Americans, and which conveys an impression of bottomless wisdom and authority. It was clear to me from the very first moment that I was facing a tremendously intelligent and agile person, the kind that picks up your train of thought and brings it to conclusion before you have even had time to finish your sentence. As I was groping half a moment for a word, he would gently interrupt and explain to me what I meant to say.

I had very little interviewing experience, and had prepared myself extensively with a barrage of questions and possibilities. I felt nervous. You can imagine my surprise, therefore, when he simply starts telling it all after my very first fragment of a question. The interview was lenient on me. For two whole hours, I essentially sat back and listened to the great man, only interjecting now and then, mainly to convince myself that this was actually an interview. On my way home, I thought about this. I had a curious, not altogether flattering, feeling that he had prevented me from doing my job, and that it was all for the best, as I knew I had a splendid interview on that tape. I was safely in the hands of a professional.

When dropping me off at my hotel, he invited me to dinner at his home. I was delighted. It gave me a chance to see where he lived, get to know him a little bit more, and to meet his wife Edith. While showing me his study he explained that he was working on a new pamphlet on "the three deficit scares," namely the Federal budget, the foreign trade and the Social Security deficits. He would send over the manuscript, he promised.

Arriving back in Sweden I found the manuscript in my e-mail. There is no such thing as delay in dealing with an Eisner. I read it and got so excited that I immediately passed it along to my editor-in-chief. He didn't like the interview. It was too academic, he said, and stripped it down to almost nothing. But, he did like the pamphlet and decided we should seek to publish it. He asked me to find out if we could, and to translate it to Swedish. There followed a mad rush to get the book out before the Social Democratic Party congress, whose delegates, thought our sanguine editor-in-chief, could be persuaded by a pamphlet of this sort. Intensely green and brashly titled copies were distributed free of charge to all delegates. I was quietly skeptical, but at least I enjoyed the diversion from the usual lull.

The best part of the sudden frenzy, from my point of view, was that it brought Robert Eisner to Sweden, on a promotional tour. And Edith came with him. There was great joy of reunion, but the tour was no great triumph. Bob was brilliant, of course, but he was met with indifference and even disrespect. A seminar at the Parliament attracted only junior clerks, and media showed an almost complete lack of interest. The Swedish establishment, as I had feared, was no longer fertile soil for these ideas. But this went beyond that. It amounted to a refusal to even hear the arguments. The case had been closed. For me personally, it brought things to a critical point. I was fed up. The environment had become impossible and unbearable. I decided that I should leave.

I wrote a brief message to Bob, indicating ever so vaguely that I had had it. He was perceptive enough to understand what I really meant, and he had also read my book and knew that "we had a lot in common," as he put it. The subsequent chain of events was truly astonishing. I have never seen anybody bend over backward the way he did to help. He wrote letters and made phone calls on my behalf until it was all but a done deal that I could move over. Having now spent six years in the United States, I thank my lucky star, whose name is Robert Eisner, for getting me here. My personal and intellectual debt to him is enormous.

It was not much later that I learned about Bob's serious illness, which he had been diagnosed with even before I first met him. I knew nothing. Learning about it put the whole interview experience in a very different light. I suddenly found myself having been entrusted with an autobiographical piece. I felt confused. In April of 1998, I met Bob at a conference here at the New School in New York,[1] and I thought he looked well under the circumstances. He gave his talk, about the fallacy of the NAIRU doctrine, and then he had to leave. I saw him sneak out the door and discretely eased my way out to say goodbye. "Nice talk" he said to me, for we had been in the same session, and we shook hands and he walked off. It was the last time I saw him. A few months later he was dead.

Robert Eisner was the greatest of the American Keynesians. When I first met him I had only a vague idea of his intellectual stature. I have been on a journey of discovery ever since, and the world of Robert Eisner never ceases to fascinate. He had a comprehensive grasp of the entire gigantic research area of macroeconomics in all its aspects and dimensions. He worked on the theory of consumption and investment behavior, on economic growth, on fiscal and monetary policy, on the relation between inflation and unemployment, on social accounting, as well as several other areas. He left no stone unturned.

Economists of Robert Eisner's caliber are few and far between in the profession. The way economics is structured today makes it virtually impossible, even for the most talented and devoted, to acquire the formidable combination of breadth and depth that Eisner had. The tradeoff may be grimmer these days, forcing most of us to choose drilling into narrow holes and remain dilettantes outside our home turf. But the truth is that very, very few are endowed with the unique combination of analytical acumen, practical capability and balanced sense of judgment that Robert Eisner possessed. He was three times blessed with the Aristotelian virtues: he had the *episteme* of a pure theorist, the *techne* of an applied econometrician and the *phronesis* of a policy adviser. His long-term perspective and stamina will stand through the changing fads and fashions of a myopic profession all too eager to adapt to what's politic. The timeless quality of Eisner's work will be borne out as time sifts and winnows, separating the wheat from the chaff.

Interview with Robert Eisner

Per Gunnar Berglund

Perhaps we should start off with some background, about your life and career that is, and I suppose the natural point to start would be to tell the story about how you became an economist. What was it that persuaded you, as a young man, to go in that direction?

Robert Eisner

Well, it's been, I am afraid, a while since I was a young man, but I will get into that in all the gory detail. What influenced me, I guess, was a certain interest in trying to improve society. I was a history major in college, but I was told by one of my favorite teachers that history did not help you in deciding anything about the present. That led me into sociology for a master's degree, at Columbia University.

Just before the war, I went to work in Washington briefly, for about a year, until I was drafted into the Army. I was working at the Office of Price Administration, and later at the Office of War Information. Served three and a half years in the armed forces, came back, got married, worked for a year again in government, was rather disillusioned by the lack of anything going on, productively, it seemed, partly because I was working in the Office of Price Administration again, which was being dissolved, eliminated, with the end of price controls.

I became active in a public workers union and worked for eleven months as a union organizer, part of the CIO's "Operation Dixie." This was tough, rough work, organizing garbage collectors and other state and city employees in North Carolina and Virginia. I remember my car was broken into once. I suspected the FBI looking for I don't know what. They found a bunch of leaflets which I was putting out. So, after eleven months I found out that I did not want to continue.

I went back to Washington with my young wife, took some courses during the summer, and then I decided to go back to get a doctorate. Fortunately, under the GI Bill, this could be done readily, with financial support from the government. My wife taught at the University of Maryland for a year, and then at high schools in Washington. I was going to go back and get a sociology doctorate at Columbia, where I had received my master's degree. I had a nice welcoming note from the late Robert Lynd, a very famous sociologist, and I had also studied with Paul Lazarsfeld. In fact I did my master's thesis on the Gallup poll on conscription with him.[2]

But, on the way to New York from Washington, one hot day, I was persuaded to stop in at Johns Hopkins, which had no sociology department. I was warmly welcomed by the late Fritz Machlup, who was a great economist and a great teacher; I ultimately did my dissertation with him. Since there was no sociology department at Hopkins, and Machlup and Evsey Domar (who just died[3]) were very distinguished people, I went and got my doctorate in economics at Hopkins, still with the idea that economics was a tool, perhaps, to help me make the world better.

Machlup somehow took to me, and I took to him. I came out of this union work, and I guess I was sort of a good, young radical. I think Machlup was very far from a radical, but something may have appealed to him, perhaps about his own youth. He had a great influence on me. You know, I was sympathetic to that anyway, but he persuaded me that it was important to get a sound base in economic theory, and that is what I proceeded to do.

My work was with Machlup mainly, and with Evsey Domar, who made me very much of a Keynesian. My dissertation was closely related to the work of Domar, but I ended up doing it with Machlup, who was a very careful reader and good critic.[4] My first article, "The Invariant Multiplier," was written while I was a graduate student, and it was published in *The Review of Economic Studies*.[5] The article addressed a small point in Keynesian theory, on the logic and the theory of the multiplier.

I guess that I should say that I am of a generation, like [James] Tobin, [Robert] Solow,[6] and others, who took economics as not just mechanics and mathematical abstractions, although I think we all recognize the importance of mathematics and logic and good theory. But economics helped you understand the economy, and then more broadly, the world. It was a tool perhaps, if you understood it right, to guide you to policies that could make things better.

We also came out of the Depression. I was a child during the Depression. I wasn't particularly hurt by it – my father was a schoolteacher and the chairman of a math department, and he had a steady salary when others were losing their jobs. So we were not that hurt, but you could see it all around you. I was brought up in the age when Roosevelt became President, and we felt that there was something government could do, and had to do, to make things better.

Berglund

Does this imply that you approached economics as a "moral science" rather than a "hard science"? Also there is a widespread feeling these days that economics has become too technical and too abstract for lay people to understand, and therefore losing some its relevance for policymaking. Some seem to think of economics as a kind of applied mathematics. It does sound like the situation was very different at that time?

Eisner

I mean, economics – I am very proud of the discipline, and I am very glad I became an economist – I think it manages to combine what talents I have, appropriately, with an interest in trying to make the world better. I guess I am no longer to be considered to be much of a mathematician by today's standards, but I was reasonably adept in the needed tools in economics when I was doing my graduate work. So, it was something that you could do that was professional, that was rigorous, that wasn't soft, that could be reasoned, and which might do some good.

Berglund

So, what happened after you got your PhD?

Eisner

I got the PhD degree, and I was offered a job at the University of Illinois, in Champaign. The university had a new Dean, who was trying to build up his economics department, which had been particularly provincial, with no international reputation to speak of. I remember that I was offered what seemed like a remarkably good salary in those days – it was $4,500 in 1950. Machlup, my professor said "That's rent! Pure economic rent!" which, of course, to the non-professional, I should explain, means that my pay was considerably more than was necessary to hire me, and that was undoubtedly true.

The Dean then, Howard Bowen, who came from the Irving Trust Company, and I guess was something of a liberal Keynesian, did undertake to bring some quite distinguished, generally younger, people like Franco Modigliani, who became a Nobel laureate, and with whom I worked on a research project while I was there.[7] The department also included Don Patinkin, Margaret Reid, Dorothy Brady, people who went on to great distinction in the profession if they didn't have it then.

But that brought on a great controversy, because these young people like Modigliani, were then being given big graduate courses in macroeconomic theory, and taking them away from the old-timers, who, frankly, didn't know much and who largely made their income on textbooks. So, a revolt broke out against the new Dean. In fact, a day or two after I arrived, I was called to a meeting with the faculty, which ended up voting, sixty to forty or something like that, "no confidence" in the Dean.

That was a critical point in a great effort to force the Dean to resign. It was joined by the local newspaper that decided that the new Dean was bringing in a lot of "pinkos," or radicals, which was rather absurd. I mean, we were of all different persuasions; several were conservatives from the University of Chicago, like the late Oris Herfindahl, I remember, who did a lot of good work in resources theory. But *The Chicago Tribune* had, under conservative hands at that time – very conservative, supported this charge that we were all a bunch of "pinkos." Ultimately the conservatives were trying to drive out the President of the University, one George Stoddard, and they succeeded.

But then, when Bowen was forced to resign, all the new people that came in realized that things were going nowhere, and we began to think about leaving. I wrote a note to Fritz Machlup, suggesting that maybe I should leave. He said "it just so happened here they had already recommended me at Northwestern, and let me know what happens." I got the job at Northwestern in 1952, and I have been here ever since.

I had a great colleague, who later became President, the late Robert Strotz. He and I collaborated on a couple of pieces, and our department got better and better over the years. Over the early years, at several points I considered leaving. I had an opportunity to go to Berkeley, also elsewhere, but I decided, for one reason or another, that I liked it here. My wife got involved in a private school, teaching right off the university campus, we had a house, raised our children, and we have been happy here ever since.

Berglund

The economics department at Northwestern, then, is a better place for young teachers?

Eisner

I am not sure I know what you mean there. No, it is just a forward-looking department, as the University of Illinois, under the chairman Everett Hagan was at that time. I recognize that seniority has certain privileges, but you can get stodgy and out of touch if you don't quickly bring in the best of the young people, and give them responsibilities. I remember when I was chairman – I had two stints as chairman here – I did get the course load to be lowered and changed, so that all people taught the same number of courses. Previously, the junior people taught more courses than the senior people. But they ultimately taught the same amount.

If you have a young person who comes in and is qualified, you don't want to say "you have to teach nothing but the principles classes." Frankly, the older professors are often better at principles classes these days. They have more experience of the economy, and the things that are interesting to elementary students. So, it has not been unusual for the new PhD's to find themselves teaching a graduate class at Northwestern, which usually has a proportion of three undergraduate classes for every one graduate class, roughly. A normal teaching load in economics is four courses spread over three quarters. Most of us would teach two courses in one quarter and two in another, and the third quarter we would not be teaching, but we would be in residence. It would mean that on the average, each faculty member might expect to teach three undergraduate classes and one graduate class.

Berglund

Let us talk a little about the "Keynesian revolution." I get the impression that it was related to a generation change at the universities?

Eisner

Well, I am afraid that is always true. I mean most of us, I am afraid, change little, and the way the profession changes is not so much that the people in the profession change themselves, but that new people come in. When you're brought up as a non-Keynesian, you stayed non-Keynesian, and the younger people, who were open to the new ideas adopted them and began teaching them to other younger people. So that is the way it is spread.

I guess I remember my own dismay in the early years at Northwestern with one or two of the faculty members who seemed to me to be terribly out of touch. They didn't understand Keynes, and they didn't understand what we were saying, and I suppose, to be honest, that a lot of the younger people may feel that about me and others. They don't understand Keynes anymore. They reject him and work instead from a Classical model, where you assume there is always full employment, the business cycles are "real," the people are always working as much as they want to work.[8] They are in a different world, where parallel lines don't cross. As Keynes pointed out, we are in a three-dimensional world where, in fact, parallel lines on a globe will cross even if they are parallel at one point.[9]

So, that does change. I am hopeful in this country now that the pendulum will be swinging again, and perhaps some of the old ideas that are appropriate are back in reasonable vigor. Many of them have never really been dropped. At the policy levels throughout Europe and the US, I think, people are well aware that there can be fiscal stimulus, that you don't always have full employment, that a tax cut will stimulate demand, or even that government expenditures will stimulate demand, and that the central bank can influence economic activity easing credit and lowering interest rates. Those ideas are, of course, essentially Keynesian, but they have been so deeply embodied in the profession now that even if you struck out the name and said "We don't believe in Keynesian economics anymore," the policies are still there, although perhaps not followed as clearly as they should be.

Berglund

Maybe you could make some remarks on the Keynesian revolution from a historical and personal perspective?

Eisner

Well, I am not sure I am the best one to do that, because remember I started my graduate work in 1948, when the Keynesian revolution had already occurred. I taught Keynesian concepts as a teaching assistant, out of the first edition of Samuelson's *Principles*, which was an essentially Keynesian text. So the revolution had occurred before I became of age as an economist.

But I do remember, when I did my undergraduate work at the College of the City of New York, I had only had a few courses in economics – I had been a history major. I don't think the faculty at City College was that advanced. I remember during World War II – I was in France at the end of war, and had the opportunity, when the war was over, to study at the University of Paris for four months. I was still in uniform, and I took a couple of courses in economics, and a couple in sociology. The economics professor was talking about Keynes and looking to me as an American who must know very much about Keynes. But that was the first time I had heard of him as an economist! I think I had been familiar with him through *The Economic Consequences of the Peace*,[10] which is a work on the Treaty of Versailles, but I had never been exposed to any of the general theories of his economics.

When I got to graduate work in 1948, as I said, the Keynesian revolution had largely been achieved. It had began to sweep through the advanced economics departments. There was the Samuelson text, Larry Klein had a book called *The Keynesian Revolution*, and he had a splendid article in the *Journal of Political Economy*, which compared Classical, Keynesian and Marxian macroeconomic theory.[11]

Berglund

Was there a lot of controversy surrounding this?

Eisner

There was plenty of controversy, and at Johns Hopkins, where I did my graduate work in 1948–1950, Domar was a very clear, advanced Keynesian, and Machlup was an old, Classical economist. But Machlup observed Keynes – he had a book on the international trade multiplier – and he helped me on this article I wrote on the multiplier, which came out of a chapter of Keynes.[12] Others in the faculty were probably less aware. I remember the then-chairman, Heberton Evans, had a textbook and taught us a course, which was almost chapter-by-chapter Alfred Marshall. I didn't take that much to that, but I guess to him, Marshall was what Keynes was to me, the great source of wisdom. We were also studying the arguments of D.H. Robertson and of Pigou, against Keynes. So there was certainly a lot of controversy in the departments, and people arguing.

Berglund

How did you relate to the so-called Classical counter-revolution of the 1970s? Did you get involved in that controversy?

Eisner

Well, only to the extent that I have been accused of trying to ignore it. I mean, for a long time I just did ignore it. The ideas didn't make much sense to me initially. But now I have experienced it, and I think, well, there has been a lot of useful work done by the new economists, if you wish. There is a lot of sense to "rational expectations," but I think it has been much overdone, or misapplied. I think there is something to [Robert] Lucas's econometric critique, but again you shouldn't go overboard with it.[13]

Early I got into what I think was a fundamental objection to the whole premise of Robert Lucas, in which he said that in effect he had been brought up as a Keynesian himself, but perceived the failure of Keynesian economics in the stagflation of the 1970s, when we had a combination of high inflation and high unemployment simultaneously. To him, this seemed to beat the idea of the Phillips Curve, and seemed to defy the usual Keynesian notion of a tradeoff between unemployment and inflation.

I have written on a number of occasions now that this was an essential misreading by Lucas of what had happened. That the stagflation – the high inflation and high unemployment of the 1970s – was simply the result of a supply shock, which means that we had huge increases in the prices of oil and energy and agricultural commodities on world markets. These increases tended to drive up prices in other sectors, and brought on inflation. Then, unfortunately, misunderstanding this, or not having the correct goals, the monetary authority and those setting fiscal policy instead of moving with this, easing and stimulating, tried to hold back the inflation either purposefully or by inaction. And that, in turn, caused a reduction in real aggregate demand. This isn't literally what happened, but if you keep the same quantity of money in nominal terms, and prices rise, then real quantity of money goes down. Similarly, if you determine that you have to balance the budget as the economy slows, you simply aggravate the slowdown.

In the late 1970s, there was this misreading: It was felt that we had a big budget deficit, and part of that was a mismeasurement of the budget deficit, not taking into account what I call the "inflation tax," the fact that we had a high rate of inflation, which was reducing the real value of the debt. We did not have a stimulatory fiscal policy – we had a *contractionary* fiscal policy. Ultimately we had a contractionary fiscal policy, and a repressive monetary policy in the face of the supply-shock inflation. That gave you the high unemployment, and that was no contradiction of Keynes at all. Of course, Keynes had not considered this possibility, that's true. In the Great Depression you didn't have rising prices, so this was not an issue.

But that is, I think, what happened and I was taking this up with some of the graduate classes I was teaching, and tried to explain both the contributions of the New Classical economics, and what I thought were some grave limitations. Rational expectations, with its conclusion of policy impotence – that there was nothing that government could do to affect the macro economy, except on the supply side – I thought very foolish. The notion that you could not change, influence, the economy with monetary policy, unless it came about as a surprise, struck me as a misreading in part. Even if you took that point of view, every change is to some extent a surprise, because you are never quite sure what is going to happen in the future. So when something changes, that is a difference.

Berglund

So you are basically arguing that the New Classical economists have been misreading Keynes?

Eisner

I think that is quite true, that they were wrong in their reading of him, and increasingly, I think, that few of them did read him! I don't think most people, many of that rising generation in the 1970s and the 1980s, really studied Keynes in graduate school, neither in the original nor in other renditions. He lingered on in terms of practical policy, but many people, economists, didn't follow him, because many of the best minds in economics, I am afraid, got into very abstract work, and the abstract mathematical work was probably easier to do if it wasn't Keynesian.

Remember that Keynesian economics, essentially, developed macroeconomics, because the microeconomics didn't seem to be giving you the answers to the macroeconomic questions. Microeconomics could frequently be very neat, if you stick to general equilibrium theory, in which you assume that all markets clear. You can develop some very elegant mathematical formulations, and it was easier then to make assumptions that worked with elegant results, than to try to make assumptions that brought you closer to answers that seemed to fit the real world.

Again, I am not objecting to the use of mathematics in any way. It is just that if you are an economist, what is important, is the answers to economic questions. You may want to get them in the most elegant fashion, and the mathematics will maybe make you more rigorous and sure of yourself. But you can't say that "I'm not going to approach this problem, or get this answer, because I can't find the mathematical formulation, the mathematical solution for it." You can maybe keep looking for it, but ultimately the issues in economics have to be with faced with whatever tools will work.

Berglund

A great deal of your work is in the field of empirical, applied economics?

Eisner

Yes, much of my work has been what you call applied, or empirical econometrics. I hardly do any theoretical work in econometrics. I did, I think, establish a bit of a name for myself with a couple of articles, such as one defending Friedman's permanent-income theory. Milton Friedman, the great Chicago conservative, became a Nobel laureate. Early on, I defended his permanent-income hypothesis against a critical review by Hendrick Houthakker, by using analysis of variance and covariance, which I had picked up in the summer before I went back to graduate school, and that came out very neatly.[14] But essentially I have done – I guess people would consider it – low-level econometrics.

My early work in applied econometrics was on the investment function. I have done some theoretical work on growth and unemployment. An article published in *The Economic Journal*, which I think had some influence, called "Growth Models and the Neoclassical Resurgence," was actually something of a critique of the work by Solow and Tobin, with whom I am usually in agreement.[15] In this case, however, I insisted that their criticism of the Harrod–Domar model was sort of avoiding the essential Keynesian assumption in it. That was my theoretical work, but then I got into empirical work to a large extent.

I worked out the distributed-lag investment function in econometrics, in which I picked up the work of L.M. Koyck on distributed lags, and developed what I thought was a Keynesian application, if you wish.[16] I had investment depending very largely on the accelerator, and found that if you gave time for changes in sales to affect investment, they did, partly because there were lags in the production process, and partly because there were lags in the development of expectations. That paper, I think, had substantial influence, and got me into a series of empirical papers on investment.[17]

Berglund

When did you start this work on investment functions?

Eisner

I think it must have begun in the late 1950s. I got access to the McGraw-Hill economic surveys. McGraw-Hill had a survey of the anticipations of business capital spending. I worked out an arrangement with them. They had to have the answers to these surveys confidential, but I worked with a person who collected them and put them together with accounting data from *Moody's Industrial Manual*. I developed a huge series, which I had on cards and then on tapes – I was an early user of computers, giant computers at that time.

So, I got into a series of papers, empirical papers on investment, that led me to collaboration with my old, good friend and late colleague and President of Northwestern University, Bob Strotz, in a monograph for the Commission on Money and Credit on the determinants of business investment. The theory was largely his – the rationale for the distributed lag in terms of the greater cost of more rapid adjustment.[18] That paper had a very considerable influence on the profession and was widely quoted; it is still widely cited.

The next major part of my work, which was not particularly econometric, was on the expanded accounts for national income and product. A lot of this work I labeled *The Total Incomes System of Accounts* – I had a book by that name.[19] I became persuaded that while the income and product accounts were great, they were limited. They didn't account for a lot of non-market activity; they didn't account for capital gains; and they didn't account for a lot of income you might get from the perquisites of being an executive of a company, whether it was a country club or a three-martini lunch. So I had the notion of developing what I called first, I think, "non-income income." Then I called it *The Total Income System of Accounts*.

Throughout my career I have had a series of grants. Initially, I had one from the Social Science Research Council – when I was a young assistant professor – that freed me from half my teaching, and paid for summers. I had a three-year grant that furthered my research. Then through the National Science Foundation, which also supported this work on *The Total Income System of Accounts* – I had a bunch of graduate students working with me. We did what I considered illustrative: We set up some accounts from 1946 to 1981, and that research was reported in a book and also in an article, a big survey article in *The Journal of Economic Literature*, which surveyed my own work and that of others. The book finally came out in 1989, but I had a number of earlier articles based on this work, bringing out parts of it.[20]

The next major part of my work was on budget deficits. You could see the Keynesian motivation here, I suppose, related in considerable part to my objection to the Lucas rejection, the Lucas–Sargent rejection of the Keynesian model, which said "you know, you've had stimulative policy, and look, all it gave you was stagflation."[21] And I said "you didn't have stimulative policy, because you aren't measuring the deficit correctly." With a young collaborator, who was a graduate student here at Northwestern, Paul Pieper, I wrote the first major article, called "A New View of the Budget Deficit," in which we adjusted the deficit for inflation. The article was published in *The American Economic Review.*[22]

As I suggested, it counted an inflation tax as a reduction of the real value of the outstanding debt. You could also do that by using a real interest rate instead of a nominal interest rate when calculating interest payment outlays. Also, I did a cyclical adjustment, and found that with these adjustments, this correctly measured deficit was related in a very significant way to what happened to unemployment and real GDP. Bigger deficits were associated with greater subsequent growth in real GDP, and with a lesser increase in, or a reduction of, unemployment. That was controversial, and I got a number of critical comments, which I suppose only increased the visibility of the article. So I think a lot of that has gotten into the profession, and I know that the Council of Economic Advisers and others all now recognize the importance of making this inflation adjustment. Indeed you see the inflation adjustment in some of the tables put out by the Congressional Budget Office.

I continued working on budget deficits. A paper I just did for a conference in France on time-series and cross-sectional analysis is in a way a reprise:[23] I found that, again, these inflation-adjusted, cyclically adjusted deficits were associated, for some 16 countries in pooled time-series and cross-sections, with greater subsequent growth in real GDP, and lesser increase or reductions in unemployment. I think this is something that should be taken into account by the countries in Europe.

Again, I don't claim that any of my econometric findings are the end of the world. I keep saying I would not really bet my life or the economy on anybody's econometric estimates, including my own. But I am confident of the fact that they do seem to fit the relevant theory and produce results which I think are correct. So I have kept pursuing the work on budget deficits, and I have also pursued it a good bit in popular writings.

I do write regularly for *The Los Angeles Times*, which is one of the major newspapers in this country, and for *The Wall Street Journal*. The *Wall Street Journal* publishes me although they have a very conservative editorial page, and I am hardly known as a conservative. But the editor, Robert Bartley, who is very conservative, a bright, able man, does share my view that budget deficits are no calamity.[24] He is quoting me on that, and he is sympathetic to a lot of what I write, which is not always on budget deficits. But I keep coming back to that topic for them and for others.

Most recently, I have been completing a Twentieth Century Fund pamphlet shortly to come out, called *The Great Deficit Scares*, in which I try to denounce the mythology and the misunderstanding on budget deficits, trade deficits and our presumed forthcoming deficit in our social security trust funds.[25]

But I have also been attacking the NAIRU, which is an acronym for the so-called "Non-Accelerating Inflation Rate of Unemployment." The concept there, which I should explain to the laymen or those who don't know, is that the economy has some rate of unemployment at which inflation will remain constant. If unemployment is above that, for one reason or another, not always very well explained, inflation will come down, and keep coming down, as long as unemployment is above that magical rate. But if unemployment is below that rate, inflation will keep rising. However, it is not just as in the old Phillips Curve argument that at lower unemployment you would have higher inflation, and at higher unemployment you would have lower inflation, and therefore a tradeoff.

The idea of the NAIRU, which is supported by the Classical economists, is that there is no tradeoff. At best you can get a temporary reduction of unemployment if somehow you would do something which would then be accompanied by higher inflation. But that's temporary, and as soon as expectations adjust, you would be back with the same level of unemployment, this so-called NAIRU – which is also called the "natural rate of unemployment" – with the higher rate of inflation that you have achieved. So any effort to keep unemployment below this so-called NAIRU means that inflation will keep getting higher and higher and higher – 2, 4, 8, 100, 500 percent – and that, obviously, is impossible. So the conclusion is that you have to leave the economy alone, and let it settle at the "natural rate."

In fact that idea, and that name, goes back largely to Milton Friedman, in his [American Economic Association] presidential address of 1968, and also to Ned Phelps at Columbia University, who simultaneously advanced the same concept. Unfortunately that dogma of the NAIRU has largely dominated thinking in this country.[26]

I quip that the NAIRU brings out the difference between conservatives and liberals of this country. For example, conservative economist Martin Feldstein, the President of the National Bureau of Economic Research, and chairman of the Council of Economic Advisers under President Reagan, has argued that the NAIRU or "natural rate" is $6\frac{1}{2}$ or 7 percent, while liberals have argued that it is maybe 6 percent, or slightly less. My colleague Robert Gordon enshrined in his textbook and in many of his writings over the years the idea that the "natural rate" was 6 percent. And that meant that both liberals and conservatives conclude that there is nothing that economic policy can do about high unemployment. You can't reduce unemployment below that NAIRU without disaster.

But there is even a worse corollary: that if somehow unemployment got below that by itself, you had better drive it up again, by slowing the economy, tightening money. Otherwise, you would have accelerating inflation. Also, once it accelerated, it would take quite some efforts to get it to stop accelerating, let alone to get it down again. To get it down again, you would have to have serious unemployment later, unemployment above the NAIRU. So, indeed, people like Friedman would say, "You know, you have no policy choice about high or low unemployment: it's just whether you want unemployment now or later."

That is a terrible doom-and-gloom view, an argument that conservatives liked: The government should do nothing, and, even worse, it should keep unemployment high. For a long time I felt, I am afraid correctly, that our Federal Reserve was much influenced by that policy, by that view, and indeed, I think the markets, our stock and bond markets, felt it was being operated by that view. As a result, every time the news was good, that the economy had grown more rapidly, or that unemployment had gone down, the stock market would dive.

People would wonder, "Why is it that the stock market goes down when the economic news is good?" I think they failed to see that the stock market was reacting, not to the good news in itself, but to how they felt that the Federal Reserve would react. If they felt that the Federal Reserve would interpret the good news as reason to raise interest rates, then anytime good news came out, a large number of investors felt that interest rates should go up. Therefore investors started to sell their bonds, which did drive interest rates up, and to sell their stock, which drove the stock down.

I am much encouraged, because just yesterday, again, the Federal Reserve refused to raise interest rates even though unemployment was 4.8 percent for the month of May, and the June report, which came out today, was expected to be about the same.[27] That would mean that unemployment has been below this 6 percent NAIRU for almost three years. As everybody knows, the US economy has been doing quite well. We grew at 4 percent the last year, which, again, is above the $2\frac{1}{2}$–3 percent which would be consistent with no reduction in unemployment – $2\frac{1}{2}$ percent, I guess, would be consistent with that.

So, I have been insisting that that NAIRU is a terrible bit of dogma, bad economic theory, and in my econometric work, I have been arguing in a number of papers that it is not supported by the data, despite the fact that there have been many, many studies which show it supported.

The reason why these studies seem to show support for the NAIRU is that they estimate a relationship between inflation and unemployment and past inflation, and this relationship seems to show that past inflation gets embodied into the expectations of future inflation, and that lower unemployment does raise inflation. One can immediately solve the estimated equations for a result which gives you a NAIRU, and the implication that lower unemployment will cause inflation to keep accelerating.

What I did in my econometric work was to try a different model, in which I separate quarters of high unemployment and quarters of low unemployment, and I found that while high unemployment does appear to be associated with lower inflation, low unemployment is not associated with higher inflation. I have a number of after-the-facts theories that I can advance for that, but those do seem to be the facts.

In fact, when I then try to estimate, not the old-fashioned Phillips Curve, but a cubic Phillips Curve, which has two points of inflection, or turning points if you wish, I find that at very low unemployment, if you lower unemployment further, inflation goes up, and very rapidly. You raise unemployment, and inflation begins not to go up. But then, there is a turning point, at about 5 percent unemployment, or $4\frac{1}{2}$ percent, and as unemployment goes up beyond that, the Phillips curve turns up, to come down again at considerably higher rates of unemployment.

Berglund

Your work on Phillips Curves suggests a skeptical approach. Does that reflect a general philosophy of yours?

Eisner

Frequently I have found it easy to criticize others, and take on something, particularly if it is by a well-known economist, who may be influential. It may be useful to subject it to a critical analysis, and I have found that to be fruitful. In terms of economic policy, it is frequently fruitful to criticize the policies being followed. I have not ever really been in a policy-making position – I have never been in the government, except as a lower level functionary and then I had no influence on policy.

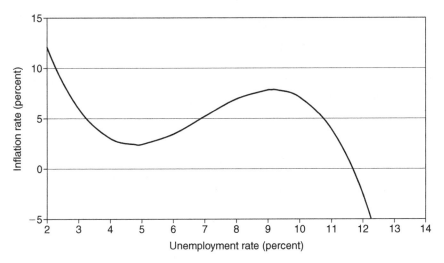

Figure 14.1 Cubic Phillips Curve based on data from Eisner (1997b).

I was an economic adviser to George McGovern back in 1972. I knew him fairly well, but he never became President, so I never got into the government then. I have frequently testified before congressional committees, and I have offered my advice to friends and people in the Council of Economic Advisers and the Federal Reserve. How much they listen is another question. I have been more of an outsider, and in that sense free to criticize.

Berglund

Let us switch gears a little. What would you consider to be the biggest economic problem of today?

Eisner

In much of the world, and certainly in Western Europe, I think the chief economic problem at the moment is unemployment and the lack of full utilization of capacity – and therefore also inadequate economic growth. A secondary problem, well maybe a major one there and a major one here as well, is the distribution of income, which seems to be getting, if anything, more unequal – the rich getting much richer, the poor getting poorer, and the middle class getting nowhere. So, those are serious problems.

On the other hand, I think many economies, and certainly the US economy, are doing relatively well. Some of them have to do more of the same, and simply not get frightened away from economic growth by misguided needs for austerity, frightened away from free international trade by misguided protectionism, or even a form of mercantilism, in which you decide you have to have a big export surplus. I think the Japanese are suffering, finally, from having pursued a one-sided policy of promoting exports, rather than investing adequately at home. But there are a lot of relative success stories in the world, the US in part, at the moment. China, which I have been to a few times, has had a remarkable growth, and even a tremendous growth; in Hong Kong, now a part of China, the growth may be, if anything, accelerating.

Berglund

So the main economic problems basically remain the same as those pinpointed by Keynes, namely unemployment and an inequitable distribution of income. What remedies, if any, are there to these social ills?

Eisner

There are two means that I would use dealing with them. One is the old Keynesian approach, making sure you have adequate aggregate demand,

and that, unfortunately, is a policy that is not being followed in Europe in particular. You must make sure that there is adequate aggregate demand. I think that a considerable part of the Western European unemployment problem is due to not applying Keynesian policies.

But the other part does involve investment in human capital. A lot of workers find themselves unemployable, partly because of a kind of hysteresis. Once they have not been employed for quite a while, they no longer have skills, they no longer have habits of work, and they even no longer have the motivation to seek work. Government programs, which have been developed to support the unemployed, may be a contributing factor: they may have sometimes been set up in such a way that it doesn't pay for the jobless to go to work. In other words, the added income you can get from working is not sufficiently greater, if greater at all, to warrant working.

On the one hand, you have to correct the policies of austerity, by adequate aggregate demand stimulus; on the other, you have to remove the structural impediments to employment, and they range from high labor costs, imposed by excessive taxes on labor, to measures which sometimes makes it difficult to fire people, discouraging companies from hiring them to begin with.

You have to have measures, then, to make sure that people are trained and mobile, and able to find jobs for which they are qualified. So, you need a considerable investment in human capital at all levels, particularly in people with relatively low income and in the jobless, and that has to begin at a very early age. You have to have early, adequate care of infants, even before they are born, and proper healthcare for children. Ideally you should have two-parent families, and you should have parents who know how to parent, who are themselves educated. We should have good preschools and nursery schools. Those things will take time to have all of their curative effects, but in the long run I am certain that they will begin to make some difference.

You do have to recognize that employment, in a modern society, is absolutely critical. I think I have written that without a job, a person is nothing, he – or she – is really essentially "out of it." People are destroyed socially, psychologically. They are easy targets for crime, either as victims of crime and lured into criminal activity. They are not really part of society. I mean, a modern industrial society, a market economy, with exchange, division of labor, means ideally, no necessarily, that people have to have jobs. They also, really, should be part of families, either forming them or being members of them. Those are critical problems for the success of society. Actually, more employment, more jobs means higher GDP, but the jobs are important in themselves, for the functioning of individuals.

I believe that we should have a fiscal policy in which we would keep as an aim, as a rule of thumb, to keep the debt-to-GDP ratio constant, and to use the deficit to finance public investment in human capital as well as infrastructure.[28] And I believe that we should have a monetary policy that makes credit freely available, that does not have what I would consider to be artificial restraints to hold back credit.

I believe in competition, in removing unnecessary regulations, which interfere with the free operations of markets, although I would recognize that many regulations might prove necessary, and these I would keep. I try to distinguish externalities, negative and positive, which may require government intervention, but these should preferably be done by taxes and subsidies, rather than by regulation.

Berglund

You identify aggregate demand as one cause of unemployment. How can one go about stimulating it?

Eisner

Through the use of both fiscal and monetary policy. The fiscal policy, I suggest, would involve maintaining a substantial, or whatever works out to be appropriate, debt-to-GDP ratio. That debt is an asset of the public. It is normally largely an internally held debt, and that gives people enough wealth to fall back on, so that they feel free to consume enough. That ratio should be allowed to fluctuate with the business cycle, going up when the economy is slow – that gives you more stimulus – and perhaps going down when the economy is very vigorous. That would be the fiscal policy.

In terms of the counter-cyclical fiscal policy, that has its limitations. I think there is something to the permanent-income theory of consumption, and to the companion life-cycle theories of Modigliani, in that people are influenced, not just by their current income, but also by expected future income and by their assets.[29] If, for example, there is a recession, if you merely cut taxes for a while, you may not have that huge an effect. It may be helpful, but not that great, if you cut income taxes.

You might, as a counter-cyclical tool, want to make use of things that will give you an intertemporal substitution, for example, a credit to businesses or individuals who are buying machinery or durable goods now, with the understanding that if they buy them later, they may not get that credit. In that way people have an incentive to spend, and businesses will have incentives to invest when the economy needs a boost.

Now, further than that, the government itself can contribute directly to jobs and GDP and spending, by actual expenditures for goods and services, rather than just transfer payments or cutting taxes, and that can be effective as a counter-cyclical tool. It can be effective over the long run in terms of keeping employment up, and it can be effective as a tool of public investment. I think one of the big things, we have to acknowledge, that kept us from anything like the Great Depression during the post-war period, was the Cold War, and the huge spending on the military by the United States, in particular, and other countries.

I think that was a terrible way of keeping employment up, but it undoubtedly did. There were a lot of government jobs created, within defense-related industries, and the people who had these jobs, in turn, spent money. That kept the economy going. We have to recognize that, and substitute for defense spending. As defense spending comes down, and I think it should come down more rapidly, we should increase the far more useful spending for education, for infrastructure, for all the things that will make us prosperous.

Berglund

The Swedish economy is suffering from massive unemployment. Would you have any advice about how to reduce it?

Eisner

I don't really know the Swedish economy, and I shouldn't be presumptuous. But in terms of general principles, I would say that it is very unfortunate, if not disastrous, if you have unemployment over 10 percent and the deficits are already down to 3 percent of GDP or below, to be trying to reduce the deficit. If anything, I would suggest that maybe the deficit should go up some again. So that, I think, is clearly the wrong policy.

There may as well be other causes to the high unemployment, related to things that I have been concerned about, where you have perverse incentives, incentives to make use of benefits rather than work, where you have other things that restrict employment. I would think from the little I know about the Swedish educational system, the society is such that the human capital is at a high state, but there may be problems there.

From the macroeconomic standpoint, with 10 percent unemployment you have no business trying to reduce the budget deficit, because aggregate demand is inadequate. Whatever public spending is undertaken will be more beneficial to demand if it is financed by deficit than financed by taxes. And if you try to reduce the deficit by reducing welfare spending, for example, social spending or insurance spending, then that also reduces aggregate demand.

To the extent that some of that spending encourages people not to work, that is another issue to be faced, and maybe that spending should be restructured and channeled in another way. So, to keep up the aggregate demand, you should not discourage people from working by saying that "Well, you can get $200 a week by not working and you'll get only $250 if you work." People therefore may rationally decide not to work.

In the United States, they may even get less, in fact, the way our system has worked until now. In many situations, through the combination of what we have called welfare benefits – grants to dependent children, low-income housing, medical benefits – people going to work have faced an effective tax of over 100 percent. They simply are worse off when they work than when they don't work. So you can hardly blame them for not trying very hard to find work, particularly because these people are not going to move from their very poor welfare benefits to a very high-paying job. The alternative is a low-paying job, which it may not pay to take.

Berglund

The emergence of the NAIRU doctrine and the changing view on budget deficits happened along with a general change of politics in a more conservative direction. Could you reflect a little on the relationship between political sentiments on the one hand and economic research on the other? Do the economists follow the political trends?

Eisner

Yes, I think there is a lot to that. I think economists tend to be behind the times. They are influenced by the realities of people's perceptions outside the economy, and of political forces. Keynesian ideas might never have taken in the profession, as well as elsewhere, if there hadn't been a great depression which made people feel that unemployment was terribly serious, and the Classical economists simply were offering them no sense of an answer.

When unemployment got much lower, people weren't as concerned about it. When they had bouts of inflation, they were concerned about that, and some groups do suffer from inflation. As opposed to unemployment, if you are retired, you are not looking for a job anyway, and inflation may be very costly to you. If you are a banker, and you have lent money out, if inflation goes up, interest rates go up, and on the money you have lent out at a low interest rate you will lose badly.

So there are important causes that can develop at different times, depending on the economic situation, to favor one set of policies or another. The Keynesian counter-revolution undoubtedly gathered weight because the problems that Keynesian economics was addressing didn't seem so severe in the 1970s. On the other hand, that may suggest a reason why Keynesian economics will come back. In Europe, with unemployment in double digits, over 10 percent, people are very much concerned about that – and more likely to listen to Keynesian prescriptions that would address themselves to the problem of unemployment.

In the United States, this of course relates to political parties. The Republicans, the conservatives, seem to be generally opposed to government action, and that makes them unsympathetic to Keynesian economics. There seems to be a failure to understand, by many conservatives, that

Keynes did not necessarily believe in, and was not advocating, much government action other than maintaining aggregate demand. He was not saying that government should be setting prices and regulating, doing this and that. It is perfectly consistent to be a free-market man, believing in free and open competition and as free a trade as you can get, and also be Keynesian in your macroeconomic policies.

But there tended to be a rejection of both. Rather ironically though, as many of us have pointed out, under Ronald Reagan, the great conservative Republican, we had probably a greater implementation of Keynesian policies than we have ever had, except during the great war, World War II. Reagan didn't call his approach Keynesian, he called it "supply-side economics," but he had, beginning effectively in 1982 or so, a great reduction in taxes, and a great increase in government expenditure for the military. That created big budget deficits, which did bring the economy out of the great, very severe recession we had in 1982–1983.

So, again, how much of the military buildup, and the cut in taxes, was induced by the fact that we had high unemployment is a good question. The one supports the other. But I do believe that economic circumstances, and therefore the mood of the people, will affect economic policy, and indeed affect economic theory. They will affect the kind of problems in economics that people address. I think there are probably many more people working now on questions of welfare economics, of health economics, of the distribution of income, because these problems are perceived by the public as pressing.

So, economics is much influenced by the prevailing ideas and affected by the times. Keynes wrote near the end of *The General Theory* that – I don't have the exact words in mind, but you can check them – that "Policymakers are influenced by the long-ago ideas of some defunct economist."[30] But economists are influenced by the economic events that have occurred in the past, which finally come up to them.

Berglund

Speaking of Keynes' aphorisms, I have one that has stuck on my mind. It says, "Look after employment, and the budget will look after itself." Is there any truth in that?

Eisner

That is largely true. In this country – it is almost astonishing – there is this huge battle, which I think is very misguided, to reduce the deficit, and to balance the budget. It is very likely that we will have a balanced budget soon; the budget is very close to balance. But it is so in considerable part because the economy is growing so well, and unemployment has gotten relatively low.

In fact, just a few months ago, our Congressional Budget Office suddenly discovered that the budget deficit was going to be about $50 billion less for this year than they had forecast. Current forecasts for this year – that we are already in the middle of – are now down to $70 billion and below, which is less than 1 percent of GDP. If the growth continues, the deficit is very likely to disappear, at least for a while.[31]

Berglund

A lot of your recent work addresses the deficit concept. Could you explain in a non-technical way the major problems with the currently used concept?

Eisner

There are several major things wrong. One very major thing wrong is that our budget does not account for the inflation tax. The impact of the deficit on the economy should be thought of in two ways: First, in terms of a flow, which means that if there is a budget deficit, the government is giving people more than what is being taken away from them. That enables people to spend more without borrowing; it increases measured incomes.

Now, to the extent that that income consists of interest payments, which are raised by inflation, if people get 8 percent interest when there is 5 percent inflation, the real interest rate is 3 percent. Unless they are guilty of what we call "money illusion," people have to recognize that those interest payments in considerable part are simply enabling them to add to their savings and bonds and money such that the wealth they have does not actually go down in real value.

Another way of looking at it is to say that the deficit adds to the real wealth of the public, in the form of government securities and of money. But suppose prices are rising. If we have a deficit of $100 billion, and people are holding $4 trillion in government debt, that $100 billion adds to their fortunes, and gives them $4.1 trillion. That means that they are wealthier and should spend more. But suppose, over the year, you have had an inflation rate of 5 percent. Well, that means that the $4 trillion is really worth 5 percent less, it is worth $200 billion less.

On the one hand, the $4 trillion you have is worth $200 billion less; on the other you do have $100 billion more in government bonds, because of the deficit – the deficit adds to the debt. But, on balance, you are $100 billion worse off. So, if we do not make that adjustment, we think people are getting wealthier and would spend more, when – unless they are fools who do not see what is happening to them, and that is a bad assumption to make – they are really worse off.

You have to make that inflation adjustment, and I found that that actually works, in my econometric analyses of the impact of the deficit on growth and employment. You get a better fit of the estimated equations when adjusting the deficit for inflation; it seems that the inflation tax does in fact affect the economy.

The second adjustment that has to be made, to understand the impact of the deficit on the economy, involves recognizing that the economy has a big effect on the deficit. You may have a big deficit, not because the government is stimulating the economy in any way, but because we have low employment, low income and production. That means that all the deficit is doing is counteracting, to some extent, the already bad situation, the slow economy you have.

But if you want to measure the impact of the deficit on the economy, you have to say, "Well, what would the deficit be, and how is it changing, for a given state of the economy?"

Herb Stein, who is now 80-years-old, and who had a fine article today in the *Wall Street Journal*, where he keeps writing regularly, was the main developer of the idea of a high-employment budget, in which you recognize that the budget deficit will depend upon the state of the economy as much, if not more, than the state of the economy depends upon the budget. One way to measure the impact of the budget on the economy is to have a full-employment, or high-employment budget.[32] Stein formulated that concept, which went on to have considerable, deserved influence and usefulness. In those days, Stein was at the Committee for Economic Development, which was a rather surprisingly liberal business-sponsored group in Washington.

It is very important to make this cyclical adjustment, or adjustment to a fixed-employment, standardized or high-employment budget. The Congressional Budget Office calls it a standardized budget deficit. I think it can be called "high" or "full." But it doesn't matter what you call it – you have to make that adjustment. So that is the second thing that is wrong with the conventional look at the deficit.

In fact, without such an adjustment, we would have rather ridiculous policies. You could say, "Well, if the deficit goes up, we have to raise taxes or cut government spending," which is exactly the wrong thing to do. If the deficit goes up, you should probably cut taxes and raise spending. On the other hand, if the deficit goes down, then the argument may be made, that "Well, that means that we are able to cut taxes and raise government spending," which – if you are really at full employment – is not necessarily the thing to do.

So there are two big things wrong with the conventional measure: We don't make an inflation adjustment, and we don't look for the cyclical adjustment to get at the structural deficit.

A third thing wrong is that we don't distinguish between different forms of outlays. It makes a difference whether you have interest payments or transfer payments, both of which are not likely to be as stimulative to the economy as government expenditures for goods and services. That distinction has to be made. Indeed, in a paper I just presented in Paris,[33] I did find that, independently of the amount of the deficit, government expenditures for goods and services had the predicted impact on the economy: The greater their proportion of GDP, the more GDP will tend to go up, and unemployment to go down. And with a lesser proportion of government purchases, GDP will tend to rise less rapidly and unemployment, perhaps, to go up. That is the third adjustment.

The fourth thing that should be done, is that we should have – and this is very important – a separate capital budget. We should distinguish between government expenditures for current use, current outlays, current consumption, and expenditures of an investment nature. The expenditures of an investment nature will help future growth and productivity. Also, expenditures of an investment nature you would probably, in principle, want to finance by borrowing, because then the services of this future capital will be paid for by the taxpayers, through their servicing of this debt, in the future.

If you require that investment spending be financed out of current taxes, you may not get enough government investment. You probably won't get enough public investment, because the current taxpayer hardly wants to pay a huge amount of money for benefits to be enjoyed in the future. Indeed, that would be the same even for private investment, or household investment. If everybody who bought a house in this country had to finance it out of current income, then most houses wouldn't be bought until people were getting close to retirement, or certainly until their children were grown, and they would hardly need them anymore.

So it is important that investment is financed, I would say, by borrowing. And it is important, then, that you separate out public investment from public consumption. We don't do that in our Unified Budget, and the budget of the Congress that the legislators consider. We have just begun to do that in the National Income and Product Accounts of the Bureau of Economic Analysis, although that still does not separate out investment in human capital. But that is, of course, a recommended procedure in the United Nations' *System of National Accounts*, and it is therefore done in many European countries. So we should make that distinction, separating public investment from consumption. Those four corrections would go a long way.

I should say when I was at the Little Rock economic conference, which was held by President-elect Clinton in 1992, I was delighted when I shook his hand at the cocktail party reception. He had met me once before, but I reintroduced myself, and he said "Oh, I'm glad you're here, I wanted you here. I have read your stuff on budget deficits and I agree with it even if nobody else does." I went around, overjoyed, telling everybody this. Of course, subsequently, he also agreed with Robert Rubin and others on reducing deficits, so I am not really sure how long this agreement really lasted.

However, then, I wasn't on the program. I mean, I was one of about 200 people invited, only about 100 of whom were being seated around the big table to make a few remarks. I was quite upset by this. I told my wife, and she said, "Do something!" So, I went up to Clinton at the first break, and I said, "You know, you ought to have me on the program, to defend you against these deficit hawks," and he said, "I will do what I can." To my astonishment, I ran into him later in the day at the cocktail reception, and he said "Bob," as if he knew me, "I think I have got you on the program." So, sure enough, the next morning Ron Brown was asked to vacate his place for me! Then Clinton gave me an introduction. He said that I was "the world's greatest expert," which is quite untrue, "on capital budgeting," and he had me talk some on that.

So, he was very much interested in that, and I know that he still is dedicated to the idea of trying to have a separate capital budget. Now, there are a lot of people opposed to that in this country, particularly deficit hawks who think it will be an excuse for more government spending. They think it will make the deficit look lower, and therefore be an excuse, again, for an easier fiscal policy.

In fact, sadly, our public investment, if you exclude investment in human capital, is so low that when you make the correction and, as you should from an accounting standpoint, include capital depreciation on the existing capital stock as a charge in the current budget, you find that making the adjustment for capital investment doesn't make much difference. The current budget would still look about the same, because the depreciation of past investment is about as big as the current investment. That's because the current investment isn't that great. But still, over the long run, I hope capital investment will be higher. And that adjustment is certainly very important if you include investment in human capital, which we should.

So, there are four corrections in the measurement I have advocated: the inflation tax; the cyclical adjustment; distinguishing between interest payments, transfer payments and government expenditures for goods and services; and a separate capital budget. And if we made those adjustments, I think they would lead clearly to much better policies. Policy would not be biased in favor of austerity, or biased in favor of current consumption at the expense of investment in the future.

Berglund

The fact that the capital budget idea has not made much headway so far, do you think that reflects a political change on the part of Clinton? And how has the general political environment, as it were, developed since then?

Eisner

Well, that was 1992, and I guess I must have gotten to some people who were handing him my articles. I tried to be very active in the 1992 campaign, in terms of writing papers and sending articles, newspaper articles, to people I knew working in the campaign, and they probably gave some of them to him. And he, I have to say, is a tremendously intelligent and well-informed man. He is really remarkable; he made a remarkable impression on me, and all of us at the Little Rock conference. Anybody, even right-wing conservatives, who saw him in action, would know he is tremendously intelligent and tremendously well informed, on economic matters and on other matters.

Now, he also is a very political person. In Arkansas, he was used to working in a very conservative state, and whatever his liberal views – and I think he is essentially liberal in the American sense of being in favor of helping the poor and having the government to do things to help the economy – he feels that he has to follow policies that he can get through Congress, with the support of the American public, so that he won't run into a blank wall and get thrown out of office. I tend to defend him against my liberal friends, who say he is a sellout, that he doesn't really have any views. I think he has views, and that he tries to be realistic. He may sometimes give up too soon in the fights I think he should undertake.

So, well, there is a political change. You know, we had the very shocking, to many of us, results of the 1994 election, which were probably due to the fact that a lot of people didn't go out and vote. There wasn't such a shift in voting among those who did vote. Unfortunately, we always have a very low voter turnout; we have an even lower voter turnout in off-year elections, between the presidential elections.

So, the Republicans won decisively. Moreover, a lot of the Republicans who won were, I have to say, not sensible, moderate Republicans, but a lot of know-nothing people who really did know nothing, with ideas that were almost anarchistic. They believe that all government is terrible, and they just want to abolish government willy-nilly. That, of course, caused some reaction when the public saw what was happening. People got quite upset by that, and Clinton acted on that wisely. Partly because of that, he was able to win his own re-election. He unfortunately didn't quite carry it to the point of winning back the Congress, and the Democrats even lost seats in the Senate.

Now, where is the political pendulum moving? It is a tough struggle. I think the public is really clearly ready for policies that I would approve of, and that Clinton would like. The public does believe in education and investment in human capital; the public does want a more equal distribution of income; and the public is certainly committed to trying to keep unemployment low. Now, to what extent these policies can get through is always questionable, because there are very powerful forces on the other side. The public is not consistently well informed; it doesn't quite know how to pursue things, is easily misled.

The political process is such that the conservatives in this country, in my view, have a tremendous advantage. They are generally much richer people, and they contribute much more money to the Republican Party and to conservatives generally. It is ironic that there is all this fuss in the United States about Democratic fundraising and how the Democrats have somehow cheated, or even violated the law, in raising funds. Republicans have raised far more money than the Democrats, and that has a big impact.

It has an impact even in intellectual, professional discourse. Wealthy Republicans have poured vast sums of money into right-wing "think-tanks." The Heritage Institute, the Cato Institute, the American Enterprise Institute – there are a lot of them – and some are very right-wing, some more moderate. These right-wing institutes have lots of money. They have staff that rewrite articles and put things out in the press. I write all my articles for *The Wall Street Journal* and *The Los Angeles Times*. I write them myself. My wife, who used to be an English teacher, may look them over and help with the English, but I don't have a professional, editorial writer editing them and sending out copies to all the newspapers.

I was just on a radio program yesterday, being interviewed about a proposal, a pamphlet, put out by two people at the Cato Institute, one of the right-wing think-tanks. They are advocating replacing the income tax in this country with a 15 percent national sales tax, which I think is an outrageous proposal. It would tremendously tilt the tax system (which is favorable to the rich already, and not sufficiently helpful to the poor) against the poor and middle-income people, and toward the rich. But they have the money to have a couple of people to write this thing and put it out, and then they get themselves interviewed; the author was interviewed along with me on the radio program.

Berglund

What do you have against sales taxes?

Eisner

The income tax is much maligned. It is sort of painful to people. In the United States it has become a tax full of loopholes and complications. So the wealthier people, who have a lot of loopholes they are trying to use, and a lot of deductions that have become very complicated, have to hire tax accountants to prepare their tax returns. With that understanding, the income tax in the United States is really quite successful, as I think it must be in some other countries. It is, as far as I can make out, the most successful tax in terms of efficiency of collection and of being able to collect the money you need to finance government. It also is a tax that, if properly done, can be done with equity, in which you can, to a considerable extent, tax people in accordance with ability to pay, make those people who are getting the most out of the system pay the most for the government services they are getting.

So I am a defender of the income tax. I have written a big article, actually in a volume published by The American Enterprise Institute, this conservative outfit, on the so-called "flat tax," which I criticized.[34] But the point that I acknowledge is that the income tax is in many ways terrible. As Churchill said about democracy, "It is a terrible system, but there is nothing better." The flat tax, as proposed, is not better – it is worse. The income tax could be improved. It could actually be made flatter and still more progressive – flatter in the sense that I don't believe the rates should be tremendously high for upper-income people. They should be considerably higher than for lower-income people, but still adequate to leave incentives to work and earn in your own country. If you make the tax base comprehensive, the tax rates don't have to be that high at any level. So I would defend the income tax.

The problem with the sales tax – and with value-added taxes to a very considerable extent as well – is that you could not easily, if at all, make them progressive. And in fact, in most cases, they tend to be quite regressive. Take the flat sales tax that was just proposed by the American Enterprise Institute, of 15 percent; it's still regressive even with a credit against payroll taxes of some $18,000 that was proposed, to match the consumption of a family at the poverty level. The 15 percent means that the percentage of income taxed would never be more than 15 percent. Under the income tax in this country for those making over $200,000, by my estimates, they're having more than 30 percent of their income taxed – nowhere near that marginal rate of close to 40 percent or even more, because it is a marginal rate, and there are many deductions. But that means that the rich will be much better off with a 15 percent flat tax, and that means somebody else – and that will be the poor and the middle-income groups – will be worse off.

The other thing about the sales tax is that, since it is a tax on sales, it is even more regressive than you would think, because the wealthier people don't consume as large a proportion of their income. They certainly don't consume as large a proportion on domestic goods. So, you will find that the very wealthy will consume a much smaller proportion of their income on articles subject to the sales tax. Bill Gates, who is reportedly worth $40 billion, I am sure, spends a very small proportion of his income. He spends much more than I do on consumption, or than you do. But it will still be a very tiny proportion of his income spent on consumption, and therefore, this sales tax would hardly bother him a bit.

Berglund

In Europe, governments rely heavily on the value-added tax and also on payroll taxes for fiscal revenue. Do you have any reflections on that?

Eisner

Again, I would hate to seem unduly presumptuous, since I don't know the details in most of these, if any of these, countries. In general, I would avoid the value-added taxes, because they are largely like sales taxes in terms of their incidence. There is a further objection to them that I have, and to sales taxing, and that is they make prices higher. Particularly as you impose them, they raise prices and cause inflation. That, presumably, will be adjusted for – the higher prices – by your exchange rate, but then it causes all kinds of distortions, in terms of products that are subject to the tax and products that are not, products on export. So one of my objections is that the relative prices get distorted.

My other objections to the value-added tax are the same as I suggested, in terms of equity and distribution of income, to the sales tax. When the value-added tax is applied in Europe, you may frequently be exempting certain items, or giving lower rates to certain items, like food, which you think should be excluded. This has been done with state sales taxes in the US. But that introduces, again, further distortions. Economists would agree that you should try to let prices seek levels which mirror their costs of production, and if you want to change the distribution of income, don't fiddle with it by changing prices, but rather by changing income directly.

An additional problem concerns administration, I would think. If you have a charge for food in a restaurant, and not for the food in a store – what if you go to a store that gives you the bread and meat and it says, "Make your own sandwich!" What if it even makes the sandwich for you? Or what if you buy an apple from somebody in the street? You get all kinds of distortions and evasions. So, I don't like the value-added tax, and I don't like the sales tax.

I also don't like our payroll taxes. In Europe, I gather, they are frequently terribly high. They are taxes on labor, and I don't want to discourage the employment of labor or the investment in human capital. It is ironic that people keep objecting to so-called taxes on capital, many of which are not taxes on capital, like the corporate income tax, which is a tax on corporate business, not on investment in capital. But while they object to that, they don't object to the taxes on labor and payroll taxes, which are clearly discouraging the employment of labor. If you have an income tax, you tax labor income, but there are other kinds of income to tax as well.

I would generally look for a more comprehensive base, which would tax more income. Indeed in the United States I would like to include the imputed income, if we could do it practically, from owner-occupied housing, as an important form of income. This income is measured in my *Total Income System of Accounts*, and we do have an imputation for that in our existing accounts. I would also want to include in the comprehensive base real capital gains – capital gains in excess of inflation – that is a very important source of income to the rich, and that would make a big difference. I object, though, by the way, in the United States just for the moment, to a move by the conservative head of the Ways and Means Committee, [Rep. William] Archer, who is promoting, along with the Republicans an index for capital gains from inflation. As long as unrealized capital gains are not taxed and costs of investment in the form of interest payments are not indexed, indexing capital gains would add new distortions and unjustified benefits to the rich.

Berglund

Some economists have argued that the current, and indeed chronic, European unemployment problem is *caused* by the "welfare state," meaning big government and high taxes. How do you relate to that argument?

Eisner

I think that's a rather confused argument. There probably is some element of truth in it, but there is more non-truth. Countries of Western Europe generally have much more comprehensive social insurance systems for support of retirement, and healthcare. I think that is a good idea. It is helpful to the public, and the public wants it – I wish we had more of that here.

To some extent, that may reduce employment, because if people can get generous benefits in retirement, they feel that they don't have to work as long. But, you know, though I say that every job is essential for a person's dignity, the job is not his entire life, and he is entitled to decide when he has worked long enough. He doesn't have to be like a professor, as I am, who likes his work and just keeps working as long as he has the health to do it.

So, it may be true that generous retirement benefits, perhaps generous unemployment benefits, do tend, to some extent, to reduce employment and encourage unemployment. I notice that France is raising its minimum wage, and I just saw a piece in *The New York Times* that with a higher minimum wage and payroll taxes, it would cost an employer $9.50 an hour to hire a minimum-wage worker. Now, that's almost double what it will cost in the United States, although taking the exchange rates literally is very questionable.

So, you do have a problem, and that problem relates, in part, to the high payroll taxes. As I have already suggested, that is a bad way to finance social insurance, and that will tend to discourage employment to some extent, both in terms of discouraging the employer, and leaving you with a situation where some workers find that it doesn't pay to work, or it doesn't pay to work legally. Many of them work, as they say, "on the side," or, you know, "underground," in ways that are not reported or detected, but that is not necessarily a healthy thing to do, and not an optimal way to proceed. You could have a generous social insurance system, and a system that pays people who might want to work to do so – without forcing them to work.

I am very much against the French moves which, to my dismay, try to force people to work less, to get them to reduce hours, and induce earlier retirements. I think people should be free to work as much and as long as they want. On the other hand, you have to have a tax and benefit system that makes it profitable to work. You may need some tax credits and subsidies to bring people from unemployment benefits into work. So, those corrections would be in order. You should avoid protective policies, which are perverse. I think I have alluded to measures to discourage firing and laying off people, because that makes employers reluctant to hire, although I was told by one French economist just a week or two ago that that problem in France has been exaggerated – there are enough loopholes, so that it is not serious. I can't evaluate how serious a problem it really is.

As to the fact that government is bigger in itself, I think, again, there is a confusion as to what government is bigger. If you simply mean a social insurance system, I don't consider that big government. I mean, in principle, you could have the social insurance system operated by private enterprise, and the government just passing over the funds. So that, to me, is not big government. Indeed, there is confusion in this country. We say government outlays have been going up, when actually the outlays which are going up are for social security, largely retirement benefits, and they are being matched by increased taxes on payrolls, which are credited to social security.

However, there is the question, then, of the role of government in two other respects: the extent to which the government regulates the economy and interferes in it, and the extent to which there is government operation, actually "socialism" in the old-fashioned sense of government ownership and operation of the means of production – I think that was the Marxian term.

Now, my understanding is that Sweden, for example, which was called by many a socialist state or a socialist economy, does not have a high proportion of the economy operated by government. On the other hand, France has had a high proportion of its economy in government hands, or operated by government, and this, I think, was undertaken, frequently, under conservative regimes, such as the de Gaulle administration, and maintained for many years. Now, whether that is desirable or not, or whether it can be improved, I think, is a pragmatic question: Can you operate a government enterprise in an efficient way in the public interest, or is it better left to private enterprise? Some things might be better left in private hands, and some things that are private might be better done by the government.

I have long believed that insurance is a terribly inefficient thing to be operated privately. Insurance should be centralized, so you have the risk being borne centrally, the administration centralized. I would socialize, if you wish, life insurance, casualty insurance, health insurance in this country. I don't know quite where it stands in Europe. Other things, you know, may not be operated that well – and I will say that I think with the French railroads maybe the workers are being paid too much, and maybe they retire too early. But you compare the French railroads with the American ones! You think you might die in an American passenger train, but when you ride in the TGV, the rapid transit trains in France, and I guess in much of Europe, they are tremendous! I don't know if they would be any better off in private hands.

The public services, take the mail services in France, and the telephone services now, are maybe considerably superior! The mail services certainly compare favorably to what they are in the United States. We have tried to operate the mail services as a government enterprise, independent directly of the government, and our mail service is terrible. The French mail service, which I presume is operated directly by the government, is excellent. I mean incredible! You have mail collection and delivery, I think, several times a day.

So, I think one should not be ideological about this. Socialism as practiced in Eastern Europe has been an awful failure. I have argued that the Russians have now managed to give both socialism and capitalism a bad name. They have made a mess of socialism, and so far, they have been making a terrible mess of capitalism. But, you know, in principle I think there is a lesson: you have to be pragmatic. I was long telling my Russian economist friends, you know: "For God's sake, how can you expect to have little retail shops, automobile repair shops, all these things, operated by the government? It just doesn't work!" You should recognize that some things are clearly effectively left to individual, free enterprise. But there may be some things that government can operate better, and I would approach each one on the issue of "Which can be operated better?" and do it that way. I wouldn't dogmatically say "Government is too big!" In this respect it may be too big, and in other respects it may be too small.

On the regulation matter, which is the other aspect of government, there may well be a tendency for many governments to act too quickly to regulate things. Regulation can be inefficient and ineffective. If there is a need for government intervention, I would always prefer to – when feasible, which is not always the case – handle it by taxes and credits and subsidies. Government regulation is clearly necessary to protect competition, to protect the environment, to try to advance information, and to protect consumers from being victimized by lack of information or misinformation – that even is true for investment. You know, we have to have information for investors in securities markets.

So there is a need for a fair amount of regulation. There may be some need, certainly, to protect the young. I am not against regulations that prohibit or penalize child labor, because I can't always trust parents to look after their children's interests, and society does have an interest in the children, who will be with us for decades to come. So, there are places where government regulation and intervention are necessary. There are many places where it is not, and where the regulation is actually not in public interest, but in the private interest of people who use the government to protect themselves against competition, against others.

Berglund

A major political issue in Europe at this time, of course, is the monetary union, EMU. What is your view on the monetary union?

Eisner

Again, this is a complicated issue, and I hate to be dogmatic. In principle, I think a common money may be useful. But it is technically difficult to establish, and it is very important that it be done in a way that does not make things worse. I have very serious misgivings about the current Maastricht agreement, and the terms under which countries would be brought into it.[35]

One set of rather obvious problems is this whole matter of budget deficits. I don't know quite how the 3 percent target was picked, out of a hat or whatever, but at this point, it is a target which can wreak great havoc. In Germany and France, the two great economies, if you wish, the deficits are clearly over 3 percent, and the effort to get them down to 3 percent could be, in my view, a disaster for the French economy. I don't know the German economy that well.

It is true that Maastricht indicates that you could be admitted, if you're not yet at 3 percent, but moving in that direction, and that may be an out for France, that the deficit is coming down. But even that is very difficult, because, given the unemployment in France, what the new government should really be doing is raising the deficit, and financing public investment, reduction of taxes on payrolls, things like that, which would increase employment and growth. So, the budgetary aspects to the effort of establishing the currency union are, I think, very bad.

In general, over the longer run, there is a problem on the budget, which is not, I think, widely understood. I'm referring to the analogy of the common money in Europe, the euro, to the dollar and the United States, and the fact that we are one economy. But it is not understood adequately that in the United States, we have state and local governments with their own policies. State and local governments can't readily run big deficits except to finance capital investment, and they are limited in that by the constraints of the market.

But, if one section of the United States economy, say New England, has a slump, then even within an overall fiscal policy – let us say a 3 percent deficit for the US economy as a whole – the economy in New England will in effect be the beneficiary of a greater deficit: In New England, the tax paid will go down as employment and income are lower, and the benefits they get from unemployment insurance as well as other transfers from the rest of the United States will go up.

In Europe, if each country has to maintain a 3 percent deficit, and the French economy slumps, there is nothing you can do. There is no compensation from the German economy or from elsewhere. So that is the problem which I don't think is sufficiently recognized. There should be ways out of that if you are going to have these budget constraints, which, in fact, I don't think you should have. Each country should be free to follow its own fiscal policy.

Another worrisome thing about Maastricht is simply in terms of the political influence of the German central bank, and maybe other central bankers, with their conservative monetary policy. You should have a monetary policy which is targeted at high employment. If the central bank is to be largely influenced by the German Bundesbank, and is terribly concerned, all the time, about inflation, because of the German tradition, then you are likely to have too austere and restrictionary a monetary policy.

Also, if that central monetary authority is not subject to any political influence, it may be – as monetary authorities, central bankers generally are – overly sensitive to the interest of bankers and concerns about inflation, and less sensitive to the issues of economic growth and employment.

So, I see those major problems. Beyond that, of course, eliminating restrictions on movement of people, trade restrictions, customs barriers, all of those things are, I think, generally quite healthy. They involve dislocations: they involve people in some industries or occupations losing, others gaining. We will hope that governments would be willing to try to compensate the losers sufficiently, so they don't lose terribly, and that, by the way, would reduce the political objections to the losses. So, that's about where I would stand on EMU.

Berglund

It is also sometimes argued that liberalized capital movements have put an end to national policy autonomy, in particular for small open economies.

Eisner

My view is that that is exaggerated. Of course, the reduction of these barriers will make it easier for capital to move, but it does not move perfectly. I mean, there have been studies, by Feldstein and others, making clear that capital does not move all that freely.[36] It makes a difference if you are investing in a place that you know, to a place that you don't know. More capital movement is desirable. The movement will not be perfect. Particularly over the short run it will not be perfectly free. It also can be influenced by government. You can have government public investment or subsidies to the extent that movement is proving disadvantageous. But, of course, much of the movement may be advantageous.

There is a lot of confusion as to what we mean by "movement of capital." The movement of capital really has to be accompanied by the movement of goods, otherwise there is no movement in this sense. For a French firm to take its French francs and buy German marks, and invest in Germany, is not a movement of capital, because they will have assets, maybe physical assets, in Germany. But then the Germans will have assets in these French francs, which they will use for something. So, there has been no movement of capital, net.

If you have a common currency, and a French firm decides to start constructing a business in Germany, there isn't a movement of capital, actually, except to the extent that the goods move from France to Germany. So, you may well have a situation where, with a common money, firms will find it easier and more desirable to invest in places that are more profitable. I can't really say that is bad! Why would you want to preserve a system where a firm can only invest in a terrible place – where it can't find workers that are qualified, where there are no resources, no railroads, nothing to service them – when it has an opportunity to invest somewhere else?

Now, there is a problem of leaving certain people behind. People will not be as mobile as capital, even if nobody asked them for their visa at the border, because they have their families, their homes, and the like. That means that with a common money, and a common market, the authorities have to be more sensitive to this, and be willing to subsidize the movement of people. Alternatively, as a last resort, it may be better to subsidize people, to pay them benefits, welfare payments, where they are, rather than subsidizing businesses to keep them working where they are. And people may be too old or too unable to move to the other country, partly because they don't know the language in the other country. You are still not going to have a common language. Well, you have a common language in English to some extent, but most people still don't speak English adequately.

Freer capital movements are not something I am going to oppose. I think they are beneficial. They are never going to be perfectly free. You have to understand what you mean by free capital movements. It is not what I think Thomas Friedman alludes to in an article in *The New York Times* today. He is a fine columnist, but his economics, I think, are sometimes shaky. He talks about the electronic transfer of billions of funds in a day. But that's not capital movements – that's portfolio management.

Berglund

But these portfolio transactions might cause disruptions in interest rates and exchange rates?

Eisner

The exchange rate is the constraint they have to avoid. Now, that's going to be a problem with a common market, with a common money. But, as far as Sweden goes, for example, if you find interest rates going up, the monetary authority should try to make credit available to keep them down. Then, of course, it is very likely that your Swedish currency will depreciate in value – and it should! You should let it depreciate. If you stick to a fixed exchange rate in the face of high domestic unemployment, you are sort of committing economic suicide for a false God, a false goal.

There is nothing sacred about any particular value of a country's currency, and in general, I am a great believer in free movement of currencies. Indeed, that is a problem with the common money they are going to have, unless they have appropriate fiscal policies within each country, and an overall monetary policy generally, to compensate for that. We have, in the United States, as I said, to some extent a compensatory fiscal policy, because we have the one federal government levying taxes that presumably are the same rates everywhere.

But, as far as Sweden goes, at this point, they should not let concern about the value of the Swedish currency constrain them. I said that this is not a matter of capital movements, but rather portfolio changes, financial transactions. They will affect the value of the currency. I mean, if people decide they want to hold the new euro, or the dollar, or the German mark, instead of the Swedish currency, the Swedish currency will go down. That will be fine. The Swedish currency will go down, which will help your exports. It will also help your employment, your output, your economy. It will make prices somewhat higher, and increase the cost of living somewhat. But real output, which is what counts, will be higher.

Berglund

So what would be your policy advice for a small European country like Sweden?

Eisner

I will give you a quick summary advice. You should stimulate the economy, with appropriate public spending and lower taxes, which will give you a higher deficit. You should pursue an easier monetary policy, which will hold interest rates as low as you can, and you should let the Swedish currency go where it will. That should give you higher employment, and higher output. It may give you somewhat higher prices – it probably will, because real terms of trade will deteriorate due to your lower exchange rate – but that is a small price to pay for the benefits that you will have.

Notes

1 The conference proceedings are documented in Nell and Forstater (2003).
2 Refer to Eisner (1942).
3 Evsey D. Domar died on April 1, 1997.
4 Refer to Eisner (1951).
5 Refer to Eisner (1949–1950).
6 James Tobin and Robert M. Solow both received the Bank of Sweden Nobel Memorial Prize, in 1981 and 1987, respectively. Tobin died March 11, 2002.
7 Franco Modigliani received the Nobel Memorial Prize in 1985. He died November 25, 2003.
8 For an overview of "real business cycle" theory, refer to Plosser (1989) and Mankiw (1989).
9 Eisner is alluding to the famous passage in *The General Theory* where Keynes compares Classical economists to "Euclidean geometers in a non-Euclidean world who, discovering that in experience straight lines apparently parallel often meet, rebuke the lines for not keeping straight – as the only remedy for the unfortunate collisions which are occurring" (Keynes, 1936, p. 16).
10 Refer to Keynes (1919).
11 Refer to Lawrence R. Klein (1947a, 1947b). Klein received the Nobel Memorial Prize in 1980.
12 Refer to Machlup (1943).
13 Refer to Lucas (1976). Robert E. Lucas received the Nobel Memorial Prize in 1995.
14 Refer to Eisner (1958a), Friedman (1957).
15 Refer to Eisner (1958b).
16 Refer to Koyck (1954), Eisner (1960).
17 Eisner (1962, 1963, 1967, 1969, 1972), Eisner and Nadiri (1968).
18 Refer to Eisner and Strotz (1963).
19 Refer to Eisner (1989).
20 Refer to Eisner (1978, 1980, 1985, 1988); Eisner *et al.* (1982).
21 Refer to Lucas and Sargent (1981).
22 Refer to Eisner and Pieper (1984).
23 This paper (Eisner, 1997c) is published for the first time as Chapter 10 of this volume.
24 Robert L. Bartley died December 10, 2003.
25 Refer to Eisner (1997a).
26 Refer to Friedman (1968), Phelps (1968).
27 The US Bureau of Labor Statistics reported unemployment at 5.0 percent for June, and 4.9 percent for July 1997. Subsequently, unemployment kept falling,

reaching 4 percent in late 1999 and remaining at that level throughout 2000. The recession and terrorist attacks in 2001 threw unemployment back up to about 6 percent throughout 2002 and 2003, from which it then receded, albeit very slowly, to today's (September 2004) level of about 5½ percent. Inflation has remained subdued. Since 1992, the annual rate of increase of the GDP deflator has been confined in an interval between 1.1 percent and 2.4 percent without any clear tendencies to acceleration or deceleration. Similar observations can be made about CPI-based inflation measures.

28 The Congressional Budget Office reports that the US Federal debt held by the public was $3,734.1 billion end of (fiscal year) 1996, and $3772.3 billion end of 1997, an increase of $38.2 billion in 1997. However, due to the brisk pace of GDP growth, the debt, when expressed as a percentage of GDP, fell from 48.5 percent to 46.0 percent. In the subsequent years, the debt-to-GDP ratio kept falling sharply, reaching a low of 33.1 percent end of 2001. It has risen since, albeit very moderately, and was reported at 36.1 percent end of 2003 (the dollar amount being $3,913.6 billion).

To illustrate the implications of Eisner's principle of a constant debt-to-GDP ratio, consider an economy with a $4,000 billion dollar national debt, and with a $12,000 billion dollar GDP. The debt-to-GDP ratio is then one-third or 33.3 percent. Further suppose, realistically, that this economy is growing in nominal terms at 5 percent per annum (say, 3 percent real growth and 2 percent inflation). After one year, nominal GDP will have reached $12,600 billion. In order to maintain the debt-to-GDP ratio at 33.3 percent, the debt must also grow, to $4,200 billion to be precise. Thus the growth in GDP implies that $200 billion dollars of debt must be added just to keep the ratio of debt to GDP intact. In other words, a *deficit* of $200 billion, corresponding to 1.7 percent of GDP, will be necessary to keep the debt-to-GDP ratio from falling in this growing economy.

While these numbers are chosen to be realistic for the US case, a different debt-to-GDP ratio and a different GDP growth rate would have resulted in a different size for the deficit required to keeping the debt-to-GDP ratio constant. In general terms, we can write the relationship as $B/Y = (D/Y)g$, where B denotes the steady-state ("required") deficit, D the debt, Y GDP, and g the growth rate of GDP – all in nominal terms. Evidently the deficit ratio B/Y is positively related to both the growth rate of GDP and the debt-to-GDP ratio. In Japan, where the debt-to-GDP ratio is currently at about 140 percent, 5 percent nominal GDP growth would imply that a deficit of no less than 7 percent of GDP be required to keep the debt ratio at that level.

A faster rate of GDP growth also works as a "lever" in the same fashion. In the US example, a speedup of the nominal growth rate to 6 percent per annum would imply a steady-state deficit of 2 percent of GDP, which is to say that a one-percentage-point speedup of GDP growth would provide room for an additional 0.3 percentage points of deficits, relative to GDP.

29 For the permanent-income hypothesis, refer to Friedman (1957); for various renditions of the life-cycle hypothesis, refer to Modigliani and Brumberg (1954); Ando and Modigliani (1963); Modigliani (1986).

30 The exact quote is: "Practical men, who believe themselves to be quite exempt from any intellectual influences, are usually the slaves of some defunct economist." Keynes (1936), p. 383.

31 As of August 1997, the deficit forecasts for (fiscal year) 1997 were $37 billion by the (Clinton) administration, and $34 billion by the Congressional Budget Office, corresponding to about 0.4 percent of GDP. The actual outcome was $22 billion, or 0.3 percent of GDP. The federal budget went into surplus in 1998, and remained there until 2001 after peaking at $236 billion (1.3 percent of

GDP) in 2000. Deficits reappeared with a vengeance in 2002, reaching $375 billion (3.5 percent of GDP) in 2003. CBO currently (September 2004) projects a deficit of $422 billion (3.6 percent of GDP) for 2004, which suggests that the deficit may have stabilized as a percentage of GDP.

32 Herbert Stein died on September 8, 1999.

33 Eisner (1997c); the paper is published as Chapter 10 of this volume.

34 Refer to Eisner (1996).

35 The third stage of the EMU, which established the common currency, was implemented in 1999. Euro notes and coins, however, were put into circulation only in 2002. The budget and debt limits, commonly known as the "Maastricht rules" or "convergence criteria" after the 1992 Treaty of Maastricht, imposed a debt ceiling of 60 percent of GDP, and a deficit limit of 3 percent of GDP, and also additional requirements with respect to currency exchange rates, inflation rates and long-term rates of interest, in order to qualify for the currency union.

Countries like Belgium and Italy, while formally in violation of the debt limit, were allowed to join the union from the start thanks to a loophole about the debt ratio moving in the right direction. Only Greece, which exceeded the debt, deficit and inflation limits, was excluded from the start, but joined the euro zone in 2001.

The Maastricht rules were subsequently enshrined in the Stability and Growth Pact (SGP), which gained constitutional status as a part of the 1997 Treaty of Amsterdam. In fact, SGP goes further than the Maastricht Treaty, and stipulates a "medium-term budgetary objective of close to balance or in surplus," implying a secular reduction of the debt-to-GDP ratio. The Commission is under legal obligation to initiate an Excessive Deficit Procedure (EDP) for countries out of compliance with the Pact, particularly with respect to the 3-percent deficit limit. An EDP may result in the imposition of fines on the erring country.

After a relatively frictionless introductory phase, the euro zone has been mired in economic stagnation and budgetary difficulties for the past three years. Germany, France and Portugal are all subject to EDP, and the Netherlands and Ireland have received early "blue-letter" warnings from the Commission. In view of the dire situation, France and Germany recently pushed through in the Ecofin Council what amounts to a suspension of SGP, which the Commission went on to challenge in court. At the time of writing (September 2004), the tug-of-war might best be described as having entered juridical limbo.

While few doubt that SGP will be subject to review and modification in the coming months and years, recent signs of economic recovery in the euro zone are likely contribute to a mitigation of the deficit situation, and thus to take some pressure off this intensely political issue. It remains to be seen whether these issues will have been satisfactorily resolved by the time the next recession strikes, or whether the currency union will once more find itself in a similar predicament.

36 The most well-known study is Feldstein and Horioka (1980).

References

Ando, Albert and Franco Modigliani (1963), "The 'Life Cycle' Hypothesis of Saving: Aggregate Implications and Tests," *American Economic Review*, 53(1), March, pp. 55–84.

Eisner, Robert (1942), *The Gallup Poll and Opinion on Conscription: A Study in Public Opinion and Polling Technique*, Columbia University (MA thesis).

Eisner, Robert (1949–1950), "The Invariant Multiplier," *Review of Economic Studies*, 17(3), pp. 198–202.

Eisner, Robert (1951), *Growth, Investment and Business Cycles: A Critique and Development of Some Recent Theories*, Johns Hopkins University Library (Doctoral dissertation).

Eisner, Robert (1958a), "The Permanent Income Hypothesis: Comment," *American Economic Review*, 48(5), December, pp. 972–90.

Eisner, Robert (1958b), "On Growth Models and the Neo-Classical Resurgence," *Economic Journal*, 68(272), December, pp. 707–21.

Eisner, Robert (1960), "A Distributed Lag Investment Function," *Econometrica*, 28(1), January, pp. 1–29.

Eisner, Robert (1962), "Investment Plans and Realizations," *American Economic Review*, 52(2), May, pp. 190–203.

Eisner, Robert (1963), "Investment: Fact and Fancy," *American Economic Review*, 53(2), May, pp. 237–46.

Eisner, Robert (1967), "A Permanent Income Theory for Investment: Some Empirical Explorations," *American Economic Review*, 57(3), June, pp. 363–90.

Eisner, Robert (1969), "Investment and the Frustrations of Econometricians," *American Economic Review*, 59(2), May, pp. 50–64.

Eisner, Robert (1972), "Components of Capital Expenditures: Replacement and Modernization Versus Expansion," *Review of Economics and Statistics*, 54(3), August, pp. 297–305.

Eisner, Robert (1978), "Total Incomes in the United States, 1959 and 1969," *Review of Income and Wealth*, 24(1), March, pp. 41–70.

Eisner, Robert (1980), "Total Income, Total Investment, and Growth," *American Economic Review*, 70(2), May, pp. 225–31.

Eisner, Robert (1985), "The Total Incomes System of Accounts," *Survey of Current Business*, January, 65(1), pp. 24–48.

Eisner, Robert (1988), "Extended Accounts for National Income and Product," *Journal of Economic Literature*, 26(4), December, pp. 1611–84.

Eisner, Robert (1989), *The Total Incomes System of Accounts*, Chicago: University of Chicago Press.

Eisner, Robert (1996), "The Proposed Sales and Wages Tax – Fair, Flat or Foolish?" in *Fairness and the Efficiency in the Flat Tax*, Washington DC: American Enterprise Institute, pp. 48–95.

Eisner, Robert (1997a), *The Great Deficit Scares: the Federal Budget, Trade, and Social Security*, New York: Century Foundation Press.

Eisner, Robert (1997b), "A New View of the NAIRU," in *Improving the Global Economy: Keynesianism and the Growth in Output and Employment*, edited by Paul Davidson and Jan A. Kregel, Cheltenham, UK and Lyme, NH: Elgar, pp. 196–230.

Eisner, Robert (1997c), "Budget Deficits, Unemployment and Economic Growth: A Cross-Section Time-Series Analysis," Paper presented at the Seventh International Conference on Panel Data, La Sorbonne, Paris, June 19–20, 1997. (Published as Chapter 10 of this book.)

Eisner, Robert and Robert H. Strotz (1963), "Determinants of Business Investment," in Commission on Money and Credit, *Impacts of Monetary Policy*, Englewood Cliffs: Prentice-Hall, pp. 59–337.

Eisner, Robert and M. Ishaq Nadiri (1968), "Investment Behavior and Neo-Classical Theory," *Review of Economics and Statistics*, 50(3), August, pp. 369–82.

Eisner, Robert, Emily Simons, Paul J. Pieper, and Steven Bender (1982), "Total Incomes in the United States, 1946 to 1976: A Summary Report," *Review of Income and Wealth*, 28(2), June, pp. 133–74.

Eisner, Robert and Paul J. Pieper (1984), "A New View of the Federal Debt and Budget Deficits," *American Economic Review*, 74 (1), March, pp. 11–29.

Feldstein, Martin S. and Charles Horioka (1980), "Domestic Saving and International Capital Flows," *Economic Journal*, 90(358), June, pp. 314–29.

Friedman, Milton (1957), *A Theory of the Consumption Function*, Princeton, NJ: Princeton University Press.

Friedman, Milton (1968), "The Role of Monetary Policy," *American Economic Review*, 58(1). March, pp. 1–17.

Keynes, John Maynard (1919), *The Economic Consequences of the Peace*, London: Macmillan.

Keynes, John Maynard (1936), *The General Theory of Employment, Interest and Money*, London: Macmillan.

Klein, Lawrence R. (1947a), *The Keynesian Revolution*, New York: Macmillan.

Klein, Lawrence R. (1947b), "Theories of Effective Demand and Employment," *Journal of Political Economy*, 55(2), April, pp. 108–31.

Koyck, Leendert M. (1954), *Distributed Lags and Investment Analysis*, Amsterdam: North-Holland.

Lucas, Robert E., Jr. (1976), "Econometric Policy Evaluation: A Critique," *Journal of Monetary Economics*, Supplementary Series, 1(2), pp. 19–46.

Lucas, Robert E., Jr. and Thomas J. Sargent (1981), "After Keynesian Economics," in *Rational Expectations and Econometric Practice*, edited by Robert E. Lucas and Thomas J. Sargent, Minneapolis: University of Minnesota Press, pp. 295–319.

Machlup, Fritz (1943), *International Trade and the National Income Multiplier*, Philadelphia: Blakiston.

Mankiw, N. Gregory (1989), "Real Business Cycles: A New Keynesian Perspective," *Journal of Economic Perspectives*, 3(3), Summer, pp. 79–90.

Modigliani, Franco and Richard E. Brumberg (1954), "Utility Analysis and the Consumption Function: An Interpretation of Cross-Section Data," in *Post-Keynesian Economics*, edited by Kenneth H. Kurihara, New Brunswick, NJ: Rutgers University Press.

Modigliani, Franco (1986), "Life Cycle, Individual Thrift, and the Wealth of Nations," *American Economic Review*, 76(3), June, pp. 297–313.

Nell, Edward J. and Mathew Forstater, editors (2003), *Reinventing Functional Finance*, edited by, Cheltenham, UK and Northampton, MA: Edward Elgar.

Phelps, Edmund S. (1968), "Money-Wage Dynamics and Labor-Market Equilibrium," *Journal of Political Economy*, 76(4), July–August, pp. 678–711.

Plosser, Charles I. (1989), "Real Business Cycles: A New Keynesian Perspective," *Journal of Economic Perspectives*, 3(3), Summer, pp. 51–77.

Robert Eisner

Biographical data

Robert Eisner (1922–1998) was the William R. Kenan Professor of Economics at Northwestern University. Eisner held this position, which was the first endowed chair in the then School of Arts and Sciences, from 1974 and onwards (emeritus from 1994). He came to Northwestern University in 1952, and served as Chairman of the Economics Department, 1964–1967 and 1974–1976.

Earlier professional appointments during 1941–1947 include the Office of Price Administration and the Office of the Housing Expediter. He served in the US Army from 1942–1946, with the terminal rank of Captain, and taught at the University of Illinois, Urbana, from 1950–1952. He was a Guggenheim Fellow in 1960, a Fellow at the Center for Advanced Study in the Behavioral Sciences in 1968, and a Senior Research Associate of the National Bureau of Economic Research, 1969–1978.

Eisner was President of the American Economic Association (AEA) in 1988, and Vice President in 1977. As a member of the AEA Executive Committee, he played a lead role in establishing the AEA's Committee on the Status of Women on the Economics Profession (CSWEP) in 1971. He also served as President of the Midwest Economics Association, 1982–1983. He was a Fellow of the American Academy of Arts and Science, a Fellow of the Econometric Society, and a Director of Economists Allied for Arms Reduction (ECAAR).

Eisner was a member of the board of editors of several leading academic journals, including *The American Economic Review*, *The Journal of Economic Literature*, *The Review of Economics and Statistics*, and *The Review of Income and Wealth*.

He received a Bachelor's degree from the College of the City of New York in 1940, a Master's degree from Columbia University in 1942, and a PhD from Johns Hopkins University in 1951. He received an honorary doctorate from University Pierre Mendes France, in Grenoble, France, in 1996.

Robert Eisner died November 24, 1998.

Robert Eisner
Bibliography

This bibliography is not exhaustive, but aims at giving a fairly comprehensive guide to the works of Robert Eisner. Minor replies, rejoinders and comments have been omitted, as have opinion pieces, newspaper articles, etc. Foreign articles are limited to a selection in French. The materials have been arranged chronologically, in six sections: (1) books and monographs; (2) articles; (3) writings on war and peace; (4) encyclopedia entries; (5) academic theses, and (6) writings in memoriam.

Books and monographs

Eisner, Robert (1956), *Determinants of Capital Expenditures: An Interview Study*, Urbana: University of Illinois Press.

Eisner, Robert and Robert H. Strotz (1963), "Determinants of Business Investment," Research Study Two in *Impacts of Monetary Policy*, prepared for the Commission on Money and Credit, Englewood Cliffs: Prentice-Hall, pp. 59–337.

Eisner, Robert (1978), *Factors in Business Investment*, Cambridge, Mass.: National Bureau of Economic Research.

Eisner, Robert (1986), *How Real is the Federal Deficit?* New York: Macmillan, Free Press; London: Collier Macmillan.

Eisner, Robert (1989), *The Total Incomes System of Accounts*, Chicago and London: University of Chicago Press.

Eisner, Robert (1994), *The Misunderstood Economy: What Counts and How to Count It*, Boston: Harvard Business School Press.

Eisner, Robert (1997), *The Great Deficit Scares: The Federal Budget, Trade, and Social Security*, New York: The Twentieth Century Fund.

Eisner, Robert (1998), *Social Security: More Not Less*, New York: The Century Foundation.

Eisner, Robert (1998), *The Selected Essays of Robert Eisner, Volume 1: The Keynesian Revolution, Then and Now*, Cheltenham, UK and Northampton, Mass.: Edward Elgar.

Eisner, Robert (1998), *The Selected Essays of Robert Eisner, Volume 2: Investment, National Income and Economic Policy*, Cheltenham, UK and Northampton, Mass.: Elgar.

Articles

Eisner, Robert (1949–1950), "The Invariant Multiplier," *Review of Economic Studies*, 17(3), pp. 198–202.

Eisner, Robert (1952), "Underemployment Equilibrium Rates of Growth," *American Economic Review*, 42(1), March, pp. 43–58.

Eisner, Robert (1952), "Accelerated Amortization, Growth, and Net Profits," *Quarterly Journal of Economics*, 66(4), November, pp. 533–44.

Eisner, Robert (1952), "Depreciation Allowances, Replacement Requirements and Growth," *American Economic Review*, 42(5), December, pp. 820–31.

Eisner, Robert (1953), "Guaranteed Growth of Income," *Econometrica*, 21(1), January, pp. 169–71.

Eisner, Robert (1954), "Conventional Depreciation Allowances vs. Replacement Cost," *The Controller*, May, pp. 134–8. Reprinted in *An Income Approach to Accounting Theory*, edited by Sydney Davidson *et al.*, Prentice-Hall, 1964, pp. 266–72.

Eisner, Robert (1955), "Depreciation Under the New Tax Law," *Harvard Business Review*, January–February, pp. 66–74 (plus duplicated mathematical appendix). Reprinted in *Congressional Record*, March 11, 1955, pp. 2264–7.

Eisner, Robert (1955), "Accelerated Depreciation: Some Further Thoughts," *Quarterly Journal of Economics*, 69(2), May, pp. 285–96.

Eisner, Robert (1956), "Technological Change, Obsolescence and Aggregate Demand," *American Economic Review*, 46(1), March, pp. 92–105.

Eisner, Robert (1957), "Interview and Other Survey Techniques and the Study of Investment, " in *Problems of Capital Formation: Concepts, Measurement, and Controlling Factors*, Studies in Income and Wealth, Vol. 19, Princeton, NJ: Princeton University Press for the National Bureau of Economic Research, pp. 513–84, 596–601.

Eisner, Robert (1958), "Expectations, Plans and Capital Expenditures: A Synthesis of *Ex Post* and *Ex Ante* Data," in *Expectations, Uncertainty and Business Behavior*, edited by Mary Jean Bowman, New York: Social Science Research Council, pp. 165–88.

Eisner, Robert (1958), "An Appraisal of Proposals for Tax Differentials Affecting Investment," in *Income Tax Differentials*, by Dan Throop Smith *et al.*, Symposium conducted by the Tax Institute, Princeton, NJ: Princeton University Press, pp. 154–71; also discussion, pp. 172 ff., passim.

Eisner, Robert (1958), "On Growth Models and the Neo-Classical Resurgence," *Economic Journal*, 68(272), December, pp. 707–21.

Eisner, Robert (1958), "The Permanent Income Hypothesis: Comment," *American Economic Review*, 48(5), December, pp. 972–90.

Eisner, Robert (1960), "A Distributed Lag Investment Function," *Econometrica*, 28(1), January, pp. 1–29.

Eisner, Robert (1962), "Investment Plans and Realizations," *American Economic Review*, 52(2), May, pp. 190–203.

Eisner, Robert (1963), "Investment: Fact and Fancy," *American Economic Review*, 53(2), May, pp. 237–46.

Eisner, Robert (1963), "Another Look at Liquidity Preference," *Econometrica*, 31(3), July, pp. 531–8.

Eisner, Robert (1963), "Forecasting Investment Spending," in *The Economic Outlook for 1964*, University of Michigan, Ann Arbor, pp. 71–95.

Eisner, Robert (1963), "An Overall View of the Model," 1963 *Proceedings of the Business and Economic Statistics Section, American Statistical Association*, pp. 260–3.

Eisner, Robert (1964), "Income Distribution, Investment and Growth," *Indian Economic Journal*, April–June 1964, pp. 400–12; French translation, as "Repartition des Revenues, Investissement et Croissance," *Economie Appliquee*, No. 3, 1963, pp. 343–60.

Eisner, Robert (1964), "Capital Expenditures, Profits and the Acceleration Principle," in *Models of Income Determination*, Studies in Income and Wealth, Vol. 28, Princeton, NJ: Princeton University Press, pp. 137–65, 172–6.

Eisner, Robert (1964), "Capacity, Investment and Profits," *Quarterly Journal of Economics and Business*, September, pp. 7–12. Reprinted in *Economics: Readings in Analysis and Policy*, edited by Dennis R. Starleaf, Glenview, Illinois: Scott, Foresman, 1969, pp. 243–7.

Eisner, Robert (1964), "An Overall View of the Model," *1963 Proceedings of the Business and Economic Statistics Section of the American Statistical Association*, Washington, DC: The Association, pp. 260–3.

Eisner, Robert (1965), "Realization of Investment Anticipations," in *The Brookings Quarterly Econometric Model of the United States*, edited by James S. Duesenberry, Chicago: Rand McNally, pp. 95–128.

Eisner, Robert (1967), "A Permanent Income Theory for Investment: Some Empirical Explorations," *American Economic Review*, 57(3), June, pp. 363–90.

Eisner, Robert (1967), "Fiscal and Monetary Policies for Growth," in *The Future of Economic Policy*, edited by Myron H. Ross, Ann Arbor, Michigan, pp. 14–27.

Eisner, Robert (1967), "Capital and Labor in Production: Some Direct Estimates," in *The Theory and Empirical Analysis of Production*, edited by Murray Brown, Studies in Income and Wealth, Vol. 31, New York: National Bureau of Economic Research, pp. 431–62, 472–5.

Eisner, Robert and M. Ishaq Nadiri (1968), "Investment Behavior and Neo-Classical Theory," *Review of Economics and Statistics*, 50(3), August, pp. 369–82.

Eisner, Robert (1968), "Factors Affecting the Level of Interest Rates: Part II," in *Conference on Savings and Residential Financing, 1968 Proceedings*, Chicago: United States Savings and Loan League, pp. 28–40. Reprinted in *Monetary Economics: Readings on Current Issues*, edited by William E. Gibson and George G. Kaufman, New York: McGraw-Hill, 1971, pp. 303–10.

Eisner, Robert (1969), "Investment and the Frustrations of Econometricians," *American Economic Review*, 59(2), May, pp. 50–64.

Eisner, Robert (1969), "Fiscal and Monetary Policy Reconsidered," *American Economic Review*, 59(5), December, pp. 897–905.

Eisner, Robert (1971), "What Went Wrong?" *Journal of Political Economy*, 79(3), May–June, pp. 629–41.

Eisner, Robert (1971), "New Twists to Income and Product," in *The Economic Accounts of the United States: Retrospect and Prospect*, 50th anniversary issue of *Survey of Current Business*, Vol. 51, July, pp. 67–8.

Eisner, Robert (1971), "What Went Wrong: Further Thoughts on Fiscal and Monetary Policy," in *Issues in Fiscal and Monetary Policy: The Eclectic Economist*

Views the Controversy, edited by James J. Diamond, Chicago: DePaul University, pp. 75–91.

Eisner, Robert (1971), "The 1971 Report of the President's Council of Economic Advisers: Inflation and Recession," *American Economic Review*, 61(4), September, pp. 522–6.

Eisner, Robert (1971), "Non-Linear Estimates of the Liquidity Trap," *Econometrica*, 39(5), September, pp. 861–4.

Eisner, Robert (1972), "Components of Capital Expenditures: Replacement and Modernization Versus Expansion," *Review of Economics and Statistics*, 54(3), August, pp. 297–305.

Eisner, Robert (1973), "Tax Incentives for Investment," *National Tax Journal*, September, pp. 397–401.

Eisner, Robert (1973), "Bonanzas for Business Investment," *Challenge*, November–December, pp. 38–44.

Eisner, Robert (1974), "Econometric Studies of Investment Behavior: A Comment," *Economic Inquiry*, March, pp. 91–104. Reprinted in *Modern Macroeconomics: Major Contributions to Contemporary Thought*, edited by Panayotis G. Korlinas and Richard S. Thorn, New York: Harper and Row, 1979, pp. 77–86.

Eisner, Robert (1974), "Business Investment Preferences," *George Washington Law Review*, March, pp. 486–500.

Eisner, Robert and Patrick J. Lawler (1975), "Tax Policy and Investment: An Analysis of Survey Responses," *American Economic Review*, 65(1), March, pp. 206–12.

Eisner, Robert (1975), "The Keynesian Revolution Reconsidered," *American Economic Review*, 65(2), May, pp. 189–94.

Eisner, Robert (1975), "Government and Inflation, or What is Wrong with the Old-Time Religion," in *The Economic Outlook for 1975*, University of Michigan, Ann Arbor, pp. 58–66.

Eisner, Robert (1976–1977), "Money and Other Illusions in Economic Policy," David Horowitz Lectures in Tel Aviv and Jerusalem, May 1976, published in Hebrew in *Quarterly Banking Review*, Vol. XV, No. 60, July 1976, pp. 33–44, and vol. XVI, no. 62, January 1977, pp. 17–28. Revised versions published in English in *Sozialwissenschaftliche Annalen*, 1979, and in *Economic Forum*, 1980.

Eisner, Robert (1976), "The Corporate Role in Financing Future Investment Needs," in *U.S. Economic Growth from 1976 to 1986: Prospects, Problems and Patterns*, Vol. 3: *Capital*, Prepared for the use of the Joint Economic Committee, Congress of the United States, Washington, DC: US Government Printing Office, pp. 16–32.

Eisner, Robert (1977), "Capital Shortage: Myth and Reality," *American Economic Review*, 67(1), February, pp. 110–15.

Eisner, Robert (1978), "A Direct Attack on Unemployment," *Challenge*, July–August, pp. 49–51. Reprinted in *Solutions to Unemployment*, edited by David C. Colander, New York: Harcourt Brace Jovanovich, 1981, pp. 177–80.

Eisner, Robert (1977), "The Outlook for Business Investment," in *Capital for Productivity and Jobs*, edited by Eli Shapiro and William White, New York: Prentice-Hall, pp. 50–72.

Eisner, Robert (1977), "Inflation," in *Full Employment and Economic Justice*, edited by John Carr, Huntington, Indiana: Our Sunday Visitor, Inc. Press, pp. 61–75.

Eisner, Robert (1977), "Government Policy and Investment, " in *Financing Economic Growth: The Problem of Capital Formation*, Center for the Study of American Business, Washington University, St. Louis, and Federal Reserve Bank of St. Louis, Working Paper No. 19, June, pp. 7–37.

Eisner, Robert (1977), "Government and Inflation," in *Stability and Inflation: A Volume of Essays to Honour the Memory of A.W.H. Phillips*, edited by Albert R. Bergstrom *et al.*, New York: John Wiley and Sons, pp. 103–11.

Eisner, Robert (1978), "Government Policy, Investment and the Return on Capital," in *Le Capital dans la Function de Production*, edited by Jacques de Bandt, Paris, pp. 239–52.

Eisner, Robert (1978), "Total Incomes in the United States, 1959 and 1969," *Review of Income and Wealth*, 24(1), March, pp. 41–70.

Eisner, Robert (1978), "More on Capital Anticipations," *Problems and Instruments of Business Cycle Analysis*, edited by Werner H. Strigel, New York: Springer-Verlag, pp. 329–90.

Eisner, Robert (1978), "Cross Section and Time Series Estimates of Investment Functions," *Annales de l'INSEE*, No. 30/31/1978, April–September, pp. 99–129.

Eisner, Robert (1978), "Machlup on Academic Freedom," in *Breadth and Depth in Economics: Fritz Machlup – The Man and His Ideas*, edited by Jacob S. Dreyer, Boston: Lexington Books of D.C. Heath and Co., pp. 3–12.

Eisner, Robert (1978), "Employment Taxes and Subsidies," in *Work Time and Employment*, National Commission for Manpower Policy, Washington, DC, pp. 275–310.

Eisner, Robert (1980), "Incitation à l'emploi plutôt qu'à l'investissement," *Revue Économique*, 31(1), January, pp. 5–15.

Eisner, Robert (1980), "Total Income, Total Investment, and Growth," *American Economic Review*, 70(2), May, pp. 225–31.

Eisner, Robert (1980), "Stopping Inflation, Reducing Unemployment, and Solving the Oil Problem," *Journal of Post Keynesian Economics*, Spring, 2(3), pp. 432–5.

Eisner, Robert (1980), "Capital Gains and Income: Real Changes in the Value of Capital in the United States, 1946–1975," in *The Measurement of Capital*, edited by Dan Usher, Studies in Income and Wealth, Vol. 45, Chicago: University of Chicago Press for National Bureau of Economic Research, pp. 175–342.

Eisner, Robert (1980), "Limitations and Potentials of Countercyclical Fiscal and Monetary Policies," in *The Business Cycle and Public Policy 1929–1980: A Compendium of Papers*, Joint Economic Committee, Congress of the United States, Washington, DC: US Government Printing Office, pp. 147–71.

Eisner, Robert and David H. Nebhut (1981), "An Extended Measure of Government Product: Preliminary Results for the United States, 1946–76," *Review of Income and Wealth*, 27(1), March, pp. 33–64.

Eisner, Robert (1981), "Expectations in Economics," in Joint Economic Committee of the United States, *Expectations and the Economy*, Washington, DC: US Government Printing Office, pp. 54–65.

Chirinko, Robert S. and Robert Eisner (1981), "The Effects of Tax Policies on Investment in Macroeconometric Models: Full Model Simulations," *OTA Papers*, No. 46, Washington, DC: Office of Tax Analysis, US Treasury Department, January. Also published as "Tax Policy and Investment in Major U.S. Macroeconomic Econometric Models," *Journal of Public Economics*, 20(2), March 1983, pp. 139–66.

Chirinko, Robert S. and Robert Eisner (1981), "The Effects of Tax Parameters on the Investment Equations in Macroeconomic Econometric Models," *OTA Papers*, No. 47, Washington, DC: Office of Tax Analysis, US Treasury Department, January. Reprinted in *Economic Activity and Finance*, edited by Marshall Blume, Jean Crockett and Paul Taubman, Cambridge, Mass.: Ballinger, 1982, pp. 25–84.

Eisner, Robert (1981), "The State of Fiscal Policy – and Some Alternatives," in Conference Board Public Policy Forum, *Colloquium on Alternatives for Economic Policy*, New York, NY: The Conference Board, pp. 28–35.

Eisner, Robert (1982), "Money, Taxes and Budgets: Demand or Supply-Side Economics?" *Economic Papers*, 1(1), April, pp. 38–48.

Eisner, Robert and Steven Bender (1982), "Differential Impacts of Tax Incentives for Investment," *Journal of Policy Modeling*, 4(2), June, pp. 143–59.

Eisner, Robert, Emily Simons, Paul J. Pieper, and Steven Bender (1982), "Total Incomes in the United States, 1946 to 1976: A Summary Report," *Review of Income and Wealth*, 28(2), June, pp. 133–74.

Eisner, Robert (1982), "Tax Policy for Investment: Implications for Innovation," in *Tax Policy and Investment in Innovation*, edited by Eileen N. Collins, Washington, DC: National Science Foundation.

Eisner, Robert (1983), "Social Security, Saving, and Macroeconomics," *Journal of Macroeconomics*, 5(1), Winter, pp. 1–19.

Eisner, Robert (1983), "Government Policy, Saving and Investment, " *Journal of Economic Education*, 14(2), Spring, pp. 38–49.

Eisner, Robert (1983), "Which Way for France?" *Challenge*, 26(3), July–August, pp. 34–41.

Eisner, Robert (1983), "Tax Policy and Investment, " in *Public Finance and Economic Growth*, edited by Dieter Biehl, Karl W. Roskamp and Wolfgang F. Stolper, Detroit: Wayne State University Press, pp. 167–80.

Eisner, Robert (1983), "The Economics of An Effective Jobs Tax Credit," in *Proceedings of the Small Business Tax Equity Conference*, New York, NY: American Institute of Certified Public Accountants, pp. 33–42.

Eisner, Robert and Paul J. Pieper (1984), "A New View of the Federal Debt and Budget Deficits," *American Economic Review*, 74(1), March, pp. 11–29.

Eisner, Robert; Steven H. Albert and Martin A. Sullivan (1984), "The New Incremental Tax Credit for R&D: Incentive or Disincentive?" *National Tax Journal*, 37(2), June, pp. 171–83.

Eisner, Robert, Steven H. Albert, and Martin A. Sullivan (1984), "Tax Incentives and R&D Expenditures," in *Leading Indicators and Business Cycle Surveys*, Washington, DC, New York: St. Martin's Press, pp. 385–419.

Eisner, Robert (1984), "Transfers in a Total Incomes System of Accounts," in *Economic Transfers in the United States*, edited by Marilyn Moon, Studies in Income and Wealth, Vol. 49, Chicago and London: University of Chicago Press, pp. 9–35.

Eisner, Robert (1984), "Inflation, Unemployment, and the Budget," in *Reconstructing the Federal Budget: A Trillion Dollar Quandary*, edited by Albert T. Sommers, New York: Praeger, pp. 150–63. Earlier version published in *Toward a Reconstruction of Federal Budgeting*, New York, NY: The Conference Board, 1983, pp. 59–64.

Eisner, Robert (1985), "The Total Incomes System of Accounts," *Survey of Current Business*, 65(1), January, pp. 24–48.

Eisner, Robert and Paul J. Pieper (1985), "How to Make Sense of the Deficit," *The Public Interest*, Winter, pp. 101–18. Reprinted in *A Nation in Debt: Economists Debate the Federal Budget Deficit*, edited by Richard H. Fink and Jack C. High, Frederick, MD: University Publications of America, 1987, pp. 87–101.

Eisner, Robert (1985), "The R&D Tax Credit: A Flawed Tool," *Issues in Science and Technology*, 1(4), Summer.

Eisner, Robert and Paul J. Pieper (1985), "Measurement and Effects of Government Debt and Deficits," in *Economic Policy and National Accounting in Inflationary Conditions*, Proceedings of an international conference in Dorga/Bergamo, Italy in January 1984, edited by J. Mortensen. Reprinted in *Studies in Banking and Finance*, Vol. 2, edited by Bertrand Jacquillat, Arnold W. Sametz, Marshall Sarnat and Giorgio P. Szego, 1985, pp. 115–44. Updated and revised version published in French as "Dette et déficit gouvernementaux: mesures et effets," *Annales d'Économie et de Statistique*, 0(3), July–September, pp. 27–52.

Eisner, Robert (1986), "The Real Federal Deficit: What It Is, How It Matters, and What It Should Be," *Quarterly Review of Economics and Business*, 26(4), Winter, pp. 6–21.

Eisner, Robert (1986), "Will the Real Federal Deficit Stand Up?" *Challenge*, 29(2), May–June, pp. 13–21.

Eisner, Robert (1986), "The Real Deficit," *Quarterly Model Outlook*, Wharton Econometric Forecasting Associates, 5(5), May, pp. 99–108.

Eisner, Robert (1986), "The Revolution Restored: Keynesian Unemployment, Inflation and Budget Deficits," *Eastern Economic Journal*, 12(3), July–September, pp. 217–21.

Eisner, Robert (1986), "Real vs. Nominal Debt," *Challenge*, November–December, 29(5), p. 58.

Eisner, Robert (1986), "Fact and Fancy on Debt and Deficits," in *Confronting the Federal Deficit*, edited by Hugh W. Long, Dover, Mass.: Auburn House Publishing Company, pp. 1–15.

Eisner, Robert (1986), "The Real Federal Deficit," in Congress of the United States, Joint Economic Committee, *The American Economy in Transition: From the Second World War to the 21st Century*, A symposium on the Fortieth Anniversary of the Joint Economic Committee, Washington, US Government Printing Office. Also published as "The Federal Budget Crisis" in *The Changing American Economy*, edited by David Obey and Paul Sarbanes, Oxford and New York: Basil Blackwood, 1986, pp. 73–107.

Eisner, Robert (1987), "The Federal Deficit: How Does It Matter?" *Science*, September 25, pp. 1577–82.

Eisner, Robert (1988), "Extended Accounts for National Income and Product," *Journal of Economic Literature*, 26(4), December, pp. 1611–84.

Eisner, Robert (1988), "What's Facing the Next President?" *Challenge*, 31(4), July–August, pp. 22–31.

Eisner, Robert and Paul J. Pieper (1988), "Deficits, Monetary Policy, and Real Economic Activity," in *The Economics of Public Debt*, edited by Kenneth J. Arrow and Michael J. Boskin, New York: St. Martin's Press, pp. 3–38.

Eisner, Robert (1989), "Budget Deficits: Rhetoric and Reality," *Journal of Economic Perspectives*, 3(2), Spring, pp. 73–93.

Eisner, Robert and Paul J. Pieper (1989), "Inflation-Adjusted Government Budget

Deficits and Real Economic Activity: Rejoinder," *Annales d'Economie et de Statistique*, 0(13), January–March, pp. 139–47.

Eisner, Robert (1989), "Debt and Deficit and Other Illusions," in *The Economics of Imperfect Competition and Employment: Joan Robinson and Beyond*, edited by George R. Feiwel, New York: New York University Press, pp. 709–20.

Eisner, Robert (1989), "Employer Approaches to Reducing Unemployment," in *Rethinking Employment Policy*, edited by D. Lee Bawden and Felicity Skidmore, Washington, DC: Urban Institute Press, pp. 59–80.

Eisner, Robert (1989), "On Keynesian Underemployment, Prices, and Wealth Effects of Government Debt," in *Money, Credit and Prices in Keynesian Perspective*, edited by Alain Barrère, New York: St. Martin's Press, pp. 162–9.

Eisner, Robert (1989), "Taxes, Budget Deficits and Capital Formation," in *Public Finance and Performance of Enterprises*, Proceedings of the 43rd Congress of the International Institute of Public Finance, Paris, 1987, edited by Manfred Neumann and Karl W. Roskamp, Detroit, Michigan: Wayne State University Press, pp. 15–29.

Eisner, Robert and Nancy S. Barrett (1989), "Fiscal Policy" in *America's Transition: Blueprints for the 1990s*, edited by Mark J. Green and Mark Pinsky, New York: Democracy Project, pp. 8–27.

Eisner, Robert (1990), "Debunking the Conventional Wisdom in Economic Policy," *Challenge*, 33(3), May–June, pp. 4–11.

Eisner, Robert and Paul J. Pieper (1990), "The World's Greatest Debtor Nation?" *North American Review of Economics and Finance*, 1(1), pp. 9–32.

Eisner, Robert (1990), "Learning About Economics and the Economy," in *The Principles of Economics Course: A Handbook for Instructors*, edited by Philip Saunders and William Walstad, New York: McGraw-Hill, pp. 10–18.

Eisner, Robert (1990), "Social Security, Saving and the Future," in *Conference Proceedings, Social Security Trust Funds: Issues for the 1990s and Beyond*, Proceedings of the Public Trustees' Policy Symposium on Social Security Trust Fund Build-Up, Washington, DC, September 16, 1988, published by Public Policy Institute, American Association of Retired Persons, pp. 25–30.

Eisner, Robert (1990), "Public Policy and Manufacturing: Back to Basics," in *American Manufacturers in a Global Market*, edited by Kenneth W. Chilton, Melinda E. Warren and Murray L. Weidenbaum, Boston: Kluwer Academic Publishers, pp. 9–16.

Eisner, Robert (1991), "The Real Rate of US National Saving," *Review of Income and Wealth*, 37(1), March, pp. 15–32.

Eisner, Robert (1991), "Our Real Deficits," *Journal of the American Planning Association*, 57(2), Spring, pp. 131–5.

Eisner, Robert (1991), "No New Taxes for S&L Bailout," *Challenge*, 34(2), March–April, pp. 34–8.

Eisner, Robert (1991), "Infrastructure and Regional Economic Performance: Comment," *New England Economic Review*, September–October, pp. 47–58.

Eisner, Robert and Paul J. Pieper (1991), "Real Foreign Investment in Perspective," *Annals* of the American Academy of Political and Social Science, July, pp. 22–35.

Eisner, Robert (1991), "Deficits and Us and Our Grandchildren," in *Debt and the Twin Deficits Debate*, edited by James M. Rock, Mountain View, Ca., London and Toronto: Mayfield, Bristlecone Books, pp. 81–107.

Eisner, Robert (1992), "Deficits: Which, How Much, and So What?" *American Economic Review*, 82(2), May, pp. 295–8.

Eisner, Robert and Paul J. Pieper (1992), "Real Deficits and Real Growth: A Further View," *Journal of Post Keynesian Economics*, 15(1), Fall, pp. 43–9.

Eisner, Robert (1992), "The Twin Deficits," in *Profits, Deficits, and Instability*, edited by Dimitri B. Papadimitriou, London: Macmillan Academic and Professional; New York: St. Martin's Press, pp. 255–67.

Eisner, Robert (1992), "Some Measurement and Policy Issues of National Saving and Investment," in *Personal Saving, Consumption, and Tax Policy*, edited by Marvin H. Kosters, Washington, DC: AEI Press, pp. 119–24.

Eisner, Robert (1993), "Measure, Theory, Fact and Fancy: The Case of the Budget Deficit," *Bulletin of the American Academy of Arts and Sciences*, April, pp. 27–43.

Eisner, Robert (1993), "Clinton, Deficits, and the U.S. Economy," *Challenge*, 36(3), May–June, pp. 47–51.

Eisner, Robert (1993), "Sense and Nonsense About Budget Deficits," *Harvard Business Review*, May–June, pp. 99–111.

Eisner, Robert (1993), "Fiscal and Monetary Policy Reconsidered, Again: Basic Lessons," *Journal of Economic Education*, 24(3), Summer, pp. 245–59.

Eisner, Robert and Sang-In Hwang (1993), "Self-Correcting Real Deficits: A New Lesson in Functional Finance," in *The Political Economy of Government Debt*, edited by Harrie A.A. Verbon and Frans A.A.M. van Winden, Amsterdam, London and Tokyo: North-Holland, pp. 255–94.

Eisner, Robert and Paul J. Pieper (1993), "National Saving and the Twin Deficits: Myth and Reality," in *The Economics of Saving*, edited by James H. Gapinski, Norwell, Mass. and Dordrecht: Kluwer Academic, pp. 109–33.

Eisner, Robert (1994), "Real Government Saving and the Future, " *Journal of Economic Behavior and Organization*, 23(2), January, pp. 1–15.

Eisner, Robert (1994), "Déficits, épargne et politique économique," *Économies et Sociétés*, 28(1–2), January–February, pp. 231–74.

Eisner, Robert (1994), "National Saving and Budget Deficits," *Review of Economics and Statistics*, 76(1), February, pp. 181–6.

Eisner, Robert (1994), "Challenge to the Natural Rate Doctrine," *Journal of Post Keynesian Economics*, 17(1), Fall, pp. 159–61.

Eisner, Robert (1994), "Deficits, Saving, and Economic Policy," John R. Commons Lecture at Allied Social Science Association Meetings, January 4, 1994, published *American Economist*, 38(2), Fall, pp. 3–11.

Eisner, Robert (1994–1995), "Keynes Is Not Dead, Just Drugged and Dormant," *Journal of Post Keynesian Economics*, 17(2), Winter, pp. 211–29.

Eisner, Robert (1995), "Our NAIRU Limit: The Governing Myth of Economic Policy," *American Prospect*, 0(21), Spring, pp. 58–63.

Eisner, Robert (1995), "Saving, Economic Growth, and the Arrow of Causality," *Challenge*, 38(3), May–June, pp. 10–14.

Eisner, Robert (1995), "How About a Really Fair Flat Tax?" *Durell Journal of Money and Banking*, Spring, pp. 8–14.

Eisner, Robert (1995), "US National Saving and Budget Deficits," in *Macroeconomic Policy after the Conservative Era: Studies in Investment, Saving and Finance*, edited by Gerald A. Epstein and Herbert M. Gintis, Cambridge, New York and Melbourne: Cambridge University Press, pp. 109–42.

Eisner, Robert (1996), "The Point of Using GDP," *New Economy*, 3(1), Spring, pp. 2–5.

Eisner, Robert (1996), "The Balanced Budget Crusade," *The Public Interest*, No. 122, Winter, pp. 85–92.

Eisner, Robert (1996), "Expansion of Boundaries and Satellite Accounts," in *The New System of National Accounts*, edited by John W. Kendrick, Boston, Dordrecht and London: Kluwer Academic, pp. 91–113.

Eisner, Robert (1996), "The Proposed Sales and Wages Tax – Fair, Flat or Foolish?" in *Fairness and the Efficiency in the Flat Tax*, Washington DC: American Enterprise Institute, pp. 48–95.

Eisner, Robert (1996), "The Marginal Efficiency of Capital and Investment," in *A "Second Edition" of The General Theory*, edited by Geoffrey C. Harcourt and Peter A. Riach, Routledge, pp. 175–87.

Eisner, Robert (1996), "The Retreat from Full Employment," in *Essays in Honour of Paul Davidson, Volume 2: Employment, Economic Growth and the Tyranny of the Market*, Cheltenham, UK and Lyme, NH: Elgar, pp. 106–30.

Eisner, Robert (1997), "State of the Union: Black Holes in the Statistics," *Challenge*, 40(1), January–February, pp. 6–15.

Eisner, Robert (1997), "Don't Sock the Elderly, Help Them: Old Age is Hard Enough," *Elder Law Journal*, University of Illinois Law School, 5(1), Spring.

Eisner, Robert (1997), "A New View of the NAIRU," in *Improving the Global Economy: Keynesianism and the Growth in Output and Employment*, edited by Paul Davidson and Jan A. Kregel, Cheltenham, UK and Lyme, NH: Elgar, pp. 196–230. Published in French as "Une autre interprétation du NAIRU," *Cahiers de l'Espace Europe*, March 1997, pp. 9–37.

Eisner, Robert (1998), "Save Social Security from Its Saviors," *Journal of Post Keynesian Economics*, 21(1), Fall, pp. 77–92.

Eisner, Robert (1998), "Damn the NAIRU – Full Speed Ahead," in *The Rising Tide*, edited by Jerry Jasinowski, New York: Wiley, pp. 61–9.

Posthumous publications

Coen, Robert M., Robert Eisner, John Tepper Marlin, and Suken N. Shah (1999), "The NAIRU and Wages in Local Labor Markets," *American Economic Review*, 89(2), May, pp. 52–7.

Eisner, Robert (1997), "Education in a System of National Accounts," Unpublished.

Eisner, Robert (1998), "A Capital Budget for Truth in Packaging," Statement prepared for the President's Commission to Study Capital Budgeting Public Hearing, April 24, 1998. Available online at: http://clinton3.nara.gov/pcscb/wt_eisner.html.

Eisner, Robert (2000), "Budgets and Taxes," in *Back to Shared Prosperity: The Growing Inequality of Wealth and Income in America*, edited by Ray Marshall, Armonk, NY: M.E. Sharpe, pp. 186–96.

Eisner, Robert (2003), "The NAIRU and Fiscal and Monetary Policy for Now and for Our Future," in *Reinventing Functional Finance*, edited by Edward J. Nell and Mathew Forstater, Cheltenham, UK and Northampton, MA: Edward Elgar, pp. 91–115.

Eisner, Robert (2006), "Budget Deficits, Unemployment and Economic Growth:

A Cross-Section Time-Series Analysis," in *The Means to Prosperity: Fiscal Policy Reconsidered*, edited by Per Gunnar Berglund and Matias Vernengo, Routledge.

Encyclopedia entries

Eisner, Robert (1968), "The Aggregate Investment Function," *International Encyclopedia of Social Sciences*, Vol. 8, Macmillan, pp. 185–94.

Eisner, Robert (1982), "Business Investment in New Plant and Equipment," "Capital Formation," "Investment Function," and "Profits in Economic Theory," in *Encyclopedia of Economics*, edited by Douglas Greenwald, New York: McGraw-Hill, pp. 105–7, 113–16, 553–7, and 773–5.

Eisner, Robert (1987), "The Burden of the Public Debt," in *The New Palgrave: A Dictionary of Economics*, edited by John Eatwell, Murray Milgate and Peter Newman, Vol. 1, London: Macmillian, pp. 294–6.

Eisner, Robert and Robert M. Coen (1987), "Investment" in *The New Palgrave: A Dictionary of Economics*, edited by John Eatwell, Murray Milgate and Peter Newman, London: Macmillan Press, pp. 980–5.

Eisner, Robert (1992), "The Gramm–Rudman–Hollings Balanced Budget Act," in *The New Palgrave Dictionary of Money and Finance*, Vol. 2, edited by Peter Newman, Murray Milgate and John Eatwell, London: Macmillan Press Limited, pp. 275–9.

Eisner, Robert (1992), "Budget Deficits: Problems of Measurement," in *The New Palgrave Dictionary of Money and Finance*, Vol. 1, edited by Peter Newman, Murray Milgate and John Eatwell, London: Macmillan Press Limited, pp. 245–7.

Eisner, Robert (1992), "The Total Incomes System of Accounts," in *The New Palgrave Dictionary of Money and Finance*, Vol. 3, edited by Peter Newman, Murray Milgate and John Eatwell, London: Macmillan Press Limited. pp. 670–3.

Eisner, Robert (1993), "Federal Debt," in *The Fortune Encyclopedia of Economics*, edited by David R. Henderson, New York: Warner Books, pp. 248–53.

Eisner, Robert (1994), "Debt and Deficits," in *The McGraw-Hill Encyclopedia of Economics*, edited by Douglas Greenwald, New York: McGraw-Hill, pp. 248–52.

Eisner, Robert (1994), "Fiscal Policy," in *Business Cycles and Depressions: An Encyclopedia*, edited by David Glasner, New York: Garland, pp. 233–7.

War and peace

Eisner, Robert (1968), "War and Taxes: The Role of the Economist in Politics," *Bulletin of Atomic Scientists*, June, pp. 13–18.

Eisner, Robert (1970), "Economics, Freedom, and The Draft, " *Public Policy*, Fall, pp. 733–41.

Eisner, Robert (1970), "The War and the Economy," in *Why Are We Still in Vietnam*, edited by Sam Brown and Len Ackland, New York: Random House, pp. 108–23.

Eisner, Robert (1991), "Macroeconomic Consequences of Disarmament," *Challenge*, 34(1), January–February, pp. 47–50. Reprinted in *Economic Issues of Disarmament*, edited by Jurgen Brauer and Manas Chatterji, New York: New York University Press; London: Macmillan, 1993, pp. 33–42.

Eisner, Robert (1994), "Quelques considérations macroéconomiques sur le désarmement," in *Les Cahiers de l'Espace Europe*, No. 4, March, pp. 53–71.

Eisner, Robert (1995), "Désarmement et chômage aux Etats-Unis," in *Reconversion des Industries d'Armement*, Paris, pp. 47–62.

Eisner, Robert (1996), "Disarmament and Unemployment, " in *Arms Spending, Development and Security*, edited by Manas Chatterji, Jacques Fontanel and Akira Hattori, New Delhi: APH Publishing, pp. 70–86.

Academic theses

Eisner, Robert (1942), *The Gallup Poll and Opinion on Conscription: A Study in Public Opinion and Polling Technique*, Columbia University (MA thesis).

Eisner, Robert (1951), *Growth, Investment and Business Cycles: A Critique and Development of Some Recent Theories*, Johns Hopkins University Library (Doctoral dissertation).

In memoriam

Bergmann, Barbara R. (1999), "Robert Eisner 1922–1998 In Memoriam," *Feminist Economics*, 5(1), March, p. ix.

Galbraith, James K. (1999), "Robert Eisner: An Appreciation," *Challenge*, 42(3), May–June, pp. 95–9.

US Bureau of Economic Analysis (1999), "Robert Eisner's Contributions to Economic Measurement," *Survey of Current Business*, January, pp. 8–10.

Index

For Product Safety Concerns and Information please contact our EU
representative GPSR@taylorandfrancis.com Taylor & Francis Verlag GmbH,
Kaufingerstraße 24, 80331 München, Germany

Batch number: 08165901

Printed by Printforce, the Netherlands